The Isle of Thanet Farming Community

An agrarian history of easternmost Kent: outlines from early times to 1993

By R.K.I. Quested

**Revised enlarged 2nd edition
brought up to 2001**

First edition 1996 © R.K.I. Quested
Second revised enlarged edition © R. K. I. Quested 2001

Printed by Intype London Ltd
Units 3/4
Elm Grove Industrial Estate
Elm Grove
Wimbledon SW19 4HE

Distributed by R.K.I. Quested,
30 Woodford Court
Birchington
Kent CT7 9DR

ISBN 0 9529147 1 9

Books by R.K.I. Quested MA PhD (London) F.R.Hist.S.

The Expansion of Russia in East Asia 1857–1860
With an introductory chapter on Russo-Chinese relations
1792–1857. University of Singapore Press 1968.
Chinese translation of the above: *1857–1860 nian E guo zai Yuan-
dong de kuozhang*, tr. Chen Xiafei, ed. Chen Zexian, Beijing, 1979.
*The Russo-Chinese Bank: a multi-national financial base of
Tsarism in China*. Birmingham Slavonic Monographs No. 2, Uni-
versity of Birmingham, 1977.
*"Matey" imperialists? The Tsarist Russians in Manchuria
1895–1917*. Centre of Asian Studies, University of Hong Kong,
1982. pp. vi, 430
Sino-Russian relations: a short history. Allen & Unwin, Sydney,
London and Boston, 1984, 1986.

In memory of my parents
Olive and Eric Quested

Table of Contents

List of Tables

Abbreviations

AC	Archaeologia Cantiana
AgHR	Agricultural History Review
AHEW	Agrarian History of England and Wales, Cambridge 1972–
EcHR	Economic History Review
EKT	East Kent Times 1897–1980
ITG	Isle of Thanet Gazette 1909–
JHistG	Journal of Historical Geography
JKBNFU	Journal of the Kent Branch of the National Farmers' Union February 1924–January 1931
JKFU	Journal of the Kent Farmers' Union 1918–January 1924
JMH	Journal of Medieval History
K	Kebles Gazette 1870–1909
KA	Kent County Archives
KCT	Kent Coast Times 1865–1896
KF	Kent Farmer, January 1952–
KFJ	Kent Farmers' Journal
KG	Kentish Gazette 1768–
KM	Kent Messenger
KP	Kentish Post 1726–1767
PP	Parliamentary Papers
TA	Thanet Advertiser 1859–1950
TT	Thanet Times 1958–
VCHK	Victoria County History of Kent

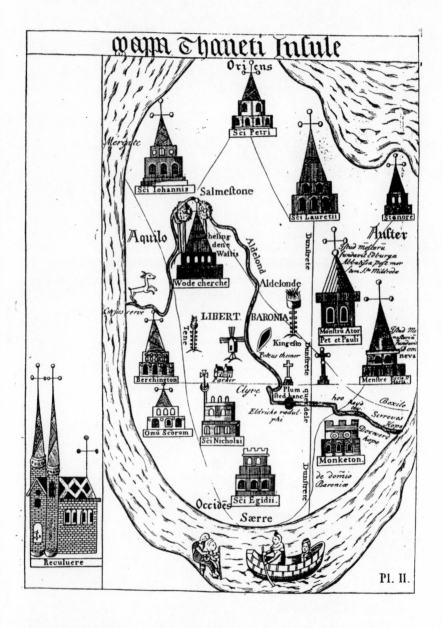

Thomas of Elmham's map reworked by John Lewis in *The history and antiquities . . . of the Isle of Tenet*, London, 1723

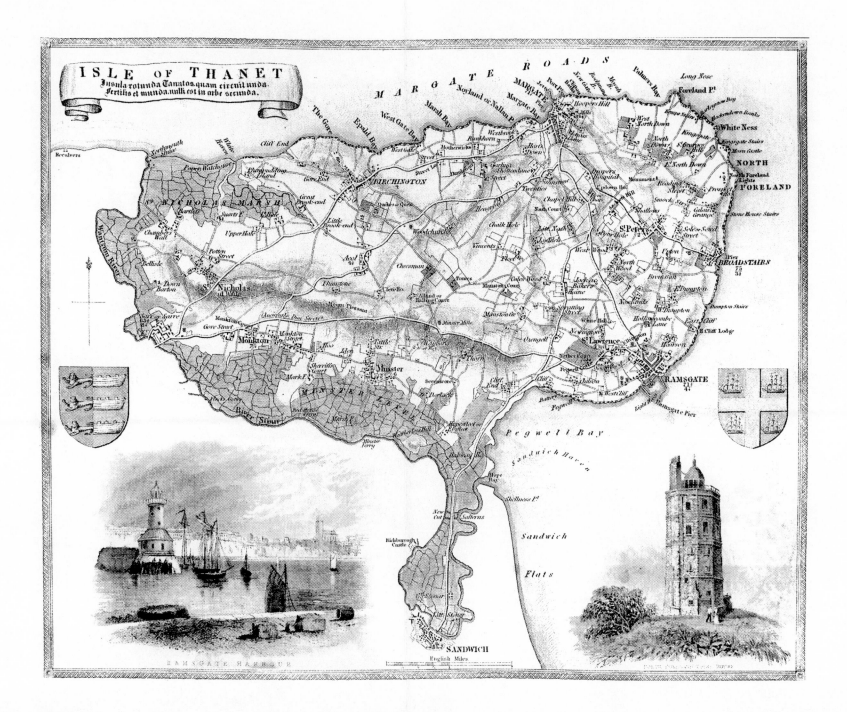

ISLE OF THANET

Insula rotunda Tanatos, quam circuit unda.
Fertilis et munda, nulli est in orbe secunda.

MARGATE ROADS

Long Nose
Foreland Pt.
White Ness
Kingsgate Stairs
NORTH
North Foreland Lights
FORELAND

St. Peters
BROADSTAIRS
Dumpton Stairs
East Cliff
B. Cliff Lodge

RAMSGATE
Light Ho. Ramsgate Pier

Pegwell Bay
Sandwich Haven
Shellness Pt.
Sandwich
Flats

BIRCHINGTON
St. NICHOLAS & MARSH

St. Nicholas
at Wade

Monkton
Minster
MINSTER LEVEL
River Stour

Woolchurch

St. Lawrence

Richborough
Castle

New Cut
Salterns

Stonar
SANDWICH

English Miles

RAMSGATE HARBOUR

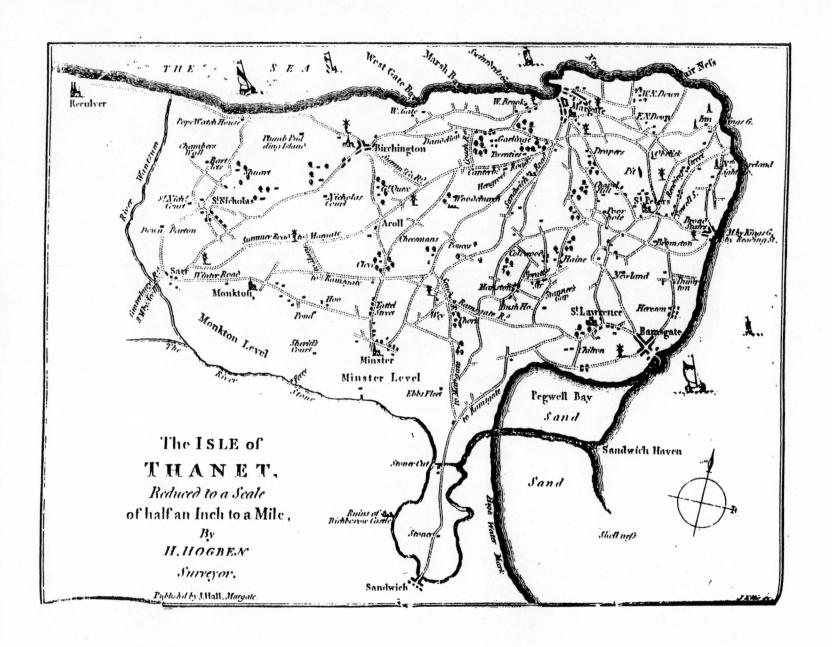

The ISLE of
THANET,
*Reduced to a Scale
of half an Inch to a Mile,
By*
H. HOGBEN
Surveyor.

Published by J. Hall, Margate.

Introduction

Nobody has attempted an agrarian history of the Isle of Thanet before, although contemporary descriptions of the farming have been made at various times, the fullest of the early ones being by John Lewis in his history of Thanet published in 1723. There has been no serious documented history of the whole island apart from Lewis' book, although there have been notable works on the history of parts of it and on its archeology.

Until the rise of the towns the history of Thanet was largely the history of the farming community, for most of the population depended on agriculture directly or indirectly. Since the late 17th century urban development has gradually increased, until now it begins to threaten much of what remains of our farmland. So this seems the right moment to look back on our agricultural past, to see how our ancestors and predecessors have fared tilling the splendid fertile soil of this unique and once beautiful chalky island.

For the prehistoric period I have given an outline of the agricultural evidence only, since the Trust for Thanet Archeology have provided us with a convenient general prehistoric survey in their *Gateway Island*. From Saxon times to the 18th century I have included some general history of the island as well, covering some of the more important events and aspects, since a documented history of Thanet for this period has been so conspicuously lacking, and the forthcoming County Council history of Kent will not include any specific Thanet volume. For the remaining years, from the 18th century onwards, I have again concentrated on the farming community, leaving the history of the towns to its distinguished experts, Alan Kay and John Whyman.

Regarding the source material, until the 18th century I have used the best available published scholarly work, and descriptions left by famous visitors of the past, helped by consultations with relevant specialists in archeology and history, and with the addition of a few fragments of my own primary research. Since the references to Thanet in scholarly literature hitherto have been so scattered, I hope that this provides a useful service. From the 18th century onwards and particularly from the end of the 18th century, I have had to rely mainly on primary research of my own, from sources published and unpublished.

An extra word is needed about the secondary material for the medieval period. Some of the sources are old, and some (R.A.L. Smith's *Canterbury Cathedral Priory: a study in monastic administration*, Cambridge, 1943, and A.H. Davis, *William of Thorne's Chronicle of St Augustine's Abbey*, Oxford, 1934) are now criticized in some aspects. I have nevertheless included material from them which seems to tie in well with the work of reputable later scholars such as Du Boulay and Mavis Mate. Although much new work has appeared in recent years on the pre-Conquest period, much primary research needs to be published on post-Conquest medieval Thanet, especially about the St Augustine's lands. This book can only attempt to give an outline of findings on some key issues to date, for the period before the 18th century.

The local historian has one advantage over those wiser in each period and over larger areas, and that is intimate knowledge of the people and terrain. This book is not based entirely on written sources alone, and was inspired by my own deep roots in this soil. I was born and grew up in the Thanet countryside a quarter mile from the legendary deer's path, and I have walked over most of the island, which is the best way to know a place. My Sackett ancestors were on the land here from the 14th century at least, and my father Eric Quested (1895–1991), farmed at Woodchurch near Birchington from 1919–1970, having learnt farming from his grandfather Barzillai Sackett at East Northdown from 1911–1914. So oral and family history comes into the later chapters, and I have been much indebted to my father's marvellous memory and to the advice and contributions of a number of other Thanet people.

Indeed this study owes much to many people. I am grateful to G.E. Mingay, Emeritus Professor of Agrarian History at the University of Kent, and to Dr Joan Thirsk, late of Oxford University, for reading the whole text and making many useful comments, and to Professor F.M.L. Thompson for advice. I am indebted to Donald Sykes, late of Wye College, for reading the last three chapters and numerous comments. All the above have made a significant difference to the work. The prehistory section could not have been written without the invaluable aid of David Perkins of the Thanet Archeological Trust and Nigel MacPherson-Grant

of the Canterbury Archeological Trust. Dr Ann Williams at the
Institute of Historical Research steered me into some basic Anglo-
Saxon sources. Alan Kay and John Whyman were kind and helpful
from their funds of knowledge, and Harold Gough provided information about medieval Latin terms. The late Martin Jackson
allowed me to see the old NFU branch archives, and the Rural,
Agricultural and Allied Workers' section of the TGWU gave me
access to their library to read their old reports and balance sheets
published for limited circulation.

Within the agrarian community in Thanet, Christopher and
Tony Powell-Cotton have been very helpful with information
and documents. Ann Linington has made available her late father's
extensive MS notes on Birchington history and other material, and
both she, Jill Smith and David Steed have made many useful
comments on the text. Jill has given me material from Marion
Smith's 19th century diary, and much information from family
documents. Michael Smith before his lamented recent death gave
me numerous articles and documents about his family's farming
and Monkton Court. David Steed and his late father Norman have
provided information and photographs. Joan Champion gave me
a copy of William Champion's 19th century diary, and another
fascinating document. The Tapp family, Norah Mallett, the late
John Ash and others too many to mention have supplied very
welcome material. It is a pity that I could not use everything that I
have been offered, because of the need to avoid undue length.

A particular word of thanks is due to Peter Linington, Mary
Tyrrel, the late Michael Smith, Jill and Peter Smith, William Friend
and the late Martin Jackson for submitting to questioning about
recent farming methods. Norah Mallett and Edwina Steed also
deserve thanks for their help with the progenitor of this book: an
uncompleted history of the Thanet ploughing match.

Penny Ward, the Local Studies Librarian at Margate Library,
and Charlotte Hodgkin, former archivist at Ramsgate, and all the
staff at Margate, Broadstairs and Ramsgate libraries have been
unfailingly helpful during the many hours that I have spent in their
premises, mostly at Margate. Like very many other people I have
benefitted from Penny Ward's patience, enthusiasm and vast store
of local knowledge; her help was particularly valuable for the
maps. My thanks are also due to Canterbury Library, Canterbury
Cathedral archives, the Templeman Library (University of Kent),
Maidstone Library, the Centre for Kentish Studies (incorporating
the County Library and the Kent Archives Office), the library of

Wye College, the library and archives of the Institute of Agricultural History at Reading University, the British Library, the University of London Library, the libraries of the Institute of Historical Research and the Institute of Archeology of the University of London, the library of the Royal Agricultural Society of England, the library of the Ministry of Agriculture and Fisheries, the library of the Royal Historical Society, the Public Record Office and the archives of the Religious Society of Friends at Friends' House.

Last but not least, I would like to pay tribute to Edward, my husband, for his patience with this obsession, and to Natasha for typing the final copy, and to Dina for being there in the background.

Needless to say, the mistakes are my responsibility. It is possible however that I may share some of the blame for error with the local newspaper sources, which often cannot be checked for accuracy. I will be very grateful to receive any further information, and especially any criticisms, corrections and suggestions, which will be left with the Local Studies librarian at Margate library for the use of future researchers.

The publication of this book has been helped by a grant of £745 from the Heritage Services Group of Kent County Council, and a grant of £250 from the Allen Grove Fund of the Kent Archaeological Society, for which I express my thanks. The maps are reproduced from copies owned by Margate Library, by kind permission.

Foreword to the Second edition

Brief mistakes have been corrected in the text, likewise any printer's errata which affect meaning, including tables 13 and 21. Other errors of mine have been gone into in the new supplement at the end of this edition, after the index. This also contains a list of minor errata, some new information and a brief update on Thanet farming at early 2001. More information on sources for further research has been added to the Appendix. I am very grateful to Kristin Slater, Natasha, and David Stevens for helping me to get the extra material on tape.

RKIQ April 2001

Chapter One: From early times to 1066

The Isle of Thanet is some eight miles long from East to West and five miles wide from North to South at its widest, about 45 square miles in extent and 55 metres (181 feet) above sea level at its highest points at Stanar Hill outside Ramsgate and Telegraph Hill above Minster. The island forms a plateau, interspersed with now dry valleys. Most of it is covered with 1–4 feet of sandy silt loam on Upper Chalk bedrock, the whole studded with flints. This soil is loess material, considered to have been blown here by severe winds in the aftermath of the last glaciation. In places on the uplands the chalk comes too near the surface, leaving only a thin cover of earth, but most of the plateau is very fertile, although Thanet's low rainfull (less than 25 inches at best) often makes it rather too dry. From Cliffsend to Monkton there is a low-lying strip of land sheltered from the North, Northeast and Northwest, with some chalk but also very fertile soils of brickearth and Thanet Beds, and there are scattered patches of these other soils else-where, especially in the Broadstairs St Peters' area and along the North coast.[1] For a very long time Thanet has been a famous agricultural place. Its dryness has been an advantage as often as not, giving rise to the old rhyme, "When England wrings, the Island sings", but since 1930 decennial rainfall totals have been declining, causing fears for the future.[2]

Thanet became an island sometime between 8,000 and 5,000 BC (estimates vary), when sea levels rose at the end of the last glaci-ation and covered the low lands now under the Southern parts of the North Sea and the Straits of Dover.[3] At that time there was probably a deep and fairly narrow salt water channel where the Stour and Wantsum now flow through the marshes, and an inlet of the sea perhaps as far as Fordwich on the mainland Kent shore. The central Thanet plateau was probably heavily wooded. The island in those times was larger, as the sea has eaten away our

Northern and Eastern shoreline, at a rate difficult to estimate, for
it has clearly varied depending on the relative hardness of the land
at various places, and the frequency of frost and storms. Thanet
Archeological Trust made one estimate of about 90 feet per
century, or less than half a mile every 2,000 years. Between Epple
Bay and West Bay the author reckons from personal observation
that the cliff receded about 20–25 feet between 1940 and 1990, this
being one of the firmer parts long thought not to warrant protection by a promenade. Recession at this rate would amount to less
than a quarter of a mile in 2,000 years, but the known advance of
the sea at Reculver suggests that there might have been soft soil
areas of Thanet beyond the chalk which might have extended
much further out to sea originally.[4]

During all the millenia of prehistory, from the remotest times,
our island was inhabited by people of whose customs, tongues and
descent little definite is known. Archeological opinion tends to
believe that for most of the time in most places cultural change
may have occurred as much or more through local initiative and
new ideas spread through trading contacts as through invasions
and migration, though these last are not to be excluded. As far as
is known, the early people settled near the shores of Thanet,
and on the downland slopes of the escarpment above Monkton,
Minster and Cliffsend. It has been considered that the central
plateau was probably heavily wooded and hard of access until
about 400 BC, but this opinion may need revising in the light of the
constant new evidence. These early people seem to have existed in
small, probably tribal groups, in gradually increasing but fluctuating numbers.

Farming has been generally considered to have started in Britain
in the fourth millenium BC (although recently much earlier
remains have been discovered in the far North of the British Isles),
but only fragmentary traces of this Neolithic agriculture have been
found in Thanet where the Neolithic dates from roughly 3,500 to
2,000 BC. As of 1993 Thanet Archeological Trust had found four
sites from the earlier part of the Neolithic, and some 350 round
barrows dating from the Bronze Age (c 2,000 – c 600 BC), but the
number of finds was continually rising and included five large new
ones not yet fully identified, (near North Foreland lighthouse, in
Manston, on Halfmile Ride near Margate, at Sarre and above
Monkton). This may mean a relatively large population at the
time. It looks as Thanet may have been important in later prehistory because it controlled the sheltered water of the Wantsum, a

natural harbour. The barrows (1) and a few henge-type (2) enclosures have been found not only near the sea, but all over the plateau, following the "false crest" of the now dry inland valleys such as the Shottendane. By 1993 the Middle and Late Bronze Age (c 1,200 – c 600 BC) had yielded at least 12 big village settlements and 15 hoards, 8 established as important, of which at least one, the Ebbsfleet Hoard, contains bronze-bladed knives and sickles, proving agriculture.

Late Bronze – early Iron Age remains found at Westgate are dominated by cow and ox bones, indicating the people were cattle breeders, but until Roman times farming small fields seems to have been the norm. It must have been laborious indeed to clear and cultivate them with stone or bronze-edged tools, even with primitive iron ones. Food gathering, notably of molluscs, was also probably important here from early times. Early Iron Age middens in Thanet often contain considerable quantities of shells of the common mud-gaper (*Mya arenaria*) which is now rare locally.

The use of iron came to Thanet around 600 BC, when like most of Britain it was probably inhabited by Celtic tribes, linguistic ancestors of modern Welsh, Irish and Scots Gaelic speakers. A small field pattern is clearly shown in the Iron Age village at Dumpton Gap/South Cliff Parade. Other Celtic fields have been seen from crop marks at Bartlett's (near St Nicholas) and Gore End farms. The oldest known plough marks in Thanet date from about 50 BC in the "Belgic" Iron Age at a Lord of the Manor (a Thanet place name) site. An Iron Age pot found in Cliftonville contained rye seeds, one grain of wheat and seeds of weeds such as plantain which accompany grain crops. Since there was a period of colder climate from roughly 1,000–500 BC with gradual warming only thereafter, rye was probably the main crop at that time, being more resistant to cold than wheat. Iron Age querns and millstones

(1) A barrow or tumulus is a mound usually of earth and rubble, raised to cover single or multiple burials.
(2) A henge, found only in the British Isles in the Neolithic and early Bronze Age, is a circular or irregular area enclosed by a bank and a ditch, usually on the inside of the bank. Some enclose pits, with or without burials, others have rings of timbers or timber buildings, and 13, including Avebury and Stonehenge but not any Thanet ones, have standing stones. (Whitehouse, Macmillan Dictionary of Archeology).

have also been found in Thanet. Clearing of the woodland on the plateau – for farming, as opposed to barrows etc. – probably began about 400 BC, after iron axe-heads became available.[5] There is no certainty when it was completed; one suspects that the tree cover alternately shrank and readvanced with the fluctuations in the prehistoric, Romano-British and medieval populations.

The first civilized, learned man known to have sighted Thanet was Pytheas, a geographer and astronomer from the Greek colony of Massilia (Marseilles), who circumnavigated Britain (in a probably 50-oared vessel) around 325 BC. According to a modern British scholar, he also went close to Iceland and into the Baltic as far as the mouth of the Oder.[6] His books on this stupendous voyage were lost in one of the fires at the great library in Alexandria, perhaps in 47 BC, but fragments have come down to us in the works of other scholars of antiquity. He described "Al-bion" (Britain) as mostly flat, overgrown with forests, thickly populated; the people tall and not so yellow-haired as the Celts on the Continent. They lived in humble houses of wood thatched with reeds, grew corn and stored the ears in roofed granges, and used chariots. There were many kings and potentates amongst them, but they were usually at peace. Pytheas reported rounding "Kantion Corner" (the Kent promontory), from whence the Continent was visible and which was opposite the mouth of the Rhine; this is the first reference to the name of a people from which derive the names of both Kent and Canterbury.[7] The few sentences about Britain are the nearest we are likely to get to an eyewitness description of Thanet before the Romans; archeological evidence supports the use of wood for dwellings here, with no signs so far of houses with a second storey before Roman times.

Agriculture and living standards must have been expanded under Roman rule, for at least 14 certain Romano-British villa-type sites and 37 homesteads had been discovered by 1993. The Ramsgate area was particularly populated, and the A253 (Sarre-Ramsgate), known in medieval times as Dunstrete, is considered to have been a Roman road dating from the 1st century AD. Then as later, Sarre must have been the main point for boat communication with the mainland. Field size increased, the climate was warmer again by then – and it must surely have been anti-cyclonic in the years of Pytheas' voyage – and wheat, barley, oats and rye were grown. Cats, dogs, and a full range of farm animals were kept, with extensive use of horses. There may be traces of a Roman water-mill at Shuart farm (St Nicholas). Bones of hares, red and roe deer and a possible wild-boar tusk have also been found from the Roman centuries, showing that perhaps woods were quite extensive.[8] William Friend, a local farmer and botanist, believes that the Romans probably introduced evergreen oaks, walnuts and Alexander brocoli to Thanet. The population may have been relatively large, since that of Roman Britain as a whole was four – six million, a peak not reached again until 1300.[9]

The Romans also left written information and data for at least one large-scale map. Julius Caesar did not visit Thanet, but his description of Kent in 54 BC suggests an enclosed landscape of largish arable fields interspersed with woodlands, and settled in a dense but unnucleated pattern of farmsteads. He also found corn in the fields.[10] Strabo (64/63 BC – AD 23/24) says that corn was amongst British exports to the Continent.[11] Salway thinks it improbable that any grain from Britain ever reached Rome itself, the distance being too great[12], but Frere states that British corn was compulsorily purchased for the Roman garrisons, and in AD 359 the Emperor Julian caused a large fleet to be built to transport corn from Britain to Gaul.[13] The geography of Claudius Ptolemy (AD 90–168? Floreat AD 130) contained data on latitudes and longitudes from which the first, inaccurate map of Europe could be produced. The Ebner MS of this geography (c AD 1460) contains a map of unknown authorship which shows Thanet as an island decidedly larger than now in relation to the East Kent promontory, but the whole map is obviously distorted. In this MS Thanet is named Conuennos or Couenos.[14] The usual Roman name for Thanet was Tanatus, or Tanatos, a Romano-British word cognate with the River Tanat on the Welsh borders and perhaps meaning Bright Island.[15] Caius Julius Solinus (3rd century AD) says of Thanet (in the Golding translation, London, 1587, ch 33): "The Isle of Thanatos is beaten upon with the French sea, and is divided from Britannia by a verie narrow cutte, luckie for cornfields and fertile soyle", and goes on to say that there are no serpents there, (though Golding thought that Solinus must mean the Isle of Wight).[16] It cannot therefore be claimed, as some writers have done without citing sources, that Thanet's corn was exported to Rome itself, but its fertility and corn-growing properties were well-established in antiquity, and its corn may have been exported to Roman Gaul.[17]

When the Romans arrived the sea-channel between Thanet and the mainland was probably still narrow and deep. Richborough was not an island, and Roman remains have been found on the marsh beyond Belle Isle, which must then have been some distance from the shore. During Roman times sea levels rose considerably (probably by a series of inundations, each followed by a smaller regression)[18], reaching the borders of the present-day Thanet marshland, and Richborough became an island linked to the mainland by a causeway.[19] These rising sea-levels swamped the homelands of the Anglo-Saxons on the Continental shores of the North Sea, and were a factor leading to their invasion of Britain.

Around 410 the Roman legions left, and the Jutes, a grouping among the Anglo-Saxon peoples, became masters of Thanet. The villa system and the Celtic language of the ancient Britons vanished, and all our old place-names in Thanet are of Anglo-Saxon origin, except perhaps for Sarre, which is considered by some to be Romano-British or earlier.[20] Some fairly recent research suggests that the conquest of Eastern England took place between 410 and 441, and that for the Romano-Britons it was catastrophic.[21] The disappearance of the Celtic names from Thanet seems to confirm this, and to hint at a mass slaughter of the peaceful civilized population by the fierce Jutish tribesmen. The population seems to have fallen steeply, leading probably to regrowth of trees and bushes.

Garlinge is possibly the earliest Saxon name here: the inge (*ingas*) terminals according to some scholars indicate a secondary wave of colonization in the 6th century at places already settled by earlier Jutish settlers, or even by the Romans.[22] The terminal "ton" (*tun*) was at one time believed reliably to indicate early settlement, but is now known to have been a living element from early Saxon times until at least the 13th century. There are twelve or thirteen "ton" placenames in Thanet, mostly in the Eastern part: Birchington, Hereson (a *tun* corruption), Salmstone (Salmanstun), Upton, Dumpton, Ellington, Newington, Chilton, Manston, Cottington, Monkton, Downbarton. A clearer case of antiquity may be Reading Street, from Rydding, meaning a clearing in the woods.[23] The name Stone in Broadstairs is considered to indicate Romano-British ruins,[24] and Bromstone is possibly cognate, but possibly a *tun*.

The division between the Jutes and the Saxons lay roughly along the River Medway.[25] In the late 5th/early 6th century the Kingdom of Kent emerged in the Jutish territory, bounded by the Medway and the Weald, with Thanet being a part of it. Later, Kent north and west of the Medway became a linked kingdom; this seems reflected in the dioceses of Canterbury and Rochester, and almost certainly is the origin of the division of Kentish folk into "Men and Maids of Kent" and "Kentish Men and Maids".[26]

Under the Kingdom of Kent, Thanet was apparently a separate lathe or administrative district. A royal palace and court was early established at Sarre, where the king also controlled the ferry to the mainland and the harbour. This is supported by archeological evidence of graves of heavily armed males of evident high status, Sarre having perhaps the richest Saxon burial ground in England.[27] The upper class in the early Kentish kingdom was wealthy from Continental trade.[28] The early Saxon pattern of cultivation was probably one of subsistence farming with small fields, a reversion to pre-Roman practice, and the extent of communal cultivation, if any, is obscure.[29] By 1993 Thanet Archeological Trust had found 21 Saxon cemeteries and isolated graves, but only one settlement, at Acol, then probably at the head of a creek or stream running down to Brooksend. It estimated the total Thanet population as at least 1,500 in the 5–7th centuries AD, but almost nothing of the life-style of those days had been uncovered, since most of the villages and homesteads probably lie underneath modern ones.[30]

Bearing in mind that all the original villages of Thanet lie near the sea, or what was the sea, it may be surmised that the oldest farmsteads were in such areas too. Amongst surviving well-known farms or farmhouses (whether still used by farmers or not) which might stand on early sites are the following, going clockwise round from Ramsgate: Chilton, Little Cliffsend, Ozengell, Cliffsend (Bethlehem), Thorne, Sevenscore, Ebbsfleet, the Way farms, Eden, the Hoo farms, Walter's Hall farm, Monkton Parsonage, Gore Street, St Nicholas Court, Ambry Court, Lower and Upper Gore End farmhouses, Dent-de-Lion, Mutrix, 16 Omer Avenue (earlier Tomlins, later Dairy farm), Holly, East Northdown, Callis, Callis Grange, Elmwood, Stone, Fair Street and Dumpton (earlier East Dumpton farm). The antiquity of Monkton Court and Minster Abbey (which still has a farm attached) are well-known. The present cores of Pegwell, Minster, Monkton, St Nicholas, Birchington, Acol, Garlinge, West Northdown and Reading Street most probably contained small farms from early times. At Sarre the village may have spread up to the higher ground, for the church was somewhere near the present windmill, though David Perkins found that Elms farmhouse contains medieval traces.[31] Gore End was a village now partly under the sea at Minnis Bay. Salmestone Grange was originally a Saxon hall. The Hartsdown, Salmestone,

King Street, St John's and Dane Valley parts of Margate seem to have particularly ancient connections, likewise the harbour parts of Broadstairs and Ramsgate and the courses of the now-vanished streams which flowed into them. St Peter's, St Lawrence, Manston and the isolated farms of inland Thanet might date from later Saxon or even Norman times, when the population had grown again after the collapse following the Jutish conquest. There remains a category of farms situated very close to the present marsh, which may be ancient sites or may date from the 14th–15th centuries after the retreat of the sea.

In AD 597 St Augustine landed near Ebbsfleet farm on his mission to convert England, and according to the Venerable Bede, before long Ethelbert, King of Kent, came to Thanet and received him "sitting in the open air".[32] In 1855 the field behind the farm was still said by the farmer of the day to have been the site of "some landing",[33] but the makers of the 1872 Ordnance Survey map and a recent investigator concluded that Augustine landed near the track called Cottington Lane, which runs from Ebbsfleet Lane to St Augustine's Cross.[34] This would have been a nearer landfall, but the field behind the farm (which stands on what must have been a promontory of the Thanet coast) would have been more sheltered.

Bede does not say, as is sometimes asserted, that St Augustine met Ethelbert under an oak, but says that the Saint met British Christians on the Welsh border beneath one.[35] It was the 18th century Thanet historian John Lewis who stated that the Thanet meeting was under an oak, but gave no source.[36] So Bede cannot be cited as authority that Thanet was then covered in oaks, as some writers since Lewis have assumed.

The Venerable Bede (AD 672 or 673–735) also left us a description of Thanet: "Now at the east end of Kent is Thanet, an isle of goodly size, that is to say containing 600 hides according to the custom of the English, which island is parted from the mainland by the river Wantsum (Vantsumu), which is of three furlongs breadth and in two places only passable, for both the heads of him runneth to the sea."[37] In Kent the local land units for taxation purposes were the sulung and the ploughland (carucate), which were nearly synonymous at least until the end of the 8th century, and nominally of 200 acres. At that time there were normally five hides to a sulung or ploughland: if this pertained in Thanet K.P. Witney estimates its area at 24,000 acres at that time. He considered that the term sulung originated with the early land seizures of the Jutes, sulungs being especially numerous in Thanet and on Thameside.[38]

Together with the rest of the Kentish people Thanet was officially converted to Christianity by the King. This had taken place by AD 600, although in fact it may have taken much longer to eradicate the old pagan religion. Traces of pre-Christian belief lingered in various customs in rural England until the present century, and are not quite extinct everywhere even today.

Our most famous legend purports to date from the 7th century. According to medieval texts about St Mildred of Thanet, it was in 670 that King Egbert I of Kent (reigned 664–673) granted the royal lady variously called Domne Eafe/Aebbe/Eormenburh as much land as her tame deer would run around to found an abbey on, as weregild (legal compensation) for his responsibility in the murder of her two brothers.

The deer's track, in early 20th century tradition in that part of Thanet, lay along St Mildred's Lynch, an unmade cart-road of which the last fragment still exists between Woodchurch Road and the Birchington – Manston Road, starting besides the water-pumping station.[39] Actually the Lynch must be the remains of an ancient track between Minster and Westgate, and in the Middle Ages the deer was believed to have run along the old boundary between Minster and Monkton parishes, which followed a zig-zag course from Westgate round to the east of Woodchurch and Cheeseman's farms, thence via Cleve to Sheriff's Court. The historian D.H. Rollason argues this convincingly from Thomas of Elmham's map of 1410 or 1411, the tithe maps of 1839–1842 and the first edition of the 6-inch ordnance survey map. This remained the boundary between the two parishes to some extent after St John's parish was carved out of Minster, for an isolated portion of Minster parish near Westgate was still shown on the tithe maps of 1839–42.[40]

According to the last part of the legend, Egbert's wicked courtier, Thunor, tried to impede the deer, but the ground opened and swallowed him, the site being marked by a *hlæw* (mound) of stones. Thomas of Elmham's map puts this spot somewhere east of Cleve and Acol,[41] but by the 20th century *hlæw* had been transformed into "leap", and the site was said to be Mount Pleasant chalkpit, now called "Smugglers Leap"! In this form the legend still survives in Thanet.

St Mary's Abbey was indubitably founded at Minster around the supposed date, for it is mentioned in a surviving summary of a charter dated 675.[42] No foundation charter has been found, but tradition says that written charters were only introduced into Anglo-Saxon England by Archbishop Theodore, who took office in 667, five years before King Egbert died.[43] The abbey was a dual foundation of nuns and priests, but always under female rule.[44] The modern scholars Nicholas Brooks and D.W. Rollason have confirmed that all the royal personae existed, and evidence suggests that the murders took place.[45]

Charters of 676 and 678 state that the original grant of land, which they confirm, was of 44 hides only (about 1,760 acres), and Witney concludes that the abbey's rights were gradually extended to cover the whole eastern half of Thanet, at which point a delimitation was held and the deer story arose.[46] The oldest text of the Mildred legend, drawing on 10th century sources, does not mention the deer. Other scholars have argued that probably the whole island was given to the abbey in the first place,[47] in which light the deer story and the Minster-Monkton parish boundary may relate to an earlier division,[48] or a division between the Abbey and the Reculver monks (see p 12),[49] or a division between the Abbey and the magnates to whom land in West Thanet was granted in the 10th century[50] (see p 15). It is also conjecturable that it relates to a division between St Augustine's Abbey and Christchurch Priory in the 11th century (see p 15). In short, it is very misty, as good legends should be.

Even the Thunor part of the legend may have some meaning, for Thunor was the name of the Saxon pagan god of thunder and the elements, so this might even be a garbled version of pagan resistance to the founding of a Christian abbey. Whilst in the realm of speculation one must say that Mount Pleasant, with its panoramic view of the sky, would make a much better place for Thunor worship than somewhere between Cleve and Cheeseman's, but the fall of a thunderbolt or meteorite could have accounted for the choice of the latter site, and indeed for the story of the earth opening.

By 748 a second abbey belonging to Minster had been established, called St Peter or St Peter and Paul. It also appears to have been called Northminster, whilst the original abbey was known as Southminster. Brooks speculates that St Peter and Paul was at St Peter's village, Everitt that it was at Monkton, and Witney considers that Southminster was at Eastry.[51] Opinion, particularly Roman Catholic opinion, in Minster itself today considers that the original abbey (Southminster) was on the site of St Mary's parish church, and that St Peter and Paul (Northminster) was at the present abbey, which lies north of the church, for both church and abbey have Saxon early parts. This is also the opinion of Newman in the Pevsner architectural history of England series,[52] and Kilburne in 1659[53] said that the ruins of the monastery were converted into the parish church. Rollason[54] considers St Peter and Paul was merely the known Norman church of that name excavated close to the present abbey, but the charter of 748 states that it was a monastery.[55]

A number of extant charters confirmed and extended the lands of the St Mary's abbey in Thanet and the Kentish mainland until about 764.[56] Some of the land in Thanet was at places called Haeg (Haine?), "by Northanuude" (Northwood), "Humanton" (Manston?) and "Sudaneie" (South Thanet?). This does not necessarily eliminate the possibility that the whole island was given to the Abbey, for these places might have been already occupied by people who contested the grant. A seventh century charter in an unnamed part of the island specifically mentioned an existing occupant named Yrminred, who accepted the Abbey as his overlord, but only persons of status would likely be mentioned by name in such documents.[57]

One of the most intriguing charters was that of 724, by which King Wihtred granted the Abbey land at Tenterden (in Anglo-Saxon *Tenetwaraden*, the swine pasture of the men of Thanet). This proves that the Abbey and its tenants had herds of pigs, at this time when clearings were being made in the Wealden forest to fatten these beasts on oak and beech mast.[58] The swine of those days were still close to the European wild boar: tall, long-legged and agile, only partly domesticated. They were possibly driven to Tenterden via Thanington (*Tenet-tun*, or the settlement of the Thanet men), where they rested en route.[59] Land on the river Rother was also granted to the Abbey,[60] indicating that carcases were brought back to Minster or despatched elsewhere by boat. In a recent article Witney considers the Wealden land may have been used for fattening oxen.[61]

Minster Abbey had its own harbour and merchant vessels, trading over the inland sea of the Wantsum with Fordwich, Reculver and Sandwich and as far as London. Several of the 8th century charters gave or confirmed toll and tax privileges for such vessels.[62] The St Peter and Paul/St Peter Abbey operated ships from Sarre.[63] According to the Latin text of the 748 charter given by the 18th century historian John Lewis,[64] one of these vessels was

bought from "Leubuco", which P.D. Hopkins has translated as
Lubeck. This is unlikely, and Birch's text of the charter[65] gives an
alternate reading of "Leubrico", which sounds like an Anglo-
Saxon personal name, or might be a place-name in England, or
possibly Friesland, an area with which Southern England then had
known ties.[66]

According to tradition the toll from the royal ferry at Sarre was
given to Minster Abbey in 726 by a King Egbert,[67] but no modern
scholar has confirmed it, and the King of Kent then was not an
Egbert. (Egbert II reigned c 775 – c 785, in a brief restoration
of the independent kingdom of Kent that was soon crushed by
Mercia.)[68]

The most famous abbess was the second one, later canonized as
St Mildred of Thanet. Witney in an early work debunked her as a
person of small importance whose reputation was artificially pro-
moted by St Augustine's monks later for their own ends, but
he subsequently accepted her legend as probably founded in a
genuinely saintly personality. Rollason and Brooks found that
Mildred's legend originated in or soon after her own lifetime,
and that the Abbey may have been a very learned and literary
foundation. The third Abbess, Eadburh, was commissioned by
Boniface, the Apostle of Germany, with whom she corresponded,
to make a copy in golden letters of the Epistles of St Peter, and
Minster was likely to have been the wealthiest of the Kentish
monasteries of this time.[69]

The first grant of land to Reculver dates from 679, when King
Hlothere gave some land in Uestanae (Western Thanet) to Abbot
Berhwald who became Archbishop of Canterbury in 692. This
formed the nucleus of the See's estates in the island, which later
came to include Sarre, Downbarton and places near Margate.[70]
The site of the 679 grant was the St Nicholas area, possibly Downbarton. The charter gave the land to the Abbot "with everything
belonging to it, fields, pastures, marshes, copses, fens, thickets",
indicating that it was not heavily wooded, and that every part of it
was being exploited in some way, by grazing animals in the copses,
and snaring birds in the thickets, etc, as well as cultivation and
pasturing.[71]

No local Saxon grain analyses are as yet available, but sheep
seem to have been important as well as pigs. By far the commonest
animal bones found in early Saxon graves in Thanet are sheep,
leading to the hypothesis that these were food offerings and that

mutton was a favourite delicacy. They are not found in later Saxon graves.[72]

Some general information is available about Kentish agriculture which may have applied to Thanet too. An 8th century document shows that rye was an important Kentish crop – a month was named after the rye harvest, *rugern*. This is consistent with the colder climate which is said to have prevailed from AD 400 to about 900.[73] Oats, wheat and beans were also grown in Kent,[74] a large range of iron tools was used,[75] and as well as swine and sheep, oxen, cattle, mules, fowls, geese, pigeons, cats and dogs were kept, with horses for the upper classes to ride. Oxen were the plough animals, and the use of horses was much less than in Roman times.[76] In the reign of Aethelston (925–939) the price of a full-grown pig in Kent was ten pence,[77] but no other animal prices have been found.

In 762 the original Kentish dynasty ended and the kingdom of Kent fell under the overlordship of Mercia, which ruled through puppets from another branch of the Kentish royal house. King Egbert of Wessex (reigned 802–839) absorbed it after defeating Mercia in 825, and in due course it came under Alfred the Great (reigned 871–899) in the united kingdom of England.[78] By some-time in the second quarter of the 9th century the Wessex kings had given away most of the royal lands in Thanet, which became part of the Lathe of Borowart (Borough), administered from Canterbury.[79] Later, probably in the 10th century, the Lathes were sub-divided into Hundreds, and Thanet became the Hundred of Thanet.[80]

St Mary's Abbey and the St Peter and Paul Abbey disappear from the records in the mid-9th century, possibly due to Wessex domination over Kent or to Viking (Danish) raids, which may have begun as early as the late 8th century. The Vikings were certainly active in Kent in the 9th century, making a severe raid on Thanet in 841, and wintering on the island in 850–851.[81] The two versions of St Augustine's Chronicle by William of Thorne and Thomas of Elmham each mention the burning of Minster Abbey with all its inhabitants, each giving a different date, but no modern scholar has so far published any definite conclusions as to this. There is one small reference to the boundary of St Mildred's lands in a charter of King Eadred of 948, and the St Mary's abbey may have made a brief restoration at the start of the 11th century. After a lapse of about 100 years, Danish armies began ravaging England again towards the end of the 10th century. Thanet was devastated in 980, and ravages were made in Kent and the southeast in 991, 994, 999, 1006, 1009, 1011, 1013, 1014 and 1016. In 1011 an Abbess Leofran of a St Mary's abbey was captured by the Danes in Canterbury according to a 12th century source; this may or may not have been the Thanet one.[82]

By tradition, in Thomas of Elmham's rendering of the St Augustine's Chronicle, King Cnut (reigned 1016–1035) gave the ruined St Mary's to St Augustine's Abbey. The dateless charter cited by the latter to prove this in the medieval period is a post-Conquest forgery, but Brooks thinks it plausible that it was Cnut who gave it to them. The extent of land they received remains uncertain; apparently they claimed to have been given only half the original lands of St Mary's.[83] At Domesday Book St Augustine's was in possession of 54 sulungs in Thanet, but the land measurements had not remained constant in size since the 8th century. (See p 18).

Both the status of the people of Thanet and their land tenure and cultivation system in late Saxon times remain shrouded in mystery as far as published work goes. It is known that over England generally the simple society of the 5th century had by this time evolved into a complex feudal or semi-feudal one. In the 9th century Kentish society already consisted of two or three ranks of freemen, three of half-free, and slaves as well, although women's status seems to have been less rigidly stratified.[84]

In England as a whole throughout Saxon times the manorial system was developing, and the 11th century saw its widespread imposition. Domesday Book (see below chapter 2) shows that it was established in Thanet before the Conquest. Manors consisting of one or more villages or parts of a village with surrounding areas, were granted with rights of jurisdiction over the inhabitants to powerful ecclesiastical or lay persons, who held them in theory at least on condition of fealty to the monarch. Sometimes they granted some of their lands to lesser people in a chain of sub-infeudation. The manor owners farmed their own demesne land in the heart of the manors, and extracted rent, special taxes and judicial fines for offences from their tenants, the rent being at first usually in the form of labour duties on the demesne and gifts in kind, later in monetary payments. All these customs, including even weights and measures, were generally very complex, due to many local and regional variations right through the Saxon and medieval periods.

Over England as a whole too the so-called Open Field system developed in middle or late Saxon times. Under this system village families each held strips, divided by baulks or headlands, in several large fields, one of which was usually left fallow each year. The lords of the manor held their demesne land in large blocks, often within the Open Fields. We know that demesne land was held in large blocks in Thanet later, in the 13th century (see p 27), and some evidence of Open Fields here also exists. Kerridge[85] states that long narrow fields of this type persisted into the 19th century, in parts of England, but gives no Thanet source. A study of the 1839–1842 tithe assessment maps however shows that a line of fields of this type then extended between Monkton and Minister on the downland slopes rising to the escarpment. There was also a similar smaller group near Pegwell village, and single long fields at Downbarton, in Birchington, extending inland from Dent-de-Lion, and a possible one near Joss Bay.[86] Detailed investigation, if feasible, might find other explanations for these fields, but they differed clearly in shape from the average of 1839–1842, which was squarish as shown in the tithe assessment maps, and it is possibly significant that they were situated in areas known to be of ancient settlement. Residual common fields have been found on the North Downs near Canterbury.[87]

In the mid-10th century land in western Thanet was given by King Eadmund (reigned 940–946) to various magnates.[88] Christchurch Priory possessed lands in Thanet in the 1030's and perhaps already in Aethelred's reign (978–1016), and later, in the 11th century, these were organized into the Manor of Monkton.[89] But the charter of 961 granting Monkton to Christchurch, confidently accepted by Hasted,[90] and also apparently by Detsicas,[91] is now considered a forgery.[92]

So by the Norman conquest Thanet appears to have been largely under the influence of three big ground landlords, the Abbey, the Priory and the Archbishop. Yet these three directly disposed of only a minor part of the island, although St Augustine's seems to have claimed overlordship over the whole of Minster parish, which as we have seen covered all the eastern part of Thanet. Hasted[93] reported that in his time, the late 18th century, the manor of Minster still claimed paramountcy over most of the former parish, and exacted a rent called Pennygavel from land owners, whilst documents in the Kent archives show that other rights were claimed for the manor into the 20th century, in areas apparently outside the original St Augustine lands. It is likely that Monkton manor did the same in Western Thanet, as in 1760 Quex Park estate was making annual payments of £4/13/4d to the Lord of

Monkton manor.[94] When the "Big Three" first acquired their lands, most of the rest of Thanet was probably still woodland or scrub, but was gradually cleared and brought under cultivation during the Middle Ages. (See pps 31 and 32)

The constant stream of archeological finds continues to confirm the Isle of Thanet's importance and relatively large population in pre-history. The *Archaeologica Cantiana* gives updatings by David Perkins, who is also preparing a new publication, but any printed work is bound to be out of date by the time it appears. Much the same applies to the historical aspects of this chapter. Recent research has begun to lift the curtain higher on the local government structure of late Saxon times, of which so little has been known regarding Thanet.

In the tenth and eleventh centuries, before the Conquest, there was already an organized system of county government based on the various ranks of nobility. Under the County Sheriff were reeves running the Hundreds and lesser landowners within the Hundreds performing functions comparable to those of later J.P.'s. Moneyers collected taxes within a centrally controlled currency system. Alan Everitt has noted a specially large number of lesser landowners in the Kentish downlands, though he does not mention Thanet.[95] The lawless incursions of the Vikings stood in fearful contrast to this society, which probably compared more favourably with the post-1066 Norman regime than historians earlier recognized.

Chapter Two: The Middle Ages: 1066–1485

From 1066 to the latter half of the 12th century: Conquest and Feudalism

In 1066 William the Conqueror's invasion army by-passed Thanet, marching from Dover to Canterbury.[1] An article by Witney reports that the Abbot of St Augustine's opposed the Conqueror, (possibly supporting the failed rising against him at Dover in 1067), and that his lands in Thanet were ravaged as punishment, but that the Thanet lands of Christchurch and the Archbishop enjoyed immunity.[2] According to some writers Thanet was also amongst the districts which the Conqueror ordered to be devastated in the autumn of 1085 to discourage the threatened invasion by King Cnut of Denmark.[3] Domesday Book (1086) descriptions support Witney's case but not that for a devastation in 1085.

Inaccurate statements about Domesday Book on Thanet have been made by many writers, and even the *Victoria County History of Kent* translation is rather misleadingly more sonorous than the brief notes of the original, which run as follows in the admirably literal Morgan translation of 1983:

(Lands of Christchurch Priory). "*In Borough Lathe. In Thanet Hundred. Monkton.*

Before 1066 it answered for 20 sulungs, now for 18. Land for 31 ploughs. In lordship 4. 89 villagers (*villani*) with 21 smallholders (*bordari*) have 27 ploughs. 2 churches; a mill at 10/-. A new fishery. 1 salt house at 15d. Woodland. 10 pigs" (ie. enough to pay 10 pigs in tax). "Value in the time of King Edward" (the Confessor) "£20; now £40."

The second church was probably St Giles at Sarre, which paid

Christchurch 7d a year, according to the Domesday Monachorum, a monastic survey of the period.

(Lands of St Augustine's Abbey)   "*In the Thanet Hundred of St Mildred, Minster.*

"The manor of Minster which answers for 48 sulungs. Land for 62 ploughs. In lordship 2. 150 villagers (*villani*) with 50 smallholders (*bordari*) have 63 ploughs. A church and priest who gives 20s a year. A salt house, 2 fisheries at 3d; a mill. Value at the time of King Edward £80; when the Abbot acquired it" (ie. after the devastation ordered on the Abbot who opposed the Conqueror) "£40; now £100.

"Three men-at-arms" (often translated as knights in other versions) "hold as much of the villagers' land of this manor as is valued at £9 when there is peace in the land: they have 3 ploughs there."[4] The statement about the value of the knights' land has been described as singular by a leading agrarian scholar.[5]

The Chislet estate of St Augustine's also held 6 sulungs at Margate, with four saltpans. Another 1½ sulungs were held in Thanet by Vitalis, a knight holding Northwood manor near Reculver, and Reculver itself (belonging to the Archbishop) held four sulungs in Thanet, according to the Domesday Monachorum and another survey related to Domesday Book.[6] No Thanet places except Sarre, Margate, Minster and Monkton are mentioned in any of these sources.

The Domesday references to sums of money relate entirely to the amounts payable in tax on the item or by the person in question. A recent definition of its use of the term sulung describes it as "a defined unit of land" (for tax purposes) "superimposed on holdings, rather like the grid on an Ordnance survey map",[7] for by this time sulung and ploughland were no longer synonymous, as is evident from the greater number of the latter in Minster and Monkton.

The mills were water-mills, fed by long shrunken or dried-up streams. The first water-mill in England was probably at Chart, Kent, in 762.[8] The mention of a "new" fishery suggests that fisheries may have consisted of an arrangement of stakes and nets in the shallow waters of the Wantsum, such as was used at Pegwell Bay in the 19th century (see p 86). It is tempting to speculate that the woodland for the swine might have been in the Woodchurch area, since this was part of Monkton parish. Lewis[9] argued from

Domesday Book that Thanet must have had at least 1,000 acres of woodland then, which is plausible, but not actually stated in Domesday, as often assumed. We do not know what percentage of the swine was required to be given up as tax in Kent, so we are left guessing as to the total number in Monkton's possession. One in seven had to be paid over in Sussex, one in ten in Hereford.[10] Nothing was said of Minster's Tenterden *den* (swine pasture), but few dens were mentioned in Domesday, and it is thought that by that time the Wealden swine pastures had become cultivated.[11] The absence of any mention at all of swine or woods in Minster's ownership is something no scholar has commented on yet, but Domesday does contain omissions.[12]

Nor is anything revealed in Domesday of the local Thanet relations between the religious bodies and the knights, villagers (*villani*) and small-holders (*bordari*). The term *villani* is now considered "a rough general one, used by the ... Domesday clerks to cover any freemen or unfree serfs who owed labour service as rent".[13] The *villani* were not slaves or chattel serfs (*servi*), nor were the *bordari*, who are thought to have occupied less land than the *villani*.

In Kent as a whole there was an average of 3.7 families per ploughteam, poorer than Sussex, Essex or Cambridge, but not as poor as Lincolnshire.[14] Thanet, with an average of just over 3.4 families to a team, was slightly better than the Kent average. The general social set-up seemed somewhat dissimilar to the rest of Kent: in the county as a whole something over half the land belonged to the Church, and something over half the population were *villani*,[15] many of the rest belonging to various categories not mentioned in Thanet. But here according to Domesday nearly all the land belonged to the Church as ultimate overlord at least, and most of the people were *villani*.

Domesday and its related surveys indicate a total Kent population of 11,753, of whom only 46 were entirely free and only 1,160 slaves.[16] Multiplication of the number of family heads by four or five is currently accepted by historians as a rough means of estimating a medieval population;[17] this would give a figure of 800–1,000 for Minster and 400–500 for Monkton, including the knights, their families and servants and such few monks and their servants as might have been present (it appears that there were never many of them here). The population may not have all been concentrated in the historic village centres, but may have been spread out over the two parishes, all over the island. The total, plus any who may have escaped the attention of the Domesday clerks, may have amounted to no more than that estimated by Thanet Archeological Trust from the burial sites of the early Saxon period (see p 7).

Minster was evidently the centre of Thanet life, since it was given the right to a market in 1115 or 1116,[18] and this right was confirmed at various times far into the 14th century (see p 34). But in the 12th century references to the other parts of Thanet apart from Minster, Monkton and Margate began to appear in the records. Tradition says that St John's church was founded in 1050, and St Lawrence in 1062.[19] In 1128 chapels of Minster parish at St John's, St Peter's and St Lawrence were mentioned in an extant document,[20] and these were enlarged in the late 12th and 13th centuries.[21] St Giles at Sarre is again mentioned by name in 1194–5.[22] All Saints' at Shuart is thought to have been started before the Conquest, but received stone form probably in the 13th century.[23] St Nicholas church dates from the 12th century in its approximate present form, but is thought to be based on an earlier Saxon one. It was a chapel-of-ease to Reculver until it became a separate parish in 1294.[24] All Saints' Birchington was a chapel-of-ease of Monkton parish until 1871, and the present church also dates from the latter half of the 12th century, tradition saying that it contains stone from an earlier one at Gore End (Minnis Bay, see p 51), which was threatened by the sea and taken down.[25] St Nicholas at Woodchurch too was a chapel-of-ease of Monkton, but virtually nothing is known of its origins, though it was probably of roughly similar age to the rest. The parish churches of Minster and Monkton were enlarged in the 12–13th centuries on Saxon remains, and a church of St Peter and Paul was built in early Norman times beside the St Augustine's abbey in Minster.[26] In short, the seven ancient Thanet churches now standing, and probably all the four that disappeared, were considerably enlarged or actually constructed in the great age of church and cathedral building from the 11th–13th centuries. This showed growing centres of population, with some leadership from prosperous if not noble families.

From pre-Conquest times until 1157, according to the only source, most manors belonging to Christchurch were leased out in entirety, either to a tenant or to a professional steward.[27] In the Archbishop's lands similar leasing probably continued to 1200.[28] The position in St Augustine's lands is not clear from the existing studies; Domesday Book indicates that it did less demesne farming at Minster than Christchurch Priory at Monkton, since there were only two ploughs on the Minster demesne to four on the one at Monkton.

Land was traditionally believed to have been leased or assigned after the Conquest to various magnates, many of whom are shadowy, as are those from whom they may have acquired their estates.[29] There seems no doubt about the de Criol family who held land at Sarre and St Nicholas from the Archbishop in the 13th and 14th centuries, some of it at least under knight's tenure at Sarre from 1210. Nicholas de Criol and his son were from time to time summoned by Edward I (reigned 1272–1307) to take military commands in France. In 1346 a Sir John is known to have held "one fee in the vill of St Nicholas and one in Sarre".[30] Sir John de Criol is claimed by Philipott to have commanded the forces of Henry V at the Battle of Agincourt in 1415, and his son Thomas to have been governor of "Gournay in Brittany"[31] (possibly a confusion with Gourney-en-Bray near Amiens). In 1248 Michael le Tenet held his land in knight's service of Margaret Countess of Lincoln,[32] but the extent and duration of her landowning in Thanet is uncertain. The Leybourne family, Counts of Huntingdon, owned the manor of Dene or Le Dene at some time, and Juliana of Leybourne gave it to St Augustine's in 1362. Dene manor appears to have been the Dane valley/St John's part of Margate, and not Lydden in its small, dry valley in the central plateau. According to Davis, Dene was given to St Augustine's with "marshes, streams, mills, services, tenements" etc., and there was marsh in the Marine Terrace/Westbrook area of Margate well into the 19th century. Dene also contained a chapel under the mother church of Minster, seemingly St John's.[33] Vincent's farm is said to have been named from Adam le Vinch, a 13th century possibly knightly occupier or founder, Flete farm from a similar de Fleta.[34] More detailed specialist research is needed to identify our placenames. Thanet Lydden has been confused with marsh Lydden between Sandwich and Dover by a leading modern medievalist, and it is easily done by scholars not closely familiar with the countryside.[35]

The size and exact location of the landholdings of the three main ecclesiastical lords in Thanet in the Middle Ages has not been clarified much yet. Possibly 9½ sulungs belonged to the Archbishop in the 13th century, but even this is uncertain since his possessions at Northwood might have been in Thanet or at the other then so-named Northwood near Reculver. Sarre and Downbarton seem to have been his only definitely known manors in Thanet.[36] There is no evidence that the Christchurch monks owned any manor outside Monkton itself except for Brooksend.[37] St Augustine's evidently disposed of the largest territory. A document given by Davis as an appendix to his translation of and commentary on William of Thorne's chronicle, which may be coeval with the chronicle's end in 1397, lists "the land of the manors of St Augustine's as measured". As cited by Davis, this document is decidedly confusing, but seems to indicate a total holding in Thanet of 4,077 acres (the virgates seem to be identical with a rod). Most of this lay between the manors of Minster and Cliffsend, but there was also land at the following manors: Hengrene (probably Hengrove farm) 203 acres 3 virgates; Salmanston (Salmeston) 99 acres 1 virgate; Newlond (Newlands farm) 126 acres; Aldelond (Alland Grange) 62 acres; Caleys (Callis Court) 59 acres 1 virgate; and "356½ acres 1½ virgates" of sacristy land.[38] As well as the directly owned land, St Augustine's claimed rights over the manor later known as Nethercourt, and "other minor manors under the manor of Minster", according to a Minster manor document of about 1750.[39]

Other known or likely candidates for minor manors under the main ecclesiastical powers are some of those mentioned by Hasted: Thorne, Pegwell, Nash Court, "Westgate alias Garling", Ozengell Grange, Manston Court, and Sheriff's Court (this last doubtful) under St Augustine's, and St Nicholas Court under the Archbishop. Hasted also mentions "Brockman's" (College Farm, which he says belonged with St Nicholas Court estate and got its name from being bought by Queen's College, Cambridge, in 1473, well before the Dissolution) and Dane Court, which Hills found had never been a manor.[40] Hasted did not mention Vincent's, Dene or Sarre in this category, although the last certainly was a manor under the Archbishop, and Dene was one under St Augustine's for a while at least. Melling observes that most Kentish manors under ecclesiastical overlords were leased to farmers and not nobles; a Court farm was where the manor court was held. Monkton Court Farm was certainly the centre of the Christchurch manor, as the present Minster Abbey was of the St Augustine's manor, and the Abbey was known as Minster Court Farm from the Dissolution to its return to a Roman Catholic order of nuns in 1937. (There is a recognizable architectural similarity between the two buildings.) In at least two surviving cases in the former St Augustine's lands there are a Court farm and an ordinary one of the same name: the two are Nash Court and Nash Farm, Spratling Court and Spratling

Farm, the latter no longer a farm. Flete Court farm was not built till after 1872, as the ordnance survey map of that year shows its site as a bare field. The remains of private pre-Reformation chapels survive at Thorne, Manston Court and Callis Court, proof of earlier status, and there is published evidence that the Thorne one was medieval. Henry of Thorne held the manor and had a private chapel there in 1300.[41]

The knights or others who may have held these minor manors were not large farmers by modern standards. An average knight on the Archbishop's estates in Kent had one or two plough teams, and was lord of eight fairly substantial village families and four or five cottagers, who could raise two plough teams between them.[42] It seems unlikely that the picture could have been much different in Thanet under any of the lords.

Under the manorial system in the early 12th century more servile conditions obtained for the average tenant, now known as a villein. In Thanet on the Archbishop's land the men had to bargain with the bailiff before they could marry outside the manor, though the custumal (setting out customary rights) guaranteed that they could not be fined more than 5/-. Frequently even those having the status of gavelkinders (free tenants) had to seek per-mission to marry off their children outside the manor.[43] Conditions were presumably similar in the monastic lands. This situation per-sisted after 1200. Gavelkind, much heard of in the post-Conquest centuries, probably had ancient Anglo-Saxon origins. It was an inheritance system whereby land was shared amongst sons or brothers; their widows could hold half the land of their deceased spouses provided they neither remarried nor bore a child out of wedlock. The parcelling of land caused by gavelkind was probably constantly cancelled out by amalgamation,[44] and the number of surviving children was seldom likely to have been so large as to make it impractical.[45]

The harshening of labour conditions after the Conquest has been roughly explained by increasing requirements of the lords and shortage of labour. It was at this time too that in many parts of England the villagers may have moved towards a more village organized system of common field management, which made more efficient use of grazing for livestock on the stubble after harvest.

In Thanet, however, it is thought that there was little or no common cultivation, but no absolute proof has so far been pub-lished. In many parts of England common use of lands lingered on into the 18th century, but in Kent it either never was or disappeared very early. Thirsk originally considered that much of the land in Kent and Sussex was never held in common, partly because of gavelkind, and that areas with plenty of pasture and woodland did not need to graze animals on stubble and therefore had less reason to abolish the baulks which divided the individual strips in the Open Fields when there was no common cultivation. She considered that enough woodland survived in Saxon and medieval Thanet to provide opportunities for gainful employment other than agriculture, thus encouraging individual farms.[46] Dennis Baker in his study of North Kent farming suggested that not only the pastures available on the reclaimed marsh in Thanet, perhaps from the 12th and certainly from the 13th century, would have precluded the need for communal grazing, but also that fishing could have provided as lucrative a dual occupation with agriculture as could forestry.[47] (Some indication of the wealth of fish available can be seen by the fact that Sandwich in Domesday Book paid a rent of 40,000 herrings a year to Christchurch Priory, which implied a total catch of about 500,000).[48] More recently Dr Thirsk expressed the view that this does not exclude the possibility that kinsmen associated through gavelkind in the subdivision of a piece of land may have engaged in some form of common cultivation amongst themselves.[49]

From the late 12th century to 1325: a peak of prosperity

With the growth of population, the more rapid circulation of money and general prosperity in the late 12th and 13th centuries, serfdom became less necessary to the lords of the manor, and the financial advantage of leasing land for money more obvious. In the Christchurch lands in Kent from 1157 letting to numbers of smaller demesne tenants, not to one large tenant as before, is said to have become common. On the Archbishop's lands letting to one large tenant seems to have continued to 1200,[50] and in the 13th century leasing of manors to individual monks was widely practised by Christchurch Priory.[51] But Roger de Cobham of Monkton, who became High Sheriff of Kent in 1262,[52] must presumably have been a lay tenant of the manor. What happened on the St Augustine's lands has not so far been revealed.

By the 14th century the free personal status of the men of Kent seems to have become fairly well-established;[53] a legal decision of

1293 declared that villeinage did not exist there.[54] Sub-tenants of the manorial tenants remained obligated to their lords for services and payments in kind at the start of this period, but these were increasingly commuted to payments in cash.

Davis concluded that the Christchurch monks were better land-lords than the St Augustine's ones; he saw the Abbots as rapacious, especially from 1259 when a huge increase in payments was extracted from the tenants. Then in 1273 the sum of £53/6/8d was demanded from Minster to buy the Abbot a palfrey (a horse then costing a few pounds), and this special subsidy was repeated twice more. Davis also claimed that the Abbot hanged seven of his tenants in one year,[55] but these opinions have been contested (to the author) by at least one modern scholar (whose verdict unfortunately is not yet in print), who considers that it is not proven that the Abbot ordered the hangings personally and that in general there was not much to choose between the various ecclesiastical landlords. Some researches by John Land suggest that there were plenty of disputes between tenants and the Arch-bishops in the St Nicholas area.[56]

But no documented evidence of unrest in Western Thanet has yet been published, whilst it has long been known that discontent smouldered in the St Augustine's lands, centering on the Abbot's requirement that the tenants attend his court in Canterbury, held once every three weeks, or pay a fine. Two different versions of the dispute have appeared. The chronicle of William of Thorne presents it as purely due to this reason, whilst Dom Pragnell's account based on the chronicle of William of Byholte views it as an attempt by Thanet notables to put the island under the direct jurisdiction of the Sheriff and not the Abbot. Perhaps the two arguments are not incompatible. The journey to Canterbury in those days was arduous and time-wasting, and only minor matters could be settled in Minster.

Complaints about the attendance at Canterbury were made unsuccessfully in 1165 and 1176, resulting then in an agreement between the Abbot and 29 men of Thanet that they would attend court. This document is instructive also for the names of the 29, which show, following the Christian names, a mixture of Norman-French style by-names, Anglo-Saxon patronymics and, rarely, early Middle English nicknames. Head of the list was Adrianus Miles (knight), believed to be a member of the de Criol family, others included Robertus de Westgaethe, Ode, Asketinus and Aelmerus de Cliuesende, Normanus de Liedienne, Aeluiath Kete (bold, brave), Aedwardus fillus Brithue, Wluricus filius Achemann, Jordanus de Dumeitune.[57]

Another unsuccessful complaint was made in 1198. In 1216 the people of Thanet, or some of them, supported Louis of France when he was invited by the barons to oust King John, and they rose and looted several Thanet manors – the references so far do not reveal which ones. In 1318, 660 tenants attacked St Augustine's manors at Salmestone and Cliffsend, cutting down trees, destroying seven carts and imprisoning two monks and servants at Salmestone and one monk at Cliffsend, later selling him for 4/-! In Minster itself they attacked the manor guards, made disturbances against the monks' bailiffs, and raised money for their cause.

This too ended in victory for the Abbot, but Edward II intervened on behalf of the tenants and saved them from imprisonment on payment of a £200 collective fine. The following year, 1319, the Abbot agreed to hold his court only twice a year, and Thanet could send representatives,[58] but the discontent erupted again later in the century.

The growing profitability of agriculture (due basically to rising population) led to the introduction of direct demesne farming through lay serjeants (stewards) by the Christchurch monks at latest by 1278, perhaps as early as 1222 in Thanet,[59] and from as early as 1200 by the Archbishop.[60] As well as the serjeants, reeves (bailiffs or foremen) and wage labourers were employed on the demesnes in this period. The position on the St Augustine's lands is unknown, but the above-cited description of the 1318 rising, though from an old source not particularly interested in the agrarian structure, suggests that some amount of direct demesne farming was possibly being carried out.

Thanks to the work of Du Boulay and the two Smiths we know more about agriculture in Western Thanet in the 13th and 14th centuries than in any part of the island before or later until the 17th century, though nothing has been published about yields and the information is somewhat sparse, since these writers were not focussing on Thanet exclusively. The sale of corn at Monkton is said to have brought in £74/6/- in 1230–1231,[61] and during the priorate of Henry of Eastry (1285–1331) the monks of Christchurch Priory were sowing 4 bushels of wheat per acre, 6 bushels of spring barley per acre, and 6 of spring oats, on their estates in East Kent, presumably including Thanet. This was nearly three times the amount sowed by their French counterparts; these large amounts of seed were an innovative attempt to overcome weeds, birds, and failure to germinate in the rough seed beds produced by the rudimentary tools.[62] In 1285 most of the arable land was under barley and oats, but the wheat acreage rose steadily from 1300 to 1325. Both at Monkton and at Brooksend frumentum (an early form of barley) and inde (a grain crop) were grown as well as wheat in 1315–16. In that year 107 seams of wheat was grown at Monkton and 27 seams 6 bushels at Brooksend; 27 seams 6 bushels of frumentum at Brooksend and 27 seams at Monkton; 37 seams of inde at Monkton and 8½ at Brooksend. The corn farming was very profitable for both monks and tenants.[63] Vetch was also widely grown, and peas and beans were introduced in the late 13th/early 14th century.[64]

In the 13th century marling was carried out on a small, perhaps experimental scale on the brick earth at Monkton – 8 acres in 1225 for the cost of £4, and 11 acres in 1252 for 19/6d, so it was getting cheaper. The land was consistently fertilized in the first half of the 14th century, though we are not told with what. Field size was large by that century in Thanet: 20 to 60 acres, sometimes even 100, and the demesne land lay in blocks, sometimes in larger fields, which is suggestive of few hedges and the possibility of some form of common cultivation. Already in the 13th century the Kentish turnwrest plough was in use in the county. It had a deeper and more pulverizing action than other medieval ploughs, and the detachable mouldboard meant the side of a hill could be ploughed well. Horses were increasingly replacing oxen in this century, about ⅓ horses and ⅔ oxen being used in the Christchurch Priory and Archbishop's estates as a whole, but the Thanet proportions are not known.[65]

It is possible that corn exports from Thanet commenced (or recommenced, remembering the likelihood of them in Roman times) in this period, for Sandwich and its limbs are recorded as exporting corn, apparently mainly to London, from 1304–5.[66]

A great boost to livestock husbandry was given by the retreat of the sea from the Wantsum Channel. The first spit of land (at first an island) to emerge from the sea seems to have been at Stonar, which must have appeared by the 8th century, and had dried out sufficiently to support a town, church and harbour, opposite Sandwich, by the 12th. Stonar enjoyed a rather important status for a relatively short period only. It suffered from sea floods in 1365, when the three miles of low land as far as Cliffsend was inundated, and in 1385 it was burned down by the French, thenceforth almost abandoned until the 20th century.[67]

Reclamation of land from the sea all along the Thanet coasts of the Wantsum went ahead busily in the 13th century. Northward of Brooksend, Hale and Shuart and off the shores of the Archbishop's land from St Nicholas to Sarre it seems to have been carried out by individual tenants,[68] but the monks took the lead or competed with tenants for the marsh in the Minster-Monkton area. Walls to enclose land from the sea were made from earth heaped around hurdles and bundles of straw, and thatched, supplemented by groynes. (The marsh language of East Kent is distinctive: dykes are called walls, and drainage channels are called dykes). The most famous monument to this endeavour by the monks is the Abbot's Wall, still bearing this name, and running north of the Stour from Minster towards Sarre as a raised earth-road to this day. By 1306 the Monkton monks had 366 acres of marsh and their tenants only 53½ acres. The furthest part of the marsh to the North towards the present Reculver–Birchington sea wall was not completely reclaimed till the 18th century,[69] and this was where the sea broke through again in 1953.

As late as 1242 however Minster still had a harbour, accessible to the sea via its own creek, for which the Abbot enjoyed toll privileges.[70] Sarre was being used for grain export as late as 1348.[71] It was a member of the Cinque Ports by the end of the 12th century, perhaps even from Edward the Confessor's reign, but the position of Minster in relation to this confederation has not been clarified by the principal writer on its history.[72] As an ecclesiastical property it does not seem to have belonged. With the ebbing of the sea from the Wantsum, Minster and Sarre lost their maritime use and the open seaports of Thanet became important. (See p 38).

Meanwhile sheep and later cattle raising began on the newly-won marsh pastures, and dairy farming became very profitable. About 1322 there were 2,000 sheep at Monkton,[73] and the monks alone had 847 sheep including 689 ewes in 1314–15, in which year they made 985 cheeses for sale.[74] Cows were milked only from St George's Day on 23 April to Michaelmas Day on 29 September, for there was no winter fodder but hay. Pigs, by now a more domestic animal, were raised in piggeries, tiled ones in the Archbishop's establishments.[75] In 1302 the Christchurch monks bought 40 pigs from their Monkton steward for £4/13/4d.[76]

Demesne farming by the Christchurch monks reached its apogee in 1285–1331. At Monkton many wage labourers were employed on the demesne in the 14th century. In 1307, according to R.A.L. Smith, 17 ploughmen or carters were paid 3/- a year and a gift of gloves. Four swineherds, two cowherds, one shepherd and a harrower got 3/- for full-time work, and a part-time harrower got 1/6d. Three stackers, three drovers and one lambherd got 2/-, a sower 4/-, a cheese-maker 3/-, with a serjeant at £2/14/-, a beadle at 13/4d and a hayward at £1/4/1 to supervize them.[77]

Prosperity and rising population brought about "an explosive fragmentation of tenure" in the 13th century.[78] Even before the chief lords (monks, magnates and Archbishop) commuted the services and gifts due to them for cash, sub-tenants in some parts of Thanet (not specified by the sources) were paying 10/8d per annum for 8½ rods of land in 1262, and at Minster in 1256 15 acres were being rented for 7/-. Prices charged varied, but these seemed fairly typical according to Detsicas.[79] In 1300–01 ploughing services at Monkton were commuted by the monks at 10d per acre,[80] and in the St Augustine's land, sometime before the end of the 13th century, service rent for an acre of ploughland could be commuted to 12d–16d, and 16/- paid per sulung in place of supplying a horse's labour for ploughing. As far as gifts went, 9d per lamb could be paid in place of a customary gift of two lambs on 24 June, but there was no commutation for 2½ loads of barley due to be paid at Easter.[81] These commutations too were offered to the tenants of the sulungs, who bore collective responsibility in each sulung for the performance of certain services or payments in cash or kind.[82] Sulung tenants are not mentioned in the Archbishop's lands after the late 13th century,[83] and no mention of them in the Christchurch lands has been found in published sources either.

In 1313 the Abbot of St Augustine's was confirmed by itinerant royal justices in the following rights at Minster – the list seems worth quoting in detail for the medieval flavour:- "Soke and sake (rights of local jurisdiction and fining), grithbrech, homsoknes, forstall, infongenathef (all rights of jurisdiction over various crimes of violence), flemenfremes (exacting penalties for entertaining banished persons), tolls and theams (these appear similar to tolls here) on land and water, and free warren, and the Hundred of Ringslow (as Thanet Hundred was renamed in the 13th century) at fee farm (fixed permanent rent), and the chattels of felons and runaways, and the tenants of the same living on their manors, wheresoever condemned, with a year and waste (for a year and a day), also chattels belonging to the King of all such felons etc; frankpledge (right to demand mutual financial responsibility from members of a manor), weif (unclaimed animals and things), wreck of the sea, thieves captured on land and arrest of thieves, and pastio over their own men (right to dispose of the followers or chattels of such arrested felons), and toll within the boundaries of manors where it is right and customary and the custom called theams" (probably in this context an obsolete phrase of varying interpretation by the end of the 12th century). The Abbot was also confirmed in the right to hold a market each Friday at Minster (see p 20) and a fair each year on the eve and day of St Mildred. The somewhat repetitive and overlapping list of rights was typical of such documents, which most of the population, being illiterate, would have found intimidating. Financial benefit would accrue to the Abbot from the rights, and perhaps from whatever powers were associated with the Hundred of Ringslow.[84] No such document has been mentioned for the Christchurch monks, who did not control the Hundred of Ringslow rights and must have held a less powerful position in the island as a whole.

Regarding the right to free warren, it may be noted that the rabbit existed in England in an earlier inter-glacial, but became extinct. It was re-introduced in the early 13th century, and remained rather rare and sought after through the rest of the Middle Ages. Wild rabbits were encouraged to breed in enclosed pillow-shaped mounds,[85] an adaptation of this method still being used in Thanet in the first half of the 19th century (see p 101). As well as the modern speckled brown kind, black and silver-grey wild varieties were found in parts of medieval England, though there is no mention of them here.[86]

1325–1485: Decline and Recovery

Despite the demands of the monks, the population must have greatly increased between 1086 and the first half of the 14th century if the Domesday record is anywhere near accurate. Not only the church building, but a tax register of 1334–1335 shows the difference. This listed in the Hundred of Ringslow 685 heads of households able to pay tax, one group (about 45%) being in the jurisdiction of the Cinque Ports (Stonar and Margate, which had become a "limb" of Dover by 1293, see p 38) and another (about 55%) outside their authority in the rest of Thanet. Sarre was listed in the Hundred of Bleangate with its fellow Cinque Ports member Reculver, together with which it had 19 households capable of tax-paying. It is impossible without specialist research to distinguish

Margate's population from Stonar's, or Sarre's from Reculver's, but if the tax-capable households constituted slightly under half the total number, as Chalklin considered,[87] and allowing 4–5 per household, there would have been roughly 5–7,000 people in Thanet and Stonar together at that time, a rise of at least well over threefold since 1086, and possibly nearer fivefold.

No estimates for Stonar's population have been found (its relics vanished into the gravel pits before any extensive archeological survey was made), but that of Sandwich was apparently very large for the period. At Domesday it is said to have been the fourth largest town in England, with 312 inhabited houses, and in 1377–1400 it had 810 inhabited houses and an estimated population of over 3,000.[88] Stonar seems to have been still thriving in 1334, and judging from the number of Thanet by-names in the group in which it was included, many from Thanet must have moved there; one would expect such a town to attract migration from the rural areas. As it had barely any inhabitants at Domesday, its growth had been even faster than Thanet's, as something like an overspill town for Sandwich.

Assessments ranged from 1/- to £1/-/2d, the average being about 3/-, except for Sarre with Reculver where it was nearly 7/-. Only 23 people paid more than 10/-. The total for Thanet and Stonar without Sarre was £106/4/4d, for Sarre and Reculver £7/9/5½d, A number of women were listed as heads of households, some said to be widows, others with no indication of marital status. In Chalklin's analysis the assessments were some of the lowest in Kent,[89] but a recent study suggests that Kent was eighth in yield per 1,000 acres at this time, with the Northeast of the county much higher than the West. Prosperity is certainly suggested by the "unusually sumptuous" 14th century tower of St Nicholas church, a twin with that of Herne.[90]

In these assessments the only titled people named (all outside the Cinque Ports so definitely in Thanet proper) were a Lady de Goschalle and a John Miles (knight). (Various people with the surname Kniht were probably titleless descendants of knights). Other East Kent Hundreds had equally few or none; Kent had held few important secular estates since the end of its independent kingdom, and in the 14th century knights became rare in the whole county.[91] There seem to have been no lay or ecclesiastical deer parks in Thanet at any time in the Middle Ages after the Conquest, which is significant as they were the status symbol of the gentry and nobility.[92] The Thanet woods may not have been particularly impressive even at Domesday, and they may have been substantially cleared by the 14th century, which would be consistent with the rising population. We know that timber was brought from Fordwich to repair groynes at Monkton around 1315.[93] We can surmise that there may still have been dwindling patches of woodland, and perhaps clumps of trees which defied the axe, for there was still a tract of apparently ancient woodland at Woodchurch until the early 18th century (see p 69)

It is interesting to see the evolution of names in this period. We have already seen that in the 12th century by-names were used in Thanet as well as patronymics. In the 13th century a number of people used the by-names de Taneto, de Tanet, de Thaneto, de Thanet, but many still had only a personal name and a patronymic. Some women bore such names as Godelifa and Waltrina amongst the now commoner Margery and Joan, etc, whilst some men were called Eilweker or the Norman Hamo as well as the already more usual Thomas, John, Henry, Richard, Reginald, etc.[94] The register of 1334–35 shows a distinct further development, with a return to more precisely differentiated by-names, such as Elizabeth de Wode, Martin de Ramsgat, John de Brokessende, and some surnames of a modern type which are current in Thanet today: Johnson, Jordon, Phylepot, Kempe, Coleman, Smyth, Saket, etc, together with others such as Queyk which later remained only as place-names or vanished.[95]

Thanet's prosperity seems to have held well into the second quarter of the 14th century. The 1334–35 tax assessment suggests this, and a market was started at Downbarton in 1337 according to Hasted,[96] though this may have been connected with the greater navigability of the Wantsum on that side of Thanet compared to Minster. The island was able to produce two gentlemen with sufficient resources to become High Sheriffs of Kent in this period – Ralph de St Lawrence in 1326 and Thomas de Brockhull of St Lawrence in 1331 and 1336,[97] possibly both minor manor tenants of St Augustine's. Ralph de St Lawrence became a knight of the shire in 1332.[98]

Yet conditions seem to have been gradually becoming less favourable. A great drought hit Thanet and East Kent in 1325–26 according to R.A.L. Smith,[99] and the European climate generally may have become colder after 1300.[100] A series of animal plagues began in 1327, with recurrence at intervals till nearly the end of the century.[101] The war with France added an economic strain: the mint at Canterbury was closed in 1324 for lack of silver.[102] In 1348 came the Black Death, a combination of pneumonic, bubonic and septicaemic plague strains, which struck at a population in many parts of England known to have been already weakened by starvation, due mainly to adverse weather.[103]

It was possibly not so here, for there is no direct report of the impact of the plague in Thanet, and Mavis Mate has established that the initial epidemic of 1348 did no more in East Kent as a whole than reduce the over-large population to a more viable level for the agriculture of the day to support, enabling the economy to function at a high level of efficiency till the 1380's. It was the many recurrences of the plague (which went on till 1670), and the series of animal plagues which gradually lowered both human and animal populations below the optimum, so that by the 1380's wages rose, prices fell, arrears started to accumulate and holdings increasingly fell vacant.[104]

In 1348 Kentish wage rates may have been as follows according to an 18th century Kentish source:- 13/8d for a bailiff with clothing once a year; 10/- for master hinds, shepherds and carters; 6/8d for oxherds; 6/- for deyes (dairymen) and 7/- for plough drivers.[105] But wages are known to have soared after 1348. At some point there was a return to labour services again at Monkton, for the sub-tenants of the manor could no longer afford money payments, and by 1390 these services were far heavier than a century earlier.[106] Wages for ploughmen at Monkton rose from 11/2d or 12/- per annum in the mid-1370's to 14/2d. in the mid-1380's.[107] In 1383–84 a labourer was paid 4d a day for working on the sea wall at Brooksend,[108] an immense wage if the source is correct, but the work may have been unpopular. Similar work at Monkton was also paid 4d.[109]

Incomplete archeological digs indicate that the decline of the villages at Shuart and Woodchurch may have been a result of the plague, although whether it happened abruptly or gradually is not known.[110] The investigations at Shuart were more extensive than at Woodchurch and suggested that at its height Shuart was probably equal in size to the St Nicholas of the time. It was made into a united parish with St Nicholas by Archbishop Winchelsea in 1310, when possibly the two villages had been expanding towards one another at this period of demographic growth,[111] and possibly it had been decided to concentrate funds on the improvement of St Nicholas church, for this was round about the date of its new tower (see p 31). St Nicholas church at Woodchurch is known from a number of documentary references between 1292 and 1544;[112]

there are traces of the village also in the appearance of the names "de Wode" and "atte Wode" in the tax register of 1334–35 (see p 32), and of the names "Robert Wodechyrch" and "Thomas Wodechyrych" in the 1441 agreement between the Abbot of St Augustine's and some of his Thanet tenants (see p 37). Both All Saints' Shuart and St Nicholas Woodchurch appear on Thomas of Elmham's early 15th century map of Thanet, together with the Norman church of St Peter and Paul at Minster Abbey, and St Giles at Sarre, and the existing old churches.

In 1362 the extensive rights of jurisdiction of the Abbot of St Augustine's at Minster were reconfirmed.[113] The position regarding leasing, labour services and rents in the St Augustine's lands after the Black Death has not been clarified in published work so far, but labour services were in force there in 1381 and the regime was evidently felt to be onerous, particularly the continuing obligation to send representatives to the court at Canterbury. This led the men of the Thanet estates to take part in Wat Tyler's rebellion, otherwise known as the Peasants' Revolt. Triggered off by the arrival of Wat and his men at Canterbury on 10 June 1381, the Thanet revolt broke out at St Lawrence and St John's on 13 June. At the latter it was led by the local curate, probably wretchedly paid by the Abbot in Davis' opinion.[114] A proclamation in the name of Jack Straw and Wat Tyler ordered that labour services should not be performed nor distraints made, and called on the people to destroy the Manston house of William de Medmenham, (a local coroner who evidently acted as representative for St Augustine's), and if possible behead him. The same day a crowd some 200 strong attacked the house, burnt "the books and muniments" and "took away and burnt the rolls" to the value of 20 marks.

On 8 July de Medmenham's house in Canterbury was also looted, and John Bocher, a Thanet tailor, carried out a raid of his own, extorting 32/- by force of arms from one John Wynnepenny at his house in Canterbury. Medmenham himself evidently escaped. The rebels levied a tax Thanet-wide to fund themselves, but exempted the tenants of Christchurch Priory, which indicates that these were not taking any action against their overlord. Witness to the above events at the enquiry was borne by the jurors of the Hundred of Ringslow William Daundelion (Dent-de-lion) and Thomas Eldrich, and three constables: Stephen Colluere (Collier), Gervase Saghiere (Sayer) and Simon Fygge. It does not appear that any Thanet men went to London with the rebels, although six from Canterbury were amongst those hanged. The demands of the rebels were not met by the government and some payments in kind continued to be exacted by St Augustine's until 1441 at least,[115] though there is no more mention of labour services in the limited published sources.

In other parts of Thanet there were rapid changes at the end of the century. The period from the 1350's to 1390 was one of experimentation by the Christchurch monks, with spells of leasing of manors or demesnes by the Priory interspersed with spells of direct management of the demesnes on behalf of the monks.[116] Thomas Stefthy paid an annual rent of £22, 40 quarters of wheat and 40 quarters of barley for the lease of the Monkton demesne alone for the six years 1391–1396,[117] but after 1390 it was usual for whole manors to be leased out.[118] One demesne somewhere was reserved for the feeding of the monks each year; in 1411 Monkton was the one kept for them, and the eight *famuli* (wage labourers) there were getting still higher wages at £1 per annum.[119] Between the 1380's and 1440 all the Archbishop's land also gradually came to be leased out again. In 1397 the Archbishop rented Downbarton manor to a farmer for £66/3/4d, although the annual value was only £44/9/5d, because nearly £150 worth of the Archbishop's livestock was included in the lease.[120] The rent of Monkton manor in 1406 was £22.[121]

Pastoralism increased in the late 14th century as it required less labour than arable, and the King's demands for the renewed (Hundred Years) war against France stimulated demand for livestock further by 1415. But this demand collapsed again in the 1430's, when there was bad weather and animal pestilence as well,[122] and multiple tenancies of manors granted from this time on may indicate a lack of farmers with much capital and a surge of poorer men eager to get on.[123] In 1431 Monkton manor was leased to Thomas Salesbury, "Jantylman", and Thomas Hyer, yeoman of St Nicholas for £26/13/4d, a marked rise over 1406, but much less than Downbarton in 1397 (although we do not know the sizes of the two manors or other comparative details). Brooksend manor was leased to two Birchington men in the same year for 14 marks, leaving only rights over waifs and strays and wreck of the sea to the Prior and Chapter of Christchurch Cathedral.[124] Corn exported from Sandwich and its limbs also dropped greatly during the later 14th and 15th centuries, falling (though with fluctuations and missing statistics) from 6,630 quarters in 1304–5 to 12 in 1399, rising to 388¼ in 1439–40 and falling to 12 again in 1464–5.[125]

Yet a moderate prosperity, which must have been based on arable, had returned to East Kent by 1440, and though grain production at Monkton and Birchington fluctuated, it held up fairly well between 1455-6 and 1472-3.[126] The cultivation of beans may have stopped at some time in this period, possibly because of labour shortage or climatic worsening. (See chapter 4, p 71). During the 15th century the weather, according to Lamb, was particularly bad, though this is contested by David Farmer except for the 1430's.[127] But corn evidently remained a relatively abundant product. Windmills were apparently increased in this period: the first is said to have been built in Monkton parish in the late 1190's and there were at least two in Monkton manor in 1431, when it was leased to Salesbury and Hyer. There was a water-mill still at Birchington in 1477.[128] (Hasted also mentions a water-mill at Ebbsfleet within the knowledge of the inhabitants in the late 18th century).[129]

A market was started at Monkton in the 25th year of Henry VI (about 1447),[130] when those at Minster and Downbarton probably closed, for markets were not supposed to be held less than 6½ miles apart,[131] and surely at this time of fallen population Thanet could not have supported three? Monkton was about equidistant from the other two, and not too far from the Stour or the Wantsum, so it would have been a rational step to have one market there. Yet it had certainly gone by 1500 (see p 50), perhaps as much because of the decline of the sea passage as anything, for medieval markets are known to have been somewhat dependent on water transport.

Some Thanet farmers of this time may have been well-off for livestock, for a William Aldelond, who fell foul of the law for some reason and drowned himself at the end of January 1445, left "as his winter minimum of livestock" five horses, 20 pigs, 8 bullocks, and 100 sheep. He also grew wheat and barley.[132]

In 1444 Parliament laid down national wages which seem similar or a little lower than those paid at Monkton in 1410-11.[133] An 18th century Kentish source gives slightly different figures for Kent in the same year, as follows:-

Bailiff 23/4d a year with meat and drink and 5/- for clothes.
Chief hind, carter or shepherd 20/- a year with meat and drink and 4/- for clothes.
Common male servant in husbandry 15/- a year with meat and drink and 3/4d (sic) for clothes.

Woman servant in husbandry 10/- a year with meat and drink and 3/- for clothes.

Child under 14, 6/- a year with meat and drink and 3/- for clothes.

In harvest, a mower 4d a day with meat and drink and 6d without.

In harvest, a reaper or carter 3d a day with meat and drink and 6d without.

In harvest women and other labourers, 2½d a day with meat and drink and 4½d without.[134]

In 1441 the Abbot of St Augustine's at last reached an agreement with his 121 sulung tenants holding 47 sulungs in "Minster and Hengrave" to commute the complicated system of rent in cash and kind per sulung to a more straightforward rent of 6½d per acre per annum for Corngavel land and 3d per acre for Pennygavel land. The new arrangements seemed less tiresome and open to abuse than the old, but any proper comment on them must await study by a specialist, which is not so far available. The reduction in the fine for non-attendance at the Abbot's Canterbury court from 6/8d to 1/- was another notable change, but may have been connected with fall in the value of money.[135] This agreement was not the end of the sulung tenants as such, for they are mentioned again some ten years later, in the 30th year of Henry VI (1451–52), when 50 tenants are known to have held "Meregate swyllung" (sulung) of 210 acres, whilst 13, 10, 20, and 15 tenants respectively held the smaller sulungs of Sayling (Garlinge?), Westgate, Syankesdon (Salmeston), and Hertesdowne,[136] all in the St Augustine's lands.

During the last period of the monasteries Christchurch at least, (and probably St Augustine's) acted as a responsible landlord, keeping the tenants' property in good repair and maintaining the sea walls. On one occasion Christchurch gave all its tenants a cloak each. The Christchurch leases generally indicated that many manorial rights were still reserved to the Prior, including "waived estrays, wreck of the sea, royal fish, warren" etc.,[137] but there is no precise information from Thanet in this respect except for the Brooksend lease of 1431.

In the 15th century there is little trace of any knights in Thanet, though some of the rich clergy were commonly called "Sir" – for instance "Sir John" Spicer, vicar of Monkton 1427–1450.[138] Sir Thomas Flete, vicar of St Peter's in 1473, may have been the same or may have been a genuine knight.[139] The pinnacle of Thanet society seems to have been occupied by the Manston and Daundelion families. William Manston was High Sheriff of Kent in 1436.[140]

Nicholas Manston (d 1444) was an armiger esquire whose brass, now illegible, is in St Lawrence church,[141] and John Daundelion (d. 1445) was another such with a brass in St John's church.[142] (An armiger esquire was a gentleman just below the rank of knight entitled to bear arms and wear armour).[143] The Queyk and Parker families at Birchington seem to have been a little lower in status, having brasses in the church, but not being armigers.[144]

Sometime before John (the last of the Daundelions) died the family built the display fortification, of which the tower gate is all that survives in the present Dent-de-Lion estate.[145] It must either have been constructed at a time of local prosperity, or else the family had sources of income other than agriculture. It may be that they were involved in shipping and foreign trade, since John brought a new bell for St John's church, which was inscribed "John de Daundelion with his great Dog, Brought over this Bell on a Mill-cog" – a dog being a type of ship.[146] Lewis mentions what may have been another gate of this kind at Pouces, long since vanished.[147]

The fishing village of Margate had become a "limb" of Dover Cinque Port by 1293. Part of St Lawrence, including the fishing village of Ramsgate, became a "limb" of the Cinque Port of Sandwich in about 1353. Gore End became one of Dover by 1373, and St John's, St Peter's, with Broadstairs small haven, Birchington and Woodchurch became "limbs" of Dover by 1424. They had been trying to acquire this status for over a century previously, probably because of the privileges involved.[148] Part of St Nicholas also came under Sandwich at some date.[149] The Cinque Ports extended their own judicial system over their limbs, which the latter soon came to dislike.

At least eleven Thanet men, including four constables of the Hundred of Ringslow, took part in Jack Cade's rebellion of 1450, which was based on Ashford. Their grievances seem to have centered on the oppression and corruption of Dover Cinque Port court, and the corruption surrounding the election of knights of the shire, of which Thanet had only one in the whole medieval period (see p 32). Thus they were not obviously economic complaints. Amongst those pardoned for participating were the following from Thanet: Thomas Tyrry (Constable), Thomas, Harry and John Rychevile (Constables), John Rychengood, John Rychefeld, Wills Manston, Thomas Seynt Johns, Nichus Sandeway, John Malyn, John Septvans "ac omnes" (and all).[150] Thanet took no part in the other risings of the 1450's according to the latest study by Harvey.[151]

The first printed reference to Thanet, in the description of England by Ranolphus Higden,[152] simply repeated Solinus, so we cannot attach too much importance to it. Yet it is unlikely that he would have ventured to get away with this plagiarism if Thanet's reputation had been otherwise. He wrote:- "Thanatos, that is Tenet, and is an ylonde besides Kent, and hath that name from deth of serpents ... There is a noble corn londe and ryght fruytfull." (Sic).

It is clear that the 13th century witnessed one of the major upsurges of Thanet agricultural techniques; so far as is yet known it was not specific or unique to the island but centred on the ecclesiastical manors all over East Kent, though perhaps more on those of Christchurch than on the rest. Tantalizingly little modern work has been published on the Thanet Middle Ages. Davis' book on William of Thorne's chronicle and Turner and Salter's mostly untranslated Latin transcripts of St Augustine's records call out for a new monograph. Beyond this, the dramatic Malthusian changes of the medieval period in this part of the world are worthy of one or more overall surveys of all their aspects: economic, political, administrative and legal. The example of the monks was believed by later observers such as John Lewis to have been very important for Thanet agriculture.

Chapter Three: Early modern times: 1485–1700

The end of the Middle Ages in Thanet; some general features of the period 1485–1700

The accession of the house of Tudor has often been taken as a political turning point in English history, heralding the end of the Middle Ages, and the emergence of the nation state. In peaceful Thanet change came more slowly than in areas where there were feudal lords with their own armies, whose power was terminated in the reign of Henry VII.

The first year of this first Tudor king, (1485–86) may have seen the end of Thanet as a real island, for according to Hasted an Act that year permitted a bridge to be built over the Wantsum at Sarre.[1] Yet in many ways island conditions prevailed for much longer, for the one small wooden bridge did not much ease the difficult journey to Canterbury and London over un-made roads, and until 1757 the only other crossing points were the ferries over the Stour at Stonar and below Minster and Monkton. (The last two ferries are still shown on H. Hogben's map of 1791). Until the latter half of the 18th century sea transport remained almost as good a way of reaching Thanet as land, and only with the coming of the railways did the land route gain an overwhelming advantage in all weathers.

Until 1538 the ecclesiastical landlords continued as before. Multiple tenancies were still found, in Western Thanet at least, particularly at the end of the 15th century and less so in the early 16th century. A large multiple tenancy of Monkton manor started in 1486–87, when five men (two from Monkton, two from Sarre and one from Minster) leased it for 11 years.[2] Rights of manorial jurisdiction were often shared still. In February 1525 Downbarton was leased to John Everard by the Archbishop for fifteen years at

£60 per annum, with all rents, services, meadows, marshes, fisheries and fowling, together with half the profits of courts, waifs and strays, and a marsh called Wademarsh, but reserving advowsons, wardship and marriage to the Archbishop. The latter was also to repair the marsh wall beyond which the salt water still flowed.[3] The Abbot of St Augustine's retained more rights than this when Minster manor was leased to Roger Bere for £127/9/6d in 1537–38.[4] These increased rights to the landlord may suggest greater eagerness to apply for leases or simply a different policy by St Augustine's; more research is needed on this. A quantity of Thanet corn was available for London by 1535,[5] which supposes prosperity.

The Reformation brought the closing of St Augustine's Abbey in 1538 and of Christchurch Priory in 1540,[6] both of them by then almost purely landlords. The Dean and Chapter of Canterbury Cathedral received (and still retain some of) the Priory lands; those of the Abbey mostly passed to the Crown, or the Archbishop, then later, mainly in the 17th century, to private landlords, amongst them Oxford and Cambridge colleges, which had already begun to acquire land here in the 15th century. The Dissolution of the Monasteries has been described as the real end of the Middle Ages in Thanet. It strengthened the secular propertied classes, sometimes in the most concrete way: stones from St Augustine's Abbey were bought by Henry Crispe to build his new mansion at Quex in 1553![7]

From now until the rise of the towns the standard inhabitants of Thanet consisted of the usually secular landlord, the yeoman (usually tenant) farmer, the husbandman (small farmer, usually a tenant), the cottager and the labourer, together with the parish clergy, the few craftsmen, traders and inn-keepers and the fishermen and seafarers in the fishing villages. A class of large farmers would seem to have re-emerged or have been re-emerging in Henry VIII's reign (1509–1547), (if indeed it had ever been entirely absent), and was to be a feature of the island until the present. A host of lesser holdings probably co-existed with them throughout this period, but it is not until the 17th century that we have proof as to this. (See p 64).

Elements of rent in kind did not entirely disappear until the 19th century, for tithes in particular remained payable partly in grain until the commutation of 1839–1842, and fat hens featured in some cottagers' rents until at least 1774.[8] But market relations, which had been developing fast in the 13th and early 14th centuries, and suffered a setback in the disasters of the later 14th and 15th centuries, now dominated agrarian life. Gavelkind was formally abandoned by most gentry families in Kent between 1538 and 1624, and partitioning of holdings is said to have become exceptional at all social levels in the 16th century.[9] Sulung tenants, with their joint responsibilities, are not mentioned after the 15th century, and it has been concluded that most of Kent was enclosed before 1500.[10] Since Thanet was generally a relatively prosperous area, it may have been early in this process.

Enclosed is not to be thought of in our case as enclosed with hedges throughout, but having the land not in strips, but in consolidated fields, in the occupation of single families. Most authorities seem to think that large hedgeless fields predominated in the lands of the major farms throughout this period, although even in the 17th century there was often much intersection and fragmentation in old enclosed property, made easier by the absence of hedges.[11] A Downbarton Court Baron held on 11 October 1714 shows many tenants still held land in small parcels of a few acres, sometimes several parcels per tenant.[12] But it appears that until the Napoleonic wars there were more hedges than now, with further destruction of them since World War II. The village farms were especially well provided with them, and even the isolated farms have in some cases retained a few until the present. Dennis Baker's study of Quex leases from 1658 to 1769 indicates a mixture of (usually) small fields enclosed with hedges near both isolated and village farms, and further out the hedgeless fields typical of Thanet in our day.[13] A 1688 estate map of Church Hill farm, Birchington, for instance, shows apparent hedges marked green;[14] the hedged fields were called "closes" from the 17th century if not earlier. Thanet was comparatively free of common waste land already in the 16th century,[15] but Minnis Bay was such in medieval times,[16] and some existed near Monkton until the Napoleonic wars (see p 101).

Although a few minor gentry were always present, and there was a sprinkling of knights again from the 16th century, nobility remained largely absent from Thanet throughout this period. Holinshed and Hooker mention no parks belonging to gentlemen in East Kent at all.[17] Philipott, writing in the middle of the 17th century, could find only one titled person in Thanet, Lady Mary St Leger, widow of a baronet, Sir Warham, who leased Salmestone Grange from the Archbishop and may not have lived there.[18] The Conyngham family, who bought a substantial part of the original St Augustine's manor at Minster in the 17th century, were ennobled to Baronet in 1642,[19] then progressively to Baron, Viscount, and Earl by 1780, but never seem to have lived in Thanet.[20] The Thanet men who became High Sheriffs of Kent at this time were all from one family of the squirearchy: 1518 John Crispe of Quekes, 1546 Henry Crispe of Quekes (a dominating person known as the little king or *regulus* of the island), 1650 another Henry Crispe of Quekes.[21] Four members of this family, starting from the *regulus*, became knights in the 16th–17th centuries.[22] In 1599 a Sir Edward Carye leased Minster manor.[23] In the 17th century there was also a Sir Adam Sprackling (died St Lawrence 1610), and a Sir Henry Compton of St Nicholas (c. 1630).[24] There were no knights of the Shire from Thanet after 1332, and a number of people apparently paid contributions to the Exchequer to avoid assuming the financial responsibilities of knighthood.[25] According to the 17th century hearth tax documents, in 1663 Thanet had only three mansions with more than 10 hearths, and all other homes had less than 9. In 1662 two were at Birchington: one belonged to the Crispes, with 17 hearths, to which were attached 424 acres in 1688, and 611 acres in 1700 when their estate was sold. The other large house at Birchington, with 12 hearths, belonged to an unidentified John Hayward.[26] (See p 60).

Apart from their earlier scarcity in Kent as a whole, already discussed, reasons for the lack of titled people are easy to suggest and hard to prove. The almost complete loss of English possessions in France by 1450 and consequent lessening of traffic with the Continent, difficulty of access and social isolation on the peninsula, and the windy, exposed position, are three obvious ones. Of these, Joan Thirsk considers social isolation to be the most important. It was very different in areas nearer London: there were upwards of sixty deer parks near Windsor in the late 16th century.[27] In Thanet too there were not enough trees for deer parks, for we know for certain that they had become few, by the density standards of the time, in the second quarter of the 16th century, nor was upland Thanet a good place for pasture.[28] (See p 52–3 for Leland's and Holinshed's visits and p 54–5 for Fiennes' visit).

After the Dissolution judicial rights, outside the Cinque Ports areas of authority, remained with the manor owners, although more serious offences came under the Justices of the Peace. The duties of a Minster manor Court Leet were updated as late as Queen Victoria's reign, empowering it to try "all offences except petit Treason and Felonies", which had to be sent to a higher court.[29] But J.P.'s, representing Crown justice, were few in East

Kent into the 18th century,[30] although there were always two
at Canterbury for the Quarter Sessions there. There paucity is
explained by the peacableness of the region and the tradition of
manor courts.[31] In the late 16th century the Crispe family at
Quekes seemed to supply the J.P.'s: the only one in Thanet in 1596
was a Crispe.[32] Many manorial rights seem to have fallen into
disuse by the 18th century, but some were still being claimed as
late as the early 20th century.[33]

The parishes gradually took over some of the responsibilities of
the manors. Under the 16th century Poor Laws the Thanet parishes
were slowly turned into administrative units, in the following
order: Birchington 1538, St Lawrence and St John's 1559, Minster
1567, St Peter's 1582, Acol, Sarre and St Nicholas 1653, and
Monkton not until 1700.[34] Under this new system they had to
appoint Overseers of the Poor to administer relief, and local
farmers featured prominently in this role. There is a description of
the introduction of the Poor Law provisions at Birchington in 1615,
though there had been previous sporadic assessments for poor
relief and Overseers had been appointed in 1604.[35] The duty of
maintaining roads was also laid on parishes by the act of 1555, and
again it was farmers who usually held the position of surveyors
until the mid-19th century. Other duties of local government, such
as supervision of apprenticeships, wage levels and grain prices fell,
at least in the less remote parts of England, on J.P.'s.[36] In their
absence here, such matters must have been left to the discretion of
the manor and later parish. Another duty of the parish from
1673–1834 at Birchington was paying for the destruction of vermin:
rooks, crows, choughs, owls, sparrows, foxes, badgers, weasels,
stoats, polecats, hedgehogs, kites, sparrow-hawks, snakes and rats,
but mainly rats and sparrows.[37] It seems that in this period the
administrative and judicial system in Thanet was a hodge-podge,
with the Cinque Ports at Dover and Sandwich, the J.P.'s, manor
owners and parishes all having some say, and the bigger farmers
playing a key role in the last two categories. Farmers may also have
held the post of Deputy of the Cinque Ports in the areas that came
under the same.[38]

There has been speculation that in the 15th or early 16th centuries some Thanet farms might have been nuclei of the proto-
Protestant Lollard movement, which began from the teaching of
Wycliffe about 1380 and continued until it was subsumed into
the Reformation, being persecuted most of the time. One of the
enigmas of the island are the underground chambers or halls,

hewed out of the chalk, to be found in various places, for instance St Nicholas Court, Woodchurch farm, and in the Margate caves. They have inset alcoves reminiscent of church windows, which may have been used for shrines, or simply for placing lights. The persecution of Lollardy might have driven its followers literally underground for their worship. Although the St Nicholas chamber probably began as a permitted private chapel, St Nicholas Court has traditionally been associated with the Lollards and from 1473 part of the estate belonged to Queen's College, Cambridge.[39] Oxford was the centre of the movement, but a connection with Lollardy through the other intellectual centre might not be impossible. The typical late Lollard of the end of the 15th and early 16th centuries was "not extreme or vulgar, quite well-off",[40] which could apply to prosperous farmers. It is more likely that the movement could have spread from the Kentish mainland. No Lollard trials involving Thanet people have been brought to light, and its main Kentish stronghold was in the Tenterden-Appledore-Cranbrook area of the Western part of the county. But known or suspected supporters were tried from Bridge (1497), Canterbury (1498), Waldershare (1511) and Herne and Ringwold (1525) – all near enough for proselytizing in the Lollard manner through friends and kin.[41] The impact of Lollardy must have been slight or well hidden, but a radical strain is known to have kept surfacing in Thanet from the 16th century onwards.

It is worthwhile looking at the politico-religious events of the 16th–17th centuries for the light they throw on the development of Thanet's character. During Henry VIII's Reformation, the return to Catholicism under Mary and the final shaping of the Church of England by Elizabeth I, most of the Thanet population apparently accepted the changes imposed upon them from above, and at first only a few took sides. Clark[42] considered that Thanet was probably a traditional area which had to be roused to Protestantism. This was no doubt true of the majority, but more recently it has been found that the Lollard tradition survived in parts of East Kent into the middle of the 16th century. There was extreme Protestant, Lollard-type activity at Faversham in 1535, at Canterbury in the 1540's, at Faversham again in 1550–51, and some of the Canterbury martyrs burnt under Queen Mary in 1555 were accused of Lollard-type arguments, though none came from Thanet.[43] In 1556 John Alchorne of Birchington denied all the ceremonies of the Church and kept illicit books, though he gave in and agreed to conform.[44]

The Vicar of St Peter's however was accused of supporting the Pope in 1537. Cranmer probably made a preaching tour here, but Serles and Shether, the more Catholic and conservative of the Six Preachers appointed at Canterbury Cathedral in 1541, preached in two Thanet churches each, and two other conservative clergy from Canterbury did likewise, on a single day. Serles (famous for having maintained that Mary gave birth to Jesus when she was fourteen because the moon comes to the full in fourteen days), was vicar of Monkton in 1552–1561.[45] Change came slowly to many: in 1569 the curate at Birchington said he had never had the Thirty Nine articles to read, nor had most clergy in the diocese ever read them.[46]

Later in the century various sectarian tendencies definitely became established here. William Claybrooke, a former lawyer living at Nash Court, owned or had read "all contentious or schismatic books at any time printed" about 1588. The Vicar of St Nicholas, a non-conforming Puritan, preached against other sectaries in 1590. By the end of the 16th century separatist or semi-separatist groups were especially active in Thanet and villages in the Dover area. In 1617–18, under a moderate Puritan archbishop, St John's was one of various parishes in East Kent given a new vicar with reforming duties – a "reformed pulpit" as it was called.[47] The Puritan movement is not mentioned again until the 1640's.

Sectarian or not, Thanet was patriotic. The inhabitants apparently paid their sess for the defence of the realm against the Armada,[48] and by tradition warning beacons were lighted at Beacon Road, Broadstairs. Many sick and wounded English sailors were landed at Margate and Broadstairs. Captain Henry Crisp (who must have been of the Quex family) commanded a company of 250 trained officers and men (probably local militia) to defend the island, being paid £169/15/6d to keep them at the ready for 22 days. Three other companies (two untrained), totalling 470 men, were also deployed here under Captains Partridge, Charles Hales and John Finch. Mr Edward Wotton was appointed overall commander, though it seems uncertain if he actually arrived here. They had orders to retreat to Canterbury if the Spaniards landed, "the Downs and Margate" being thought the likeliest landing places, but neither Canterbury nor the Cinque Ports ever sent in details of possible landing places to the government as they were supposed to do.[49]

What is known of Thanet in the Civil War period (mainly regarding

Minster and Birchington) suggests that it was rather a backwater at that time as in the Reformation. At least three local men, including William Crispe from Quex, joined the rebels at Faversham in the rising against the Covenant imposed by Parliament in 1643. But after that the island duly sided with Parliament, like the rest of Kent; only Birchington was a Royalist nest under Crispe domination, but no reprisals are as yet known to have been made. It became a wedding centre for those disliking the Puritan wedding service, which its Vicar did not introduce for some time.[50] Minster petitioned against its Vicar, Merle Casubon, for being too High Church, also for raising tithes 50%, which may have been the stronger grievance. His successor in 1642, Richard Culmer, was even more unpopular, although a rampant Puritan who was involved in the destruction of the medieval stained glass in Canterbury cathedral, and in Minster church of the glass and the crosses, and the globe and great wooden cross then crowning its spire as well.[51] Extreme Protestant clergy were appointed to Monkton, St Lawrence, St Peter's and St John's too, but seem to have met with no opposition. A political incident which aroused great interest in local historians was the kidnapping by Royalists of Henry Crispe at Quex for a large ransom in 1657.[52]

In 1660 the Rev. Peter Johnson, ejected from St Lawrence at the Restoration, set up a congregation of dissenters at Ramsgate,[53] and at the end of the century a few Quakers and Anabaptists were active, especially in Birchington and Margate.[54] The number of Thanet dissenters listed in the 1676 census was small (though likely larger than the census admitted), and largest in St Lawrence and Ramsgate (see p 49). Since politics in the early modern period was largely conducted in a religious guise, we can thus note that Thanet's 20th century political pattern was well-established already by 1676: everywhere a conservative majority, but an opposition minority centred on Ramsgate. The most radical movements (Quakers and Anabaptists in the 17th century, Green Party today) were and are scattered.

According to the Birchington records at least the Restoration was greeted with the relaxation of behaviour traditionally associated with it: for there was much eating and drinking. The Great Plague of 1666 did not affect the island, but plague or other epidemics occured frequently in Birchington throughout the 17th century, the early part of which was much worse in this respect in this village than the late 16th century.[55] At Minster too, of 33

upland holders in 1635 only 17 appeared to be still there in 1640.[56]
Presumably other parts of Thanet were likewise afflicted.

Not only plague but marsh fever was a serious problem in the
low-lying southern and western parts of the island after the retreat
of the sea. So bad was it at Sarre that it became almost depopu-
lated.[57] Almost certainly this was *plasmodium vivax* malaria from
the mosquito *anophiles (maculipennis) atroparvus*, which lives in
coastal salty marshes. It was a rarely fatal but weakening disease
which diminished as the marshes became less saline through
drainage and as more livestock (which the *atroparvus* prefers to
bite) became available.[58] In the 19th century it virtually vanished
from Thanet, but still raged in the Hoo peninsula and the Sheer-
ness area as late as 1917.[59]

The population seems to have taken long to recover from the
many recurring outbreaks of plague, as well as the effects of
malaria. Regrowth is perhaps indicated by the successive regis-
tration of parishes as administrative units. Yet Archbishop
Parker's census of 1563 gave a figure of 442 Thanet households
liable for church rates,[60] 243 less than those listed for tax in 1334–35
in Thanet and Stonar without Sarre, Stonar being practically
empty in 1563.

The per capita wealth may have increased in the intervening 228
years – although the effect of inflation remains uncalculated – for
according to Lambarde the total tax to be paid in 1563 was £103/
13/7, only £2/10/9 less than in 1334–1335. In 1563 there were
the following numbers of Thanet households by parish liable for
church rates: St Nicholas 33, Monkton 15, Minster 53, St Lawrence
98, St Peter's 107, St John's 96, Birchington 40, Wode
(Woodchurch) none.[61] A 1566 shipping survey gave a figure of
331 houses in the fishing villages of Margate, Broadstairs and
Ramsgate alone (see p 65), but this may have included some of
their hinterlands. If not, it suggests a population fall prior to 1563,
or the existence of a high proportion of poor people not liable for
rates, and in any case is a reminder of the uncertainties of these
early statistics.

The 1563 census showed the end of the village of Woodchurch.
Even the farmhouse seems to have been abandoned, if this account
is correct, being restored, it is thought, early in the following
century. The church was disused by 1563 according to separate
evidence, and was pulled down with the adjoining schoolroom in
1602–1604 by one Thomas Rowe of Birchington, on orders of
Henry Crispe, who must have been the landowner. The lead and

some timber went to Quex, and the flint stones (of which like the other ancient Thanet churches it was built) by tradition form the stables and probably some other buildings at Woodchurch farm. The church site and the churchyard became the farmer's hen run, orchard and vegetable garden; a small ruin of the church remained there until the 1980's, by which time the whole area had become a paddock for horses.[62]

Barrett found a surplus of 87 funerals over baptisms at Birchington from 1538 to 1553, which indicates demographic decline as suggested above, even without men lost at sea, for instance. The registers for the next ten years were missing, but from 1564 to 1700 births significantly exceeded deaths in the village. There was a surplus of 120 baptisms over burials from 1564–1600, of 89 baptisms over burials from 1600 to 1649, and of 153 baptisms from 1650 to 1700.[63] No doubt this was the general long-term trend, but the hearth tax assessment for 1663 lists, in one document, only 305 houses in the Hundred of Ringslow,[64] although there were apparently 73 households in Birchington.[65] The accuracy of these tax figures may be doubtful, though it is known from Barrett's study that epidemics did not hit all parts of Thanet at once, and some houses may have been occupied by more than one family. (See p 60 for more analysis of the hearth tax figures).

The Compton census of 1676 for the first time counted heads, and showed such a large increase over the 1663 hearth tax as to cast more doubt on the latter.

According to the Compton census the population was as follows:-

Table 1[66]

	Conformists	*Non-Conformists*
St John's (adults)	737	15
St Lawrence (adults)	70	50
St Peter's (adults)	590	24
Minster (adults)	250	3
St Nicholas (adults)	160	
Birchington (with children)	317	
Monkton (with children)	154	

The St Lawrence figure seems exceedingly low, especially as it included Ramsgate, and the non-conformist totals are also suspected of deliberate under-return, but if the numbers are correct and assuming 40 children for every 60 adults in all parishes, this census indicates a total Thanet population of around 3,635, which again might be below that of 1334–35. In England as a whole the population is considered to have grown by 75–100% between the mid-15th and mid-17th centuries,[67] which if Thanet were similar shows just how far it might have dropped here at the lowest ebb of the 15th century.

A low population is suggested by the lack of markets. The medieval markets at Minster, Downbarton and Monkton by the Wantsum had disappeared by 1500, and Thanet was without any till towards the end of the 18th century.[68] Hasted stated that there was a market at Margate "as long ago as 1631 . . . but this seems not to have lasted long . . .".[69] Kilburne in his 1659 book mentioned only a fair at Monkton, two fairs in St John's and two in St Peter's and none in St Lawrence, which is consistent with its small population return in 1676.[70] Eventually a weekly market was allowed in Margate in 1777; it also sold corn till at least 1798.[71]

A feature of Thanet parishes from the 16th century, if not much earlier, was the appearance of charitable endowments for the poor, often including the provision of schooling for them.[72] A workhouse and an almshouse was established in Minster in the mid-17th century,[73] and all parishes must have had poorhouses of some kind by the end of the 17th century. By 1660 St Nicholas and St Lawrence were amongst the 85 Kent parishes having charitable endowments of over £400 (£659/18/ – and £974/8/ – respectively).[74] The schoolhouse pulled down at Woodchurch in 1602 must have been started well before the church became disused 40 years earlier. At St Nicholas in 1636 Thomas Paramore gave £6 to found a school for ten poor children of that parish and Monkton.[75] As early as 1541 42% of the settlements in Canterbury diocese had a permanent school, and by 1640 50%,[76] but in Thanet only St Nicholas and St John's had schools in 1660. Yet there was some teaching by the clergy even without a special school building: the Monkton curate taught in the parish in 1617, and in 1686 the Minster curate had a school in the North aisle of the church.[77] From the mid-17th century schools gradually increased. Elizabeth Lovejoy who died 1694 left £40 for a schoolmaster to teach 20 poor children in St Peter's parish.[78] How well the schools were maintained is another matter. Education in St Nicholas, for instance, was "haphazard and improvised for two centuries after the Paramore bequest" in the justified comment of Anneli Jones.[79] On the other hand the establishment of grammar or endowed schools at Canterbury, Ashford and Wye in the 16th century meant that richer farmers' sons could be sent to them, lodging with families in these towns.

The most ambitious effort educationally in Thanet was that of a Henry Robinson, gentleman, who in 1642 gave a messuage at Upper Gore End (possibly the site of the present farm), for the maintenance of two fellows at St John's College, Cambridge, and two scholars at King's School, Canterbury, all to come from Thanet. But the value of this land having sunk to £50 pa by 1652, it was decided to abandon the fellowships and maintain four scholars at King's School.[80]

With the end of the Wantsum channel the ports of Ramsgate, Margate, Gore End and later Broadstairs gradually came into more prominence, but for long they were poor fishing villages. In early times when the cliffs extended out to the end of the Nayland Rock at Margate and to the end of the corresponding chalk rocks on the east of the pier, Margate bay with its creek running inland through the present old town and past the "old" house must have offered good shelter from all but due northerly winds to the small vessels of the day. By the end of the Middle Ages these cliffs seem to have been largely eaten back by the sea, and a wooden pier was made at an unknown date. This was frequently damaged or destroyed by storms, and the little harbour at Gore End (where the sunken greens now are at Minnis Bay) was more reliable until ships became too large for it in the 16th century. The most dangerous winds in these parts were considered to be the north-easterlies; Gore End gave protection from these, and the wooden piers at Margate, Broadstairs and Ramsgate were designed against them. John Whyman has established that Broadstairs' first pier was built in 1587, those at Margate and Ramsgate being much earlier.

It has been claimed by some writers, citing no sources, that the oak woods of the island were cut down to make Henry VIII's navy. Gnarled hedgerow oaks were in demand for naturally curved timber for ship-building,[81] so to this extent it is plausible that Thanet's wind-swept specimens might have been purveyed to civil or naval shipyards. But none of the naval history sources recommended by the librarian of the National Maritime Museum and Library indicate that Thanet was ever a source of supply. Under the Lancastrian kings, only Southampton and the New Forest are mentioned in the records surviving.[82] Under Henry VII the yards were at Deptford, Rye and Smallhythe, drawing on the Weald in all probability. Under Henry VIII the shipyards were at Portsmouth, Woolwich and Deptford, which would draw on the New Forest or the Weald for timber. The Kentish weald was the usual source for the Chatham dockyard, which came into use between 1560 and 1570 under Elizabeth I.[83] In the 17th century Blean Woods near Canterbury were used for oak supplies.[84] Whatever timber Thanet may have had was probably mostly used up by the reign of Henry VIII, as a contemporary account shows.

Descriptions by visitors of the 16th and 17th centuries

John Leland visited Thanet sometime between 1535 and 1543; the following were his most useful comments: "Gore End, a 2-mile from Northmouth (or Genlade)" (mouth of the Wantsum), "and at Gore End a little staire caul'd Broadstairs to go daune the clive, and about this shore is a good taking of mullettes. The great ragusseis" (large merchant ships) "ly for defence of wind at Gore Ende." "At Northmuth where the entry of the sea was, the salt water swelleth yet up at a creeke a myle or more to a place called Sarre, which was the common ferry when Thanet was full iled. . . ." "*In the isle is very little wodde*" (author's italics). "Margate lyith in St John's paroche yn Thanet a v. myles upward of Reculver, and there is a village and a peere for shyppes, but now sore decayed." "Margate lyeth a mile from Sandwich haven", "Ramsgate a iiii Myles upward in Thanet, where as is a small Peere for Shyppis". Thus he amalgamated Gore End and Broadstairs, and was confused about Margate and Ramsgate; perhaps he never went far into Thanet.[85] His testimony about the ragusseis at Gore End contrasts with Barratt's findings that in 1565 Gore End had "neither shippe nor boate", and that in 1584 it was certified to Dover Cinque Port as having "no harbour or shipping, but onely three fishermen, Henry Brabourne, Ralphe Linche, Steven Knight who usually saile at Margate". Possibly Gore End silted up rapidly after Leland's visit.[86] Leland was also erroneous in saying that both Birchington and St Nicholas were daughter parishes of Reculver, making processions there at certain festivals. Until 1294 this was true of St Nicholas, but Birchington was until 1871 a daughter parish of Monkton, as St John's, St Peter's and St Lawrence earlier were of Minster. He noted that there were three decayed churches in Thanet and eight remained: since seven ancient ones still stand, the eighth must have been St Nicholas at Woodchurch, pulled down in 1602.

Holinshed said of Thanet in the 1570's "this Iland hath no wood growing in it except it be forced, and yet otherwise it is verie fruitfull, and beside that it wanteth for few other commodities, the finest chalke is said to be found there."[87]

Camden, who visited a decade later, was more explicit: "All the isle standeth upon a whitish maile, full of goodly cornfields, and being a right fertile soil, carrieth in length eight miles and four in Bredth." "Neither must I pass over in silence that which maketh for the singular praise of the inhabitants of Tenet, those especially which dwell by the roads or harboroughs of Margate, Ramsgate, and Brodstear. For they are passing industrious, and as if they were Amphiby, that is, both land and sea creatures, getting their living both by sea and land, as one would say with both these elements: they be Fisher-men and Plough-men. . . . According to the season of the years, they knit nets, they fish for Cod, Herring, Mackerels etc. they saile and carry forth Merchandise. The same again dung and manure their ground, Plough, Sow, harrow, reape their Corn, and they inne it; and thus they go round and keepe a circle in their labours. Furthermore, whereas that otherwhiles there happen shipwrackes there . . . these men wont to bestir themselves lustily in recovering both ships, men and merchandise endangered."[88]

Some vivid pictures of our island have come down to us from the later 17th century. On 27 March 1672 John Evelyn visited Margate to make arrangements for the treatment of wounded from the wars with the Netherlands. He made no comment in his diary on his journey from Sandwich to Margate, where he "was handsomely entertained and lay at my deputy's Captain Glover". He then returned to London via Rochester, describing the first part of his journey thus: "I came back through a country the best cultivated of any that in my life I had anywhere seen, every field lying as even as a bowling green, and the fences, plantations and husbandrie in such admirable order, as infinitely delighted me, after the sad and afflicting spectacles and objects I was come from; observing every tall tree, to have a weather-cock on the top bough, and some trees half a dozen, I learned, that on a certain holy-day, the Farmers fete their servants, at which solemnity they set up these cocks in a kind of triumph etc."[89] Nobody else has mentioned this, and Evelyn might have been referring to the country round Faversham and Sittingbourne, which was also famous for fertility and good husbandry. It certainly suggests a picture of farmers treating scarce labourers well, and there is no doubt about the May entries in his diary on Thanet.

"17 May.   Took horse for Margate from Dover, where from the North Foreland lighthouse top (which is a *pharos* built of Bricque, having on the top a Cradle of yron, in which one attends a greate sea-coale fire, all the yeare long when the nights are darke, for the safe-guard of sailors), and we could see our fleete as it lay at Anker . . .
                        19 May. I went to Margate church where one Mr Chunie the Minister made an excellent sermon on 14 Apos. 7.

20 May.   I was carried to see a gallant widow, a Farmoress and I think of *Gygantic* race; rich, comely, and exceedingly industrious, she put me in mind of *Debora*, and *Abigail*; her house so plentifully stored with all manner of Countrie provisions, all of her own growth, and all her conveniences so substantial, neate and well understood; she herself so jolly and hospitable, and her land, so trim and rarely husbanded, that it struck me with a kind of admiration at her Oeconomie.

21 May.   This towne much consists of Brewers of a certain heady Ale, and deale much in mault etc: for the rest 'tis raggedly built and an ill haven, with a small fort of little concernment, nor is the Iland well disciplin'd" (ie. possibly the militia), "but as to husbandry and the rural part, far exceeding any part of England, and I think of the whole world for the accurate culture of their ground, in which truth they exceede even to Curiosity and emulation. We passed by Richborow, and in sight of Reculvers, and so came thro a sweate garden as it were to Canterbury."[90]

In the reign of William and Mary, possibly in 1697 (for she hardly put any dates in her diary), Celia Fiennes rode from Deal to Sandwich and glimpsed Thanet from afar: – "You go along by ye seaside in sight of ye Isle of Thanet, which is just over against Sandwich, and is so near to it you see ye lands and inclosures" (presumably hedges) "woods and houses. I suppose it is not a quarter of a league from Sandwich; this is a sad old town all timber building – but its run so to decay that except for one or two good houses it's like to drop down, ye whole town."[91] Her reference to enclosures and woods suggests that perhaps to modern eyes Thanet in the 16th century would not have looked so bare and treeless as it appeared to Leland and Holinshed, as the whole of England had far more trees and fewer people then. Dutch elm disease struck England in the 17th century, with what results in Thanet is not known, but it is a proven fact that in 1760 there were 4,305 timber trees on the Conyngham estate at Minster.[92] At the present time there are on a rough estimate nearer a hundredth of that number.

The farmers' standard of living

The evidence shows a slow but marked improvement in the farmers' standard of living, which changed from primitive to much more comfortable in this period. There seems to have been a great move to establish new farmhouses or rebuild old ones with brick, in the wake of the collapse of feudal services and rents, which must have lifted a burden from the population. It is noteworthy how many present or former Thanet farms stand very close to the marsh: Watchester, Sheriff's Court, the Sarre farms, Downbarton, Belle Isle, Wagtail, Chamber's Wall, Bartlett's, Shuart, the Hale farms, the Brooksend farms. It seems unlikely they were all built there in the days when the marsh edge was the sea-shore, though in the case of the Elms farmhouse medieval origin is known, more probable that some at least were founded on the spring line when the sea had safely retreated, and so a 15th century date is plausible. In fact many Thanet farmhouses now standing are believed by tradition, and in some cases archeological examination, to have originated from that time, although a few including Cleve, Wood-church, Hoo and Way are said to date from the 14th century. Perhaps significantly, none of these is by the marsh. An exception may be the old hall house at Nether Hale, which is thought to be of 14th century date, and may have been connected with the use of Hale Creek as a port in the later Middle Ages. Many of these houses may stand on the remains of earlier wooden or wattle-and-daub dwellings. Sheriff's Court is literally built round an ancient cottage with very thick walls, which must have been connected with Sheriff's Hope creek.[93]

We may get some idea of how the houses evolved from the archeological examination of Durlock Grange, Minster, when it was demolished in the early 1960's. In the 15th century it consisted of a brick-built central hall open to the chimneyless roof, with a smooth clay floor, a central hearth of a rough circle of flat stones four feet wide, and two great windows 10' and 7', which had sliding shutters on their lower halves and hinged ones on their upper. It must have been smoky, dark and grimy inside – the black carbon on the rafters could be flaked off with a knife. All the posts were made of inverted oak trees. A buttery and pantry led off the main hall. There were no bedrooms, or other rooms except the hall. This was a typical farmhouse of the superior, Wealden type in the 15th century.[94]

During the 150 years from 1575–1725 a housing revolution occured amongst English farmers, who became the best housed of their class in Europe.[95] Probably in the 16th century two small rooms with oak panelling and lofts over them were added to Durlock Grange, one either side of the hall, and in 1613 a complete upper floor was built.[96] Elsewhere in Thanet there is more remarkable evidence of the improvements of this time. There are the fine Elizabethan timber-frame houses of Gore Court farm and Wayborough Manor, half-timbered Callis Court, and Margate "old house" in King Street. At Nether Hale Old Farmhouse timber seems to have been added to the outside and panelling to the inside in a re-building of the earlier, late 14th century timber-frame hall house, with solar wings, of which the crown posts still remain. At Woodchurch farmhouse 17 layers of wallpaper and two successive fireplaces were stripped away from the dining room by the present owner to reveal Elizabethan oak panelling and an open fireplace. This room contains what seem to be the original oak beams, very rough hewn and once covered in thick Victorian brown varnish paint, and formerly contained a small wooden spiral staircase of uncertain date, but certainly ancient, for it gave amazingly little headroom.[97] Many other old Thanet farmhouses must contain similar features, discovered or as yet concealed. Some, like Shuart, date from the 16th century but are not timber-frame.[98]

Before 1660 in East Kent, farm as well as domestic servants were increasingly boarded in the enlarged farmhouses, and the inference is that it was done at Durlock Grange and Woodchurch. At Woodchurch there were five bedrooms in the old part of the house, probably rebuilt more or less in its present form in the 17th century, and a loft up in the widely sloping roof, giving sufficient space for boarding by the cramped standards of the past. Most old Thanet farmhouses have similar or greater accommodation. After 1660 a brewhouse, bakehouse and wash-house were added to Durlock, and probably at a similar time a small building, tradition-ally known as the wash-house, was added at the North end of Woodchurch farmhouse; it is still there. There was also a stone-flagged area at the West side of the house which seems to have been used for a dairy or brew-house, and the underground chamber in the chalk underneath the neo-Georgian wing at the front might also have been used as a dairy at some time,[99] (but see p 44–45).

Thanet yeomen were amongst the wealthiest in Kent in the 17th century. By the mid-17th century a middling farmer and shop-keeper in Minster, Thomas Sackett, enjoyed the comfort of a feather-bed (a prestigious item in those days), some "joyned" furniture (made by a joiner expert in furniture-making and again prestigious), pewter dishes, two bibles and two testaments.[100] In 1692 Richard Mockett of St Peter's left *inter alia* in his will ten pairs of sheets, four "pillowcoats", one dozen of napkins and four towels.[101]

Position of the agricultural work force and the poor

Labour shortage was surely the reason for the survival of the institution of covenanted or yearly farm servants (farm workers), noted in the Middle Ages (p. 28–29, 33). It is mentioned in Kent in the 15th century[102] (and obvious from the 1444 wages rates quoted above page 36), and was not to disappear in Thanet until after the First World War. Providing the farmer with tied labour, it brought certain advantages to the servant too, if his master was good. It was distinct from apprenticeship, which did exist as a separate status, at least in the 17th century when several cases occurred in Birchington. For example, in 1634 Valentine Arthur was appren-ticed by Birchington parish to Thomas Corner, yeoman of the Ville of Wode, to learn "the art of husbandry" until he was 24.[103] There is no information about the conditions of yearly servants from the earlier centuries, but later it is known that they were both single and married. They were only allowed to leave their jobs at Michaelmas, when they received their year's pay, although from the late 18th century at least there were various changes.

A statute of 1496 tried to peg wages nationally at somewhat

below the 1444 level, but no published information is available about Thanet or Kentish wages from the Maidstone figures of 1444 to 1531, when a labourer in Birchington was paid 4d a day and 2d worth of food, and an artisan 6d. The labourer's 4d represented an appreciable rise over 1383–4, for it was a normal and not an extraordinary wage, but it was the same as that prescribed for mowers according to the 1444 statute, suggesting that there had been a long period of stagnation in wages (see p 37). In 1535 workmen at Dover struck for 6d a day and their "ringleaders" were jailed, and from 1531 at Birchington there began a long rise.[104]

Wages for all Kent were laid down at Maidstone in 1563 as follows:

"Bayliff taking charge 50/- and his Liuerie",[(A)] or 56/8d without, per annum
Best man (head ploughman) 40/- and liverie, or 46/8d without per annum
Second sort 33/4d and liverie, or 40/- without per annum
Best woman 26/8d per annum
Second sort 20/- per annum
Boy 14–18 years 20/-, or 6/- a quarter without food and clothing.
Labourer: Easter till Michaelmas 4d a day and food, 9d without.
            Winter 3d and food, 7d without.
Mower by day 6d with food, 11d without.
       by acre, grass 6d, oats 5d, barley 6d, without food.
Binding and "copping" sheaves: oats 8d per acre, barley 10d.
Reaping by day: a man and his mate 6d with food, 11d without; a woman 4d with food, 7d without.
Reaping, binding and "copping" sheaves by acre: wheat 14d and food or 2/- without.
Rye the same.
Peas or tares 20d without food.
Threshers and cleaners by the quarter: wheat and rye 4d and food, 10d without. Oats and barley 2d with food, 5d without.
Thatchers: 6d a day and food; thatchers mate 4d and food.[105]
(A) OED 8/1055 says liverie means either food or produce *or* clothing, but the statutes of 1378 and 1444 had prescribed both food and clothing for bailiffs and yearly servants. Such may be the meaning of liverie here but it is not explained in the source.

These figures suggest that Thanet rates were probably ahead of the Maidstone prescriptions. By 1594 certain artisans' wages in Birchington were some 75% higher than in 1560, and wages rose by almost the same percentage in the 17th century.[106]

From the 17th century yearly servants, presumably when single, were provided with free board and lodging in the enlarged farmhouses,[107] (see p 56) and with the commencement of lodging the provision of clothing may have ceased. The older, married yearly servants appear to have farmed a small acreage and kept a few livestock as well as working for a farmer. At various times either single or married yearly servants seem to have predominated.

In 1657 Richard Mockett of St Peter's paid his head waggoner £7 per annum and the wool of four "dry sheep" to sell; the "second man" (number two waggoner) was paid £3/10/- and the wool of two "dry sheep" to sell. This was not riches, for in the same year a sow and 10 piglets were bought for £2/10/- and lambs for 4/- in St Peter's.[108] It is clearly suggestive of married yearly servants, as some of those taking yearly payments at earlier times must have been. No other 17th century wage information relevant to Thanet has been found, and so far no study has been made linking the rise of wages locally to population trends, farming methods or general inflation in the 15th–17th centuries.

Dennis Baker found that in 1690 John Wallis, a labourer of Monkton, owned two bonds worth £110, and cites this as an example of the affluence of at least some of them.[109] Private lending through legally witnessed personal bonds was the standard method of agrarian financing, as there were no banks in Thanet till the late 18th century, and many examples of these bonds are to be found in Kent, Canterbury Cathedral and University of Reading archives relating to Thanet. Though nothing more is known of boarded yearly servants' wages till the 18th century, manpower dearth must have kept them sufficiently attractive, and the single yearly servants may have used their enforced savings to join the army of smallholders with which Thanet seems to have been stocked until this century, even if they did not continue as married yearly servants. (See p 107). In Dennis Baker's view in the 17th and 18th centuries most labourers whether yearly servants or not had a small-holding as well as labouring; they had the best of both worlds and were better-off than the smallholder without wages.[110] Married yearly servants in this position might have found that their annual pay-days encouraged saving and enabled them even to lend money on bond.

At the same time there is evidence of poverty in the partially published statistics of the 17th century hearth tax. At Birchington in 1662, 73 houses were chargeable and 27 "persons" (presumably households) (37%) were exempt as they were in constant receipt of alms from the parish.[111] The 1663 hearth tax assessment found that of the alleged 305 houses in Thanet only 168 (55%) were chargeable.[112] In East Kent as a whole 38% were exempt in 1663,

Table 2

A.				Number of hearths							
	1	*2*	*3*	*4*	*5*	*6*	*7*	*8*	*9*	*10+*	
Birchington 1662[111]	25	20	13	6	4	5	2			2	(John Hayward 12, Thomas Crispe 17) (Total 77)
All Thanet 1663[112]	189	38	25	19	11	2	8	1	3		(Total 296)

B. *Number of hearths and exemptions 1664 according to Harrington transcript*[114]

	1	2	3	4	5	6	7	8	9	10+	% households exempt
St Nicholas											
chargeable	9	4	6	3	3	1	1	–	–	1	
not	None										–
East St Lawrence											
chargeable	19	9	4	3	1	–	–	–	–	–	
not	48										57
West St Lawrence											
chargeable	10	6	6	2	1	1	2	–	–	–	
not	17										37.7
Minster											
chargeable	6	6	3	6	1	–	2	–	–	–	
not	37	5	2	1							65.2
Monkton											
chargeable	12	4	–	3	4	–	2	–	–	1	
not	7										21.2
Way											
chargeable	7	2	3	2	–	1	1	–	1	1 (shared by 3 families)	
not	17	1									47.3

and the J.P.'s were suspected of undue leniency in allowing exemptions for 45% in Thanet.[113] There must also have been more than 305 houses island-wide in 1663, because the 1664 surviving returns show 297 houses excluding Birchington, Sarre, St Peter's and St John's! These 1664 returns give interesting figures for the remaining parishes, indicating concentrations of poor people in Minster, Way, and St Lawrence, and greater prosperity in St Nicholas and Monkton.[114]

At least in Birchington receipt of alms did not necessarily mean misery, and one widow obtaining poor relief for 14 years died in possession of a comfortable home, including a featherbed, in 1669.[115] Findings for the early 18th century treatment of the poor in St Nicholas suggest that they were probably not dissimilar there in the 17th century.[116] It may have been different in the poorer parishes. The commonest causes of poverty must have been widowhood, orphaning, handicaps, old age, injuries and sickness, which from all accounts were common enough. Bad weather and animal and plant disease seem to have been a less frequent cause (but see p 63); there should have been no lack of work for those able to do it. At harvest time in the late 16th and 17th centuries poor kinsmen used to come from far away to help – examples are cited of men coming from Canterbury to Sarre and from Romney Marsh to Thanet.[117]

Agriculture and maritime activities from Henry VIII to 1700

The process of innovation known as the Agricultural Revolution in England started in the 16th century, being arguably an aspect or off-shoot of the Renaissance. By the mid-17th century some parts of England had been well caught up in it, and from this time farming was subjected to new pressures. There remained the age-old erratic problems of plant, animal or human disease, and unfavourable weather, war or population growth bringing scarcity and high prices for farm products, and good seasons, peace and stable or falling population bringing lower prices. Now came a new cycle overlying this, for the speed of change began to quicken, and new crops and techniques were introduced, tending of themselves towards over-abundance and a fall in prices. The interaction of these two processes has conditioned our agriculture ever since the 16th century, but in the beginning the changes in Thanet farming practice were slow.

Differing contours have been given by different historians to the price patterns of the 16th-17th centuries, but it seems established that there was a general rise in food prices from the beginning of the 16th century to the mid-1650's, and thereafter a fall, or series of falls due to abundance, leading to bounties having to be paid to encourage corn exports from 1673. Reduction of the population by plague must have played a part in reducing demand.

The main agricultural improvements of this period were the

introduction of new fodder and forage crops, and the change from
a system of permanent tillage and permanent pasture to one of
field-grass husbandry – a system of permanently cultivated arable
alternating between temporary tillage and temporary ley. This was
already established in Kent in the early 17th century,[118] but the
only firm date we have for the first sowing of a ley crop in Thanet
before 1700 is sanfoin in 1680.[119] Clover and trefolium were also
grown by 1723,[120] but Dennis Baker does not include either in his
cropping tables from probate inventories from 1680–1760, so the
amount sown may have been small.

This could be taken to suggest that the fertility of Thanet
and its success in corn-growing, together with the marsh grazing
and the fishing, made the farmers rather slow to experiment
with leys. The eye-witness reports of Camden and John Evelyn
(see p 53–4), give a picture of an extremely industrious and
enterprising farming community in this period, so if they did
not move into ley farming very fast it was probably because they
did not feel the need. The main crops in this period were still
grain.

The preponderance of arable in the uplands is seen in the
example of David Ealneare of St Lawrence who in July 1603 had
101 acres of corn and only one cow.[121] In the reign of James I
(1603–1625) we hear of a farmer offering to pay £1 an acre extra
rent for the right to plough up marshland near Margate (there was
still marsh in the Westbrook and St Mildred's Bay, Westgate,
areas).[122] Early in the 17th century malt became an important
item of export: a group of prosperous Thanet farmers sent it to be
marketed in London through city factors who were nephews and
cousins. A network of farming gentry in East Kent, all relatives or
neighbours, supplied the London market with wheat and barley.
They bore such names as Philpott and Paramore, and some of
them may have come from Thanet. Some rich maltsters lived at
Birchington in the 17th century.[123]

In the latter part of the 17th century barley was apparently
grown more than wheat, no doubt to make malt. On the basis of
probate inventories for the parishes of Minster, St John's,
St Peter's and St Lawrence, Dennis Baker concluded that this
area was 78.3% cropped with cereals in 1680–1710: 48.2% barley,
28% wheat, 2.1% oats, 6.2% beans, 1.1% tares, 5.3% peas and
9.1% a mixture of peas, tares and oats.[124] According to Lewis
(1st edition 1723) beans were "a very late and recent improve-

ment" in Thanet. This was independently confirmed in 1763 (see p 78).

The drill and horse-hoeing culture of beans in Kent, which will be described in more detail in the next chapter (pages 71), was considered by the famous agricultural improver Arthur Young (1741–1820) in 1781 to have been established there "above a century" and to be unique to the county. Dennis Baker considers it to be Kent's original contribution to the Agricultural Revolution.[125] It is not known when tares were first grown here. Commercial seed growing, mostly canary and flax, was also carried on by 1696, on reclaimed marsh at Minster and Monkton, but was secondary to grain.[126]

Much grain was shipped out of Thanet (see p 65, 67), but much was also milled locally. Philip Symondson's map of Kent of 1596 shows 39 windmills in the county, of which five were in Thanet: at St Nicholas, Birchington, above Minster, at Nash Court and St Lawrence. The mills were probably tower mills, the earliest reference to which is to a stone one at Dover castle in 1294–1295. If the contemporary maps are accurate, the 17th century saw a fall in the total number of windmills in Kent to 23, but an increase to 8 in Thanet – 1 at Dent-de-Lion, 2 at Birchington, others at Reading Street, Minster, Monkton, Margate and Lydden.[127]

Bad weather seems only occasionally to have ruined crops, though this may be a false impression due to the weakness of the sources. Famine occurred at Birchington in 1621 and 1630–31,[128] and in 1685 "the extream hard and long frost, such as (in the judgement of all men) had not been in many years, if ever before" killed most of the wheat seed in the ground.[129]

The value of the marsh nearly doubled between 1600 and 1641 at Minster and Monkton,[130] which is evidence of improved drainage and greater use. Reference to drainage of the Stour marshes is made in publications in 1662 and 1665.[131] In the late 17th century sheep were folded on fallow land on the uplands, but also kept on the marsh. Ralph Greedier (sic) of Sarre had 331 on his death in 1696, but most flocks were small. Wattle folds were in use by 1680, probably earlier.[132] Pigs were kept in field enclosures as well as in sties. John Welby of Dent-de-Lion had 40 store pigs in 1680, apparently one of the larger herds.[133] Horses had entirely supplanted oxen well before the end of the 17th century. Thomas George of Monkton was probably unique in owning ten plough oxen at the time of his death in 1682. Farmers bred their own horses on the larger farms, and sometimes asses as well, (perhaps to supply their milk to invalids). Usually just a few cows were kept for family needs, but Thomas George was unusual again in having ten, with six followers, four steers and 26 cheeses maturing in his cheese-house.[134] Dennis Baker made the following table of the average number of livestock on Thanet farms 1680–1710 on the basis of the probate inventories:[135]

Horses	Pigs	Sheep	Cattle
5	9	20	3

Farm implements included shims, brakes and brake ploughs (variant adaptations of the Kent plough) which were in use from 1680 at least.[136]

We do not know how far it was local prosperity and how far it was the general 16th century inflation which caused rents, like wages, to rise in Elizabeth I's reign, but Sir Edward Carye paid £998 rent for all the demesne lands of Minster manor in 1599. Amongst these, a 7-acre field near Colleswood, Manston (present Coldswood farm area) let for 6/8d an acre, salt marsh at Minster for 2/- an acre and freshwater marsh for 18/- – possibly because of its value for growing canary and flax. There is little more Thanet information about rents till the 18th century, but at West Langdon in the 1660's a rental of 8/- per acre for 500 acres is mentioned.[137]

Tenancy seems to have predominated over ownership at this time as earlier, and in the 17th century many farms were small, though some were nearly 400 acres. The Cliffsend and Northwood rate books record holdings ranging in size from 16 to 273 acres at various times in the 17th century.[138] At Birchington in 1688 there were three over 100 acres, five from 33 to 100, and twenty-five small occupiers holding 199 acres in all.[139] In Monkton in 1691 there were 14 owner-occupiers of farms with rentals (sic) assessed at £67, and 57 leased farms with rents assessed at £1,178 in all.[140]

Edward Philpot, St Nicholas yeoman, left £1957/11/8d. sometime in the 17th century. John Welby of Dent-de-Lion had 382 sown acres and his personal estate was valued at £1,284 when he died in 1680. By comparison, John Prince of Margate, a brewer, maltster and owner of parts of vessels, left about £1,000. George Christian of Minster had 200 acres at least and his personal estate was £903 on his death in 1699.[141] At Minster in 1635 William Skinner and John Turner held 320 and 310 acres of upland respectively, and in 1633 William Skinner had 51 acres of marsh as well, and John Turner 92 acres. In 1635, two others each held over 200 acres of upland, and six between 100 and 200 acres; nine other holdings under 100 acres on the upland ranged between 84 and 2 acres. The 60 holdings on the marsh in 1633 were between 166 and 3 acres in size, 33 of them under 20 acres.[142] We do not have any farm size data for St Peter's, St John's and St Lawrence from the 17th century.

As there were no markets on the island, the surplus produce must have been sent by sea or Stour to Sandwich or Canterbury, or in the first part of the period to Reculver, and from an early date London became an important outlet. As early as 1535 certain Londoners brought up "a great quantity of" Thanet corn, but the Lieutenant of Dover Castle asked Henry VIII's chief minister, Thomas Cromwell, to countermand this purchase, apparently as an unfair cornering of the market.[143]

Lewis states that grain was shipped out of Margate in Queen Elizabeth's reign.[144] According to a survey made in 1566, Ramsgate with 125 houses had 14 vessels: two of 16 tons, three of 12, one of 10, the rest from 8 to 3 tons; these employed 70 men in the carrying of coal and fishing. Margate with 108 houses had 8 vessels: four of 18 tons, one of 16, the rest of 5, 4 and 1 ton, employing 60 men in the carriage of grain and fishing. Broadstairs had 98 houses and eight vessels: two of 12 tons, one of 10, the rest 8–2, employing 40 men in fishing only.[145] In 1572–1573, 112 quarters of corn were being exported from Sandwich only.[146]

Another document of perhaps dubious accuracy would suggest that a great increase in vessel size took place in the next twenty years. In 1584 Margate had 14 ships totalling 455 tons burden: one barke (70 tons), one crayer (28 tons), five fishing vessels (10–25 tons) and seven hoys (25–60 tons). Each had a master and two "common sailors and fishermen" (which seems a questionable statement). Twelve of the ships, including the barke, were all owned by twelve joint owners, and two by a single owner each.[147] By 1665–66 nine hoys were registered at Margate as against eighteen at Sandwich, and by 1699–1700 eleven at Margate and only seven at Sandwich, showing the predominance of Margate in the corn trade.[148]

Dennis Baker's researches confirmed the important role in the latter half of the 17th century of fishing as a tandem occupation with agriculture in Thanet, first noted by Camden but surely of ancient origin. Both small and largish farmers owned shares in sometimes as many as seven different vessels, and a considerable amount of fishing tackle. In the period 1660 to the end of the century, as in 1584, most boats were jointly owned, at this time in shares of 1/8, 1/16 and 1/32, and ownership was not confined to coastal parishes. In 1665 John Grant of Minster owned 1/16 of a ketch, but fishing interests were naturally more prominent in Birchington, St John's, St Peter's and St Lawrence. Labourers fished in the intervals between the main surges of farm work, and conversely men mainly employed as seamen sometimes worked on the land in harvest.[149] The intimate ties between land and sea are symbolized by the ancient ship's beam in the ceiling of the living room in Nash farmhouse.

Another increasingly important maritime occupation from the late 17th century was smuggling. The various privately owned "cuts" down through the cliffs to the sea, and the legendary caves reputed to lie under many Thanet farms must have proved useful for this. There are still intact examples of these "cuts" at Coleman Stairs Road at Birchington, Botany Bay, Dumpton, etc. The entrance to a very small narrow tunnel running to an old well at Little Cliff's End farm could still be seen at Pegwell Bay beach in 1990.[150]

The fisheries fluctuated a good deal, due apparently to periodic over-fishing and foreign competition. A few Margate and Broadstairs ships fished off Yarmouth,[151] but in the Channel in the mid-17th century Dutch competition and wartime harassment was severe. Forty-eight mackerel fishermen from the North and South Forelands petitioned Oliver Cromwell for a convoy and naval escort in 1656. The fishermen of Ramsgate, Margate, Broadstairs, Dover and Folkestone reported that they had 100 sail ready to fish off the North Foreland and that hundreds of the poor were only preserved by this fishing. Margate had better post services with Sandwich and Canterbury from 1660, but in 1661 the East Kent fishing towns were said to be greatly decayed, and in 1662 Dutch herrings were selling in Kent much cheaper than English.[152] The Dutch fleet bombarded Margate on 15 October 1665.[153]

Margate's wooden pier was dilapidated again in 1662 and no normal harbour dues were being collected.[154] As Evelyn noted, prosperity came in the 1670's from the ale, called Northdown ale since it was brewed with water from the famous well at Grapevine Cottage, West Northdown (Holly Lane now). Later it was known as Margate ale. Twelve bottles of this kept Samuel Pepys and his friends "laughing and very merry" until the early hours when at anchor in the Downs in May 1666, but it soon lost popularity to North country brews and Margate languished again.[155] In 1679 pier wardens were appointed, but in 1690 the port was again in debt and the cost of repairing the pier was estimated at £2,500. Finally it was repaired towards the end of the century, when the local fishing improved again and herring exports were started in about 1695.

Ramsgate by contrast found much greater wealth from about 1688, with the development of the trade with the Baltic. It had always been of more use than Margate as a cross-Channel port and harbour of refuge, though Margate had the advantage of a better route to London. The Thanet ports shipped about 7,000 quarters of malt, 3,500 quarters of wheat, 500 quarters of barley and a small amount of fish annually to other English ports in 1676–1696, in which years seven out of eight ships arriving in Thanet brought Newcastle coal, by then extensively burned here for lack of wood.[156]

John Evelyn's testimony shows that in the late 17th century Thanet and some other parts of East Kent led the nation in the excellence of their field cultivation, and Dennis Baker believes that Kent led in the techniques for growing beans (see pps 63 and 71). This arouses curiosity as to the source from which these things may have been learnt. The only published evidence available suggests that the inhabitants of this region may have copied the good practices of local Dutch and Flemish settlers and their descendants. It has long been known that the Dutch introduced canary seed to East Kent.[157] The first large group of Protestant refugees from the Low Countries came to Sandwich in 1561; most were craftsmen but a few were gardeners who grew flax, canary and teazle on the fertile reclaimed marsh near the town.[158] It was precisely flax, canary and other seed crops which were being cultivated on reclaimed marsh at Minster and Monkton in the late 17th century (and maybe as early as the late 16th, in view of the high value of the fresh water marsh then. See page 64). The Flanders area possessed intensive light-land husbandry techniques.[159] The Flemish gable is found in many Thanet rural houses of the 17th and early 18th centuries (see p 84), though the "Dutch" influence on Sandwich is far more concentrated. But there seems no sugges-tion so far that the Kentish bean culture innovations had a continental origin. Whatever the findings about this, the 17th century may have claims to be the start of another high-water mark period for Thanet farming. In spite of the earlier agricultural achievements of the monks, the known descriptions of the island before Evelyn's had not specifically praised the skill of the inhabitants as cultivators.

Chapter Four: The Eighteenth Century to 1792

John Lewis' Thanet

John Lewis, vicar of Margate from 1705 and of Minster as well from 1708, to his death in 1746, has left us the first detailed contemporary description of Thanet farming in his history of the island published in 1723. It is one of our local treasures, and we can do no better than let Lewis speak for himself, where space permits. (Unless otherwise stated, references are to the second, 1736 edition, which is clearer to read, and almost identical).

"The situation is very bleak and open, especially towards the sea side, where there are very few Hedges or Trees. Those that are growing thereabouts are, for the most part, scrubby and unthriving, being so much exposed to the sea-winds, which often blow very strong and blast almost everything in their path.[1] The timber growing here is mostly Elm, which in the lower part of the island about Mynstre and Monkton, grows to a good Height and Bigness, if let alone. But it is not so thriving where the Trees stand within reach of the sea-winds and very near the chalk. Just by a farmhouse called Powssis" (Pouces, later the RAF C.O's house at Manston) "is a little grove of oaks, but the unthrivingness of them shows how unkind either the soil, or the situation is to them".[2]

"The air here is very salubrious, but we so often have too much of it".[3] "Antiently, a good part of the Island was Wood-land, which is now almost all grub'd up and converted into Sowing-land. Several of the little Vills hereabouts still preserve the memory of these Woods, Westwood, North-wood, South-wood, Colis-wood" (now Coldswood farm, Manston), "Wood or Villa-wood" (Woodchurch), "corruptly pronounced by the Inhabitants Willow-wood, which last seems to have been indeed a Wood. . . . Part of this Wood was grub'd about 20 years ago" . . . (between 1708 and

1718 according to Barrett)[4], Besides these woods were "Brisket-wood near Hoo and a Wood called Bobdale in St Nicholas, and Manston-wood, a Copse of about five Acres, which is the only Woodland now left".[5] Wood farm seems to be on the site of Manston Wood.

"At present there are about 14,000 acres of Sowing-land"[6] – which supposed 10,000 acres of pasture, marsh, wood, waste or buildings. "There are 600 families or 2,400 souls in St John's parish" (Lewis' main parish), "with about 2,200 families in all Thanet, or perhaps 8,800 persons."[7] This suggests either a great rise in population since the Compton census of 1676, due to inward migration, or mistakes in the figures somewhere. "The present Inhabitants, those of them that occupy Farms, as they are often Persons of good Substance, so they live in a very generous and hospitable manner".[8] But "there is not one Gentleman of Estate left nor any Justice of the Peace, which last is no small misfortune for the Inhabitants". "There were many antient seats here, inhabited by Gentlemen of very good Family and large Estates; but their Seats are now all except two, turned into Farms".[9] The two seats were Nash and Quex.[10]

Margate was very poor and much decayed, but "Ramsgate is all the time growing, almost half of it new built, and their Pier considerably enlarged, so that there are many wealthy Persons among them". Ramsgate's prosperity was due to its overseas trade, "for the North Sea fisheries have done badly in recent years".[11]

"The farmers have sometimes good Crops when other parts of England miss theirs, and thereby have the advantage of selling their Corn at a very good Price. They have likewise the privilege of sending their Corn by water to London market at an easy rate, where they have ready Money for their Commodity".

"But they find it hard to get Servants because so many go to Sea or to the Hop-gardens; they give very great Wages to their Servants and day-Labourers, and are at a great expense in getting Compost and Manure for their Land, add to which high Rents, which have risen in late Years due to high prices of Grain, and have not fallen since, and their being obliged to trust to Factors and others selling their Corn".[12] "Poor people come from East Kent for the Harvest".[13] Women were employed only in pulling beans, but boys in a variety of tasks.[14]

As in Camden's time, the ordinary rural people were part fishermen, part farm workers or small-holders. They fished in the mackerel season in early May, and in the herring season at the end of harvest. "Those who work on small farms bargain with them to go to the Herring fishing".[15] Shrimps, soles, mullet etc. were also caught in Pegwell Bay,[16] and the people "paultered" (plundered) stranded ships. (Camden had not accused them of this).

"The Farms are generally large except in St Peter's".[17] "There are more large farms in Mynstre than in any other parish in Kent, and the Farmers here are generally Men of Ability, being otherwise unable to occupy Farms whose Rent is so great, and for Stocking which, so much is required".[18]

Wheat was grown all over, "the common red wheat".[19] "The Yield is seldom less than three quarters to the Acre, very often four or five. Barley of the common sort is grown, and yields five, six or even seven quarters". Sprack barley was formerly grown on reclaimed marsh, yielding up to seven or eight quarters per acre, but had been abandoned, for reasons unstated.[20] As already mentioned, "beans" (ie. horse beans), "are a very late and modern Improvement".[21] This was independently confirmed in 1763 (see chapter 4, p 78), but they must have been reintroduced before 1680 for Dennis Baker found them then. (See p 36 for the likely time of their abandonment or curtailment, and page 63 for Baker's finding). Wheat was grown after fallow, beans or peas, clover or trefoil ley. Lewis does not mention barley in the rotation, a serious omission on his part, but suggesting that not much was grown when he wrote his book. Tares and vetches were also grown, but very little oats. Those whose land was good enough did not fallow.[22] Sanfoin had first been sown about 1680 as mentioned earlier, the seeds having been obtained from France.[23] Canary was still being grown on land newly cultivated from the marsh, and fruit trees did very well between Ramsgate and Sarre on the low ground.[24]

Horses were entirely used for traction, and worked two shifts a day, 6–10 am and 2–6 pm in summer, from light till dark in winter. The horsemen had a snack of bread and cheese after each shift as well as three meals a day.[25] The farmers began to plough early in December, "when the Wheat season is over".[26] Lewis lists and illustrates ten types of farm tool and horse-drawn implements, including the Kent plough and the bean shim,[27] of which Thomas Johnson of Hayne (Haine) had a specimen in 1705.[28] There was also a rudimentary bean drill in the shape of the "seed-box" from which a man sprayed beans into the furrows by hand, if not enough women were available to drop them in individually, which was the preferred practice. The hink and the twibil (a hook and a curved slasher for grasping and cutting the ripe beans) were also local inventions of Thanet or East Kent.[29] Tares and vetches were furrowed too, and hoeing was done with a hand hoe as well as with the shim or Kent plough with its weeding attachment.[30]

"The man who reaps, makes the bonds and binds all the sheaves". The harvesting process was the most laborious as horses could not help until the fields were cut, when they were raked with a horse rake.[31] The wheat was all put in barns, but barley, oats and beans were stacked if there was no room in the barns. Threshing was done with the shovel and fan, afterwards the grain was run "through a wire Scry".[32] Cutters and boxes were used for preparing horse feed.[33]

Another particularly laborious job was the sowing of canary seed, which appears to have been done on small farms using family labour.[34]

Sheep were folded on trefoil and clover. "When the Corn is carried the Hogs are let loose in the Grottens or Stubbles, in this open Country where there are very few Enclosures, and which they call Havast, or Haywast".[35] There is little mention of cows. "About October there come hither a sort of grey Birds which the Inhabitants call Bun-Crows", which stay all winter and "do a deal of Mischief, preying on the newly-sown Corn, so the Farmers have to hire Boys to keep them off. This they do by crying 'Haw, Haw!'"[36] No other reference to these birds has been found, but the description fits well enough to crested plover, which in the 1940's when winters were often hard, used to come here in some numbers still and feed on arable fields, ahead of the severe weather.

Thanet farmers of Lewis' day paid great attention to fertilizing their soil. Apart from horse, sheep and hog-dung, malt dust (20 bushels to the acre), pigeon dung, and marsh-mould (silt from the dykes) were used, and sea-waur – a type of seaweed "which waves on top of the water at high Tide" – had recently come into use. Seaweed was not used on the Minster-Monkton side, but their crops were very great.[37]

Windmills had become numerous. Lewis gives a copy of Harris' map of Kent showing them at Downbarton, near Quex, between St Nicholas and Monkton, at Pouces, St John's behind the church, Northdown, St Lawrence, Nash Court, Broadstairs and Callis Court" – ten in all.[38] Dennis Baker considered the volume of flour they produced would have been too great for local consumption and must have been sold outside the island.[39]

Other sources confirm Lewis' account. Harris[40] refers to the value of the marshes to the inhabitants for "Fatting their Cattel and providing them with Butter", which Lewis had not mentioned. Harris also says that "many Yeoman and Farmers of Thanet are Men of good estate as well real as personal" (ie. owning land) "who live in a very gentleman-like Manner", and that 20,000 quarters of all sorts of grain were shipped to London by a weekly hoy service from Thanet in the course of a year. Daniel Defoe[41] speaks of a vast amount of corn shipped to London from Thanet, most or all of it grown there. Hopkins notes rents on the Con- yngham estate at Minster were 18/--24/- per acre, when the Kent average was 10–15/-.[42] In 1726 a collection of £11/17/11d was made in St John's parish for "the poor that suffered in the Fire at Wapping", and who but the rich farmers and maltsters could have contributed that much? St Peter's only raised £2/7/-, consistent with its known inferior soil and smaller farms.[43] (The particular interest in Wapping makes one wonder if it had some connection with the corn trade.)

The continuing "amphibian" tradition is also confirmed. In 1717 Nicholas Sampson of St Peter's owned 1/16 of a pink and 1/3 of a fishing vessel.[44] In 1701 Margate had 37 ships totalling 2,909 tons weight, and 138 men employed on them, Broadstairs had 17 ships totalling 731 tons and 90 men, and Ramsgate (15th in British ports) 45 ships totalling 4,100 tons and 388 men.[45]

Lewis never mentioned wages, but on 14 April 1724 the fol- lowing rates were laid down for Kent at Maidstone General Quarter Sessions, to run for the year from that date:[46]

Servants in husbandry by the year:
Head ploughman £5
His mate £3
Boy 14–18 40/- There is no mention of food or
Best woman £3 perquisites for yearly servants, but
Second sort 40/- they certainly continued.
Labourers by the day: Summer 14d, or 7d and food
Winter 10d, or 5d and food
Mowers by the day: 16d, or 9d and food
by the acre: upland grass 20d
marshland 20d
oats 12d, or 6d and food
barley 12d, or 6d and food
Reapers by the day: Man 2/-, or 12d and food
Woman 12d, or 6d and food
Reaping, binding and copping by acre: Wheat 4/-
Rye, peas and tares 4/-
Laying in band, binding and copping,

per acre:	oats and barley 12d, or 6d and food
Harvestmen, best sort:	55/-, or 35/- and food
second sort:	50/-, or 30/- and food
Threshers and cleaners by quarter:	wheat and rye 20d, or 10d and food
	oats and barley 12d, or 6d and food
Thatchers by day:	Summer 18d, or 9d and food
	Winter 16d, or 8d and food
Thatcher's mate:	Summer 12d, or 6d and food
	Winter 10d, or 5d and food

The middle and later 18th century

The 18th century was one of great developments both in British national history and in Thanet's local story. Like the late 15th century it marked a national watershed, though there is no con-venient single year which can be regarded as a particular turning point, as 1485 might be. By 1780 however the industrial revolution was under way, Canada had been won from France in the Seven Years War (1756–1763), Australia and New Zealand claimed for Britain by Captain Cook, and a strong presence established in India, whilst the loss of the American colonies (the "First British Empire") had provided a salutary lesson on which the Second British Empire was to be successfully based. Thirty-five years of struggle with France for maritime supremacy and overseas possessions lay ahead, but a new, Imperial era was opening. In Thanet the commencement of sea-bathing for health reasons in the 1730's was a very significant milestone in the life of our towns and ultimately of the whole island. Developments in the fishing industry through the mid-century also affected the rural com-munity, but marked change was not to be noticeable on the land till the 1790's, and especially after the wars with France resumed in 1793.

The fashion for sea bathing and seaside holidays, as a change from visiting spas, started amongst the upper classes, and soon catapulted Margate and Ramsgate to fame as rival select resorts within easy reach of London by sea. Sea bathing began at Margate in 1736, and soon after at Ramsgate. By 1776 Margate was claimed to be "in great vogue among wealthy citizens of the metropolis and the most respectable class of gentry in this kingdom".[47] According to a local inhabitant however, "both the houses" of

Ramsgate "and the company which resorts to them" were "of superior description to Margate".[48]

The fashionability of the Thanet resorts led to some improvement in the roads and coaching services. Communications with the mainland were facilitated by the rebuilding in brick of the small bridge over the Wantsum at Sarre in 1743,[49] and a large Dutch-style bridge with a wooden lifting section made over the Stour at Sandwich in 1757.[50] This was the "toll-bridge", still so-called though rebuilt and no longer a toll. By 1796 during the season two diligences, one post-coach, one coach and two night coaches plied each twenty-four hours from Margate to London and the same number from London to Margate. Others connected Margate with Ramsgate.[51] Some at least of the numerous chalkpits on Thanet farms are thought to have been made or enlarged to provide material for the "good chalk roads" of this time.[52] But many of the growing number of visitors preferred to come by sea, and the island atmosphere continued.

All parishes in Thanet had local charities and most had a charity school of some kind by the end of the 18th century. Margate had 9 charities, more than anywhere else in the island.[53] This suggests it had the largest number of poor, an impression strengthened by a report of January 1775 that "in this inclement season three gentlemen of Margate" (two farmers and a maltman) had given a bullock of 26 score to about 100 poor inhabitants in and about the town. Mr J. Bennet, butcher, slaughtered and distributed it for 1/- drink money.[54]

Already in 1763 a private boarding school for young ladies and gentlemen is mentioned in Ramsgate, precursor of many.[55] By the end of the century boarding school had become common for the children of Essex farmers,[56] and although no reference has been found this early in Thanet, it is likely that the prosperous gentlemanly farmers of this island too sent their offspring to such places by that time. Less affluent farmers sent their sons to board with families in Ashford or Wye, so that they could attend the grammar or foundation schools there.[57]

With increasing contact with the mainland and education came the disappearance of the old Thanet dialect, a distinct variant of the Kent one, about which little information is available except in Lewis. In the 17th century the Kentish squirarchy still knew or understood the Kentish dialect,[58] but in Lewis' time the Thanet one had survived only in the pronunciation of "th" as "d", and in 116 words which he lists.[59] By 1763 even this much of it: "had fallen greatly into disuse",[60] but a few words, and above all a distinctive accent and intonation have survived until the present day in some older people (see p 273).

It seems that the mid-18th century saw the decline of the ancient "amphibian" tradition in Thanet. Dennis Baker cites no examples from Thanet probate inventories after 1720, though their scarcity after 1740 prevented him from investigating the years when the crucial change probably came. Lewis' second edition of 1736 is the last clear reference to it as a contemporary situation. When Dr Richard Pococke visited Thanet in 1754 he reported that the island's men "are esteemed as good fishermen as well as husbandmen, all over the island", but he may not be very accurate as he went to Reculver and wrote that it was in the Isle of Sheppey.[61] The unproductiveness of the North Sea fishing was stressed already by Harris in 1719,[62] and though Hasted in his 1800 edition spoke of it as recently revived for the visitors, he said that "amphiby" existed only on the rural coast.[63]

In the mid-century the Broadstairs fishermen, like the Ramsgate ones earlier, began to look further afield, when they started cod fishing off Iceland. This seems to have been sparked off partly by a medical enthusiasm for cod-liver oil. Thirteen sloops were sent in a good year as late as 1779, but it was already waning then because of a slump in the demand for the oil.[64] Icelandic fishing and the Baltic trade were work for full-time professionals, not men coming ashore for long periods each summer. Small-scale inshore fishing has however continued to the present time, so other factors were at play too, such as the growth of population in the coastal areas seeking employment. A 1799 guidebook states that "the increase of the commerce of Britain has long ago divided their operations" (ie. fishing and farming).[65] Yet in St Peter's in the 1780's farmers were still being "induced" to invest perhaps £10–20 to freight ships, and sailors helped with harvest in 1797,[66] so the amphibian tradition lingered, perhaps longer in St Peter's coastal hamlets.

Apart from the loss of that distinctive feature of Thanet life, farming saw a gradual development in this century without any startling changes till the end years. The introduction of new crops and the maintenance of high standards of cultivation lay behind the doubling in the value of Thanet farms between 1680 and 1740, but 1740–1750 was a difficult decade in East Kent, with many tenancies advertised.[67] It is said that shortly before 1750 both rents and corn prices nationally were the lowest since 1585, but thereafter there was a steady rise, offset only temporarily by bad years.[68] If the sources are correct a great fall may have taken place here after 1743, followed by a quick recovery: in that year Minster Court farm of 328 acres paid £350/2/4d rent, and Durlock farm of 227 acres paid £173/14/3d.[69] In 1768 – though the source is dubious – three of the principal farms, Manston Court, Pouces and Thorne, are said to have been let for 7/- per acre per annum "on average",[70] but this may not be true, for Arthur Young found considerably higher rents in 1770 (see p 79–80).

There seems no doubt about the high standard of cultivation here in the 1760's, when the tradition in this respect was evidently still very much alive. A letter of 10 October 1763 from "Rusticus" to the Royal Society already mentioned by Dennis Baker, merits quoting again: "It is extremely pleasant, towards the end of summer, to ride over this little island; I don't imagine there is a more improved spot in the kingdom; the fields are all kept so clean of weeds that they resemble a well-kept garden; they grudge no expense in hoeing, weeding, plowing or manuring; and experience has long convinced them, that they pursue a right method. . . . The land here in general is very rich and fruitful, owing to the good tillage, and the quantity of manure they enjoy, yet at some distance from the sea they have land which is very barren and thin by nature; nevertheless, even this land they farm to the greatest advantage."[71]

Dr Richard Pococke, visiting in 1754, reported the rotation was barley, wheat, beans, oats and a year's fallow. Horse rakes were used after barley, but he does not mention wheat in this connection, which leaves open the possibility that gleaning had started.[72] Rusticus, writing in 1763, declared that there was no fallowing, the lands being kept constantly cropped.[73] Whatever the exact truth, there appears to have been rather more barley grown and further development of beans and canary seed over the first sixty years of the century. One writer states that hop-gardens were established in the Minster area in the 18th century,[74] but Dennis Baker has produced no evidence of this. Between 1711 and 1760 he estimated the sown area in Minster, St Lawrence, St Peter's, and St John's, on the basis of the probate inventories, to be 29.6% wheat, 40.2% barley, 1.8% oats, 18% beans, 0.4% tares, 0.1% canary, 2.1% peas and 7.7% a mixture of peas, tares and oats (dredge).[75]

In 1764 Francis Buti of Birchington was awarded £5 by the Royal Society for growing one acre of madder, and in 1767 John Neame of Birchington received the same sum for growing one acre of lucerne, which seems to mark the introduction of these crops into Thanet. Henry Jezzard of Minster did better, for in 1771 he obtained a silver medal and £5 for growing 5 acres 3 rods and 33 perches of "turnip-rooted cabbage" (kohl-rabi), and writing a series of letters to the Royal Society describing his successful cultivation of it from 1769 and its good effect on his sheep and cows. In 1769 he got 40 tons per acre and in 1770 44 tons. By 1771 other Thanet farmers were buying it from him and beginning to see the utility of the crop. Jezzard had the land for this kohl-rabi ploughed 5 times between Michaelmas and May, to a depth of 9–10 inches the first year and 8 inches later, and had it given one hand hoeing and three horse hoeings. The hand-hoeing had to be done by special turnip hoers from East Kent, for lack of local skill.[76]

Another innovation of this time was the famous Thanet walnut, grown originally from nuts washed up from a wreck on the Nayland Rock and planted at Northdown and Hartsdown by James Taddy Junior, who died in 1764. East Malling Agricultural Research Station took cuttings of the Northdown one about 1929.[77]

Rusticus was much impressed with the row cropping and hoeing of beans, and thought the Thanet method of cultivating them to be "the most perfect of any that I have ever seen", as "they follow Mr Tull's instructions almost literally". He described the Thanet practice: it was exactly the same as Lewis had described 40 years before, with the addition of an extra ploughing in March. (Had they added this in obedience to Tull, or had Lewis simply omitted to mention it? In any case Jethro Tull (1674–1741) published *The new Horse-houghing Husbandry* in 1731, so the methods described by Lewis cannot have been inspired by it, rather the other way round.) Rusticus confirmed that horse beans had been introduced "not a great number of years since". The only criticisms he made were that sheep were turned onto wheat in spring to firm it, but rolling would have been better, also that the sanfoin seed had degenerated and should be replenished from France.[78]

What most impressed the famous agricultural improver Arthur Young when he visited Thanet in 1770 was "the great numbers of drilled crops of barley and wheat – the peas universally so" in the area between St Nicholas and Margate, and the use of the "great shim of the Berkshire kind". By this he seemingly meant the broadshare plough for weed-shearing. Having been pioneers with the bean drill it is not surprising that the Thanet farmers were also pioneers with the corn drill, though it was not invented here. "Full three fourths of the crops are now drilled, and in ten years all will be," wrote Young. Barley and wheat were drilled 9 inches asunder; horse-hoed once or twice with a 4 or 5 inch shim, and hand-hoed besides, the crops were kept infinitely cleaner than any broadcast crops could be. Much less seed was also required for drilling: 2½ bushels of barley per acre compared to 4 bushels when broadcast. The Thanet farmers' "cleaning of the pea stubbles for wheat with the great shim" was "a practice in praise of which too much cannot be said".

The rotation was beans, wheat, barley – the reverse of Pococke's findings, but it all depended on which individual farmers they consulted. "Many throw in a summer fallow once in four, five or six years". Yields were much the same as in Lewis' time – wheat 4 quarters, barley 5, beans 4–5, though on the low ground at Minster oats produced 4–10, average 7. This does not after all say so much for the efficient weeding, but Young thought that more turnips should be grown instead of fallowing. Only a few were grown, and apparently not many tares. Hops were not mentioned. Sanfoin lasted now only 6–10 years. Carrots had been tried on rich, deep soil, but would not do – this Young could not understand. 150 acres of canary were grown for seed around Minster, some broadcast, some drilled, and hand-hoed twice, producing 2–3 quarters an acre. Young criticized the 4-horse turnwrest plough, for a discussion of which see Chapter 5, pp. 97–9.

Sheep flocks rose to 200–300, fed mainly on clover and trefoil. It seemed that the marsh was not much used in winter: bullocks were fattened there in summer, one to the acre, and only "a few sheep in winter." Perhaps the winters were too severe and the water-level was still too high. Sea-weed was much collected, mixed with earth and dung in the manure heaps.

The farms were particularly large and rich at St Nicholas and Minster; at the latter Young acquainted himself with Henry Jessart and a Mr Pett. Perhaps one of their farms might have been Minster Court. Young gave the following particulars of an anonymous farm, probably either Jessart's or Pett's: – "440 acres. 100 acres wheat, 40 sanfoin, 100 barley, 50 clover and trefoil, 50 peas and beans, 80 fallow, 20 turnips. 16 horses, 200 sheep in summer, 4 cows, 6 men" (must have been waggoners, but were they married yearly servants?), "4 boys", (probably yearly servants), "8 labourers".

Young only hinted at the existence of a poorer kind of agri-culture in the smaller holdings and less favoured soils, when he noted that rents were around £1 an acre at St Nicholas, 14–20/- in Minster, and not over 10/- in the poorer land to the north of

Minster. In general he concluded that the Thanet area "has long been reckoned the best cultivated in England, and that it has no light pretensions to that character. . . . It must astonish strangers to find such numbers of *common* farmers that have more drilled crops that broadcast ones and to see them so familiar with drill ploughs and horse-hoes". . . . Despite high rents, tithes, compositions and "extravagant" poor rates, these "excellent farmers make a greater profit from one acre than the slovens in 9/10 of the kingdom do from five".[79]

The influx of summer visitors may have stimulated livestock breeding, for numbers rose somewhat, the average per farm in the four parishes of Minster, St John's, St Lawrence and St Peter's in 1711–1760 in Dennis Baker's calculations being 6 horses, 11 pigs, 29 sheep, and 4 cattle.[80] Market gardening – then simply called gardening – is also mentioned in an advertisement in the *Kentish Post* in 1750: "Thomas Smith, gardener at Margate in the Isle of Thanet, intending to leave off business at Michaelmas next . . . has a large garden, well-watered, the soil rich, fit for Collyflowers, a pond well stocked with fish, summer house, lodge, Hog place, frames, and other glasses near the house, the common sewer of the place" (probably the King Street stream) "runs close to the garden, of which he has 9 years lease to come."[81]

Farmers fertilized their land so assiduously that when two whales beached and died in 1762, one at Broadstairs and one at Birchington,[82] the Broadstairs one at least was carried away by them to enrich their fields – a stench even worse than seaweed or the King Street stream.[83] Dennis Baker found a probate inventory in which the deceased, William Pett of St Nicholas, was claimed to have carried 1,200 loads of dung and "mould" (marsh silt) onto 9 acres of fallow shortly before he died in 1742.[84]

Thanet was not short of agricultural plagues and pests in this century. There was an outbreak of rinderpest near the island's East coast in 1781,[85] and in 1792 one of the notorious weeds, lesser wall mustard, locally known as kinkel (*diplotaxis muralis*, earlier classified as *brassica muralis*), arrived with a ship wrecked at Kingsgate.[86] Rats appeared in great numbers: in Birchington in 1770 £8/12/4½d was paid out by the parish for the killing of 4,137 at ½d per head.[87]

Smuggling became a great Kentish and Thanet industry in the latter half of the 18th century. It is dealt with extensively elsewhere; just by way of illustration 30 smugglers were said to have fought with two excisemen and a soldier in Sarre chalkpit at the end of

January 1771. Such affrays between smugglers and the law or more often between smugglers were not rare. It was a source of profit for farmers who used their carts and barns in the business, and also a cause of labour shortage in farming – the labourers finding it more profitable to join smuggling gangs.[88]

Labour remained in short supply on the land until towards the end of the century. In 1763 it was reported that "the wages of labourers and servants are very high, and in time of war so many men go into the navy in the certainty of better pay, or in hopes of prize money or preferment that it is no easy matter to procure hands for carrying on the common business of agriculture at any price".[89] Country people probably continued going to East Kent for hopping too – in 1746 families from St Nicholas and Sarre went to the hop-fields in the Nunnery Fields area then just outside Canterbury.[90] The *Kentish Post* (1726–1767) and *Kentish Gazette* (1768-) featured announcements of rewards for those returning yearly servants who had "eloped" from their masters, in various parts of Kent. Rewards offered rose from 5/- or unspecified "satisfaction" in 1726 to a guinea by 1768. As an example, two from Chislet were sought in October 1768.[91]

Fifteen years later the announcements had become more menacing. In 1783 Francis Simmons, tenant of Woodchurch Farm, advertised for his waggoner's mate, Robert Hancock, "about 18, 5'3" tall", stating that "whoever harbours or employs him will be dealt with as the law directs".[92] At this time the well-to-do were alarmed about possible insubordination of the lower classes. In 1775 Thomas Fagg, labourer, had to publish an apology in the *Kentish Gazette* for stealing fruit from Mr Cowell of the Dane, Margate, gent., who in return promised not to prosecute.[93]

Fear of the lower classes is also shown in reactions to the spread of Methodism. The first Methodist convert in St Nicholas, a Mr Coleman in 1767, was not allowed to preach in the street and eventually drummed out of the village. When a room was built as a chapel there in 1778 or so, the farmers resolved to punish any of their men who attended the services. One evening three young farmers were on watch, and the preacher told them to desist or each would meet an untimely end, which apparently all three did. Coleman left the village in 1780 and the Methodists of St Nicholas then walked to the chapel in Birchington, (3 miles) until a new one was built in St Nicholas in 1822.[94]

But by 1792 the farmers had gone back to offering rewards for the return of runaways. In November that year, Richard Sayer of

Smithwood, St Lawrence, advertised for "Henry White, 17 years old, about 5 foot high, stout made, wearing a short gaberdine, a blue jacket, leather breeches". Only half a guinea reward was offered.[95]

Wages for a waggoner yearly servant in East Kent generally in 1766 were about £5 pa according to John Boys,[96] which is the same as 1724, but in St Peter's payments were apparently largely in kind at reduced prices – wheat for grist, corn for a pig etc., which lends weight to Dennis Baker's view that the married men had small-holdings of their own.[97] Arthur Young must have been looking at the larger farms when he reported Thanet wages to be as follows in 1770:–

Head man (Head waggoner):	£11 or £11/11 – per annum, hence a yearly servant
Next man (Second waggoner):	£10 – per annum, hence a yearly servant

Lad's wage:
£3–£6 (probably a yearly servant)

Labourer – in haytime:	1/6d–2/- per day
– in winter:	1/4d–1/8d per day
– in harvest: (ie for general work)	2/6d per day, but commonly £3/10/- or £3 for 5 weeks

(Young does not mention board or food, but the lower rates for lads and labourers may have been given with food, and board for lads.)

Reaping:	6/- –12/-
Mowing and binding barley or oats:	4/-
Mowing alone:	2/-
Hoeing barley:	5/- –7/-
Threshing wheat:	1/6d–3/- per quarter
Threshing barley and oats:	1/2d–1/4d per quarter
Threshing peas:	1/- per quarter

These wages were "much higher than formerly", and the "extrava-gant" poor rates were 2/- –3/6 in the pound £.[98]

After that, however, there is evidence that wages did not rise much more. A Garlinge farmer in 1833 claimed that his father "fifty years ago" (ie. in 1783) paid his labourers 1/6 a day, 9/- a week if a six-day week was worked. He also maintained that at that time "every (married) man had a barrel of beer in his cellar", but that clothes were expensive and women had to knit the family hose.[99] The remarkable shortness of the absconding 17–18 year old yearly servants in comparison to modern heights may not have been due to undernourishment by the standards of the day, as the whole population was shorter at that time (viz. the corkscrew stair at Woodchurch). Yet it is likely to have been linked to nutrition in some way, for increasing height is a world-wide phenomenon occuring in many affluent countries now.[100] It has been estimated that the calorific content of Britain's food has risen at least 25% since the late 18th century.[101] By the mid-century wheaten bread was the staple diet of the labouring class even in poorer parts of England, most of their clothing being bought from shops except stockings as noted.[102]

The bigger farmers lived in greater comfort now than in the 17th century, but still relatively simply. By 1750 the larger Kentish farmhouses usually contained four or more bedrooms, and a good number of outhouses for brewing, pickling, baking, laundering, dairy work etc. We know that in the 18th century Durlock Grange was enlarged by a wing at the rear containing a bread oven and copper, and a pump seems to have been installed for the well outside the back door.[103] When the Grange was sold in 1775, the household goods included a variety of feather beds and hangings, mahogany chairs and tables, sundry brewing utensils and other effects, waggons, carts, harnesses, ploughs, harrows etc., with nine good horses, two cows, 29 fat sheep and a number of hogs.[104] This shows the occupant, evidently largely an arable farmer, to have been very fashionable, as William Cobbett says that the English farmers as a whole had only got to the mahogany furniture stage in 1821.[105]

Sales such as that at Durlock Grange were very rarely advertised in the press; tenant farmers' live and dead stock normally changed hands by valuation, as happened at Flete farm in 1755, valued at £107/16/3d. The acreage is not known, but cannot have been great: there were three horses, two cows, one sow and eleven pigs, two ploughs, one shim, four harrows, two carts, two hand shims and odds and ends. The limited farmhouse furniture, including bed-steads (one for the farmer, two for servants) and bedding were included with the agricultural items. There were seven pairs of sheets but no mention of featherbeds. This seemed to be a poorish farm whose occupant lived less well than the rich farmers had in the preceding century.[106] Another sidelight on the farm lifestyle mentioned later is that cowslip wine was a favourite in Kentish farmhouses in the 18th century; this was probably potent, at least one quart brandy to three quarts fermented cowslip brew, according to one recipe.[107]

There was a good deal of rebuilding of farmhouses and construction of small mansions in the Thanet countryside. Walter's Hall, Monkton, was built by Captain Proud in 1700, (the large house which stood near what is now Foxhunter Park, not the older farmhouse).[108] Ozengell Grange was rebuilt in 1711.[109] Chilton farmhouse was built in the early 18th century;[110] it has the distinctive Flemish gables also seen in Reading Street and Sarre in several dwellings and scattered in other parts of Thanet. Sevenscore farmhouse has a Queen Anne front imposed on an older structure.[111] East Northdown farmhouse and St Nicholas Court were built (or more likely rebuilt) and the old hallhouse at Nether Hale given a brick front in this century as well.[112] The most striking surviving house of the time is the "new" mansion at Cleve Court, erected on the remains of a much older dwelling by Josiah Farrer, who bought the old house in 1748.[113] By 1760 Josiah's son, S.F. Farrer, was keeping a pack of hounds for hare hunting, later to develope into the Thanet Harriers.[114] S.F. Farrer became High Sheriff of Kent in 1773, but afterwards lived abroad.[115] The Crispe family had "daughtered out" by 1680, and in this period the Elizabethan mansion at Quex was in decay. In 1763 it is described as "a venerable mansion which still boasts many remains of the good old English hospitality, but like most others of the same rank in the neighbourhood is now crumbling very fast to ruin and is sunk to the dwelling of a tenant."[116]

More J.P.'s were appointed here in the later 18th century, chosen still from the gentry, who were urban or semi-urban now as much as rural. St Peter's and St Lawrence were favoured areas for them, as well as other outskirts of Ramsgate, as tombstone inscriptions show.

In 1764 Thanet briefly acquired a resident nobleman at Kingsgate in the person of the disgraced Paymaster General of the Forces, Lord Holland, father of Charles James Fox, who was later the first, *de facto* Leader of the Opposition. Thomas Gray wrote of Holland:

> "Old and abandoned by each venal Friend,
> Here Holland took the pious Resolution,
> To smuggle some few Years and try to mend,
> A broken Character and Constitution."

Thanet's pure air gave him ten years (he died in 1774), and he gave it the original Kingsgate castle (rebuilt more or less in its present

form in 1913), the Captain Digby inn and other follies, in a then
bleak part of the island, of which Gray also wrote in 1766:-

"Here reign the blustering North and blighting East,
No tree is heard to whisper, bird to sing" . . .

Holland bought up the remains of the Crispe estate as well in
1767.[117] In 1777 Charles James Fox sold all his Thanet lands to the
Cashier at the Pay Office, John Powell, who had acted as Holland's
land steward and owned an estate in Kilburn. He became the
founder of a new gentry family at Quex, esteemed in Thanet to
this day.[118]

Thanet: a beautiful, unspoilt island

Late 18th century and early 19th century Thanet was still almost a
natural paradise and this period was the last before the works of
man gradually destroyed its charms. Man had denuded it of trees
by then, but replaced them with a cover of good agricultural crops,
and there were still many birds, fish and sea-shells. Taken for
granted down all the centuries since Roman times at least, the
island's natural beauty now began to be vaunted, in part artfully
for the attraction of visitors, and in part genuinely, due to the new
perception of Nature which was stirring educated Europe.

H. Hogben's map circa 1791 (see p ix) shows that almost the
whole island was still farmland, apart from the tiny villages and
urban areas with their affluent visitors. In summer, the golden
cornfields swept down to the sea almost everywhere. The Rev-
erend William Gilpin found Thanet "without any picturesque
beauty" in 1774,[119] but most people raved about it, perhaps partly
because of the great contrast with the smoke and stench of
London. Hasted, the famous author of a multi-volume history
of Kent, described it thus in the late 1790's:-

"The general face of the country (excepting the marshland
towards the South) is high land, exceedingly beautiful, consisting
of fertile cornlands, inter-mixed with those sown with sainfoin,
clover and vetches, mostly open and un-enclosed, with gentle hill
and dale frequently interspersed with small hamlets and cottages,
most of which being built, as well as the adjoining walls, with chalk,
the general soil of the country, have a very cheerful appearance. . . .
Many bridle, or horse paths, which are almost without number,

across the lands, are most beautifully enriched with continual prospects over the intermediate country and adjoining Channel, which . . . has constantly on it a variety of shipping."[120] It must be remembered that the ships had sails, did not belch smoke or leak oil, and being small were far more numerous than today's. "The pink blossoms of the sanfoin are very beautiful."[121] Hasted like Lewis also mentioned rosemary hedges of a considerable length,[122] and went on to write enticingly of the Margate seaside:-

"Margate is a weather shore during the greater part of the summer or in other words, the southerly winds, which generally prevail in that season, blow off from the land; by which means the sea is rendered perfectly smooth and the water clear to a considerable depth."[123]

Many lesser writers enhanced the picture:

"There are many seaweeds of beautiful colours",[124] and "an abundance of beautiful shells", including "the stout tellina, of nearly 20 different colours", and 28 varieties more.[125] Despite talk of failed fishery, "at Pegwell Bay, the inhabitants catch shrimp, lobsters, soles, mullets, etc. and a delicious flat fish called a prill, much sought after."[126] The fish were caught with vast nets pegged into the sand:[127] this method had probably been used in the Wantsum at the time of Domesday Book (see p 18).

"The nightingale is a constant visitor in spring. There are great numbers of quails, partridges, hares and rabbits, but no pheasants. Excepting the pole-cat, there are no vermin of any consequence: fox, badger and otter are rarely seen. There is an abundance of wildfowl in a severe winter, the bargander goose often frequents the marshes."[128] "You can easily hear 50 nightingales in an evening walk in Thanet".[129] Sparrows, rooks, stoats, weasels and pole-cats were lavishly killed for small sums paid by the parish at Birchington, particularly in the early 18th century. Buzzards and sparrow-hawks were also paid for then.[130]

Well-known writers besides Hasted noted the splendid views: one has the impression that the atmosphere, like the sea, may have been clearer than it often is now. William Marshall,[131] a critical visitor, speaks of the almost incessant throng of shipping on the surrounding seas, and the broad open views northward to Sheppey, the Nore, the Essex coast, the high ground of East Kent, and the Continent. William Cobbett writes in a matter-of-fact way that the Essex and Suffolk coast was in full view from above Dover on 3 September 1823.[132]

Other descriptions are almost, or truly sentimental, and do not look at conditions in the cottages, yet still indicate that we have lost something since that time. "Garlinge is a pretty little hamlet of 20 houses".[133] "St Peter's is very pretty and surrounded by trees, rather uncommon in these parts".[134] "St Peter's consists of 35 hamlets or knots of houses".[135] "The pleasant and romantic little village of Manston, where country life still exists in all its purity . . .".[136] "Margate affords romantic walks along the dry sand, with the ocean on one side and the caverns and grottos in the chalk cliffs on the other".[137] "Minster is one of the prettiest villages in all England, cottages neatly white-washed and clean", with "perfume diffused from its numerous gardens."[138]

E.W. Brayley's account of Thanet in 1817 contains a picture of ramshackle thatched cottages at Birchington, apparently made partly of timber, partly of chalk, which he obviously considered picturesque, but must have been rather squalid as dwelling places.[139] There were definitely two sides to the beauties of Thanet at that time: the worst sufferings of the poor actually began in the 1790's, and were contemporary with all the above-quoted praises of the island.

Yet in some ways the middle 18th century was a minor "Golden Age" in our history. The island had its unspoilt charm, enriched by wealthy visitors in still small numbers. Although life was hard for the poorer the great epidemics had gone, and there was not the horrific difference between the classes that the end of the century was to bring. Thanet farmers enjoyed prosperity, and their awards from the Royal Society and praise from visitors like Arthur Young showed them to be still nationally outstanding. We of our time would not enjoy living with their hygienic and medical facilities, but the picture of the island conjured up by the writers who extolled it is something to be treasured in the imagination.

Chapter Five: The Napoleonic War Years: 1792–1815

General position of the farmers

The long wars with France brought great demand for grain, especially wheat, and coincided with particularly bad weather. In the winter of 1793–1794 snow covered Thanet for 71 days. There had been exceptionally bad harvests nationally in 1756, 1766, 1768 and 1789 (four in 34 years), but in the next 28 there were seven: 1795, 1799, 1800, 1809, 1810, 1811 and 1812. In June 1795 60 newly shorn sheep died of cold at St Nicholas, belonging to farmers Evernden and Curling. The 1792 summer was also cold, wet, windy and dark, with severe frost in September in much of England, but the harvest was not an absolute failure. Runs of good seasons had occured in 1758–1765 and 1775–1779, but in the war years only 1801 and 1813 were really favourable. These factors led to record wheat prices, especially in the worst years. In 1813 wheat was still selling for over 100/- a quarter in London.[1] London prices continued to be usually somewhat higher than in Canterbury market, but in some years. Canterbury prices were higher than Mark Lane. Thus during the threat of invasion in 1804, when many troops were stationed in East Kent and special barracks were constructed at Margate and Westgate, wheat at Canterbury market on 16 October was 70/-–82/- a quarter and at Mark Lane only 57/- –75/-; oats were 30/-–34/- at Canterbury and 25/-–27/- at Mark Lane, and only barley was dearer at Mark Lane at 32/-–47/- to Canterbury's 38/-–41/-.[2]

Rents fixed for a number of years were not raised till the term expired, which benefitted the farmers still more at first. When Sevenscore Estates (1,200 acres), part of Minster parish, were sold in 1805, it was stated that the expiring rents were £1,720 pa, but estimated to be now worth £3,000.[3] By 1805 most rents had risen enormously,[4] and at the peak of the war prosperity were 50/- an acre or more.[5] Yet larger farms continued to make money. Tenancies were quickly grabbed all through the war period,[6] and amalgamation of farms "started" about 1800 according to a local observer.[7]

One farmer's progress can be seen from the account book cum diary of John Bridges of St Nicholas. Starting to farm on his own at twenty in 1779 at a small farm at Chamber's Wall, with debts of £1,414/14/- and an income of £199, he had an annual turnover of over £10,000 by 1813 at St Nicholas Court. But some of this was derived from rents, tithe collection, interest on loans to others, government bonds, shares, marriage settlements and inheritances, for he was an all-round businessman and the family usually married money. Such a farmer also had to meet heavy public charges: in 1800 Bridges paid out £600/12/8d for rent, tithes, poor rates, highway composition charges and taxes.[8] John Mockett, of Hopeville farm, St. Peter's, a smaller farmer, paid about £200 pa in property tax during the war period.[9]

Bridges himself attended Wye Grammar School and Ashford School only till he was 15½, but spent a great deal educating his only son privately in the homes of clergymen. In 1822 the boy was still being taught at 17 for 200 guineas pa (and £10 more for his washing!) in the home of the Rev. Godfrey Fawcett at Harefield.[10] This son, John Thomas, ended living as a rentier gentleman at Walmer, and became the father of the Victorian Poet Laureate Robert Bridges.[11]

Wealth did not necessarily bring health, however, for the mortality in the Bridges family was very heavy. A number of still births were followed by a son who died in infancy, and only the one son survived. John Bridges' father had died at 37 in 1765. His mother broke her hip falling in the garden at 59, an early age for a fracture suggestive of osteoporosis, which until recently in the 20th century affected women a decade or more older:[12] she suffered constant pain from this injury until her death at 72. Two sisters died of consumption at 15 and 23, a promising nephew at 20 and a niece at 24. His brother died in the prime of life, and several brothers-in-law in middle age; John Bridges himself had gout at 53 and died at 63,[13] though his wife lived to 78. His son John Thomas died at 48, but improved the family stock by marrying a woman who lived to 90, and had nine surviving children before remarrying after John Thomas' death.[14] The general mortality patterns were still reminiscent of today's Third World, with high death rates in children and young people, but some lived to be very old. John Mockett had lost six sons and daughters and his wife by 1824,[15] long before his own death at a late age. He was still farming in 1843 after 60 years at it.[16]

During the war period a large number of wattle and daub or brick Thanet farmhouses were rebuilt or enlarged with elegant Georgian front wings. Of the well-known ones, Hoo is perhaps the grandest. Some, like Eden (Minster) and Downbarton, just have Georgian "false fronts". Some others, like Watchester, Wood-church and Flete in their Georgian front wings, and the whole of the Hoo and Plumstead farmhouses, are roofed with distinctive blue slates, not native to Thanet or Kent, and unknown in rural roofs here from earlier periods,[17] from which we may surmise that the rebuilding probably started in the early years of the 19th century. In 1804 the firm of A.H. Spratt advertised that they had imported "a cargo of best Bangor slates, equal to Westmoreland or Patents", which were being offered for sale in Canterbury, Thanet and Faversham – precisely the richest agricultural areas.[18] The outstanding rural building of Thanet of this time is Quex House, completed in 1813,[19] and also roofed with the blue slates, which remained popular into the next century. Amongst gentry houses, Way House is also Georgian, built onto an old farmhouse like Cleve Court.

Furnishings inside the farmhouses grew finer too – by 1794 "nothing can exceed their general neatness and even elegance" in John Boys' of Betteshanger's view. When Thomas Harnett of Monkton sold part of his furniture in 1804 it included a Turkey carpet, "an exceeding good 8-day clock" and mahogany tables.[20] Money was also spent on the farms: both John Bridges and John Mockett had new brick barns by 1815, the former two, one for beans and one for barley.[21] At Downbarton the entire land, both arable and marsh, was surrounded by a ring-fence,[22] and we know from later references that other farmers did this too. A hare hunt was begun in 1813 (see p 109), showing that the farmers had money to spend on good riding horses.

Another novelty was the Isle of Thanet Yeomanry, founded in 1794 under Captain Garrett of Nethercourt, which some 60 farmers and gentlemen of the island joined. George III reviewed them with other Kent regiments at Mote Park, Maidstone, in 1799, and afterwards presided over a huge dinner with 2,200 dishes. The regiment was disbanded in 1828, never having seen action.[23] Humbler, horseless citizens joined the Cinque Ports Volunteers, and arrangements were made during the invasion threat in 1803 for them to be conveyed by waggon to their muster points at Nash Down (for Margate men), Rumfields (for St Peter's), Upper Court Field near Nethercourt (for Ramsgate) and Mount Pleasant (for Sarre).[24] One wonders why able bodied men could not have marched to these places! The Prime Minister, William Pitt, Lord Warden of the Cinque Ports, attended a defence meeting at Margate town hall on 18 October 1803, and Nelson landed at Margate on 11 August 1800 to recruit French coast pilots amongst the local smugglers.[25]

The Land Tax redemption assessments for 1798 provide a very rough guide to the agricultural landholding patterns in the villages for which they are available, as shown by Table 3. Since they do not distinguish between agricultural and other properties they are not of much use for St Lawrence and St John's, and even in the villages they certainly also contain some non-farmers, especially in St Peter's and Birchington.

Table 3: Landholding 1798 according to Land Tax Redemption Assessments[26]

Owner occupiers assessed at £1 or over		0/0 assessed at under £1	Tenants assessed at £1 or over	Tenants assessed at under £1
St Nicholas	4	7	10	37
Monkton	23	26	38	25
Minster	17	32	41	69
Birchington	10	11	21	45
St Peter's	27	93	24	231
St Lawrence	20	44	25	81

Occupiers of the same name are treated as the same individual in cases where their holdings are listed consecutively and they are not otherwise identified (as by Senior or Junior). Individuals are classified as owners or renters according to which mode pre-dominates in their holdings. Even making allowance for inaccuracy of comparison, it would seem that some increase of holdings and thus of population had taken place since 1691, when Monkton had 14 owner occupiers and 57 tenants as against 49 owner occupiers and 63 tenants in 1798. The data also confirm Lewis' statement that farms were small in St Peter's. This parish, with its 35 hamlets and only a few gentlemen's houses, obviously had a large number of small farmers, and cottagers with a little land.

Condition of small-holders and farm workers

As the farmers became richer, some small-holders gave up the struggle with rising rents, and the farm labourers became much poorer. Rising prices and years of dearth meant hunger for them, especially as a population explosion took place, transforming the labour shortage of earlier times into a glut of labour within not many years. This was partly caused by a fall in mortality, which has been attributed partly to widespread inoculation (later vaccination) against smallpox and the absence of other killer epidemics after the 1740's.[27] The tuberculosis which struck the families of rich farmers and bourgeoisie may not have had such an impact on the labouring class who lived more in the open air. It is also apparent from the parish registers that more babies were being born, or born alive, due perhaps to earlier marriage and perhaps because the women were less weakened by infectious disease. At Birchington, for instance, a steady rise took place, though the birth surplus over burials in 1700–1750 was less than it had been in 1650–1700:-

Table 4: Birchington parish registers summary 1700–1851[28]

	Marriages	Births	Funerals	Surplus of births
1700–1750	52	651	512	139
1750–1800	226	962	614	348
1800–1851	270	1,774	938	836

In 1796 John Boys reported the greatest scarcity of labour in East Kent "we have ever known", and "much worse along the coast",[29] due to the war, but in 1797 John Mockett of St Peter's noted that men were no longer needed to come from outside Thanet to help with the harvest, as sailors (still?) worked on the land outside the fishing season and the apprentices of carpenters, blacksmiths' and shoemakers were given a month off for harvest.[30] As early as 1795 a considerable part of the wheat was gleaned by women after being mown,[31] and in 1817 as many as 30 women could be seen in a field.[32] Gleaning, suggestive of poverty, was never mentioned by Lewis, who said that the harvest fields were raked with horse rakes, though Dr Richard Pococke only mentioned barley fields being raked and was silent on wheat.[33] A return to horse rakes was actually advised by a visiting agricultural expert in 1798. (See p 100 for William Marshall's report).

By 1801 the Thanet population had risen to 12,890, of which 7,876 was in Ramsgate and Margate and 5,014 in the villages, including St Lawrence and St Peter's; in 1811 the population had risen to 16,305, of which 10,347 was in the towns and 5,958 in the villages, a rise of 18.8% in the latter in the ten years. By far the largest increases were in St Lawrence and St Peter's, as Table 5 shows; this must have been partly due to immigration. In St Peter's 42.9% of families were not engaged mainly either in agriculture, trade, handicrafts or industry, hence seafaring may still have been important. Some of the migration to the towns and St Lawrence and St Peter's may have been of farm labourers seeking housing, in view of the known shortage of farm cottages until the 1870's (see p 141).

Table 5: Population 1811 census

Number of families chiefly employed:

	In agriculture	In trade, handicrafts, and industry	Other	% population rise since 1800
Margate	164	325	792	28.3
Ramsgate	9	472	409	35.7
St Lawrence	145	101	49	32.5
St Peter's	151	97	187	23.9
Birchington	78	22	19	14.3
Woodchurch/ Acol	(total population given only)			12.4
Minster	92	24	41	16.5
Monkton	53	6	4	10.6
St Nicholas	75	13	17	–7.6
Sarre	23	10	5	10

(VCHK 3/357–358; PP 1801, 1801 census enumeration 1/147, 157; PP 1812, 1811 population enumeration abstract, 138.[34])

Famine struck Thanet like most of Britain in 1795. The Birchington vestry book recorded that from 1 June all labouring men with four or more children were sold rough meal at 7/-a bushel. From July bread was also distributed. On 3 August wheat was 126/-a quarter at Birchington, and though by September it had fallen to 90/-, and distributions ceased,[35] it was an average of 104/2d in Thanet again by 23 November.[36]

In that month farm workers at Monkton held a meeting and demanded higher wages and cheaper bread, threatening to strike against the inclusion of ⅓ barley meal in their bread. After negotiations they agreed "to be served with wheat meal at 1/- the gallon, as they had hitherto been accustomed to receive, to have beans for their hogs at 3/- the bushel, and an advance of their wages from 1/6 to 2/- a day."[37] This unrest must have referred to both married yearly servants and day labourers as well as boarded yearly servants.

The unrest may have spread beyond Monkton, for on 23 November Thanet farmers as a whole agreed to raise wages and reduce the price of wheat and beans for their men by the amounts stipulated at Monkton – though John Mockett, when noting this in his diary, said nothing of any trouble with the workforce.[38] As noted wheaten bread was the staple diet of the labouring classes even in the poorer parts of England by the mid-18th century.[39] One writer maintains that by 1795 no labourer could live on his wages,[40] but according to John Boys, Betteshanger farmer and author of a survey of Kent farming published in 1794, with second and third editions in 1796 and 1805, the picture was very different.[41]

He quoted the following commodity prices:

	December 1795	1803
Half peck loaf best wheaten bread	2/-	(1/5½d *Kentish Gazette* 8/8/1803, 4)
Mutton per lb	6d	8½d
Beef ditto	5½d	8½d
Pork „	7d	7d
Veal „	8d	10d
Bacon „	8d	–
Butter „	1/-	–
Good Cheshire cheese	7d	–
Potatoes per nearly 200 lb sack	8–10/-	10/6
Coals per 36 bushels	36/-	48/-

For wages, Boys gave:

	1794 (Isle of Thanet)	1803 (East Kent generally)
Boarded yearly servant waggoner	£10–£13 pa	£11–£15 pa
Married waggoner	10/--10/6 pw	10/6 pw
Boarded 2nd ploughman	£9–£11 pa	£11–£15 pa
3rd ditto	£8–£10 „	£10–£13 „
Waggoner's mate	£6–£10 „	£7–£11 „
2nd ploughboy	£4–£7 „	£5–£7 „

3rd ditto	£3–£6 „	£4–£6 „
Bailiff	£12–£16 „	£15–£20 „
Dairy maid	£4–£6 „	£4–£6 „

Much work was piecerate, for example, spreading dung per 100 24-bushel cartloads 3/6–4/-; hoeing turnips 5/—6/- per acre; other types of hoeing from 4/—4/6 to 1/8–2/- per acre; reaping wheat 8/—16/- per acre; mowing barley and oats 1/8–2/6 per acre; threshing wheat 2/—3/- per quarter.

Other wages are given only for 1794 by Boys, the 1805 edition did not update them.

Labourers per 10-hour day	1/6–2/- (9–12/- pw)
Shepherd	9–10/6 pw
Woman weeding	8d–10d per day
Children 10–14	6d pd
A harvest man for 5 weeks.	
with board	£3/10/-
without board	£5/5/-[42]

In 1810–11 women and children were paid 1/- a load of stones picked from fields and sheepwalk at Birchington.[43]

In the 1796 edition Boys observed that "upon the whole, the price of labourers is nearly double 30 years ago", but this is not borne out by comparison with Arthur Young's 1770 Thanet data. Boys claimed that in 1795, "unless he has a large family the sober and industrious labourer cannot properly be called a poor man" and that the East Kent labourer was "comfortably clothed and well-fed."[44] Many must in fact have had more children than would permit this, and it can hardly have been true for any family men later. Only the single, boarded servants may have continued to fare better than the married labourers living in rented cottages. The enormous increase in the price of coal in particular cannot fail to have hit the latter, and the small-holder too. Moreover the rent of an agricultural cottage was £2–£3 pa in 1795,[45] and by 1803 "few good cottages with gardens" were let for less than £4. The farmers' rising rents may have continued to spread down to those they charged their men. Meal was distributed again at Birchington in 1804.[46]

It may be noted from Boys' information that married waggoners were paid weekly by 1794, presumably because of the inflation in food prices; but this did not necessarily mean that they had lost their yearly servant status, for some married yearly servants existed in the later 19th century and early 20th century on a contract but receiving a weekly wage (see p 175–6). However, the married servant with a small holding of his own seems to have vanished in the Napoleonic period, except possibly in St Peter's or St Lawrence.

Boys' omission of daily wages in 1803 in his 1805 edition may have been due to the arrival of the Speenhamland system of poor relief in East Kent. It acquired its name from a Berkshire parish where the magistrates, in the famine year 1795, provided a supplement to wages from poor relief funds, dependent on the price of bread and the number of dependants of a labourer. This system rapidly spread all over Southern England.[47] John Bridges' accounts suggest that he was making use of it by 1799 when 17 labourers cost him £303/7/- and in 1801 19 labourers cost him £318/-/8d, or about 6/6d a week each, indicating that like many farmers he was reducing wages because the parish was paying the "supplement". In 1803 20 labourers cost Bridges £520/10/6 or about 10/- a week each, which as the price of bread had fallen at that point might mean that Speenhamland was not being operated. Bridges also employed "day labour" (casual labourers) and yearly servants, but does not give their numbers so their wages cannot be calculated from his gross expenditure on them.[48] According to a later report, Thanet wages rose to 18–21/- during the war period.[49]

But in 1800–1803 Thanet overall poor rates had risen nearly 100% over 1792–1795, the increase being greatest in St John's (over 100%), St Peter's (over 75%) and Woodchurch (Acol) (150%), whilst the St Lawrence increase was less than 50%. The average annual Thanet-wide expenditure was £4,805 in 1792–1795, and £9,218 in 1801–1803.[50] A new poor house was built at St Peter's in 1805[51] and a "fine new poor house" at Birchington for the parishes of Birchington, Acol, Monkton and Sarre in 1794 (these parishes united for the purpose under the terms of the Gilbert Act of 1781–2).[52] New cottages for the poor were built at Birchington in 1810–11.[53] Educational opportunities for the bright poor child had only slightly improved by this time, but by 1807 all Thanet parishes except St John's had access to a school of some kind.[54] Not many village children would have been able to take much advantage of this, but one who did was the outstandingly clever blacksmith's son John Lyon of St Nicholas (1735–1817), who became a teacher, then was ordained and became Vicar of St Mary's Dover, and wrote three books on electricity. He died worth £10,000, but never married,[55] so perhaps personal happiness eluded him.

A farm labourer born at Birchington in March 1795 described the food in his youth to his son, born in 1837, as rough meal at a guinea a bushell, meat almost unknown, "just a plain Dumpling and a few Potatoes in the week, and a red Herring on Sunday, and for supper go and find a swede turnip field, pull one up, peel it and eat it, the law was not so strict on that sort of thing then as it is now."[56]

Agricultural developments

Agriculture was crucially important in this war greater than any Britain had yet fought (465,000 men were in the armed forces in 1811, or 1/5 of all males 15–49.)[57] The government called for reports from all regions, a rather complacent one being made for East Kent by John Boys afore-mentioned, in 1794. A more critical account of Thanet was also published by a visiting agricultural expert, William Marshall, in 1798. From them we have a comprehensive picture.

In 1794 a 7-row corn drill cost £14/10/-, harrows with six or seven iron teeth in each 11" beam cost £1/1/-, rolls £3/-/10d, (not mentioned by Lewis, nor by Rusticus in 1764), turnwrest ploughs £5/5/-, corn waggons £21/-/- with wooden axles and £26/5/- with iron ones, dung carts £8/8/-, horse rakes 18/- to £1/4/-, wheat stubble rakes £2/2/-.[58] It is not certain whether these early drills were locally made, like the rest of the horse-drawn and hand-wielded farm implements, but they probably were. A specific mention of a patent factory-made device appeared in a Downbarton farm sale announcement in 1811, when "a new 5-share Wellard's machine drill" was advertised amongst the deadstock, apparently as a choice piece.[59] A Nash Court sale in 1815 mentions a "two-furrow drill plough" and "a 5-furrow machine", whatever these may have been.[60] Local inventions there certainly were, as early as 1799 Mr Neame at Birchington had "a curious mill" for threshing clover and trefolium seed, which appeared to be his own creation.[61]

By far the most important piece of farm equipment was still the ancient Kentish wooden turnwrest plough, which now attracted nationwide attention. This seems a good point at which to discuss it, although it had been in use since the 13th century at least (see p 27). From the mid-17th century onwards British farmers had experimented with a multiplicity of different ploughs, both iron and partly iron, but Thanet was only to begin to abandon the turnwrest in the late 19th century. It was a development of the Anglo-Saxon plough, without its excessive depth.[62] Walter Blith, an early agricultural improver, castigated it in 1652, saying "it surpasseth for weight and clumsiness" . . . "all the ploughs I ever saw".[63] To William Marshall it was a monstrosity: "its component parts and the names assigned to them are nearly equal in number to those of a ship"; he considered it was "a crime to continue to plough" (in Thanet) "with four horses and an implement altogether improper to be worked in broken ground".[64] Arthur Young found it too shallow, as the chisel point at that time varied from 2–4 inches with a heel of 9–10 inches, which tended to drive weeds underground,[65] but the Thanet turnwrests of the later 19th century and early 20th century normally had a chisel point of 4 inches (viz. Barzillai Sackett's plough at the Brook Agricultural Museum, Wye College). Young also found the use of four horses unnecessary in the light Thanet soil.[66]

In 1911, after the turnwrest had been under attack for about 260 years and was still in use by some farmers in Thanet, the agricultural experts A.D. Hall and E.J. Russell delivered a balanced judgement, pointing out that despite its wastefulness of labour (three to four horses, a boy to lead and a man to hold), it was very adaptable, serving as a plough with a mould-board, and as broadshare when the mould-board was replaced with the broad flat point, 14–18 inches wide, in which guise it was used both to shim (shear off weeds) and to form a good seed bed in light soil, firm below and crumbly above. It also went very well among the flint stones with which the Thanet soil is scattered, producing a steady, even furrow 7, 8 or 9 inches deep.[67]

In 1958 Captain Mallett gave the old plough a moving requiem in an address to the Herne Bay Fortnightly Club: "The old wooden plough, with its complicated adjustments, could perform every cultivation required by any crop" (of its day), "it was most adaptable. It was built entirely by the local wheelwright and blacksmith . . . and it could be repaired by the waggoner with materials found at home. The waggoner always carried, on the axle of the plough, an old leather boot and a few horse-nails. A bit of this boot and a few horse-nails were all that was required to effect fine adjustments of the swinging "coulter" and the "point". The entire considerable weight of the plough was carried, not on its wheels, but pressed directly on the subsoil. When used as a broadshare for spring cultivation about 3 inches deep, it pressed and crushed the soil into good capillary contact with the subsoil. The great difficulties of farming upon chalk are firstly, to retain moisture in the subsoil, and secondly, to produce good conditions which will induce this moisture to rise, by capillary action, to the benefit of the crop."

"I do not know of any modern implement which will so well produce these conditions; the principle of consolidation of the soil with the subsoil seems to have been neglected, if not lost." (Here one may observe that Arthur Young on his 1770 visit was surprised at the effectiveness of the shallow turnwrest, and did not appreciate its consolidatory action.) "In these times it might not be possible to find a ploughman whose physical condition is such that he could lift this plough and carry it round a half-circle at the end of every furrow, for a period of 8 hours day after day. This means 80 times a day for one acre, with a furrow ten chains long." In this way had the Thanet ploughmen laboured since medieval times. A full technical description of the Kent plough is given by John Boys.[68]

The Thanet crop rotations quoted by Boys are much fuller than those Lewis gave: by 1794 some did peas, barley, beans, wheat, or wheat, barley, beans, wheat, fallow. Radish for seed had become a common crop (early, short, top, salmon and turnip-rooted varieties). Spinach seed and kidney beans were also new departures, but the biggest innovation of the late 18th century was the potato, "more and more cultivated each year" by 1795.[69] By 1817 the harvest was estimated at nearly 50,000 sacks.[70]

In 1795 the agricultural expert William Marshall visited Thanet on his nationwide tour for the Board of Agriculture. He approved the barley (long and short-eared sprats and a local variety, "the famous Thanet barley"),[72] and most crops, although some beans were "foul and ill-managed". But he was very critical of the practice of hoeing corn, instead of prior fallow, beans etc and ley to reduce weeds. This was done before barley but not wheat, which was not even hoed much, often "thin and foul in the extreme".[73]

He came specially to see "the famous Thanet drills at work", but was very disappointed to find that of every three acres, only one was drilled in 1795 and the rest still sown broadcast by hand. In general he considered Thanet one of the best-cultivated districts in Britain, yet found "much foul, bad farming" as well, "even in a cursory view". "It has no claims to that exclusive right of superiority, which celebrity has given it; and which it may, heretofore, have deserved."[74] This is a marked change from John Evelyn's impression in 1672 (see p 53–54) and those of Rusticus and Arthur Young in 1763 and 1770 (see pps 77 and 78). Had high wheat prices induced slackness, had there been a generational decline, had Marshall looked more closely than earlier visitors at all Thanet? John Boys in 1794 considered that the Thanet farmers could hardly be surpassed, stressing that they had greatly improved their soil in the past fifty years by seaweed application – 40–45 cartloads per acre. High land which had been poor sheepwalk or corn yellow with charlock within memory was now much better.[75] Mockett also noted that by 1796 all labourers had been taught to hoe turnips.[76] So progress there had been, but the question remains open.

Boys was an East Kent farmer showing solidarity with his fellows. His only real criticism was of tithes collected in kind, which he felt should be commuted (some chalky land, several score acres at Nash Court, for instance, had "probably never been manured" because of tithes), and of leases. These were often handed down over several generations unchanged, by farmers some of whom understood them "no more than Latin or Greek, if they ever read them", and badly needed simplifying and updating.[77] Marshall's appraisal was more independent, if confined only to one year. He further observed that enclosures would help a better rotation of arable and ley, but might spoil high-quality Thanet corn which gained from the openness of the country. Woods should be planted for shelter, however, and more farmsteads established on the mid-levels, for too many farms were crowded into the low areas. The farmers should give up hoeing corn crops, rake the fields instead of allowing gleaning, and abandon the four-horse team and the Kent plough.[78]

Livestock breeding evidently continued backward, though Marshall was more sharply worded about it. Horses were the highlight, as they no doubt had been for one or two hundred years at least. There were many fine teams of four black horses, 15–15½ hands high, some locally bred from old local stock, others a cross of Kent mares and Midlands stallions, or half-bred Flemish. But they they were often too fat to do the quantity of work they should[79] (due to their owners' excessive fondness).

Mongrel cows were kept for the farmers' own household needs.[80] Lean Welsh cattle and sheep were fattened on the marshes, and there were several flocks of 100 or more sheep folded on the upland clover and trefoil leys; mostly Romney Marsh with some Dorset or Southdown.[81] "Thin-carcassed, ill-bred swine of mixed colours and breeds",[82] "the smaller ones crossed with the Chinese breed", were fed in large numbers on corn stubbles (as in Lewis' time) and killed at 3–4 months for butchers. Others were fattened to 10–25 score at 18–20 months for the farmers' households,[83] who evidently had a taste for fattier pork than the townspeople. There were no rabbit warrens in Thanet – the wild rabbit may have passed the point of no return from asset to pest. But John Mockett of St Peter's bred tame ones in the ground under a "brick arch" in semi-medieval style (see p 30) for 51 years at least, and kept bees for over 35 years. All farmers also kept fowls – Mockett's were half-bred game (cock-fighting being a popular "sport").[84]

The war brought various innovations. In 1801 the Board of Agriculture attempted to get the clergy in each parish to make the farmers report their acreage under each crop, but it was not fully successful and was not tried again until 1867, and then not through the clergy. Birchington and St Peter's (like Maidstone) submitted no returns at all, and in the other parishes the returns were suspected of under-reporting! Only figures for wheat, barley, oats, peas, beans and tares or rape were required; clover, sanfoin, radish, canary etc. were not included. As far as the returns meant anything, it appeared that rather more wheat was grown than barley, except in Minster where for some reason twice as much wheat was grown, and in Monkton a little more barley than wheat.[85]

Marshall found "few enclosures or trees" in 1795, but some hedges were certainly grubbed out during the Napoleonic period. A Quex Park terrier refers to the removal of one from a field called Lamming's Piece on the site of the present day Zeila farm in 1804.[86] A surviving piece of common wasteland above Monkton mentioned by Hasted[87] probably also vanished at this time, as it was cultivated arable in the Monkton tithe assessment of 1840.[88] Various other upland grazing areas also seem to have come under the plough. In 1774 there had still seemed to be a fair amount of these on poorer soil. Land in the Southern part of what is now Quex Park was called the Downs in the terrier of that year, as well as land towards the sea near Joss Bay and Whiteness Bay, but all this was cultivated in the 1840 tithe maps.[89] It must have been the profitability of wheat which led to extended cultivation, but some sheep walk remained – in 1810–1811 a Mr George Friend's sheep walk at Birchington is mentioned.[90]

Victory celebrations

Despite the farmers' gain from the war, victory seems to have been
patriotically welcomed. At Sarre 18 people (including the Dennes,
Collards and Champions, the big farmers of the time) subscribed
£27/6/5d for a dinner on 14 July 1814 for the whole village. They
consumed 84 twopenny loaves, 72 gallons of strong beer, beef, suet
puddings, potatoes and "etcetera".[91] At Minster the whole village
dined in a meadow on the edge of the marsh, over 700 in all.[92]

In some other places the celebrations seem to have been more
elaborate but less democratic. At Birchington John Powell Powell,
the Neames, Friends, Tomlins and sixteen others subscribed £30/
11/6d for firing of guns on 27 June, with singers, drums and fifes,
supper for 73 men with 300 pots of beer, and donations to the
women and children. Someone was paid 5/- to dress up as
the Emperor Alexander of Russia.[93] 436 poor people at St Peter's
were dined in John Mockett's new brick barn, whitewashed, and
decorated with flowers by the ladies of the neighbourhood. There
was "an excellent band" and "the flags of various nations were
flown", the gentlemen acted as stewards. Afterwards 4,000 people
attended rural sports and fireworks in a meadow. The whole cost
£90/10/7d – comparing the costs one wonders whether the sustenance was less good than at Sarre? The ladies of St Peters then
suggested an impromptu rustic dance in the barn, so one was held
there a few days later for the gentry and farmers.[94]

No further dinners are recorded after the victory of Waterloo in
1815, but collections were made for wounded soldiers and families
of the dead and wounded, £80 being raised house to house in
Broadstairs and St Peter's in September,[95] and John Powell Powell
began planning his Waterloo bell tower at Quex, completed in
1818.[96]

The Napoleonic war period was one of stark contrasts, with great
hardship for the labourers and exceptional prosperity for the
farmers through low wages and high prices for corn. Perhaps times
were too easy for the farmers, for from the late 18th century
Thanet no longer attracted national attention for the excellence of
its agriculture.

Chapter Six: From Waterloo to the Repeal of the Corn Laws: 1815–1845

General Position of the farmers

Peace and a period of better weather brought lower corn prices, but some protection was given the farmers by the Corn Law of 1815, by which no imports were allowed till home crops of wheat sold at 80/- a quarter (there were modifications of this in 1828 and 1842). It did not prevent a collapse of the inflated market. Prices had dropped to 44/--70/- for new white wheat in Canterbury market in February 1815,[1] and though in 1817 the average wheat price throughout the country was again 96/11d, it then fell steadily to an average of 44/7d in 1822, most of this year being a low ebb on Canterbury market and the London corn exchange, apparently the main Thanet outlets.[2] The 1815 Corn Law was unpopular too with the town population: on 4 March 1815, 1,076 Margate citizens of all ranks completed a petition to the House of Commons against it,[3] but to no avail.

The price falls hit the farmers sharply. T.C. Curling of Shuart Farm, St Nicholas, stated in reply to a circular letter from the Board of Agriculture in 1816 that three farms in his neighbourhood were empty, despite a 35% rent reduction, and poor rates and unemployment were high, as the farmers had been laying off men.[4] John Bridges' balance sheet peaked at over £14,000 in 1818–19, then fell to over £8,000 in 1821 and just over £7,000 in 1822.[5] In February 1822 John Powell of Quex announced that he was postponing his rent day "from Michaelmas to April next" (meaning 1823?).[6] Some small farmers like Daniel Curling, tenant of 26 acres at Minster, went bankrupt.[7] The style of living the larger ones were trying to defend is indicated not only by Bridges' diary but by the content of farm sales. One at Ozengell Farm in October 1822 included Brussels and Kidderminster carpets, featherbeds, mahogany four-posters and tent beds, mahogany dressing tables and basin stands, mahogany and japanned chairs and a sofa. When Daniel Swinford sold up at Sarre in the same month, he also disposed of mahogany "night tables" (commodes) as well as all the range possessed at Ozengell.[8]

Yet the distress passed. Canterbury wheat prices, normally higher than barley, rallied at the end of 1822, and like national averages remained over 50/- from 1823 to 1834, giving a period of stability. Thanet farmers seem to have maintained a fair prosperity in this period not only through the low wages and relatively high corn prices but from "high farming" – the use of more labour and more manure, viz. John Cramp's statement to the Parliamentary Commissioner in 1833 that he employed more men than his father did as "I farm in a higher style".[9] Some entirely new methods were also tried out (see below Section 4 of this chapter). When Woodchurch and Cheeseman's farms (both typical good medium-sized farms) were valued for their owner Francis Austen in 1828, they were found to be worth £7/10/- and £9/6/- respectively more per annum than in 1806 (when Woodchurch was worth £132/2/-)[10] and the rents were raised accordingly. Both farms were said to be in an excellent state of cultivation, and there was no suggestion of tenant hardship; both occupiers were said to be worthy "of any reasonable indulgence" as regards repairs and improvements to buildings.[11] In the same year land at St Peter's was selling at £100 per acre.[12] By the time Woodchurch was bought by John Powell Powell of Quex in 1837, the new wing had been added to the front of the farmhouse, and probably a greenhouse too.[13]

Thanet was not at first badly affected by the renewed agricultural crisis of the 1830's, caused by oversupply of corn. John Cramp of Garlinge, farming 300 acres, was quoted in the Second Report of the Select Parliamentary Committee on Agriculture in 1833 as saying that "most (Thanet) farmers are men of property and capital", owning their own land. "They are an exception to the general rule of distress in the country." "They get their outlays back, but no rents" (profit). "During the war they accumulated property beyond what their fore-fathers left them. But now their affluence is very much curtailed and the tenantry very much more so. I have a farm to let now and but two applications, twenty years ago there would be 20 in less than 48 hours. . . ." "Most rents are fixed too high" (at about 40/-), "30/- an acre would be reasonable. There are not more than two or three farms over 350 acres and very few over 500 acres, and lately the land has been neither amalgamated nor sub-divided." Yet he noted that land continued to sell readily, though two tenants had "broken up for a destruction of their capital" – men of "frugal, prudent habits", "whose families were in comfortable and good circumstances." "Now they are breaking stones on the roads".[14]

Three years later in the Third Report of the same Committee, Cramp claimed however that "the farmers are in a much worse condition than in 1833, perhaps not obviously so as the greater portion of Isle of Thanet farmers are cultivating their own estates." He noted that rents had been reduced to an average of 30/- an acre, but claimed that only two leases had been granted since 1829, with "expenses borne jointly by landlord and tenant.[15]

Wheat prices at Canterbury had indeed begun to fall in 1834, reaching 38/2d by the end of September 1835,[16] but after a bad year they were back to 50/4½d by 5 July 1836[17] and continued to rise, averaging 78/9½d for the week ending 14 August 1838.[18] They then appear to have remained generally over 50/- until the repeal of the Corn Laws. In 1835 John Mockett noted candidly in his diary that in his twenty years' experience as a valuer and appraiser of stock etc. he had always found persons willing to take a farm "*at any price*", which had not been the case before the Napoleonic Wars, although the farmers in 1835 complained bitterly about high rents and taxes and the price of labour and tradesmen (blacksmiths, carpenters, thatchers etc.)[19] Although Mockett maintained in the same year that the only way forward for Thanet agriculture was through sub-division of holdings and moderate rents,[20] this did not come about in his time, presumably because the need was not felt. The *Kentish Gazette* revealed only three Thanet farming bankruptcies in this period, all in 1837: the well-publicized case of owner-occupier John Boys of Hengrove (probably one of the then prominent local family),[21] tenant John Sidders of Little Brooksend,[22] and a small tenant farmer at Plum Pudding Island.[23] But the publication of farm sales, for whatever cause, was only just becoming common, and many small ones may not have been advertised in a newspaper, or probably still changed hands by valuation.

So a certain question mark remains about Cramp's 1836 evidence as to the general bad state of Thanet farmers. His statements about the ownership and size of farms are also open to doubt. He did seem on the other hand to have a good case for the commutation of tithes. He noted that only 4,000 acres in Thanet were liable for Lesser or vicarial tithes (already compounded for money payment), and the rest were under Greater or rectorial tithes (taken in whole shocks of corn usually by tithe farmers). The system obviously favoured these latter and was open to abuse: Cramp's resentment seemed directed to the tithe farmers, not the clergy.[24] John Mockett complained in his diary in 1836 that "we are paying 16 times as much tithe for our best lands as in 1819 and for forty years before, when we paid only 3d per acre for lands and but very little for houses and gardens". But he acknowledged that the clergy in St Peter's now worked much harder than twenty years before,[25] (and clergy were influential amongst farmers to 1914).

Lack of credit facilities was another complaint voiced in both Cramp's 1833 and 1836 reports. In 1833 he stated that if money were lodged for personal security in a bank, two or three must join in it, not an individual alone unless he were known to be a man of substance.[26]

The farmers' lot was eased by the new Poor Law of 1834 (see p 117) and they seem to have been at least partly satisfied by the re-assessment and commutation of tithes which took place between 1838 and 1842 (median year 1840) in all Thanet parishes (original documents in Canterbury Cathedral archives). Yet tithes still remained nearly double combined rates and government tax (see p 131). The re-assessment and the 1841 census bequeathed posterity a rare glimpse of conditions at that point, although census deficiencies leave it incomplete.[27]

The biggest landowner was the absentee Marquis of Conyngham, with 1,324 acres in Minster and 154 in Monkton. John Powell Powell of Quex followed with 1,276 in St John's, St Peter's, St Lawrence, Acol and Birchington. Sir John Bridges was a non-resident, although he retained ties with St Nicholas and was buried there. He sub-let 555 acres which he leased, mostly from Queen's College, in St Nicholas, owned and let 133 acres in Monkton and Birchington parishes, and other members of the family owned 283 acres in St Nicholas and 83 in Birchington, a total of 1,054. Edward Royd Rice Esq., an absentee, owned 964 acres in Monkton. Robert Tomlin owned 730 acres in St Peter's and St John's and a home farm. The Archbishop of Canterbury, the Dean and Chapter of Canterbury Cathedral, Corpus Christi College Oxford, and St John's and Queen's College Cambridge each owned lesser amounts, and there were a host of smaller landowners, some of them gentlemen with other sources of wealth, but many seemingly renting out only one house, or a few cottages or a few acres.

Amongst farmers proper, four occupied over 700 acres, and one

Table 6: Number of farms 50–500 acres according to tithe assessments

	50–100	100–200	200–300	300–400	400–500	Total by tenure categories
Entirely owner occupied	6	6	1	–	2	15
Mainly owner occupied	1	–	2	3	1	7
About half rented and half owned	–	–	–	1	–	1
Mainly rented	1	3	3	1	2	10
Entirely rented	20	18	9	3	4	54
Total by acres	28	27	15	8	9	87

Table 7: Occupiers of arable or pasture 1–50 acres

	St Lawrence and St Peter's			
	1–5	5–10	10–50	Total
Owner occupied	12	7	7	26
Rented	48	15	21	84
Total	60	22	28	110

Table 8: Occupiers of arable or pasture 1–50 acres

	All other Thanet parishes			
	1–5	5–10	10–50	Total
Owner occupied	9	5	5	19
Rented	28	9	16	53
Total	37	14	21	72

family of these over 1,000. Gibbon Rammell of St John's (the name of his farm is not given in either census or tithe assessment) and his son Gibbon at Nash Court owned 556 acres and rented 456, total 1,012.[28] James White of Monkton Parsonage, with three unmarried sons, may have occupied as much as 917 acres in the parishes of Monkton, Acol, St Nicholas and Birchington. (Another James White is however identifiable at "Hale farm", St Nicholas in the 1839 tithe assessment for this parish and the 1840 one for Monkton, where he occupied marsh, so the Birchington holdings may have belonged to him, although he had disappeared by the 1841 census, when the only James White in St Nicholas was a labourer).[29] All but four of the 917 acres were rented. Henry

Collard of Monkton occupied 752 acres, predominantly rented. Edward Gibbens of Minster occupied 718 acres, including 156 acres of "waste", almost all rented. John Friend of Birchington occupied 420 acres nearly all rented, but owned and let out 215. Later the family moved definitely into the gentry class. Charles Taddy Hatfeild of Hartsdown seemed in the same semi-gentry category, occupying 206 acres and owning and leasing a considerable number of small dwellings and holdings. The usual size for a gentleman's home farm was about 40 acres (viz. Robert Tomlin, Sir Moses Montefiore etc.). The remaining occupancy pattern is shown in Tables 6–8.

All the occupiers have been identified by their separate names, except in the James White case and in two others, where it seems likely that there were two John Paramours, one holding Sheriff's Court farm and the other a small farm in St Lawrence, and two Richard Harlows, one in Minster and one in St John's, both small occupiers. In the few shared tenancies, none of which involve much land, the shared land has been credited to the individual having the greater amount of other, unshared land, for the simplification of the tables.

According to the 1831 census there were 130 occupiers of land employing labour and 43 family holdings not employing labour, total 173.[30] No definition of size was given, but the figure is very close to the 1867 figure of 172 occupiers of land provided by the first agricultural returns (see below Table 18), which is identical with the total for holdings 5–500 acres in Tables 6–8, though this can only be a fluke. The present study does not extend to unravelling which of the various smaller holdings of any size were truly farms. Obvious private houses with large gardens have been excluded, but the term "garden" still included market gardens at this time. Moreover many persons not gaining their main living from agriculture then occupied some pasture or arable as a side-line, in an age when the town-country divide was still often blurred, and only parts of Ramsgate and Margate were as yet really urban.

The tithe assessments show that a great concentration of holdings had taken place in Monkton, where there were 17 owner occupiers and 17 tenants, including cottagers, in 1840, as against 49 owner occupiers and 63 tenants in 1798 and 14 owner occupiers and 57 tenants in 1691. They also confirm the indications of the land tax assessments and Lewis' earlier statement that there were many more small occupiers in St Lawrence and St Peter's than in other parishes.

The continual growth of the seaside towns stimulated small farms in their vicinity. Cramp reported in 1833 that holdings of 10–20 acres near towns were let "to carriers, cow-keepers etc." for £3 or £4 per acre, much more than would be asked for any farm over 100 acres. (But during the Napoleonic wars such small holding rents had been £6 per acre). All land near towns was more productive because of the better manure available,[31] but poorer basic soil quality near St Peter's and St Lawrence may have been another cause of small farms there, since there were far fewer of them near Margate.

Various signs indicated the larger farmers' and Thanet's prosperity and standing. The Isle of Thanet Harriers were set up at Mount Pleasant in 1813, meeting three times a week throughout this period. The huntsman wore a red coat and the members green ones; the founding officials were all farmers and it was mainly run and supported by farmers until about 1873 (see p 136)[32] The ploughing match from 1836–1845 (see p 119) reflected the farmers' good status in society. The St Peters' Association for the Protection of Property gave sumptuous dinners for its members (who included John Mockett and other farmers) in 1826 and 1831.[33] John Powell Powell of Quex was High Sheriff of Kent in 1822,[34] the last one from Thanet.

From this period comes the first definite local proof of boarding school for farmers' daughters as well as sons – the younger son and daughters of Thomas Champion of Sarre (139 acres) went to one at St Margaret's Bay in 1839.[35] In the 1840's we know that a similar farmer was sending his daughters to such a school. (See p 131).

Local jollifications in these years included shooting. On 4 March 1845 it was reported that Mr J. White of Monkton (the son of James, probably) had undertaken for a wager to shoot at 500 penny pieces and to hit 495. He hit 494 in a paddock at Cleve, the seat of Benjamin Bushell Esq, who provided "a very excellent lunch" for White and his friends afterwards.[36]

The 1841 census revealed the beginning of the end of boarding covenanted yearly servants in the farmhouses. This was still usual in the inland villages and outlying farms, but starting to die out in the neighbourhood of towns. For example, at St Nicholas Court, Ambrose Collard and his wife Mary had four children, three female servants and four farm servants living in. At Nether Hale there was a very youthful household, with a 20-year-old farmer John Palmer, his 55-year-old housekeeper, and three female servants and six covenanted servants all aged between 15 and 20.

In the large farmhouse at Great Brook's End farm lived Elijah Emptage (a bailiff), his wife, nine children and six farm servants aged 15–25. But the sophisticated Mr and Mrs Richard Smithett at Hengrove farm with three children maintained a governess, two female servants and one male one in their home, and six farm servants were boarded with a married labourer. This was to be the eventual norm.

The festivities for Queen Victoria's coronation in 1838 were not so lush as those in 1814 – a tea party for the village at Sarre in Thomas Champion's barn, and elsewhere apparently only dinners in the towns organized by townsfolk.[37] William Champion (Thomas's son) did not mention any local events in his diary except his father's tea, but went into detail about the huge Conservative dinner at Canterbury in the same month, with 150 lobsters etc.[38]

Condition of the labourers 1815–1830

For the farm labourers this period continued to be very grim. The village population of Thanet, having risen by 18% between 1801 and 1811, rose only another 11% by 1821 to 6,663. But by 1831 it had grown again by more than 15.7% to 7,714, whilst Margate and Ramsgate at 18,324 had nearly doubled. In 1841 the villages had reached 9,455 by a 22.5% rise, the greatest ever shown in this period, but Margate and Ramsgate had slowed up to reach 21,918 altogether. St Lawrence and St Peter's have been included in the villages for these calculations, even though they contained many non-agricultural families and must have been subject to more and more immigration due to their nearness to Margate and Ramsgate, and Margate has been excluded, even though it is known to have included many agricultural workers by 1851, for in this way a rough indication of the predominantly agricultural population can be obtained.[39]

All the sources from 1816 on speak of a great surplus of labour. T.C. Curling of Shuart farm in that year replied to a Board of Agriculture circular letter of enquiry that there was a great want of employment, and large numbers of labourers were mending the roads, as an alternative to poor allowance, "really earning no more pence than they are paid shillings." Single men were employed by farmers for preference as being cheaper, "but the young are not deterred from marrying as they know that the Poor Law will provide". Some benevolent characters were now employing the men paid off by the farmers, but this he thought could not continue.[40] In St Peter's a large sum was raised, mostly by farmers, for the unemployed poor in 1816, but when tithes were raised in 1820 labourers' maximum pay was cut from 2/6 to 2/0, and "tradesmen's" (craftsmen's) pay from 4/- to 3/- a day. Mockett stated in 1830 that "it is true the numbers of labourers exceeds the means of the farmer, the cause being over-population, and the farmer, because of high rents, burthen of parochial taxes and heavy charges of tradesmen, cannot employ as many labourers as he needs". In 1822 he had noted that "Six children is a fair average for the labourer";[41] twelve children were not uncommon.[42] Married waggoners seem to have been much less employed, or not at all, for they were re-introduced in the 1860's as a novelty. (See p 140). Married yearly servants again are not specifically mentioned in the sources between 1803 and 1892. John Powell Powell of Quex was paying 2/6 a day (15/- a week) to "30 men, married and single", during the Swing riots in 1830, and consequently received "neither injury or insult – the reverse",[43] but wages as low as 8/- or 9/- may have been common at least in East Kent. (See p 116). The granting of perquisites partly in lieu of wages perhaps never ceased, for John Mockett was writing disapprovingly of this in 1836, although the reason for his disapproval is not made clear.[44]

The unemployment of the labourers was worsened by the introduction of the horse-powered threshing machine. Invented in Scotland, it became widespread there in the last quarter of the 18th century,[45] but was still unknown in Thanet when Marshall visited in 1798. It was advertised in the *Kentish Gazette* in 1815 and widely used in Thanet by 1817, though the flail was still being used too.[46] In a typical machine, the horse gear resembled a large windlass with five horses attached to it, and a man was seated on a stool in the centre with a long whip to keep them to their work. The horse gear wheel was 12 feet in diameter and had about 120 wooden cogs, which worked into a cast-iron nut with 14 or 15 cogs on the end of a horizontal shaft. The actual machinery which did the threshing was inside the barn and driven by this revolving shaft. Horses might become giddy from the uneven draft of the device, which was later condemned as cruel. It cost 25% less than flail threshing, and was quicker and cleaner, threshing three quarters of wheat in an hour.[47]

John Mockett of St Peter's never had a threshing machine to 1836 and probably they were not usual in the small farms of that parish, since there were no disturbances there in 1830.[48] But William Cobbett found seven at work at Monkton and Sarre on 13 September 1823. His description of Thanet on that day deserves quoting in full, for it has often been partially cited with misleading effect.

"When I got upon the cornland in the Isle of Thanet I got into a garden indeed. There is hardly any fallow; comparatively few turnips. Most of the harvest is in: but there are some fields of wheat and of barley not yet housed. A great many pieces of lucerne, and all of them very fine. I left Ramsgate to my right about three miles, and went right across the island" (ie probably from Lord of the Manor through Haine) "to Margate, but that place is so thickly scattered with stock-jobbing cuckolds, at this time of year, that, having no fancy to get their horns into me, I turned away to my left when I got about half a mile of the town" (ie probably at Salmestone). "I got to a little hamlet, where I breakfasted" (Acol?) "but could get no corn for my horse and no bacon for myself! All was corn around me. Barns, I should think, two hundred feet long; ricks of enormous size and most numerous; crops of wheat, five quarters to an acre, on an average; and a public house without either bacon or corn! The labourers' houses, all along through this island, beggarly in the extreme. The people dirty, poor-looking; ragged, but particularly *dirty*. The men and boys with dirty faces, and dirty smock-frocks, and dirty shirts; and, good God! what a difference between the wife of a labouring man here, and the wife of a labouring man in the forests and woodlands of Hampshire and Sussex! Invariably have I observed, that the richer the soil, and the more destitute of woods, that is to say, the more purely a corn country, the more miserable the labourers. The cause is this, the great, the big bull-frog grasps all. In this beautiful island every inch of land is appropriated by the rich" (author: this is certainly an exaggeration). "No hedges, no ditches, no commons, no grassy lanes: a country divided into great farms; a few trees surround the great farm-house. All the rest is bare of trees; and the wretched labourer has not a stick of wood, and has no place for a pig or cow to graze, or even to lie down upon. The rabbit countries are the countries for the labouring men. There the ground is not so valuable. There it is not so easily appropriated by the few. Here, in this island, the work is almost all done by horses. The horses plough the ground; they sow the ground; they hoe the ground; they carry the corn home; they thresh it out; and they carry it to market; nay, in this island they *rake* up the straggling straws and ears; so that they do the whole, except the reaping and the mowing. It is impossible to have any idea of anything more miserable than the state of the labourers in this part of the country.

"After coming by Margate I passed a village called Monckton and another called Sarr. At Sarr there is a bridge, over which you come out of the island, as you go into it at Sandwich. At Monckton they had *several men working on the roads*, though the harvest was not quite in, and though, of course, it had all to be threshed out; but, at Monckton they had *four threshing machines*; and they had three threshing machines at Sarr, though there, also, they had several men upon the roads. This is a shocking state of things. . . . At Sarre, or a little further way back, I saw a man who had just begun to reap a field of canary seed . . ."[49]

Cobbett, the farm labourers' champion, is probably to be believed in his account of the farmland through the centre of the island, but his picture may well not have been so true of St Peter's and St Lawrence at which he never looked. Small farms existed in St Peter's in the early part of the 18th century (see p 71) and in plentiful numbers in both parishes in the late 18th century and in 1840 (see pp 91, 107) Could they have vanished by the 1820s only to return again by 1840? It seems unlikely that Napoleonic war aggrandisement could have gone so far and unravelled so fast, so Cobbett's statement that every inch of Thanet belonged to the rich seems an exaggeration.

If the Thanet report to the Select Parliamentary Committee on Labourers' Wages of 1824 is true, the island was now free of the worst abuses of the Speenhamland system. The report asserts that no labourers employed by farmers received the whole or any part of their wages from the poor rates; that it was not usual for married labourers with children to receive assistance from the poor rates; that it was not usual for the overseers of the poor to send round to farmers labourers who could not find work, to be paid partly by the employer and partly out of the poor rates; that the number of labourers seeking assistance had diminished and the lowest daily pay of an unmarried labourer in the past year had been 1/6d (10/6 pw) and the usual wage rate 12/- pw.

Other sources show that benefit clubs were trying to help the employed. In one formed at St Peter's in 1821 6d a week was paid by members, for payments of 12/--16/- weekly in sickness and £10 funeral benefits for both husband and wife.[50] Many such clubs however fell apart.

The Captain Swing riots in 1830

1830 was a year of revolution in various parts of Europe, and in England was marked by the anti-threshing machine movement rumoured to have been plotted by a mythical Captain Swing. The resentment of the labourers boiled over against the biggest replacer of manpower, the horse-powered threshing machine. A "thresher" was broken up in Norfolk in 1822, and in 1830 a wave of unrest spread through the South, starting at Lower Hardres in Kent in late August. The labourers worked as usual by day, but banded together at night to attack machines and – much more seldom – stacks and farm buildings. Daytime disturbances were unusual and normally carried out by non-locals. The Marxist historians Hobsbawm and Rudé insisted that the riots were entirely spontaneous, but Charlesworth found that most of them broke out along the main London coach routes, and Margate was certainly on one of these, receiving over 80 coaches a week. He also found that literate lower middle-class men played a key role in the movement.[51]

In early October the able-bodied East Kent farmers were sworn in as special constables, liable to be called out at dead of night for six months to come.[52] The *Kentish Gazette* editorial for 8 October declared that "The County of Kent is at length become the scene of a system of crime and outrage as terrific perhaps as any that can possibly infest the peace and well-being of society" (sic), but the first Hop Market dinner of the season took place at Canterbury the same week, at the Rose Inn,[53] and for the most part life seems to have gone on normally. A correspondent to the *Kentish Gazette* considered that insurance (now widespread amongst the bigger farmers) "contributed powerfully to paralyzing the farmers' exertions to protect their property".[54] But Charlotte Powell, wife of Squire John, shows in her letters at this time how eery and scaring the situation was for the farmers and gentry, even those like the Powells who had nothing to fear from their own well-paid workers. There was general discontent in Thanet against the Church as well. "Margate and Ramsgate new churches" (ie. Holy Trinity and St George's) "are still threatened to be burnt", wrote Charlotte Powell, on 10 December . . . "they" (the clergy) "having brought such heavy Rates on the small tradesmen, poor people and all ranks indeed who were satisfied with their old large church". "Greater sacrifices all ranks will have to make, especially the rich supine clergy, who deserve it and want any form of feeling for their poor curates", who had "wretched stipends".[55]

Thanet was probably not much affected until November. A dozen men, three of them well-dressed, are said to have visited Major Garrett's farm at Margate at midnight on 6 October and threatened to destroy his machines, but this appears not to have been followed up for some time at least.[56] Early in November a straw stack and an outhouse of the poor house were set alight at Birchington, but these acts were directed against the overseer.[57] On 15 November a 30-ton sanfoin hay stack was burnt down at George Hannam's farm at Alland Grange.[58] By 26 November the *Kentish Gazette* reported that "the Isle of Thanet is now the scene of confusion, agitation and alarm from the nightly appearance of gangs with their faces whitened" (with chalk) "and armed with bludgeons etc.".[59] On 10 December Charlotte Powell wrote that "not a day passes but some of the people about here on suspicion of Breaking Machines are taken up",[60] but only nine were brought to trial at Dover Sessions just before Christmas, perhaps because two of their companions gave evidence against them. William Reed, Thomas Hepburn, Thomas Overy, Richard Oliphant, Stephen Bushell, William Hughes, Thomas Golder, William Bushell and William Brown were sentenced to seven years transportation for breaking up the threshing machine of Hills Row of Vincent Farm on the night of 21–22 November.[61] The same party (40–50 in all) is said to have been responsible for breaking up George Hannam's machine at Alland Grange, either on 22 November,[62] or on 24 November.[63] Hannam was waiting for them with "thirty peace officers and others, including Lidbetter, the Bow Street officer", according to the first Kentish Gazette report, but only with six peace officers and three farm servants according to an amended one.[64] Whatever the size of the protecting force, the assailants did their work and got away, and the nine were accused of having broken at least six more machines on different farms at Minster, Monkton, Gore Street and St Nicholas two nights later. According to the *Times*, some of the men were in female attire. They were armed with "sticks, axes, saws, hammers and bludgeons" and had their faces blackened.

The nine accused were said to include ploughmen, threshers, waggoners, shoemakers, and a brickmaker from "Margate, Birchington, Garlinge, Woodchurch, Cleve, Acol etc.". Although they were reliably reported to have met at 10.30pm on the 22nd at the Powell Arms, Birchington,[65] and thence gone to Vincent Farm – a round walk of 5–7 miles for any of them – it is an open question if they were responsible for all the other attacks, for which no evidence was cited in the press, and one also wonders if the people in female attire really were males. The participation of small tradesmen lends weight to Charlotte Powell's opinion that the discontent was not purely agrarian, and it is these who may have supplied the literate element. George Hannam received written threats against his house and stacks after the destruction of his machine, signed "Swing".[66] He was a young man, a magistrate for the Cinque Ports and the County, who farmed at Alland Grange c. 1829–1844, when he retired to Bromstone Court on the death of his father, but remained a magistrate in Ramsgate until his own death about 1890, and a regular supporter of the Ploughing Match. According to the *Kentish Gazette*, "a more liberal landlord and master than he does not exist".[67] Charlotte Powell had a different view of him: "I am sorry to say he grinds down the poor and together with being an arbitrary Magistrate and never laying anything out with his neighbours and actually having everything from London has made" (Hannam) "I fear a marked man." "In these fearful times", she went on to say, "we employ specially our Village Shop Keepers and in this I deal entirely with the Tradesmen of Thanet."[68] But the threats against Hannam were not carried out and there was seemingly no violence against the person in Thanet, although in Herne district an attempt was said to have been made to assassinate some farmers out on patrol.[69] The affair seems to have died down by the end of the year, and the farmers to have agreed to the labourers' demands to dismantle their machines and raise wages. A fair wage in Kent was now said to be 12/-–15/- weekly, "though if men can be found to work for 8/- or 9/- what is to prevent farmers employing them?" asked the *Kentish Gazette* editor.[70] A woman called Elizabeth Studham was deported to Australia for starting the fire at the Birchington poorhouse, and several others involved gaoled,[71] but there were no other convictions. The farmers went back to threshing by flail – a winter-long job for a number of men. (For a description of flail threshing in Thanet, see G.H. Garrad, account in the catalogue of the "100th" Thanet ploughing match).

The available evidence suggests that in Thanet Swing was directed mostly against threshing machines and larger farmers who paid lower wages than they could have afforded. But a smaller farmer, Thomas Sidders, had a "plough butt broken in pieces by mischievous persons", for which Birchington parish paid him £3/

8/-,[72] and the discontent against the church and those who did not buy locally suggest elements of a general revolutionary situation.

Labourers' Conditions 1831–1845

The Swing riots were a factor prompting the new Poor Law of 1834, which reversed the previous system in a bid to make relief for the able-bodied as unpleasant as possible in order to lessen the burden on the middle classes. Relief was reduced to the level of the poorest paid work, or less, and strict, new, large poor-houses were established to serve groups of parishes. The Thanet parishes were united with effect from 20 April 1835 to run Minster Workhouse (soon known as the Union, and later to be Hill House Hospital), which was then specially built. Its grim outlines dominated the Northern skyline above Minster until 1989. St Peter's petitioned against the amalgamation, to no avail, and on 15 March 1836 its paupers were moved to Minster, "against the general wishes of the inhabitants and to the sorrow of the paupers". (A "comfortable" new poorhouse had recently been built in St Peter's). After this, poor rates fell markedly – by £416/9/7d in St Peter's alone in the first year.[73] But John Cramp considered they fell only in previously mismanaged parishes.[74]

In 1833 John Cramp (of Garlinge or Dent-de-Lion) told the Parliamentary Committee that he usually paid 2/6d a day (15/- a week) or 2/3d a day (13/6d a week) to able-bodied men employed all the year, whom he "never let lose a day's work". Their wives and children were generally employed too. Supernumary men got 2/- a day (12/- a week). He stated that wages "had not increased since" the Swing riots in Thanet: it is unclear whether this means that they had not been raised in response to Swing or had then been raised and not increased since. The latter seems more likely. Cramp further stated that a great many labourers were unemployed, and the morals of the working class greatly demoralized by unemployment. Some food however was cheaper – low Dutch cheese 6d a 1b instead of 8½–9d in 1812 and bread 10d, compared to 15d average during the war. Clothing was also cheaper; manufactured stockings were cheaper than the home-knitted ones of 20 years previously, and labourers now preferred cotton clothes to wool. Other items of food were dearer or the same price. Ale was only 4d a quart as against 6d in 1812, but the labourers drank one quart in 1833 to three in 1812.[75]

Wages were reduced again in 1834: John Cramp reduced his to 12/- for his steady labourers and paid others "according to their ability". There was still a great many unemployed, and most labourers were much worse off than fifty years before. But he claimed that "the steady, constant labourer on 12/- a week without a large family is as well off as at any time in the past 20 years".[76]

Wages were still 12/- a week in 1845 (£31/4/- per annum if every week was worked), and cottage rents £4–£5 per annum – double or 2/3 higher than in 1795 when wages were 9/- or 10/-.[77]

In 1843 a report to the Special Assistant Poor Law Commissioners on the employment of women and girls in agriculture gave detailed information about the work of women and children in Thanet. Women were employed at spudding and hoeing weeds in corn, working from 7–5, with an hour off for meals, and paid 10d a day. But their dress, after the corn grew high, was inconvenient for this work. They were also employed on hay-making, stone picking and thistle pulling, for 10d a day. Boys were employed from 8 years old helping with threshing at 5d a day, bird-scaring for 4d. From 9 to 15 they hoed and spudded corn, for 6d–10d a day; there was the greatest demand by the farmers for this, and often more labour of this kind was needed than could be found. From 9–12 years old they cut, picked and carried turnips to sheep in folds, or were used in hay-making, for 6d a day. From 12–13 they could be used for stacking at 1/- a day, and from 13 to lead horses for ploughing and harrowing at 6d. A boy's normal working hours were from 6 am to dusk or 6 pm. Girls were sometimes employed to weed corn, pick stones, top turnips, scare birds or reap, for which they might earn 4d–8d a day, but they were generally sent to school till 11 or 12 and then kept at home to look after younger siblings.[78] The schools to which these girls were sent were generally dame schools, charging 4d per week in East Kent; there is no specifically Thanet information.[79]

This report is also interesting for its description of the way families were employed as teams for reaping. The father contracted to reap for an average of 10/--13/- per acre; he did the sickling or scything and bound the sheaves and the others picked up the corn stalks. His wife might earn 1/6d a day of the money, and his sons from the age of 6 about 3d. Men and their sons also lifted potatoes at wages paid per acre, and women and their sons pulled and topped turnips at 10/--12/- per acre. Girls featured little in this family work for the reasons mentioned.[80]

Tradtional paternalism, especially in the inland villages, must have softened the labourers' lot a little. Although the festivities for Queen Victoria's coronation in 1838 were rather subdued – see p 110 – perhaps because of the memory of Swing, perhaps because 1837 had been a difficult year, the farmers' had not abandoned the tradition. Even through the Swing riots, it remained usual for the farmers to give their men joints of beef for Christmas.[81] Thomas Champion gave a "big dinner for all our people" to celebrate Queen Victoria's marriage in 1840 and a harvest supper every year. Mr Swinford of Sarre also gave a harvest supper, presumably all the bigger farmers did.[82] George Hannam gave his employees at Alland Grange a dinner when he left to succeed his father as a gentleman of means at Bromstone Court in 1844.[83] The ploughing matches from 1836 (see next section) provided a little prize money for some, and relatively generous sums for the outstanding few. In this period trees and hedges seem to have been cut, possibly for labourers' firewood. (see p. 127).

The early Thanet ploughing Match

The Kent Society for the Encouragement of Industry and Agriculture (later Kent Agricultural Association) had been set up in 1793, and occasionally gave prizes to worthy labourers. A small one-off ploughing match was held at Maison Dieu near Dover in 1815,[84] and from 1831 many local agricultural associations were formed in the county and started matches. Thanet was not the first association, though it was four years ahead of the Nonington one (later East Kent).

In 1834 and 1835 small ploughing contests were held at two or three places in the island, with entries restricted to the immediate locality. At one of these in 1834 John Cock of Sarre, employed by Thomas Champion, won first prize (£1/10/0d).[85] The Isle of Thanet Association for the Encouragement of Agriculture seems to have been established in 1834,[86] and in 1835 the Duchess of Kent became Patroness, "feeling an anxiety to become associated with the gentlemen farmers in the formation of such a society."[87] John Powell Powell of Quex was the first president, and Captain Cotton his vice-president. The aims of the association, as stated in the chairman's speech at the first dinner,[88] were "to reward honest and industrious servants, also to encourage ploughmen, to teach young farmers the best mode of cultivation of their farms, and perhaps to somewhat abate the prejudices of the old farmers!"[89]

On Tuesday 6 December 1836 the first all-Thanet Ploughing Match was held on George Hannam's land at Alland Grange; Thomas Champion was the moving spirit behind the expansion of the event and became Treasurer of the Association. Forty-five ploughs were in the field – 28 four-horse, 12 three-horse and 5 two-horse. The day was fine, and the soil turned up well, to the enjoyment of about 2,000 people who came to watch. The prizes were awarded in the field by Thomas Champion at 1 o'clock as follows:

Class One

Four horse teams	£	Ploughman	£	Driver	Employer
First prize	5	John Philpott	1	James Butcher	T. Garrett Nethercourt.
Second prize	3	Henry Fuller	15/-	John Huskstep	Mr White Monkton.
Third prize	1/10/-	John Cock	7/6	James Ralph	T. Champion Sarre.
Fourth prize	1	William Hollams	5/6	H. Young	Mrs Wootton Thorne.

Class Two

Three horse teams	£	Ploughman	£	Driver	Employer
First prize	3	J. Rye	15/-	J. Denly	Mr Mockett St Peter's.
Second prize	2	H. Eastling	7/6	John Chandler	Mr Hannam Alland Grange.

Class Three

First prize	3	Thomas Philpott			N. Bradly
Second prize	2	George Brenchley			Messrs. Fowler

The unsuccessful ploughmen got 2/6d each and their drivers 1/-. These were higher than some Kent ploughing match prizes and over double the Nonington (later East Kent) first match prizes in 1840. All ploughing match prizes were attacked in the national press for years by liberal writers as shamefully low, but considering the meagre wages the Thanet ploughing ones seem generous, and were probably a reflection of local prosperity and the support of the rich townspeople.

At 5 o'clock about a hundred gentlemen, many not farmers and including several clergy, sat down to a good dinner at the Albion Hotel, Ramsgate, according to the press report. (But the Association records said 150 had attended).[90] T. Mayhew Esq. took the chair, supported by Sir Brook Bridges, (the sociable landowner from Goodnestone Park who was much in evidence at the Nonington matches),[91] the Ramsgate Deputy (of the Cinque Port of Sandwich and equivalent of mayor), J. Powell Powell, service officers, clergy etc. The menu[92] was "various kinds of soup, sirloins of beef, haunches of mutton, fowls, hams, plum pudding etc. in the greatest profusion", accompanied by wines and professional singers.

The chairman quickly called the company to charge their glasses, and observed that "they had met that evening from conviviality and good will, and not, as was sometimes the case, for noise and shouting, and, therefore, they would perhaps allow him to suggest dispensing with cheering. But when he saw before him so many Englishmen, and when so many of them were Men of Kent, he could not think of making them restrain their loyalty upon the first toast. After that, it was to be understood there was to be no cheering." The King's health was then drunk, "with three times three hearty good cheers", and the national anthem sung by the singers.

Further toasts to the royal family followed. It was noted that Princess Victoria had recently selected Ramsgate as her marine residence, and her mother had honoured the island by visiting it eight times. Frequent and finally deafening applause greeted the chairman's tribute to the Duchess of Kent's charitableness and consent to become the Association's patroness.

Prizes were then distributed in Class One to three labourers from St Lawrence for bringing up large families without poor relief – first prize of £5 to Isaac Danton with eleven children (this donated by the Duchess of Kent), and the third Stephen Tucker, who had raised twelve "with the least assistance from the parish" (this was donated by J. Friend Esq. of Birchington). Six other labourers got long service awards up to £5 for from nearly sixty to five and a half years' employment with the same master.

In Class Two, three yearly servants got long service awards ranging from £2/10/- to £1 for service ranging from 19 to seven years. Class Three was for female servants apparently employed on farm work: £2 to 10/- for periods ranging from 25½ to four years. The wording of the citation rings oddly to the modern ear: "To Ann Sackett, Monkton, for living eight years with Mr Bushell,

Cleve." In Class Four three widows and one widower received from £2 to £1 for bringing up families or surviving themselves without parish relief.

The prize-winners, who had been waiting apparently without food to get their awards, then left. A toast was given to the Archbishop of Canterbury and the clergy of the diocese, after which many other toasts were given and speeches delivered, "with some excellent singing, and the company did not separate till a late hour."[93] This was a typical ploughing match dinner until about 1847. Public dinners often lasted till one or two am,[94] but the diners were not necessarily drunk, for Francis Cobb had noted at the celebration for the laying of the first stone for Margate pier in 1810 that "though we did not break up till 2 o'clock, I desire to be truly thankful that not one appeared to be the worse."[95]

There must have been heavy drinking by some at these long match dinners nevertheless, and one gets an impression that a battle may have been going on about this between the clergy and the farmers. From 1838 it was customary for the principal guests to depart after the formal toasts and speeches ended; some years most of the company are said to have left with them and other years only some.[96] In 1842 they all seem to have left early after a last official toast by the Rev. Sicklemore,[97] but in 1843 and 1844 the late night sessions resumed, under a new chairman after the main one left.[98] Then in 1845 the clergy appear to have boycotted the dinner, their total (unprecedented) absence being resented, and although the entire company apparently took advantage of this to sit till a late hour,[99] before long a marked change began to come over the event, as will be seen.

The match was held at Alland Grange for the first eleven years, with Hannam as host till he inherited Bromstone Court in April 1844, when his place was taken by a Mr Neame. For some time the matches were very popular: the field "studded with booths like a fairground"; horses' manes decked with ribbons, and large numbers of ladies' and gentlemen's carriages to be seen. Hannam and Neame after him threw open the house with "real old English hospitality" to give lunch for their friends and visiting farmers and gentry, and the heavy dinners (costing 5/6d) followed at 4 or 5 o'clock in a Ramsgate or Margate hotel alternately. A peak was reached on 13 December 1838, with 60 ploughs and 2–3,000 spectators: a warm day when "the sun shone with great splendour", and there were 22 official toasts at the dinner attended by 120. (The price of wheat was over 70/-). But then entries began to drop until by 1845 there were only 33 ploughs. However, even in 1846 nearly £100 was distributed in prize money, with £20 left in the kitty, regarded as very favourable.[100]

There is no mention of any sustenance provided for the ploughmen in these years, but the amount and number of the prizes increased. Prizes were given down to the ninth best ploughman in Class 1 from 1839, introduced for shepherds, domestic servants and stack-building in 1839, and for tending horses in 1840. When John Cock won a first in 1840 for caring for a team of four for 23 years, as well as winning the four-horse ploughing, he took home £10, equal to about 1/3 of his yearly wage or more.[101] In 1842 the Association gave Cock an engraved tablet for having won nine first prizes in all, ending with an East Kent championship in that year against seven other champions.[102] Applicants for the awards had to fill in a printed form with 21 questions, to be witnessed and guaranteed by a member of the Association or a clergyman.[103]

In 1838 the 158 ordinary subscribers included the Archbishop of Canterbury, the Marquis of Conyngham, Sir R. Burton, Cobb & Sons bankers, Cobb & Sons brewers, surgeons, solicitors, military and naval officers, the Right Hon. Sir William Garrow M.P., a number of clergymen, and last but not least Sir Moses Montefiore, the only one still to be majorly commemorated in Thanet in the 1990's. The only woman subscriber was Mrs Mary Wootton of Thorne, the occupier of 471 acres, almost all owned, in the 1840 tithe assessment, and 95 years of age in the 1851 census. Women did not attend the dinners. Evidently at this time the Association was well organized: 13 people besides the Secretary and Treasurer collected subscriptions. The minimum charge for entering a plough was 10/-, although a few only paid 5/-, and John Powell Powell and his lady and a few more paid £1.[104] For the term of its life, the press reports of the match were to be a fairly but not totally accurate barometer of the general state of Thanet farming.

Farming practices

The crisis of the mid 1830's and the knowledge that the Corn Laws might be repealed stirred some of the farmers to investigate new methods, but the pace was slow, another indication of adequate prosperity.

John Mockett was feeding oil-cake to his cattle in 1834,[105] and

William Champion (son of Thomas) mentions it in his diary in 1839 (300 were bought in March).[106] Two cakes per cow per day were fed in St Peter's in 1843. In 1845 it was very dear: £12 per thousand.[107] The Champions tried bone dust as fertilizer from 1838, but it gave disappointing results.[108] The indiscriminate use of seaweed had given way, in John Cramp of Garlinge's case at least, to applying fresh weed plucked from the rocks in June as it decayed better. Cramp also mentioned the use of artificial manure, but it is not clear if it was being used in Thanet.[109]

William Champion twice mentions bleeding cattle and lambs as a veterinary remedy, in 1839 and 1849, carried out by himself or his father; unsurprisingly it did no good and is not mentioned thereafter.[110] He also mentions dipping sheep in Bigg's composition in 1839,[111] the use of a horse-powered threshing machine again in 1840 (hired from Mr Holman of Sarre mill),[112] and the growing of swedes in 1845.[113] Two kinds of deep cultivator were used by the Champions at Sarre in 1839 and 1840: a "hop-garden plough" which followed the ordinary Kent plough and went 4″ deeper ("produced a very good crop of beans"), and a Rackheath sub-soil plough pulled by five horses ("never saw that it did any good").[114] An oddity of this time was John Cramp's attempt to feed his stock entirely on carrots – with unknown results![115]

Apart from swedes and trefolium (see p 126) no other new field crops are mentioned in the sources. But we know that in 1829 Ramsgate market supplied a wide range of fruit and vegetables in the summer, as well as flour and eggs, fish, beef, mutton, lamb, pork and fowls. Rhubarb, figs, raspberries, black, red and white currants, gooseberries, cherries, French and broad beans, peas, cabbage, turnips, potatoes, lettuce, shrimps, skate, soles and weaver fish are also listed in a visitor's account book of that year. No mention was made of ham, bacon or sausages. The island evidently did not produce a sufficient abundance to saturate the summer demands, for London butter and French eggs were also on sale. In June 1828 French eggs poured into Ramsgate and sold at 30 for 1/- in Canterbury. In 1833 the Ramsgate market was frequently visited by "persons from the French coast with fruit, eggs, and other articles",[116] Unfortunately the visitor's account book rarely mentioned quantities, so the prices of the produce cannot be ascertained.

An added trial for farmers in these years was the spread of the most detested of all Thanet weeds, hoary pepperwort, also known as devil's cabbage, chalk-weed and earlier as Thanet weed

(*Lepidium* (*Cardaria*) *Draba L*).[117] It is believed to have come in the bedding-straw used by invalid troops evacuated from Flushing during the ill-fated Walcheren expedition of 1809; in 1829 it was reported as rampant in St Peter's and in 1835 at Ramsgate, and continued to advance throughout the century, being well-established inland by 1901.[118] It added to an already weedy situation: the island was reported "covered in clouds of smoke from the hetacombs of weeds" in September after harvest in 1817.[119] On the other hand Birchington parish ended its payments for the killing of vermin in 1835, though this was probably taken over by the farmers.[120]

An Isle of Thanet Farming Club, meeting at Mount Pleasant, was established in 1839. Thomas Champion was first chairman, and membership cost 5/-.[121] It tried, apparently unsuccessfully, to get all Thanet parishes to petition Parliament to preserve the Corn laws indefinitely,[122] and discussed wheat cultivation at its first meeting.[123] Efforts by some younger farmers to introduce new types of plough at the ploughing match and to discuss at the dinner abandoning the four-horse plough failed in 1841 and 1842.[124] But the St Peter's Farming Club, founded in 1841, was probably livelier than the other one, and held talks and discussions on the following topics amongst others: dairy management, pig breeding, preparing wheat for seed and sheep-keeping. Crop rotation was discussed on 7 February 1843: it was recommended that no farm should be bound by any particular system, but as a guide, wheat should not be sown on the same land more than twice in eight years, and not more than three white clover crops running. A fair rotation would be wheat, potatoes or turnips, barley or clover, clover or spinach, wheat, winter tares, and peas, barley, radish or beans. In April 1843 the club vowed to reduce tradesmen's charges by whatever means it could.[125] William Manser (see p 130) was president and James Smeed secretary; dinners were held at the Wheatsheaf, Northdown and presumably the meetings too.[126]

St Nicholas and Sarre sheep-shearing meet was begun at Sarre in June 1838, with eleven shearers.[127] By 1842 it had become the Isle of Thanet Sheep Shearing Meet and was reported in the *Kentish Gazette*. It attracted great crowds, being a novelty at a time when the public was perhaps tiring of the ploughing match. Prizes were given for shearing and wool-winding and sweepstake prizes for the farmers for several classes of sheep. Merchants from the Continent attended, and Thomas Champion gave a big lunch. In the first few years farmers and labourers dined separately after the meet at the Crown Inn, but in 1845 they all sat down together for a joint meal. They always seemed more democratic at Sarre, but one wonders how they all squeezed into the little old Crown[128] – did they sit outside?[129]

The conservative old farmer John Mockett made a little survey of local farming and his own methods in his diary in 1836, when he seemingly handed over some responsibility to his sons. He noted that he had always sown wheat broadcast, though he used a drill for other grains. Since he took over from his father in 1797 he had averaged seven quarters of Norfolk Common barley an acre on 70 acres, and had never exceeded 9 quarters 3 bushels, though his father had reached ten quarters. Barley was then the least profitable grain in Thanet. Potatoes were a precarious crop but had now become widely acceptable as food. Not many years before yearly servants would refuse them, preferring the traditional cabbage and turnips. Many acres of radish and spinach were grown for seed, but spinach seed only paid for "industrious yeomen who farm a few acres", like John Kirby of Upton, who grew 12 quarters to the acre and more. But the price had fallen from 8/-–10/- per bushel formerly to 3/6 to 4/-. Radish was much more profitable, contracts being given the farmers for 16/-–21/- per bushel, and 20–30 bushels were produced per acre. Red clover had supplanted white, which had been repeated too often. Tares and vetches exhausted the land, and should be grown only for cattle. Lucerne lasted 12–15 years, often cut three times a year. Trefolium was a new and much admired crop, but not proven. Sanfoin had increased tenfold in his time. Fennel was no longer grown much as London gardeners now supplied the capital's fishwomen who used to come to Thanet to buy it.[130] Trefolium (sown in the 1700's) must have been readopted.

Another perspective was given by George Buckland's report on Thanet agriculture for the Royal Agricultural Society of England, completed on 14 February 1845.[131] He noted a widespread use of Ransome's scarifier, a deep-cultivating machine hired out by a Faversham firm. Early in the 20th century its successors went to a depth of 18″,[132] but the 1845 depth is not known. Chevalier malt barley was now grown, with Gold Drop and Seer wheat. Average yields were wheat four quarters, beans 3½, peas 4, barley 5, oats 6, hardly up on Lewis' time, and evidently few could equal Mockett's barley. Fallowing seems to have disappeared, the common rotation being wheat, peas and turnips, barley, clover and beans, and presumably oats, though not mentioned (much shorter than the St Peter's farming club model). In 1833 Cramp had noted that fallowing was already little done except on some larger farms with sheep, before or after turnips.[133]

Buckland also noted that some small farmers often followed a rotation of wheat, barley and clover, wheat, barley and beans, which needed more manure and exhausted the soil faster. Sanfoin was only left up to four years by the best farmers. It produced 30 cwt of hay per acre in the first year, 40–50 in the second and third, then failed fast. Italian rye-grass and trefolium incarnatum had been tried but not established. Seed-growing had declined, only radish being grown in places and carraway by John Cramp at Garlinge. Most threshing was done by flail.

Livestock breeding remained backward apart from the horses, though shorthorn cows had been partially introduced and a few Alderneys. Swine were still inferior, though "not so coarse as before." (Since Marshall had accused them of being too lean, it seems there must have been a very fat phase earlier in the century; Mockett also said that the pigs were smaller in 1836 than "the fine Kentish hogs we used to have"). Rents were 30-45/ an acre.

Lastly, Buckland noted recent felling of "such trees and hedges as there were", found "widespread broadsharing of weeds after harvest" "the greatest improvement of the past 20 years in Thanet", and called for better education for Kent farmers and their men.[134] The tithe assessments showed that there was still in 1840 no less than 27 acres of woodland in Minster parish, divided between several small woods, also nearly three acres of nut-trees in Thanet, and over all the island a certain amount of wasteland. No total can be reached as it was classified with buildings in many parishes, but 56 acres of waste in the area now Westgate must have been real waste, as this town was not started till 1870. Perhaps it was unprofitable land, since the Monkton common was now cultivated. Many farms also had "plantations" of trees, apparently round the farmsteads and adjoining pastures. The greatest of all plantations was the tree belt round Quex Park, laid out by John Powell Powell in the Napoleonic years. But there are no tree statistics for 1845.

There was never any complaint about marketing arrangements. In 1833 John Cramp reported that Canterbury market was the best, but in 1836 indicated that most corn went to Mark Lane by hoy, only a lesser amount going to Canterbury or Sandwich.[135] It was probably desire for high compensation which lay behind the decision of a meeting of owners and occupiers of land held at Mount Pleasant on 30 January 1844 to oppose the coming of the

Southeastern (London-Canterbury-Dover-Sandwich) railway to Ramsgate and Margate.[136] In October 1846 John Cramp and Thomas Coleman, surveyors, estimated the compensation due by the railway company to the owner of Sevenscore farm at £1,300, and £684 to the tenants, plus a thoroughfare across the line at the railway's expense, but it is not known how much they actually obtained.[137] The gentry G.E. Hannam and J.A. Warre, who had home farms but did not derive their income from land in Thanet, attended a meeting of townspeople in Ramsgate which welcomed the railway.[138] (Re Hannam, see p 116 and for Warre, p 158). Most Thanet farmers would not have been more than three miles from a station after the completion of the line in 1847.

A substantial amount of wheat must have been milled locally. The first ordnance survey map (1819–1843) showed 14 windmills in Thanet out of a total of 226 in Kent: 3 at Birchington, 2 at Broadstairs, 1 at Reading Street, 3 at Margate, (1 at Drapers and 2 in Cliftonville), 2 at Ramsgate, 2 at Minster and 1 at Sarre. This was the maximum deployment ever. The Minster and Cliftonville ones, and one at Ramsgate, were the new smock mills.[139]

George Buckland found Thanet's farming "on the whole thorough and clean", "highly creditable", and the farmers had evidently reverted to an exemplary rotation before wheat, but like Marshall he did not seem to find them leaders. In calling for a better system of education he even seemed to hint that they and their fellows throughout Kent needed some stimulation. Although their wartime wealth had ended, the relatively good wheat prices after 1815, except for the erratic immediate post-war years and 1834–36, still did not call for as much effort from them as had been required before the late 18th century, or so one would understand from John Mockett's comments in 1835 (p 105). True, farmers in the period to 1845 applied still more manure and employed more labour (the essence of the "high farming" of this time, as John Cramp pointed out (see p 104), but there was plenty of both to be had cheaply, especially near the expanding towns. Broadsharing of weeds in corn stubble, their greatest advance, had been widely used after legumes since the mid-18th century at least (p 78). The Dutch tradition (if such it was) of very careful cultivation seems to have died out for a significant proportion of Thanet farmers by Marshall's visit in 1795, and although Buckland's remarks suggest that this "tail" may have become smaller again in 1845, even the

commendable majority were not very innovative then. Agricultur-
alists elsewhere in Britain had progressed considerably meanwhile,
particularly in the North where less abundant labour encouraged
new thinking.

At least one Thanet man, the tenant of Drapers farm, seems to
have been farming, if not innovatively, yet with some meticulous-
ness from 1841 to 1859, if his manuring charts and cropping tables
are a guide, as will be seen in the next chapter. Moreover, James
Yeomans "of Cheeseman's farm Thanet" bought a steam threshing
machine at the Royal Agricultural Show in 1842 or 1843, their first
trials there having been held in 1841. But he seems to have been a
lone pioneer, unnoticed by Buckland, although a letter to the
Kentish Gazette of 2 January 1849 (p 3D) stated that he was the first
in Kent to own one, and it was still in use, for "grinding, dicing and
crushing corn" as well.

Obviously most Thanet farmers had not become worse, and
some may have improved since 1795, but as a group they seem to
have failed to regain the renown they earlier enjoyed, perhaps
because they had no incentive to do so.

Chapter Seven: From the Repeal of the Corn Laws to the Agricultural Crisis 1846–1892

With the repeal of the Corn Laws in 1846 began a new phase in the history of British agriculture. For the first time the British government largely lost interest in the country's farmers, relying on imported food to feed the growing population. This situation was to last until the First World War, and bring much trouble to the farmers, although Thanet as usual fared better than many regions. The new order is reflected in the sources: after George Buckland's report of 1845 it was 109 years before there was any authoritive survey of Thanet agriculture again. (See p 251).

The general position of the farmers 1846–1892

The repeal of the Corn Laws did not take full effect nor begin to bite until 1849. Initially prices were often still high (3,680 quarters of wheat sold at an average of 85/8d at Mark Lane on 8 May 1847.)[1] But by the week ending 7 July 1849 the average price of wheat at Canterbury market was 47/9½d,[2] and by the week ending 4 January 1851 it was 39/10d.[3]

Speeches at the 1849 ploughing match dinner revealed the differing impact of the repeal on larger and smaller farmers. William Manser (farming 270 acres at East Dumpton in the 1851 census) declared that better management was all that was needed to survive, giving his budget as follows (tabulated by the author):

	Average per annum over preceding six years £	Projected for 1850
Income	£2,500	£2,000
Rent	930	744
Labour	500	400
Tithes	170	136
Tradesmen	120	96
Seed	110	88
Manure	140	112
Rates	70	56
Direct Tax	25	20
Oilcake and other artificial feed	70	56
Sundries including turnpikes	15	12
Servants' board	80	14
Profit	270	

Other farmers strongly disagreed with Manser. Thomas Mayhew (250 acres at Nethercourt in the 1840 tithe assessment, but by the 1851 census he occupied 515 at Sevenscore), said the value of his produce was about £10 per acre with corn at 51/-, but now his profit was gone. Wages might be reduced by 1/8d or 1/4d but not more, the only hope was for rent to come down. The Treasurer of the Thanet Agricultural Society, poor Thomas Hooper (Chilton farm with 154 acres in the 1840 tithe assessment and the 1851 census), "with less productive land and a family to maintain", confessed himself to be in real straits. He had put down his horse and walked to the ploughing match (at Hoo Farm, Minster, 3–4 miles), and had been obliged to remove his daughters from boarding school and make the elder instruct the junior, "and this was the portion of farmers generally" (cries of Hear, Hear!).[4]

At the end of January 1850 a pro-Corn Law rally was held on Penenden Heath, Maidstone, in front of the Shire Hall, attended by waggons-full of "respectable yeoman and Protectionists", but was disrupted by a huge mob yelling "Cheap loaf!" Such was the chaos that Thanet farmers Thomas Champion, John Swinford (Minster) and William Mascall (Minster) could not gain entrance.[5] The Thanet Farmers' Club petitioned Parliament in March for the tenant farmers to be taxed on Schedule D like tradesmen; for parochial and county rates to be levied on all property holders (they were still levied only on land); for tithe reduction; removal of tax on malt, hops and bricks; uniform duty on all manufactured imports including flour, and reduction of salaries of all civil servants and of pensions, since the price of all commodities had fallen greatly. Though presented to both Houses of Parliament by the East Kent Conservative MP, W. Deedes, and Lord Stanley, it achieved no more than the petition to the Queen or the earlier Margate citizens' petition against the Corn Law had done: nothing.[6] But as potatoes were not a major Thanet crop, their blight disease of the late 1840's was not a widespread blow, though it did come here, even returning in March 1846 when it was believed past.[7]

1850 saw seven Thanet tenancies and two owner-occupied farms advertised in the *Kentish Gazette*, at least one due to death.[8] Yet after this shake-up there were no more than three or four advertised per annum at most, usually only one or two. Many small farms coming vacant were perhaps not advertised, although the practise seems to have become pretty widespread for those over 50 acres by this time. In any case, cowkeepers and market-gardeners relying on the local resorts for a market were hardly affected at all, indeed their prospects bettered as the towns grew and cheap rail fares from 1869 brought growing masses of holiday-makers.

The rest of the farmers were saved from ruin in the 1850's and 1860's by a recovery in corn prices, by better farming methods and by keeping more livestock, especially sheep. Thomas Mayhew prospered at Sevenscore (see p 153). William Manser evidently did as well as he expected; he was a judge at the ploughing match in 1865,[9] distributed the prizes in 1869,[10] and was chairman of the Board of Guardians of the Thanet Union in 1875.[11] A description of his farming about 1870 is given on (p 155). Even Thomas Hooper became an enthusiast of the iron plough and chairman of the Board of Guardians,[12] remaining in business at Chiltern until his death in 1869,[13] and when his widow died in 1874, she left a houseful of good furniture (see p 135).

The Crimean War and the American Civil War in turn raised prices, and for various reasons until 1878 the weekly wheat average at Canterbury was seldom long below 50/-, and often much more, though it fluctuated greatly due to conditions in Britain and the exporting countries. In March 1868 it was as high as 70/-,[14] but by early July 1878 it was only 47/1¾d.[15] From about this year the price of malting barley was sometimes higher or not far behind that of wheat. In 1880 it was around 40/-–45/- in early January and July when the wheat trade was sluggish.[16] By January 1885 wheat price was 34/8¼d and barley 36/-.[17] A low ebb was reached in the week ending 22 October 1887, when new wheat at Canterbury market averaged 29/9d, but by the week ending 7 January 1888 it was back to 30/--35/- and malting barley was 39/-.[18] After this prices did not improve much and malting barley continued to lead wheat, consequently by 1891 nearly three times as much barley as wheat was being grown in Thanet. (See p 152).

Livestock prices rose by 85% for mutton and 58% for beef between 1858–1873[19] but then fell sharply in the rest of the 1870's and especially in the 1880's, due to the introduction of refrigerated sea transport from North America and the Antipodes. In response to this sheep and pig keeping diminished in Thanet. These falls were offset by the remarkable buoyancy of Kentish hop prices, which averaged £6/17/6d per cwt from 1826–1854, £6/7/6 from 1854–1882, and £6/3/- from 1882–1895.[20] Malting barley, hops, broccoli and dairying (see below section 3) came to the rescue of Thanet farmers in the agricultural depression which started over Britain as a whole in 1874, but which did not hit Kent hard until 1878, nor Thanet till 1893. However, an extraordinary tithe on hops from June 1886[21] somewhat trimmed their profit.

There was a bad patch too in 1884–85. In January 1884 British hops were selling at £5 per cwt due to disease, and foreign ones at £8, and in 1885 the hops failed completely in Thanet.[22] The Vicar of Monkton, which was heavily engaged in hops, remitted the extraordinary tithe for the year,[23] but there are no reports that other Thanet vicars did the same. There were five farm sales in 1885, but one was due to a fire.[24] A brief description of local farming published that year said the farms did not look so flourishing as formerly, and a leading article in the *Kebles Gazette* (Margate) said only small farmers doing part of their own work and the old tenants on the large estates were doing well[25] – but this meant much of Thanet!

Early in 1881 an attempt was made to form a branch of the Farmers' Alliance in Thanet, Basil Hodges of Vincent Farm being a Vice-President of this already. He seems to have been the first Thanet farmer to hold high office in a national farmers' organization. The Alliance represented the interests of both landowners and tenant farmers, seeking a reform of the tenancy and game laws, a fair apportionment of local taxes by making businessmen liable for rates, "a legitimate share in County government", railway freight charges lower to farmers, and effectual application of the current cattle disease regulations.[26] In all these areas there appear to have been justifiable grievances, though to consider them in detail here would be unwieldy. The South-Eastern railways treated the Thanet farmers particularly badly. Basil Hodges reported to the Royal Commission on the Agricultural Depression in the same year that French fruit, vegetables and hops were carried cheaper by rail to London than Thanet ones, and charges for the conveyance of milk were higher than on the Midland Railway.[27]

Since the Alliance seems to have come to nothing much, and petitions had proved useless, Thanet farmers now tried the more sophisticated approach made possible by the development of national networks of political party branches. Indignant meetings of the Conservative Association were held at the Bell Inn, St Nicholas, in October 1886, with an address to Lord Randolph Churchill,[28] and at the hop oast, Monkton, in November 1887, at which it was complained that with corn at about 30/- a quarter and the price of hop labour high, the tenant farmer needed help.[29] Then as always, most farmers seem to have been staunch Tories.

Yet in 1888 things had swung back to such an extent that the ploughing match, abandoned in 1874, was revived with some panache – though this probably had more to do with labour relations than anything (see p 159). Four tolerably good years followed, bolstered by better hop prices and dairying. In 1891 Eden Hall Farm, Minster (43 acres let at £167 less 10%) was put up for sale at £2,500 and sold for £3,950, and parcels of arable at Mount Pleasant – certainly not hop land – put up at £700 fetched £1,000. On the other hand the World's Wonder small-holding (on the edge of what is now Kent International Airport) did not fetch its asking price on the same occasion,[30] and there were five tenant sales that year.[31] Sackett's Hill estate (8 freehold acres of farmland, vegetable garden, stables, etc.) also did not reach its reserve and was withdrawn at £5,350 in May.[32]

Independent evidence showed Thanet was one of the most favoured farming areas in Britain in this 46 year period. A Church of England clergyman in the late 1850's found it far more advanced and prosperous than Dorset from which he had recently moved.[33] The fact that the 1881 report of the Royal Commission on Agriculture included nothing about Thanet but Basil Hodges' railway complaints speaks for itself. The Assistant Commissioner of the Board of Agriculture for the ten Southern counties, William Little, gave evidence to the Royal Commission in 1882 that the Isle of Thanet and the extreme West of England showed least effects of the depression.[34] No mention of Thanet was made in the reports of the 1894 Royal Commission on Agriculture, which had been compiled earlier – had they been of that year it could certainly have merited attention. Only two bankruptcies seem to have occurred amongst Thanet farmers from 1846 to 1892; W.H. Brown of Minster in 1884[35] and Richard Fright of Chilton in 1890.[36] But there were thirteen agricultural bankruptcies in East Kent in 1886 alone.[37] One farmer at least amassed great wealth: George Collett of Walter's Hall left over £66,000 when he died on 21 February 1882 – a great fortune for that time.[38]

Boarding in the farmhouses declined but had not totally disappeared even by 1891,[39] (married waggoners being increasingly required to do the boarding – see p 174–5), and something of the farmers' evolving lifestyles can be glimpsed from farm sales. When Mrs Susanna Hooper (widow of Thomas) died at Chilton Farm in 1874, her effects included iron, French and other beds, oak and painted washtables, mahogany chests of drawers and wardrobes, first-class feather beds, a hair mattress, a mahogany cottage piano, a mahogany dining table extending to nine feet, mahogany, rosewood, birch-frame and other chairs, "handsome carpets", Burrows' encyclopedia and "a few valuable books", a Copeland's dinner service in spode, cut glass, a handsome pair of mahogany card tables.[40] This may or may not have been above average, as farm sale advertisements usually did not list furniture at that time. It was not quite up to the best urban middle-class levels, where walnut drawing-room suites were *de rigeur*, but probably her children took her choicest pieces, for one notices there was no sofa in the sale at all. The sale at Dent-de-Lion farm in 1872 included 100 greenhouse plants.[41] When George Finch sold up at St Lawrence in 1881 (a small farmer with three carthorses, 33 swine and 100 poultry) he still had four-poster beds, but boasted a spring mattress, a sofa and much mahogany furniture.[42]

In this period the first water-closets were probably installed in the smarter farmhouses. The gentry had adopted them much earlier: when Dane Court was let in 1860 one of the attractions mentioned in the advertisement was already "WCs both upstairs and downstairs".[43] There was one at the New Inn, Minster, in 1870; a fire started in it from the ashes of a pipe.[44] But Val and Marion Smith of Acol Farm were surely exceptionally go-ahead when they acquired a bath with piped water in 1892.[45]

Yet in this period the farmers' social position declined somewhat. Something of this can be seen in the ploughing match dinners (see p 160). In part it was not so much an absolute decline as the change to a new era where the middle-class town population of Thanet was much bigger, and the farmers no longer the largest group in the island with a certain level of education and income, as they had been in earlier times. Margate races, which in the 1820's had been a three-day event at Dent-de-Lion well patronized by farmers, changed to two days, then by 1871 to one day with only six races, and thereafter were discontinued due to the sale of Shottendane farm where they were then held.[46] Although most of the members of the Thanet Harriers seem to have been farmers in 1872[47], the pack passed out of their ownership in 1873, when Captain Tomlin took it over.[48] (He lived at Dumpton Park, then a mansion with a deer park).[49] In 1887 it was stated that the pack was almost entirely supported by non-farmers.[50] Richer farmers like Thomas Mayhew II were still hunting in 1888,[51] but many seemed to be supporting the Thanet Coursing Club, started by Captain Henry Perry Cotton in 1851 (or at least that was when he took out his first party). In 1871 Mr Gardiner of Ash Brewery was vice-president, when a magnificent presentation of silver was made to the Captain by the club; facts suggestive of strong non-farming support too, as presentations were not yet customary in farming connections locally.[52]

The Sarre Pink Feast is not mentioned after 1847.[53] There were many Pink and Polyantha Feasts in East Kent in the 18th and early 19th centuries: flower shows and dinners held at inns, attended by men only. Their place was taken by the Thanet Horticultural and Floral Society, which held annual shows from 1837[54] and was town dominated from the start. The later shows in each town and village were its off-spring.

After Margate received its Charter of Incorporation in 1857 more JPs were required, but farmers were not yet appointed, nor were they in Ramsgate when it got its Charter in 1884. Yet Thanet farmers continued to supply most of the Guardians of the Poor and members of the highway boards in this period, and after the reorganization of local government in 1880 they began to serve actively on the new rural government councils. There was prestige attached to the first and last roles, as well as the sense of public service and perhaps the pleasure of exercising authority, but the highway work seems to have been more of a chore, especially after the parish arrangements were taken over by the Isle of Thanet Highway Board in 1865. By this time it had 156 miles of road to look after, and no proper map, and was faced with growing sanitary problems – for instance the cottages in Birchington near the church in that year were "very thickly inhabited and have nowhere to throw their refuse but on the highway"! "The want of proper sanitary arrangements causes a great nuisance", it was further said.[55] But gradually over this period non-farmer members of all these bodies became more numerous, and they became more professional through the appointment of a medical officer to the Board of Guardians[56] and sanitary inspectors (one for Margate in 1871) and a qualified surveyor to the highway board in 1865. Even this had its teething troubles, for steps had to be taken to force the first surveyor, Thomas White Collard, to live in Thanet as his contract required![57]

This period saw some new tenancy developments, probably caused by the greater difficulties of farming. A letter to the *Thanet Advertiser* of 19 March 1870[58] complained of empty Minster farm-houses and absentee tenants, caused by engrossing and the passage of farms into the hands of rich town-dwellers. The last is certainly indicated by the sale of Watchester farm in 1867 as a gentleman's summer residence with a farm of 115 acres, pleasure grounds, vineries, greenhouses etc., the land being suitable for building.[59] There are no more reports about this engrossment, though the censuses show that from 1841 some men were occupying more than one farm.

In the 1880's Basil Hodges shared the tenancy of Vincent farm with a Mr Chapman, who seems to have been more in the position of a risk-and-profit sharing bailiff. They are mentioned as co-tenants in 1886,[60] but Basil Hodges was often in the public eye in various capacities, and the other man never. This somewhat reminds one of the Salesbury and Hyer tenancy of Monkton manor in 1431 (see p 35–).

From the 1870's partition not engrossment prevailed. A steady decennial increase in holdings in Thanet is shown by the agricultural returns – which was the reverse of the national trend.[61] Although the returns from 1885 through 1921 showed holdings by physical unit and not as units of all land in the occupation of one individual, the rise in numbers obviously started well before 1881, and reached its decennial peak in 1901 (Table 18). In view of John Mockett's opinion earlier quoted that sub-division was the way forward, it looks as if there was a period of considerable partition here, and there is a strong local tradition that this was so too.[62] Rents however appear to have remained at round about 45/- an acre for large farms to 1860.[63] In 1885 they are said to have averaged nearly 50/- an acre, some being considerably less, but many small-holders paid £5–£6 per acre, unchanged from 1871.[64]

A certain amount of tension between tenant farmers and landowners in this period can also be surmised from the ploughing match speeches. It seems to have arisen not only over rent, but over who should build the farm cottages now needed, and who could shoot game on the farms, but it never came out into the open in the way the farmer-labourer tensions did (see sections 2 and 4 of this chapter).

From this period we have at last indisputable proof of a number of women farmers in Thanet. Bagshaw's *History of Kent* 1847, lists three in Margate, two in Minster (see p. 123 for Mrs. Wootton), one in St Peter's and one in Acol.[65] In 1881 five were selling corn to a local grain merchant. Three may have been widows or daughters winding up a farm, for they did not continue for long, but Mrs Paramor of Garlinge sold from 1879–1891 and Miss Mummery from 1878–1891. The merchant's record ends in 1891 so we do not know what happened later.[66] Mrs Paramor, evidently a kind and popular woman, had been farming on her own at least since 1860, for her waggoner Thomas Smith won 2nd prize in the four-horse class at the ploughing match that year,[67] and her obituary in 1892 mentions the early death of her husband, with whom she originally lived at Sheriff's Court.[68]

Position of the farmworkers

After 1841 the overall rural population either ceased to grow so fast by natural increase, or, more likely, was checked by outward migration. Between the 1841 and 1851 censuses the total in the villages (still including St Peter's and St Lawrence) rose by less than 800. But the 1851 census revealed for the first time how large a proportion of agriculture workers may not have been in regular employment. Table 9 shows the disparity between the numbers claimed by the farmers to be employed by them and the number of people declaring themselves to be farm workers and not paupers.

By the 1881 census St Lawrence and St Peter's had grown and urbanized to the extent they were scarcely rural villages any more. Minster and Birchington also grew fast by in-migration after the coming of the railways (Canterbury and Dover line to Minster, Ramsgate and Margate in 1847, Chatham and Southeastern line to Birchington in 1863). But the four villages of Monkton, Sarre, St Nicholas and Acol had slightly decreased in population compared to 1851, even though the new town of Westgate (started 1870) was

Table 9: Numbers of farm workers according to Census returns in Margate library, (including all categories except bailiffs and thatchers)

	Minster	Monkton	St Nicholas	Birchington	Sarre	Acol	St Peter's	St Lawrence	St John's*
No. of farm workers 1841	125	101	134			Totals not available			
No. of farm workers 1851	149	103	125	123	43	37	128	216	228
No. claimed by farmers to be employed by them 1851	108+	73	106	80	28	12+	128	106	147+
No. of farm workers 1881	189	91	136	125	32	52	116	95	155
No. claimed by farmers to be employed by them 1881	166	70	134	31	44	(inclu. Westgate) 76	102	90+	149

+ Not stated for a few farms
* including Garlinge, part of Westgate in 1851, Northdown and outlying central districts

Tables 17–29 based on agricultural returns; PRO
MAF 68/1329, 1899, 2469, 2754, 2868, 3030, 3570, 3981, 4129, 4240, 4351, 4728, 5228, 5907, 6061, 6112
Note: Figures under different headings in the agricultural returns do not always correlate exactly.

partly included in Acol census returns. Thus, these four villages had a total of 1,440 in 1851 and 1,401 in 1881. Overall the proportion of farm workers claimed to be employed by the farmers relative to the total had risen by 1881. It had sunk in Birchington and St Peter's but in Northdown, the other outlying districts of St John's and Acol labourers were obviously coming in daily from outside, as the ratio of men to employment had reversed. The very bad figures for Birchington may indicate an under-return by the farmers. Margate had apparently a reservoir of agricultural labourers, who had moved there to find cottages and obviously had to walk a long way to work (see p 141). In the 1851 census only a few married men, notably in St Nicholas and the hamlet of Stone near Broadstairs, described themselves as waggoners. The typical waggoner then was a yearly servant in his late teens or early twenties, but by 1881 this had changed.

This period of nearly half a century brought definite betterment to the farm workers, due to the fall in their numbers, generally increased demands for labour, the drop in food prices, and the workings of the middle-class conscience. A possible early sign of a lesser abundance of labour was the "substantial dinner" given the ploughing match award winners in 1862, though it is not mentioned again, and the newspaper's repeated reference to these winners as "the poor men" suggested it was charity. Wages were still 12/- a week in 1849,[69] but the sharp fall in food and clothing prices which then began raised their real value. In 1860 they were 12/---13/-.[70] By 1863 they were 13/- or 14/-,[71] and in August 1867, according to a report by John Kennet Esq of St Lawrence, to the Parliamentary Commission on the employment of children, young persons and women in agriculture, they were 15/- a week "for ordinary labourers, and they probably earn at piecework in cutting sanfoin and corn as much as £7 or £8." Kennet also said that the farmers had "adopted the plan of having married waggoners on our farms", and made plain this was being done because of the difficulty in finding good men.[72] A revival of yearly servant status for married men in the 1870's is suggested by the start of ploughing match awards for this category from 1892, the service of those awarded never going back beyond 1873. (See p 160). In 1872 wages ranged from 13/- to 15/-, with a few employees paying as much as 18/-.[73] (It is unlikely that in 1867 they were as uniform as John Kennet seemed to suggest). By 1872 a labour shortage was openly admitted at harvest time, and increased wages were given for hop pickers.[74] Not for some 80 years had labour been in short supply in this way. Overtime pay is also mentioned for the first time ever in this period, which must have been connected to labour shortage too: it was 4d, 3d, or nothing an hour![75] The only information about yearly servants' wages in this period comes from East Kent: about 1860 an 11 year-old boy starting work got £4/10/- p.a. and board.[76]

A Minster court case as early as 1864 mentions cloth suits, felt hats, calico shirts and neckties as usual off-duty wear of yearly farm servants, also that they were normally given credit at village shops from Michaelmas to Michaelmas (but see p. 147 for smocks).[77] Working clothes may still often have been ragged in the early 1870's.[78] The position of women had also eased marginally, in that by 1867 they were said to be becoming unwilling to work because their husbands would be paid more for the same tasks, and they were evidently in a position to refuse because of the fall in the labour force. Yet their basic poverty is shown by the fact that "in some cases women could only be forced to work under threat of gleaning being refused them".[79]

Wages soon fell again, for in November 1878 a meeting of the Fleece (Canterbury) Farmers Club decided that because of the price falls wages in East Kent should be reduced by 1/6 a week, but should not fall below 15/-.[80] In Thanet they appear to have fallen to 13/- to 16/-, though after further price falls in 1879 they do not seem to have decreased much more.[81] High wages were still paid for the hop harvest: in 1883 1/6–2/6 per five bushels,[82] and in 1887 the total wages for the hops were said to be £4,000, much of which went to imported London pickers.[83] It was still the same in 1892.[84]

Back in the late 1840's at least some of the clergy, landowners and farmers began to be concerned about the terrible housing of the farm workers. The Rev G.W. Sicklemore, vicar of St Lawrence, stated in a ploughing match dinner speech in 1849 that he was pained to see the deplorable state of many cottages he visited during the prevailing cholera epidemic.[85] Many had only one bedroom, he noted again in 1863 at the dinner that year.[86] Moreover, many farms had no cottages: the men had been forced into the towns and had to walk three, four or five miles to work.[87] This is well proven by Table 9. Prizes for well-kept cottages and gardens were given at the ploughing match from 1852.[88] Talk went on at the match dinners through to 1873 about the need for better cottages with two or three bedrooms, yet until then wages were so low that it was impossible to charge economic rents for them.[89] As a solution, it was claimed at the 1869 match dinner that "very comfortable" two-up and two-down concrete cottages could be built for only £60.[90] Concrete never seems to have been used, but as early as 1860 the Rev Sicklemore apparently demolished four cottages and certainly built two new 3-bedroomed ones with 12 perches of land each at a cost of £230, which he let for 2/6d per week, paying the poor rates and water rates himself.[91] But three years later he said in a match dinner speech that even 2/- a week rent was too high.[92] In 1865 he built two more cottages at Cleve, which he held, and Mr Rammell – perhaps the grandson of the big landowner of the 1840 tithe commutations – built four very small, "unpleasing" cottages, with "very small windows" at Thorne.[93]

By 1867 needs gave a prompting to consciences: the St Lawrence farmer John Kennet told the Parliamentary Commission that cottages were needed to retain labour. He said that there were very few between Minster and St Lawrence, and the farms had only one where they needed three or four. There were repeated requests, or hints, at the match dinners that the landlords should build the cottages,[94] and this is what appears to have happened in the end. Captain Cotton announced in 1870 that he had started building some three-bedroomed ones with good living rooms,[95] and others followed suit, encouraged by the rising wages which must have been part of a commonly agreed policy, and the availability of Government loans for land improvement and cottage building from 1872.[96] The fall in wages in the late 1870's, in so far as it occurred here, was offset by falling prices, the cottage building programme not being disturbed as far as the evidence goes.

By the end of the century the chalk hovels of earlier times had disappeared.[97] At Woodchurch farm, for instance, there were no cottages in the late 18th century,[98] nor are any mentioned in valuations of 1806, and 1828.[99] The two bedroomed flint cottage in the chalk-pit (now 3-bedroomed and covered in pebble-dash), seems to date from the 1840's, since it resembled a modest version of Quex farmhouse, which was built by John Powell Powell's orders in 1838.[100] Two small, semi-detached two-bedroomed cottages called Shepherd's Delight had appeared on the hillside about a quarter of a mile South of Woodchurch farm by the 1871 census.[101] There were two more called Drover's Delight in Minster;[102] possibly both pairs were built by some town philanthropist, as neither seems to have belonged to Quex Park estate like Woodchurch farm. By 1876 there were four cottages at Woodchurch, a four-roomed wooden "bungalow" having been added.[103] Most of the new cottages everywhere were probably two-bedroomed, but not a few had three. Pairs and rows of cottages dating from this time can be identified all over Thanet; the Closes outside Westgate are an example, and there is a particularly clear one at Sackett's Hill with the year 1875 on the front.

During the phase of intense religiosity in the 1850's and 1860's some farmers tried to force their men to attend church on Sundays. Most apparently did not go to such lengths, but "closed their stables during divine service". Stephen Swinford certainly obliged his men to attend in 1865, but no later reference has been found.[104] Church attendance in Thanet towns and villages was unusually high at this time. In 1851 Margate had eleven places of worship, including Roman Catholic, and Ramsgate had sixteen, including Roman Catholic and a synagogue; attendance at the Thanet churches was estimated at 76.4% of the population against a Kent average of 50–60%.[105]

The general health of the labourers in the earlier part of the period is indicated by Table 10, which shows mortality rates in St Peter's from c 1782–1856 amongst the labouring class, as recorded by the then vicar of the parish.

Table 10: Death rates in St Peter's amongst 1,839 labouring class people born there before March 1838, from birth to December 1856[106]

Age	No. quit parish	No. died	% of stayers died	Age	No. quit parish	No. died	% of stayers died
0–1	9	178	9.72	36–40	126	18	3.10
1–5	40	138	8.56	41–45	111	14	2.41
6–10	30	31	2.19	46–50	84	24	10.80
11–15	33	27	1.95	51–55	66	14	10.60
16–20	86	56	4.4	56–60	51	3	4.47
21–25	180	66	6.42	61–65	35	6	20.68
26–30	182	48	6.15	66–70	14	3	37.5
31–35	121	31	5.07	71–75	6	0	0

The high mortality in the group 16–35 was explained by child-bearing in females, and in males by naval and merchant navy service, fishing, and "hovelling" (going out to ships in distress), as well as horse and farm accidents. Disease affected all age groups, but mortality was usually higher in males until 40. Amongst 1,056 clergy of Canterbury diocese the commonest age at death from 1 June 1779 to 1 January 1849 was 70–80, with no peak in youth, but a steady rise in mortality from 40 onwards. Three lived to age group 95–99. No figures for childhood mortality amongst clergy families were given. In 1874 27% of all deaths in the Thanet Rural Sanitary Area were of children under five.[107]

In 1865 the Kent and Sussex Agricultural Labourers' Protection Union was founded, and began to recruit in Thanet in 1872, a year when the labourers must have been feeling bolder than for over three generations in the light of rising wages. Alfred Simmons, the founder, held open-air meetings at Minster in August (attended by about 200),[108] and at Birchington in September (attended by about 100).[109] These meetings were somewhat differently reported by the Ramsgate *Thanet Advertiser*, which seemed to reflect conservative and farmers' views, and the Margate *Kebles Gazette*, which was more liberal and supportive of the labourers. At both meetings, Simmons argued against the great differences in wages paid by different farmers, and the lack of recognized overtime pay, and of guaranteed pay when bad weather prevented work. He claimed that the value of wages had fallen greatly due to price rises. Some farmers paid for wet or frosty days and some did not; the same applied to overtime. A small group of farmers and landowners attended each meeting and tried unsuccessfully to dissuade the labourers from forming a branch. This group included Thomas Mayhew of Sevenscore, Basil Sicklemore of Cleve Court (son of the vicar of St Lawrence), and at Birchington Captain Cotton. Thomas Mayhew was particularly active on each occasion, claiming that his profits over the past eight years had averaged 8½%, whilst Simmons claimed that profits had risen 30% in the past ten. Mayhew (who was certainly making money from hops, see p 153) threatened to give no help to any of his men who joined, and to turn them away in winter if there were too many for the work available. He was shouted down with such cries as "Lay down, pig, your wash isn't ready!", and both meetings voted by a show of hands to form a branch of the union.

According to two of the leading agrarian historians of the period, the farmers in England generally reacted with fury at the union,[110] and Thanet seems to have been no exception. At the ploughing match dinner Captain Cotton said that "a fellow" (ie. Simmons) ought to be ducked in the horse-pond for trying to set the men against their masters. The Rev. Sicklemore implored the farmers to treat their men kindly and said that he had found that Thanet masters did treat them fairly and honestly (so by implication a union was not needed).[111] Labour relations became so strained that the ploughing match was stopped (see p 158), and four farmers made lock-out threats against union members. Simmons held another meeting at the New Inn, Monkton, in May 1874, at which these men were identified, (Collard senior, Bartlett, Chilton and Solly). He noted that the Thanet branch had fewer members than any other, and hoped these farmers' threats would increase its size. But the threats had been withdrawn already and no farmers spoke at the meeting, which ended with three cheers for the farmers as well as for Simmons.[112]

Only one further mention of the union is to be found: in May 1879, about a hundred members of the Margate and Garlinge branch together attended a service at the new St James' church, Garlinge.[113] After that it seems to have faded out, and it is perhaps significant that it seems to have taken strongest root in the Margate/Garlinge area, since we have seen that there was still a concentration of farm labourers in Margate in 1881, and that they must have had a long way to walk to work in most cases, without always a guarantee of a day's wages.

Though this period saw the turn of the tide, the status of the labourers remained very low by later standards. A few examples will suffice. It is not perhaps so surprising that almost a year after the terrible fire at Monkton Court farm in 1871, "the labourers who saved the produce of 800 acres, farm premises, two large residences and the church", and who were fire-fighting "from 2 o'clock Saturday afternoon till Monday morning", "spoiling their clothes", had "never been paid a penny by anyone". A letter to the *Thanet Advertiser* suggested that the fire office (insurance company) ought to give them something, and if not the writer offered to start a subscription for them.[114] But these men were presumably regarded by the farmer as having been saving their own employment as well as his property.

Still the public conscience had been aroused to some extent by the 1880's, and it was regarded as shocking when in 1889 nine persons including two babies were found to be sleeping in one room in the home of a "labourer looking after Mr Austin's horses" at 3, Park Lane, Birchington.[115] In 1885 it was said that the cottages at Monkton "do not reflect credit on the landowners. They are badly off for sanitary arrangements, many being without back ways or a perch of garden ground". (It sounds as if they had no privies.)[116] As late as 1892 the condition of a row of obviously newish three-bedroomed farm cottages was far from good. The back bedroom in each had no fireplace and was reached through another room. (It must be added that there were many bedrooms in farmhouses much later of which this could be said too). The front bedroom in each cottage was very damp. All the gutters were choked and some pipes broken; the roofs leaked in high winds. Yet in general they were well-appointed for the time, for they had a well, a cesspool for their sinks, and each had an earth privy, a parlour and a living room. These cottages were called Alexandra Cottages, near Pouces Farm, and appear to be what are now called Pouces Cottages.[117]

There was still no hint of relief for unemployment except charity or of a regular minimum wage. In February 1886, because of the hop failure the previous year, 50 families were being given soup twice weekly in Minster from a soup kitchen. Before that the wife of Wm. Smith of Watchester farm and the Vicar were distributing it. In January 1891, after weeks of hard frost, a sudden thaw released flood water from melting snow, which could not be absorbed by the still frozen soil and swept in a torrent through Acol to Brooksend, inundating many farm labourers' cottages. The *Keble's Gazette* noted that "this case is a most pitiful one", since the labourers in question had "been unable to work for some weeks owing to the long-continued frost", and called for charity to be given them.[118]

Draconian penalties for trivial crimes were ending. In a perhaps unique late reference a runaway farm servant was sentenced to prison in 1866 unless he return to Ambrose Collard,[119] and in 1864 a fine of 9/6 each or 14 days was ordered for two men stealing turnip tops at St Nicholas.[120] But by the 1890's fines alone were often imposed. For instance two men were fined 1/- each for stealing two gallons of apples in St Nicholas in 1892, though they had stolen them from a shepherd, not a farmer or gentleman, which might have occasioned greater leniency.[121]

Education for the labouring class improved somewhat but still left much wanting. By 1868 H.M. Inspector of Schools noted in his report on Kent that there were no areas without schools within reach; these must have been largely Church of England, as the Diocesan Inspector agreed, in his report of the following year, that if the State were to take over responsibility for providing them, very few more would be required.[122] But the schools were not fully used. In 1867 the Vicar of St Nicholas reported to the Parliamentary Commissioners investigating employment of women and children in agriculture that a quarter of the 100 children of primary school age in the village were not attending the Church of

England school, and boys were usually removed to start work at 9. As a result the girls were much better educated. In St Lawrence however a large farmer, John Kennet (already quoted), considered that boys were only occasionally employed on farms, and seldom below 12 or 13, as they were rarely competent to lead horses below this age. But he thought it important that boys start work young, and complained that the "smartest" boys had many sources of employment open to them in his area and did not choose farming.[123] Compulsory school attendance introduced in Thanet in 1881 was of limited value to the labourers' children, since the schools were still not free, and only 250 attendances were required after Standard Three.[124] When the vote was given to the labourers in 1884, it was a long time in England generally before they could be persuaded that it was genuinely secret, and they were reluctant to vote against the farmers' known political preferences. Lack of education made the men even more conservative than their masters. Their opposition to the iron plough obliged one farmer to hold the stilts of his himself at first, and another had to import ploughmen from Norfolk.[125]

It was in this period, probably in the 1870's, that the farmers began to stop giving harvest homes to their men, but to give overtime or extra harvest payments instead.[126] (See p 174). A *Kentish Gazette* report from Ramsgate in 1861 mentions harvest homes as routine: "the Lord of the Manor meets his tenants on Court days, the landlords at the rent audits, and the farmers their men at the harvest homes".[127] Thomas Pointer describes in detail two given by Stephen Goodson of Upton farm: one at the George Inn in Broadstairs in 1858, and one in a barn at Upton in 1860, followed by games and races in a meadow.[128] But gradually they decreased; for instance Barzillai Sackett, who started farming in the 1880's, never gave one, and Eric Quested could not recall having heard of one in the years 1911–1914 in North Thanet.[129] Yet the custom did not vanish entirely until after the First World War.

Routine and special entertainments for subordinates are well authenticated. The Cottons at Quex always gave rent dinners for their tenant farmers; in 1865 one was held at the Hussar, Garlinge.[130] Mrs Molesworth of St Nicholas gave a rent dinner to "her farmers and cottage tenantry and labourers on her estate" in 1859,[131] but this seems to have been rather unusual. In 1863 "all the tenants and workmen" of Upton Farm, St Peter's, were given a dinner in a barn and white favours to wear on their smocks, to celebrate the marriage of the Prince of Wales.[132] The weddings of

rich farmers' or landowners' children were occasionally marked
by large dinners for the employees, for instance, the wedding of
George Collet's daughter to a London business man in 1862, when
Monkton was decorated from end to end.[133] Henry Powell-Cotton
arranged tremendous festivities for the tenants, and the local shop-
keepers, aged and children to mark Percy Powell-Cotton's twenty-
first birthday in 1887, winding up with a servants' ball.[134]

Farming practices

In this period Thanet farmers responded rather faster to the on-
going stimulus of the agricultural revolution. At a ploughing match
dinner speech in 1850 they were advised to improve their farming,
rather than "to keep very accurate accounts and transfer from
Schedule C to Schedule D for income tax".[135] There was clearly
some improvement in response to the repeal of the Corn Laws
from the start.

Before the practice was criticized at the 1849 ploughing match
stacking competition, stacks, in the centre of the island particularly,
were "crowded together, full of vermin, and not put up on
stones".[136] Steam threshing machines were commended by an 1854
match dinner speaker, who hoped that the flail and "the cruel old
horse threshing machine" would be banished from Thanet farms.[137]
By 1860 it was stated at the dinner that "all farms had machinery
and very many steam engines",[138] and a threshing prize was given
at the match from 1867.[139] A Garrett 2-horsepower threshing
machine appeared in a Bromstone farm sale in 1869, one of the
first sale ones.[140] Yet displays of farm machinery were held at
the East Kent ploughing match from 1854, with thirteen types by
1857,[141] but none were displayed at the Thanet match till after
World War Two.

When the Royal Agricultural Show was held at Canterbury in
1860, four agricultural stallions and two pieces of locally designed
and made machinery were entered from Thanet, but won no prizes.
There were far more entries from most other Kent towns. Thanet
farmers pinned much hope on their two Kent wooden plough
entries winning in a class against iron ploughs, but this contest was
not held for some reason.[142]

There was a class for reaping machines in the 1861 ploughing
match, won by two employees of J.S. Swinford of Nash Court,[143]

but it was not repeated. There were still under twenty in use in Thanet in 1872,[144] and not many appeared in farm sales to 1892.

Continued efforts were made to get the four-horse Kent plough team replaced by three or even two-horse iron ploughs. In 1866 two iron ploughs were entered by manufacturers for the ploughing match,[145] but they were excluded again the following year.[146] However they were tried again in 1873,[147] and re-appeared out-numbering the wooden ones in the revived ploughing match of 1888.[148] (See p 159). A solitary steam plough was entered in the 1865 and 1868 matches, jointly owned by farmers Harnett and Collard, but it had no other to compete against.[149] By 1869 Captain Cotton had one too, and in 1870 Harnett had "added a mill behind his plough". Though there were never any more at the match, by 1871 there were four in Thanet, three of them hired at 12/- per acre exclusive of coal and water, or 14/- all found, with 1/- extra for 10″ instead of 8″ ploughing.[150] Quite a lot of steam ploughing was said to be done in 1885, apparently by contractors; it was not cheaper, but quicker.[151] Scarifiers seem to have rather gone out of fashion in this period, but were included in a Minster Abbey sale of 1875.[152]

The Quex farm sale of 1877 probably included the most modern equipment then available, apart from the wooden ploughs, and was attended by many buyers, who paid high prices.[153] The sale included lavish horse-drawn vehicles for private use. Thomas Sidders, the tenant, who was retiring through illness, had married the apparently wealthy London widow Mrs Lambert in 1871.[154]

Sale at Quex Park – September 1877
8 draft horses, two horses for Brougham or light van work, 2 cobs.
1 8 hp steam engine by Tuxford of Boston, Lincs.
1 new straw elevator by Holman & Collard, Canterbury.
1 first class Boby corn cleaner (with blast complete) and man-turned handle.
1 new Boby hay tedder.
2 cleaning machines.
1 winnowing machine.
1 first-class umbeller.
1 patent reaper by Salmeston.
1 mowing machine.
1 capital 13-chep Suffolk drill by Garrett.
1 5-chep and 1 3-chep drill.
1 2-furrow turnip drill.
1 first-class 3-cylinder iron roll with double shafts.

1 first-class double cylinder roll.
1 first-class ring crusher with double shafts.
4 capital wood rollers with single and double shafts.
4 excellent 4-horse waggons with iron axles.
2 4-horse wheeled ploughs. (ie. Kent ploughs).
2 2-horse wheeled ploughs.
2 4-horse nidgets complete.
4 pairs Yorkshire harrows.
1 first-class chain drag.
A patent chaff-cutting machine for steam or horse power.
Spring cutter boxes.
A patent sack lifter.
Oil cake and bean crushers.
Double action turnip cutters.

At another Quex Farm sale in 1891 the machinery included Wood's self-binder, Biddell's bean mill, and a Davey Sleep double-furrow iron plough.[155] There were also 16 horses, 30 cows, 1 bull, 16 followers, 182 sheep and 30 pigs. At a sale at Nash Court in 1875 some curiosities had appeared: a Gooday's thatch-making machine, and a portable forge.[156]

Progress was made in improving the skills of farm workers: by 1863 most farmers had trained one or more or their own men to thatch, so no longer needed to pay expensive professional thatchers.[157] Some surprisingly modern things also surfaced, sometimes as isolated rarities. A sample of silage from Thomas Mayhew's farm at Sevenscore was shown at Canterbury corn market on 22 November 1884,[158] and an Aspen potato planter was tested at Cripp's farm, Acol, in 1876.[159] Six different kinds of patent manure were advertised in the Kentish Gazette in 1866.[160]

The agricultural returns required annually from the farmers from 1866 were apparently less grudgingly made than in 1801. In 1866 the forms demanded to know the acreage of wheat, barley, oats, rye, beans, peas, potatoes, turnips, swedes, mangolds, carrots cabbage, kohl rabi, vetches, lucerne, and "other crops". To these had been added by 1891 rape, beet, tares, clover, sanfoin, orchards, market gardens and nut gardens. The crops listed were not a reliable guide to new developments, but represented a "catching up process" by the Board of Agriculture, as it gradually became aware that certain things were being grown. Sanfoin for instance had been grown since 1680 in Thanet, and clover since at least the early 18th century. But sanfoin may have lapsed.

John Bennett, who farmed 71 acres at Drapers' farm, kept a meticulous account of his cropping from 1841 to 1859: it was similar to Buckland's findings. His rotation on one piece of land was as follows: 1841 all wheat. 1842 beans, clover and oats. 1843 all wheat. 1844 canary, turnips, barley and rye (mostly barley). 1845 turnips, radish, clover, canary, and a very small piece under potatoes. 1846 all wheat. 1847 wheat, and a small amount of peas. 1848 peas, radish, lucerne, and 5 acres of potatoes (proving that the disease striking much of the country was not then in Thanet). 1849 wheat with a little lucerne. 1850 barley, small piece of tares. 1851 all clover. 1852 wheat and a little barley. 1853 wheat, turnips, peas and ? 1854 barley, oats and turnips. 1855 barley and wheat. 1856 turnips, clover, a small piece of swedes and a very small piece of potatoes. 1857 all wheat. 1858 all barley. 1859 a small piece of potatoes, rest canary or turnips. He grew swedes (yellow tankard) for the first time in 1856 and trefolium for the first time in 1859 – 16 species of crops in all. Nothing is known of his garden or his livestock. His manure register for 1843 showed precise distances of 8 or 7 feet between each pile to be placed in the fields for spreading, depending on the crop. About 1871 a typical Thanet rotation was somewhat less intensive, being roots, barley, clover, wheat, peas, barley, oats, as in 1845.[161]

Little has been found about yields. In 1859 roots were giving 40 tons to the acre, as against 20 in Dorset,[162] and William Manser often obtained 6 quarters of Kent white-strawed red wheat, and sometimes 8. Artificial manure was fairly widely used by 1871 (superphosphate of lime on rape is specifically mentioned), but seaweed "in enormous quantities" (see p 156) and town manure at 2/6d a cartload, and oilcake were the preferred off-farm fertilizers.[163] 20 tons of farmyard manure and 5 cwt of artificial were used to produce the prize-winning roots at the 1865 ploughing match.[164]

With the fall in wheat prices there was a strong swing by the 1860's towards barley, oats and green crops. (See Table 11)

Steam milling started in Ramsgate in the Hudson family's mills by 1878, and the number of windmills in Thanet dropped sharply.[165] One crop which later disappeared was nut trees: 70 walnut trees with nuts were offered for sale in Birchington in 1874,[166] and 9 acres of nut trees were listed in the 1891 returns, as against three in the 1840 tithe assessments.

Livestock breeding changed its emphasis under the impact of resort growth and falling prices for meat; and the decline of sheep and pigs was balanced by the increase in cows. About 1871 the

Table 11. All-Thanet main crops. Acres excluding rods and perches
(Agricultural returns, PRO MAF 68/132, 759 and 1329)

	Wheat	Barley	Oats	Potatoes	All green crops (including rotated grasses)*
1867	4,014	4,101	1,246	480	6,782
1891	1,958	5,556	1,367	524	7,500

* Returns do not distinguish between table and fodder vegetables

state of the marshes was not very good, due to heavy grazing and
hay cutting. They were used to fatten some Welsh or Irish cattle,
and lambs in summer until mid-August, when they were taken to
the uplands to feed on sainfoin, the stubbles, and later rape and
turnips.[167]

Table 12: Total Thanet livestock
(Agricultural returns, PRO MAF 68/132, 759 and 1329)

	Cows and heifers	Working horses	Breeding mares	Sheeps and Lambs	Pigs
1867	846	Not available	Not available	26,298	3,786
1881	1,041	872	4	20,184	2,813
1891	1,213	943 (includes market-gardens and farms)	14	20,934	2,958

Poultry were kept in some numbers here and there – 130 geese,
ducks and fowls featured in a Nash Court farm sale in 1878,[168] and
as noted George Finch at St Lawrence had 100 poultry in 1881 (see
above page 135).

The increase in numbers of agricultural working horses and
breeding mares suggests more intensive cultivation and self-suf-
ficiency. Improved shorthorns were increasingly used in the better
dairy herds; for instance a sale of shorthorns "from all the principle dairy districts of the country" was held at Newlands Farm in
June 1881.[169] A national policy to contain animal epidemics began
in this period. When cattle plague visited Thanet from November

1865 to March 1866, prayer was the only real hope, though Ramsgate had a MRCVS vet by 1866. The Champions at Sarre lost 49 cows by January 1866, and special services were held in the Ramsgate chapels in March, after which the plague rapidly disappeared![170] But when pleuro-pneumonia struck other parts of England in 1879, all dairymen and cowkeepers had to register with Margate council from 1 May,[171] and when it finally hit Thanet in 1880, the Privy Council sent an officer to inspect Margate dairy premises, and found them better than London's cowsheds.[172] (Yet quite how bad the excellent Margate dairies actually may have been may be surmised by later known conditions – see below page 183). When swine fever broke out at Newington Farm in 1882 all the pigs had to be slaughtered.[173]

The great crop innovations of the time were hops and broccoli. Hops were a fleeting phenomenon in the upland parts of the island, and grown purely as a response to the agricultural depression. It is not known when they were first grown in Thanet: Lewis does not mention them, neither do any other 18th century writers on Thanet. D. Baker mentions 3/4 acre grown at Ramsgate by a brewer, maltster and farmer who died in 1740.[174] The 1840 tithe assessment lists only a "hop-garden field" at Acol, running from the cross-roads by the pub along the South side of the Brooksend road, where the village green development now is. There is no indication if hops were actually grown there or merely had been in the past. But Thomas Mayhew at Sevenscore was growing hops on the sheltered lowland to the value of £525 pa in 1858, paying 23% tax.[175] In the first agricultural return of 1866 the Thanet total was 11 acres, rising to 18 in 1867, 282 in 1881 and 423½ in 1891 (Imperial statute acres, not hop acres). Hop gardens and oast houses sprang up in unlikely places in upland Thanet, as well as sheltered Monkton and Minster. There was a garden at Northdown south of the park,[176] an oast at Yorkshire farm (until recently untouched), gardens and an oast at Elmwood farm (again the oast still stands), and more at Fair Street farm, the oast now a private dwelling. There is a huge converted brewery oast in Cannon Road, Ramsgate and until 1993 there were the ruins of another oast at the former Nethercourt farm, now a housing estate.

There were hop-gardens at Dent-de-Lion, to the South of Quex Park (possibly the 1840 Acol field), at St Nicholas,[177] and at Alland Grange. At Woodchurch farm the hopfield lay to the West of the present manure heap, with twin oasts on the site of the present large private residence on the South side of the Birchington road, opposite the old flint cowshed.[178] London hop-pickers came regularly to Thanet – 600 came to Monkton and Minster in 1882,[179] and Mr Willett of Quex farm gave a supper to his 50 pickers and their wives in that year.[180]

"Collyflowers" had been a market-garden crop since at least 1750 (see p 80), and Walcheren broccoli, which had only a three-week season in April, had probably been here for as long or longer. Alexander broccoli, planted as partridge cover, had maybe been here since the Romans.[181] The seed of longer-lasting spring varieties, mainly Roscoff and some Anger, was brought to Thanet by Barzillai (Bar) Sackett of Northwood (1844–1918) and Augustus Brockman of Haine (1849–1942), two young market-gardeners with adjoining land, who went to Brittany together and bought it there. Local and family tradition gives the leading role in this enterprise to the older Bar Sackett.[182] The exact year is not known, but might have been 1869. In June 1870 a court case showed that broccoli were then being cut on the outskirts of Ramsgate, and regarded as an expensive rarity. About 1871 they sometimes fetched £40 an acre in May and June.[183] Anger broccoli (usually pronounced to rhyme with "banger" locally) proved rather unsatisfactory, but Roscoff did well.

Bar Sackett founded his fortunes on the broccoli. Having inherited only 15 acres from his father,[184] he was occupying 34 acres, with three men working for him, by the 1881 census.[185] In 1884 he began selling wheat,[186] indicating he had moved definitely into farming, and he began to take over the tenancy of larger farms in the decade of the '80's. He was the first to take broccoli into large-scale arable farming in Thanet;[187] previously it had been a market-garden crop only. Augustus Brockman, his friend, was also a remarkable man. Originally a waggoner at Haine, and never able to read or write, he went into business on his own as a market gardener in 1869 with £30 capital, later became tenant of Updown farm and "head of one of the best-known and most skilful farming families in East Kent".[188]

In June 1891 a sheep-shearing match was revived in Minster by the Thanet Agricultural Association; the contestants were all under 18, and the champion, George Harlow, under 16.[189] Ambrose Collard said that in the past two years his sheep "had been sheared in a disgraceful manner, but the work today was wonderful". In the 16–18 year old shearers' class prizes were £1/10/- and £1. The sheep-shearing was repeated in 1892, with a cattle and horse show as well, for which the prizes ranged from 2–8 guineas, donated by non-farmers with the exception of Thomas Mayhew.[190]

The youthfulness of the shearers highlights the increasing tendency to employ boys instead of men. This has been mentioned earlier, (in connection with wages and education, see p 146–7), as having been widespread since 1833, and probably well before that. According to one source it was becoming commoner in Monkton after 1851[191] and probably reached its apogee around the early 1890's. The census returns do not give a break-down of men and boys employed by individual farmers in many cases, except in 1881, so an island-wide analysis is not possible with much accuracy. But the 1881 census showed that the proportion of boys varied greatly, evidently according to the farmer's tastes rather than the size of the farm, ranging from nearly 2/3 boys in extreme cases to only 1/4, with 1/4 or 1/3 boys being the commonest figure. There did not seem to be any particular difference in parishes, and the 1891 census did not give details of farmers' employees, so the denouement is not yet known.

With the arrival of the railways the hoy service to London ended. Probably under the impact of the railways, an attempt was made in 1864 to start a corn market in Ramsgate. It was held weekly for two hours in the Bull and George Hotel; the first day over 300 quarters were sold and merchants came from Sandwich and Canterbury,[192] but it does not seem to have lasted even as long as its 18th century predecessor at Margate.

William Manser's farming about 1870. (From H. Evershed, *The farming of Kent, Sussex and Surrey.* London 1871, 50–52). *St Peter's parish.*

"260 acres of arable, consisting of good loam 1 foot to 12 foot deep, resting on soft white chalk. Cropping: One half of the farm is in cereal crops, ie equal quantities of wheat and of barley, with a few oats; the other half is sown with a variety of green or pulse crops, including potatoes, lucern, sainfoin, clover, mangel, peas etc. As the land is kept in high condition with town manure, the fallow crops are grown chiefly for sale, not for use in the farm-yard. *Potatoes* are the principal cleansing crop; they follow oats or wheat after lucerne etc. The usual tillages for potatoes are (1) a deep autumn ploughing (2) a light spring ploughing to cover the heavy coat of dung put on during the winter (if the dung could be got on before the first ploughing Mr Manser would prefer to plough it in then); (3) baulking at two feet apart, splitting the baulks to cover the seed and rolling down (4) horse-hoeing, hand-hoeing at 4/-, moulding up with the potato-earthing plough, and weeding. *Mangels*: a deep and a light ploughing, and 20 tons of dung, as for potatoes, and the seed drilled on the flat, in rows 2 feet apart; crops great, and even on excellent land 30 tons of cleaned roots must be considered a great crop. *Lucern* is drilled in close rows, in wheat, after mangel, or in some other corn crop which is not so bulky as to injure the lucern. 25lbs of seed to the acre; 4 lbs of trefoil are sown broadcast to give a crop of hay the first year. The lucern is cut twice the first year, and three times afterward; it pays for a coat of dung every year. Lucern is never hoed; when broken up with one ploughing there can be no better tilth for wheat. *Peas* are grown, unmanured, after clover-lea wheat which had been dunged. . . . The yield falls off very seriously if they are sown on the same land more than once in eight years. *Turnips* are seldom grown, as their value is trifling. A piece of rye or trefolium is sometimes taken and followed by turnips after several ploughings to get the land 'gentle'. *Kentish white-strawed red wheat* is drilled (2 bushels) from the middle of November till Christmas. When wheat is sown at Christmas, it is never root-fallen, which it will certainly be if sown early. The crop is strong, and is mown at 10/- or 12/- an acre. Mr Manser has frequently exceeded 6 qrs. on his breadth of 60 acres, and on a larger breadth, when he was farming more land, he has grown 8 qrs in some fields. *Barley*: 2 bushels per acre of Chevalier are sown as soon as the land is dry in February. Mangel is the best preparation for barley, with one ploughing, and the seed-bed prepared by cultivating; peas also make a good barley-tilth, with a little manure if possible. *Manure*: seaweed and town manure enable Mr Manser to be quite independent of artificial manures. Superphosphate has been tried as an experiment, and it started the turnip and mangel plants rapidly, but did not increase the weight of the crop . . . (Seaweed) is collected in large quantities by farmers, as well as by carters, who sell it at a distance of 2 or 3 miles from the coast at 2s.6d or 3s. per two-horse cart-load. . . . I believe I have seen a thousand cart-loads of sea-weed lying under the cliff within a distance of 1 mile; and as a change of wind often takes the whole away in one tide, farmers must set all hands to work with horses and carts to move the weed to the top of the cliff. Sea-weed is seldom applied to the land in its raw state, but is placed in the mixens (manure heaps) in layers with the other dung. It soon decomposes after the heap has been turned, and is then applied to the land. It is thought to be more beneficial at a distance from the sea on land that is not naturally impregnated with saline matters, and is not often dressed with this manure.

"*Steam-ploughing.* Practical men inform me that they have not observed any benefit from ploughing to a depth of 10 inches. . . . There is no doubt that the oats which best withstood last summer's drought were on an 8-inch steam-ploughed seed-bed. (but) . . . oilcake and dung best fortify light soils in adverse, and especially in dry seasons. A good seed-bed for oats after a corn crop may certainly be obtained on most soils by 6-inch ploughing; and very frequently, when an extra depth is supposed to have been beneficial, the benefit is really due to the (extra) dung.

Seed-time. Thirty years ago most persons used 3 bushels of seed-wheat; now a smaller quantity is used. The seed-time is late. The land is pressed heavily for wheat, after steam-ploughing.

Canary. This has been given up since the new tariff; and whereas formerly men did not like to thresh it, on account of the dust irritating the skin, it is now said they will not thresh it at any price.

Farm retail sales. Near a town a farm is quite a retail shop as regards the sale of produce . . .'"

This account has been included as it is less well-known than Buckland's or the 18th century writers' descriptions of Thanet agriculture; also it is the only one specifically about St Peter's parish. Evershed's account of Thanet farming as a whole was patchy and unsystematic.

The Thanet Ploughing Match

The match went through various ups and downs in these 48 years. There was a sharp downturn following the repeal of the Corn Laws: 31 ploughs in 1848, and in 1849 only 60 at dinner, mostly not farmers, though the ploughs were back to 39. From 1852 to 1860 there were generally 42–49 ploughs competing, though in 1856 there was no match for reasons unknown. Then things improved with some fluctuations, reaching 60 ploughs again in 1868, but numbers immediately declined again, reaching 26 in 1872, and "a low number" in 1873.[193] In 1874 no match was held, but in 1875 a few farmers held a low-key mini-match at Minster, with only ploughing classes and a small display of roots.[194] The response was evidently disappointing and the match then lapsed until 1888.

Even the Isle of Thanet Agricultural Association was wound up,[195] and the Thanet Farmers' Club went into abeyance even earlier.[196]

In the 1850's the tone of the dinners changed markedly, becoming exceedingly solemn and respectable; often they broke up early and the old late-night roistering after the main guests had departed seems to have ceased. From 1860 there were not usually professional singers in attendance. But from 1861 the tone became a little mellower again, the clergy (who must have been behind the change to greater respectability) seemingly realizing that they might have gone a little too far, and starting to crack jokes. The Rev G.W. Sicklemore often presided at the dinners after 1860. The President of the TAA for many years was J.A. Warre, the popular and wealthy M.P. for Ripon who lived at Westcliffe Lodge, Ramsgate, and wore a blue jacket with brass buttons in the style of an 18th century squire. After his death in 1860,[197] the Marquis of Conyngham held the office, but only attended the dinner three times, and resigned in 1867. Sir Edward Dering, Bt. was president in 1868,[198] but does not seem to have lasted long. There was no president then till J.T. Friend of Northdown was chosen in 1871,[199] and titled gentlemen stopped coming to the dinner. This was in marked contrast to the earlier picture: in 1863 the dinner guests had included five knights or baronets, an untitled Knatchbull-Hugessen, two serving military officers and two volunteer ones, as well as the Mayor of Margate and the Deputy of Ramsgate.[200] In 1850 six titled men had been present.[201] In 1873 the Earl of Mountcharles was president and attended the dinner, but only one "Sir" came with him.[202] All this may have reflected landowner-tenant tension, or the increasing unfashionableness of Thanet, or both.[203]

Prize money was several times reduced and raised again, and this may have depended on the number of members as well as the state of farming. Generally prizes were given for drilling, thatching, stacking, long service, and raising families without poor relief, as well as ploughing. In 1869 prizes were restricted to ploughing only, and the prize money was reduced.[204] Both landowners, tenant farmers and the general public seem to have lost interest in the match by this time, and the affluent townspeople did not support it so much. Only the richer owner-occupiers seem to have kept it going. The farm labourers, for their part, seem to have started to regard it with contempt. At the 1872 dinner, the secretary, Mr Harnett, complained that there was "a coldness in the affair that he should like to see removed".[205] By this time too the organization had become very scrappy. There was no committee, and since 1865 at least the secretary and treasurer alone had struggled on, sometimes sending out "150–170 circulars and getting only four or five people to the business meetings".[206] The attempts to form a labourers' union in 1872–3 must have been the last straw, and the disappearance of the match is not surprising.

Yet after fifteen years, in 1888, the Isle of Thanet Agricultural Association and the ploughing match were re-started in entirely changed circumstances. There was still a committee of only three: Ambrose Collard chairman, G. Goodson treasurer, and F.R. Benecke honorary secretary. But the KSALPU had collapsed, and there was a labour shortage due to the hops, so that both farmers and men felt more need to be nice to one another. Some tensions remained between landowners and tenants. Looking back on the early 1870's Ambrose Collard said at the dinner that he regretted the end of the old Association, but "there was a cause and a very serious one. . . . They had agitators going up and down the land setting the labourer against the farmer and attempting to set the farmer against the landowner. They failed in the latter and did very little in the first (Hear! Hear!)". The old Association "had dropped solely because of the adverse steps of the labourers towards the farmers", but now "the landowning class was the only one which had not supported the revival of the Association". He remembered "at the Wingham Association, when Lord Fitzwalter distributed the prizes for the last time, the men went up to receive their prizes in such a manner that they all felt that it was quite time that that Association ceased".

The atmosphere was now said to be very altered; and there were many young men present. Some of the farmers sang songs to entertain the rest at the more frugal dinner, but the menu was more modern and already reminiscent of the 1930's. After a variety of soups and fish dishes, Thanet saddle of mutton and ribs of Thanet beef were followed by tartlets, Genoese pastries, maids-of-honour, custards, jellies, blanc-mange and pineapple creams as well as the traditional plum-pudding.

Prizes were only given for ploughing, but as already mentioned, the largest entry was in the double-furrow iron plough class, for which a first prize of £3 was given, and only £2 for the winner of the four-horse Kent plough class. The iron plough winner, G. Goodban, employed by J.W. Smith & Sons, (Val Smith at Acol farm), was regarded as the champion.[207]

In 1889 at Cheeseman's Farm, prizes for shepherds, thatchers, stacking, hopsampling and long service were given.[208] By 1890 at Manston Green Farm the match attracted 52 ploughs and "an immense concourse of spectators, nearly 1,000 labourers", and "the sides of the road were lined with the stalls of itinerant vendors" (like the 1830's). 160 farmers lunched in a barn. Prizes were back for drilling, raising the largest families without relief, and domestic servants' long service. Dinner at the Foresters' Hall, Margate was attended by the Mayor, Henry Powell-Cotton, a number of clergy and J.T. Friend. The local landowners had come round, but there were no titled people present any more.[209] In 1891 at Vincent Farm prizes for yardmen (cowmen) were added, there were "nearly 50 ploughs" and 200 to lunch, with dinner for 60 at the Royal Hotel, Ramsgate in the evening.[210] Business meetings were well attended by both committee (now larger) and sub-scribers, and the president was the then Vicar of St Peter's, the Rev. A. Whitehead.[211]

The ploughing match of 1892 was the most lush of the new series: £100 was distributed in prizes, there were prizes for married yearly servants as well as single, and nearly a hundred to dinner at the Cliftonville Hotel, which included roast pheasant. Subscriptions had increased, there was a balance of £20 in hand, and the principle guest was the Conservative MP for East Kent, James Lowther. His speech however struck an ominous note: he suggested wages should be put on a sliding scale, as the wheat price was down to 28/-.[212]

Thanet farmers were indeed nearing one of the most difficult times in their recent history, but this period, 1847–1892, had seen a marked turning-point from the conservative mentality before the 1870's, when reapers and iron ploughs were not allowed in the ploughing match, to the much more innovative approaches later, with burgeoning dairy herds, upland farmers going into hops, and the broccoli marking the start of the later large-scale vegetable cultivation. The end of the over-abundant supply of cheap labour and falling prices for the traditional Thanet products had brought this about, and the former factor too more than any other saved the farm workers from the worst of their sufferings.

These years saw the start of the ascendancy of urban over rural England and great progress in workers' housing, public health and local administration in both town and country. Perhaps too they marked the ascendancy of a more cynical attitude by the urban public towards farmers. At a point in the 1870's, when the latter's laments did not seem to be much supported by local evidence, the editor of the *Kebles Gazette* stated an opinion which was to be echoed down the years with varying degrees of justice or injustice, when he observed dryly in an editorial "It is amazing how much ruin farmers will bear."

Chapter Eight: From the agricultural crisis to the Armistice – 1893–1918

General position of the farmers

As well as the fall in corn prices Thanet had to contend with a disastrous drought in the winter of 1892–93 and early summer of 1893. William Champion noted in his diary in June: "100s of acres in the Isle of Thanet not cropped and many not ploughed since last year. The corn in many fields as bad as could be, particular the late sown. On our land about 3 acres not ploughed. (Regular dried out. The plough could not burst it up) and many not cropped. Wm. Broadley St Nicholas Court 140 acres not cropped and many of them not ploughed. John? ammill?, Buss, Hancock, Palmer and many others had many acres not ploughed or cropped with corn. Clover, sanfoin and hay about 5 cwt per acre."[1]

Yet hops, dairying and sheep came through 1893 fairly well; sheep were making a come-back. The Minster show, with strong urban support, had much increased attendance, and featured a new 5-class cattle section. Abbot's Dairies opened in Thanet in November, supplying to all the towns from a 90-cow herd at Ebbsfleet farm,[2] after the previous tenant, Robert Gibbons, had gone bankrupt (but he had only been in business since the previous December with borrowed capital).[3] Many herds were smaller; 32 mixed "home-bred", Shorthorns and Alderneys at Woodchurch farm,[4] 23 of no specified breed at Manston Green and Spratling Street together.[5] £4,000 was again estimated to have been paid to hop-pickers, with one grower paying £400, nearly double 1892.[6] The M.P. James Lowther, now chairman of the Central Association of Chambers of Commerce, and himself a farmer, made a gloomy speech at the rather down-beat ploughing match: agriculture was being crushed out of existence. He supported the current forma-tion of the National Farmers' Union, but in view of his position felt he could take no part, and that in any case "any organization based on one class alone was utterly inadequate."[7] 1894 began with a severe frost and brought the farming crisis to Thanet with a vengeance: hop prices collapsed and there were eight farm sales, four of them large farms, including that of Ambrose Collard at Walter's Hall.[8] At Woodchurch G.W. Warren, who had only been there perhaps seven years,[9] advertised a leaving sale, but then postponed for another year. The Minster horse and cattle show disappeared, but the ploughing match was held without the dinner, though with an unusually fine lunch. (See p 189). Thanet made a small mark at the Royal Counties' Show at Canterbury, where F. de B. Collard was a sheep judge and Thomas Champion of Sarre (grandson of the founder of the ploughing match) won 2nd prize for jumping with a mare or gelding.[10]

The winter of 1894–95 was very severe, and there were eleven farm sales in 1895. One was due to bankruptcy (Flete),[11] two to death (Nash Court and Way),[12] two to retirement (Gore End and Shuart, both occupied by A.W. Rammell),[13] and some to reasons yet unknown: Monkton Court (John Hogben), Dent-de-Lion (A.S. Padley),[14] Monkton Parsonage (Bartlett and Clutton), Alland Grange (A.L. Paterson).[15] But Val Smith who left Acol Farm to concentrate on his town saddlery businesses returned to farming in 1897, and G.W. Warren who left Woodchurch turned up at St Nicholas later.[16] However, the ploughing match followed the Minster show into abeyance after 1894, and some of the sales might have been caused by rather premature retirement, since in former times farmers had tended to continue until they died, even at advanced ages. In November 1895 Lieut. Colonel Alfred Copeland wrote to the *Kebles Gazette* stating that 5,000 acres in Thanet had been placed under notice to quit by tenants and only 2,000 acres re-let. He suggested growing tobacco here (it was being tried at Malling, Wye College and other places in Kent).[17]

In 1896 there were another eleven sales, some not likely to be due to retirement: Thomas Mayhew II at Sevenscore, who disposed of four hunters, was only 30 in the 1891 census,[18] but John Swinford at Minster Abbey retired, and possibly John Kennett at Nethercourt.[19] G.K. Burge left Hengrove to move to the larger Dent-de-Lion,[20] and the death of D. Clark caused the sale at Thorne.[21] Most notably however Woodchurch, Shuart, Nash Court and Gore End were re-advertised, no tenants having been found for them the previous year. In the interim they had been farmed by foremen or managers acting for the landlords (the Powell-

Cottons at Woodchurch, St John's College Cambridge owned the
other three). At Woodchurch 17 steers and heifers had replaced
Warren's dairy herd. It is believed that Bar Sackett bargained with
the Powell-Cottons to take on Woodchurch at a reduced rent when
it was offered for the second year, and no doubt other farmers did
the same with other landlords.[22]

1897 saw only seven sales, but two of these, Alland Grange and
Monkton Court, were being offered for the second time by the
Ecclesiastical Commissioners.[23] Between 1893 and 1898 an
unusually large number of serious farm fires were reported in the
press, in some cases the farmers were said to be insured and in
some cases not fully. Whilst it is perhaps not to be excluded that
the insurance money might have been a motive on occasion, it is
equally likely that the reporters simply became interested in fires
at this time when mains water had been laid on in the villages and
the urban fire engines were consequently better able to attend
farm fires – although the pressure was often too low to be very
effective. Thomas Pointer observed in his autobiography written
about 1912 that almost every farm in Thanet had been totally or
partly destroyed by fire within the past fifty years; it may always
have been so.[24] (Some comparison with earlier periods is needed
but unobtainable, as insurance was being taken out by farmers as
early as 1830).

The indications that some farmers were making money from
livestock was reinforced by the house-warming ball which Mr and
Mrs F. de B. Collard gave in January 1897, after they took over
Minster Abbey (Court) farm: sixty people attended, many arriving
in carriages.[25] Bar Sackett, living in a much more frugal style, was
also doing well from livestock and broccoli. Having taken on
Woodchurch and Chilton for his sons, by 1899 he had progressed
from West Northdown farm to Yorkshire farm, and a little later to
East Northdown.

In 1898 the number of sales was back to three, one due to
death and one a hobby farm at Whiteness, Kingsgate.[26] When
C. Whitehead visited Thanet in 1899 he reported to the Royal
Agricultural Society that "there are comparatively few indices of
agricultural depression in Thanet, it is still well farmed."[27]
However, there were five sales that year, and the price of corn,
which stood at 42–45/- per quarter for wheat, 40–44/- for barley
and 18–22/- for oats at Canterbury in June, collapsed again to
26–30/-, 25–28/- and 14–20/- for the three grains in September.[28]
Sale numbers were again normal in 1900.

Dairying and livestock probably continued to give the best return (apart from broccoli which needed specialist know-how), so that the numbers of all animal species here remained high to 1911, though horses and sheep declined somewhat over 1891. (See Table 21). A reasonable but low-profile prosperity seems to have been maintained until the outbreak of war in 1914. The ploughing match was revived in 1903 and continued till the war, in a modest way unlike its earlier manifestations. 1904 was a bad year with ten sales,[29] but this seemed to be only a flash in the pan, and the reason is unclear, as corn prices were no worse than usual. But after that, until 1914, there were very few auction sales, suggesting take-over of tenant right and stock by valuation was widespread, possibly because the results of the 1904 sales had been poor, possibly because of increasing engrossment after 1901.

Chilton farm sale fetched only £73/7/- for the dead stock and £917/18/- for ten horses, forty cows and a bull in October 1904, but the smaller Reading Street farm sale in 1911 produced £105/11/- for the dead stock and £721/17/3 for six agricultural horses and one cob, 32 cows, a bull, 14 swine, 30 poultry, 2 geese and 10 ducks and drakes – even though four horses and five cows found no buyers at all.[30] Woodchurch farm, with tenant right, (ie. right to the remaining term of the tenancy), all crops and live and dead stock was valued at £2,423/-/6d in November 1910,[31] which may be compared with £140/12/- excluding tenant right in 1828 (see p 104). By contrast Sarre Court was valued at £1,100 for insurance purposes in 1906; this would not have included tenant right.[32]

The agricultural scientist A.D. Hall noted Thanet's "considerable local reputation for its barley" in 1910, even though crops all over East Kent were indifferent that year due to the excessive rain.[33] On this visit he made a classic contemporary description of the island, suppressed from his book and articles in the *Times*, but known in some other version to a Major Salt, author of an article in the *Journal of the Kent Farmers' Union* in February 1927, which noted: "Hall found in Thanet a certain dusty, business-like harshness, due possibly to the prevailing East Wind atmosphere, possibly due to the ever-present sight of chimneys and garish villa residences." (East winds have been much less common of recent years, even rare, at least until the winter of 1995–6, but used to impart a definite character to the island).[34]

Various things suggested that the farmers, even perhaps the richest ones, were rather a marginal social group amongst the Thanet bourgeoisie at this time. From the 1880's Thanet moved into its second heyday as a resort area, with the masses still thronging to Margate and Ramsgate, and the select townships of Broadstairs, Westgate and Birchington now in favour as quiet holiday places for persons of taste, particularly those with children. These places, with Cliftonville, Kingsgate and parts of Ramsgate were also popular residential spots for wealthy rentiers and retired people, moneyed people with health problems, some ambitious medical men, and businessmen and even professionals commuting to London. The big hotels in Cliftonville were filled with a lively and no less affluent clientele, not only in summer but at Christmas, when there were great festivities. There was plenty of money in the towns, to be spent at such good shops as Bobby's department store in Margate and the Cliftonville branch opened in 1913, Lewis and Highland's in Ramsgate, Lovely's the art dealer in Margate and so on. The Margate municipal philharmonic orchestra and international orchestras attracted large middle-class audiences to the Winter Gardens, opened in 1911.

In 1898 the East Kent Agricultural Show was held at Margate, the Mayor presided but James Friend made an optimistic opening speech, as cereal prices were now somewhat higher. Local farmers did the stewarding, and five firms of Thanet farmers won prizes.[35] When the show came to Ramsgate in 1901, five Thanet farmers again won prizes, including Percy Powell-Cotton for a Berkshire sow and Mrs H.S. Buss of St Nicholas for butter. At Ramsgate once more in 1905 F. de B. Collard won seven agricultural horse prizes including one first, for animals of various ages from foals up.[36] His successes were continued at this show, its three fairly rapid visits here suggesting that Thanet was doing better than most other parts of East Kent agriculturally. But the modest ploughing match seemed to be rather outshone by the Isle of Thanet Horse Show started in 1903, where splendid silver cups were donated by towns-people and won by farmers for farm horses. In 1904 Bar Sackett won a fine large chalice, donated by S.S. Simpson Esq., at the Thanet show, for mere 2nd and 3rd prizes for carthorses Dimple and Captain.[37] F. de B. Collard did far better in this show too, but it was about two-thirds a non-agricultural event, featuring good hacks and hunters belonging to well-off people. During the 1890's the Thanet Harriers gave some magnificent hunt breakfasts for its members at the home of a wealthy man in Westgate. In 1895 ten of the largest farmers were present, though only one, Thomas Mayhew II, brought his wife and is known to have hunted himself, which suggests that the others were guests. Ambrose Collard, the

master, had retired from farming the previous year.[38] The following
year the farmers were apparently all guests, and their names were
listed separately after those of the members in the newspaper
report, which gave a faint whiff of charity to their presence.[39] At a
meet in December 1905 only two womenfolk of the largest farmers
took part: Mrs Broadley (wife of William Broadley of St Nicholas
Court) and "Miss Norah Val Smith", one of Val Smith's daughters.
Two Friend ladies rode that day too, and a number of members of
the affluent Cobb family of Margate. No farmers' names were
reported at the hunt ball, except for Norah Smith and her brother
H.A.[40] These two also attended a fancy dress ball at the Queen's
and Highcliffe Hotel on 28 December 1908, she in a Russian
costume and he dressed as "Rats"![41] The higher status of the
bigger farmers is suggested by the fact that a few of them were J.P.s
towards the end of the 19th century. Basil Hodges was one in
1891, but may not still have been a farmer. Kelly's Isle of Thanet
Directory 1898 lists A.S. Padley and J.Kennett as such, giving their
old addresses at Dent-de-Lion and Nethercourt, from which we
know they had already retired (see p 163). Since these directories
were notoriously prone to copy old material, the position is
unclear. John Kennett had earlier been mayor of Ramsgate, and
like Val Smith may originally have been a businessman. G.K.
Burge who succeeded Padley at Dent-de-Lion and E.S. Goodson
of Upton farm were magistrates in 1909, and in 1913 there were
three: Burge, Goodson and F. de B. Collard of Minster Court
farm.[42]

Living styles of farmers varied greatly. The modern-minded Val
Smiths (who had had a bath with running water installed in 1892)
were at Christmas 1893 exchanging such presents as the works of
Dickens, chocolate creams, silk handkerchiefs, prayer and hymn
books, silk stockings, slippers, gold bangles, and checked aprons.
Their children received shut-up scissors, a doll's hymn book,
crackers, boxes of toys, handkerchiefs, oranges and sachets.[43] Bar
Sackett's older and more down-market household exchanged only
money gifts, if any. Bar did not have a bath put in, but in the 1900's
the Friends, his landlords, enlarged East Northdown farmhouse
for him with two new rooms and a first-floor W.C.; his son Vincent
at Woodchurch had a W.C. next to the coal-shed a few yards from
the backdoor, replacing the old earth privy. Bar kept his privy; at
East Northdown it was a pit about 8 feet deep with a wooden
seat. When it was about half full two men would come with a
wheelbarrow to empty it, the contents probably went onto

labourers' or smallholders' manure heaps, or even directly onto their plots.[44] Water supply both at East Northdown and Wood-church consisted of one cold tap in the scullery, the mains pressure being too weak for more. No bathrooms appeared in many Thanet farmhouses till after World War I, and many were lit only by lamps until even later, but gas was laid onto East Northdown far back in the 19th century, due to its proximity to Northdown House and the older East Northdown house opposite the farm.[45]

There is little information about furnishings from sales. At East Northdown traditional mahogany reigned till 1919. Some beds there were feather, some spring, some had eiderdowns, some disliked them. John Hogben of Monkton Court sold a rosewood sofa and a walnut dining suite in 1895[46] and in 1905 Wood farm, Manston (5 horses and 100 pigs) had some contemporary urban middle-class items: Arabian and brass-rail French bedsteads, and a drawing room suite in plush, plus feather beds and an antique carved bookcase.[47] In general improvements took the shape of adding more rooms, and W.C.s, replacing feather beds with spring mattresses and acquiring upholstered drawing room suites.[48]

The diet in Bar Sackett's house contained a great deal of meat: always eggs and bacon for breakfast and in winter fat pork instead, a joint every day for lunch, always served with a yorkshire or suet pudding and three kinds of vegetables, followed by a fruit pie. Tea was white bread and butter, supper cold meat and bread and butter, with generous salads in season. Soup was not made: vegetable water, whether laced with soda or not, was regarded as unwholesome and thrown away. This was probably typical of many farm households. Vegetables were naturally overboiled in the traditional English manner

With rare exceptions farmers in those days drank little alcohol – the mid-19th to mid-20th century was unusually abstemious – and attended church regularly. Bar and his wife Sarah went twice on Sundays, and this was quite common. He used to stay with his Covent Garden salesmen, the five unmarried Foord brothers and sisters, in London every year, but although it was rumoured that one of the brothers liked "to go on the town",[49] it is doubtful if Bar did. According to an unsolicited tribute by I.J.C. Friend, as well as the family, he was "trusted and loved, very honest and loyal"; it was his loyalty to the Queen which prompted his violent exploit during the Boer War (see p 170). He may have been particularly mindful of his reputation because he was born out of wedlock, a status which it seems was technically never reversed, although he was brought up as a legitimate son. Amongst country people in 1844, the year of his birth, it may not have amounted to much more than it would now, but it was shocking to the true Victorian middle class into which he rose. It must have been widely known, as it is to Sackett family history researchers now, and there is some evidence that it was sniggered about in his later lifetime. All farmer families' misdemeanours and disadvantages no doubt always have been, for as Jane Austen's Mr Bennett observed in *Pride and Prejudice* "For what do we live but to make sport for our neighbours and laugh at them in our turn?"[50] Farmers may be far more useful than Jane's gentry, but share the same territorial conspicuousness.

In this period medicine was beginning to become more effective, especially for those who could pay. Internal operations began to be performed on middle and upper-class people in the late 1890's and early 1900's, though at first they nearly always died soon afterwards. For instance in 1906 Herbert Harlow of Nash Court farm had his appendix removed and died, leaving a large circle of mourning friends and relatives.[51] But in 1911 the author's mother, then aged about 16, survived an appendectomy performed on the kitchen table of her home, without any complications or infection.

The gentry suffered financially in the Depression, for land values nationally fell by an average of 65% between 1879–1895. Although they levelled out in the late 1890's, the fall from 1873–1911 was 37%.[52] Yet this was an age of caring landlords here. Percy Powell-Cotton built a number of farm cottages, for instance when the hops were given up at Woodchurch in 1894 the oast was converted into twin three-bedroomed cottages, with sitting rooms, and W.C.'s just outside the entrance doors.[53] The landowner of Thorne farm had built six 3-bedroomed cottages with sitting rooms by 1899.[54] The old farmhouse at Alland Grange belonging to the Ecclesiastical Commissioners was replaced with a new one, late Victorian style, and Cheeseman's acquired a similar-looking extension. East Dumpton farmhouse merely gained a small frontal accrescence of this style, sitting prominently on the old flint house. After the Boer War Percy Powell-Cotton created six entirely new small farms on his land, with new houses and buildings, to let to ex-soldiers: Zeila farm and another outside Garlinge, Sparrow Castle and its twin on the Manston corner of Quex Park, and Acol Hill farm with its twin. The Friends at Northdown were so gentlemanly that they declined their farm manager's suggestion that they grow broccoli, lest it seem an affront to Bar Sackett![55] Another prominent gentry family was the Hatfeilds of Hartsdown, who had a home farm like the others and took a keen interest in local welfare. Captain and Mrs Hatfeild were presented at Court in June 1905.[56] For some reason similar families seemed lacking on the Ramsgate side of Thanet, the Conynghams being absentee landlords.

The gentry were naturally leaders in many ways. Their sons attended public schools, and Irvine Friend was the first member of the Thanet agrarian community, as far as is known, to graduate from an agricultural college, in 1907.[57] In 1912 the family appointed a young farmer's son from the Isle of Wight, E.S. Linington, as farm manager.[58]

Chauvinism ran high in the late 19th century, fuelled by the idea of belonging to the world's mightiest imperial race. During the Boer War in March 1900 Margate and Ramsgate were amongst many towns around Britain where "patriotic" riots took place, with attacks on the property if not the persons of people with pro-Boer sympathies or perhaps merely having some Dutch connections. The affray in Ramsgate is known only from a bare mention in the *Times* on 16 March,[59] but the *Kebles Gazette* reported that at Margate 3–4, 000 people had rioted (which may be an exaggeration) on 14 and 15 March. The object of their rage was said to have been a second-hand furniture dealer and eating-house keeper, W.J. Powell of 48–50 King Street, who had expressed sympathy for the Boers and hung out a Dutch flag. "A large crowd gathered outside his premises, singing patriotic songs such as 'Soldiers of the Queen' and 'Sons of the sea'." "Windows were broken and furniture exposed for sale damaged".[60] But there was more to it than that. The author was told on unimpeachable authority that Bar Sackett and one of his sons "had to lead a crowd of men and sack the shop of a Dutchman called Maas" in King Street, Margate, "because he had hung out a Dutch flag". At that time Henry Jacob Maas was probably a junior partner in Ferdinand Sauer's bakery at 75, King Street, as he did not trade under his own name, and it seems plausible that the Germanic Sauer would likewise have been sympathetic to the Boers. There was no other bakery in King Street or the old town then.

Later Maas & Son had bakeries in Dane Road, at 7, King Street and by 1933 also at 3, Fort Road, opposite Lloyds' Bank. This shop bore the family name many decades after the father's death in 1923.[61]

The full details of what happened on those two days remain obscure. At Margate police station on 21 March two men were fined £1 each for assaulting policemen, and three ordered to pay 5/ 6 costs. But Bar was not among them.[62] The M.P. for Sheffield Brightside, Maddison, asked in the House of Commons on 29 March if the Home Secretary was aware that two men had been released by the Chief Constable at Margate on condition that the crowd dispersed, and the Home Secretary replied that three men had been released, "and in the difficult circumstances in which the police officers found themselves placed I see no reason to doubt that the action was judicious".[63] It is not known if any other members of the agrarian community took part. On 24 March 1900 Bar Sackett was elected Overseer of the Poor and a member of the burial board for Northdown parish, proving that his status had not been affected.[64] On the contrary, he seems to have been a local heroe.

Similar, though unpublicized attacks on German-owned businesses took place in the First World War, but Bar was not involved. The war was met with enthusiasm, and the years leading up to it brought rising militarism and patriotic concern, as the nation became more conscious of the threat to its huge empire from other European powers, above all Germany. Val Smith's three sons, Bar Sackett's grandson Eric Quested and the son of F. Wellard of Cleve Court farm all joined the Royal East Kent Mounted Regiment (Royal East Kent Yeomanry) in the years before 1914. They went to camp every summer for two weeks, riding their own horses. Herbert (H.A.) Smith, the eldest, completed his stint before war broke out and was exempt from further service, but the other four were mobilized on 6 August 1914. All survived, although Alan Smith was badly injured in a riding accident, and Eric – saved from Passchendaele by being recalled for a commission – was gassed at Cambrai in 1918. Others were not so lucky: of the 600 men in the first line Yeomanry regiment and another 450–500 in the second line regiment formed in 1914–1916, only some 240–250 served to the Armistice.[65] At least four Thanet farmers' sons were killed: Private Brockman, son of Arthur Brockman of Westwood farm and grandson of Augustus,[66] Sergeant Culmer of Flete farm,[67] Lieut. R.W. Stennett RAF, son of R.W. Stennett, Alland Grange,[68] and Lieut. Frank Lake who was killed after the death of his father James Lake of Sheriff's Court.[69] Lucy, daughter of W.H. Nicholas of Bromstone farm, was one of only three Army nurses saved out of nine from the torpedoing of a hospital ship in the Channel in May 1917,[70] and another army nurse, granddaughter of John Swinford formerly of Minster Court farm and daughter of Frederick Swinford of Way, was on board the troopship *Transylvania* torpedoed in the Mediterranean in July that year. Apparently she was saved. Her father had five sons in the forces and another daughter nursing besides.[71]

Farmers' sons exempt from call-up served in the East Kent Mounted Constabulary: the B troop commanded by H.A. Smith was commended for its efficiency.[72] At a more senior level H.T. Willett of Monkton Parsonage farm was on the Food Control and Distribution Committee for S.E. London district.[73]

Thanet farmers' sons do not seem normally to have been regarded as immediate officer material like the 18 and 19-year olds of the upper and upper-middle classes: they were soon made NCO's but do not usually seem to have been given commissions until the officer casualties became very heavy in 1916–17.

The gentry made proportionally greater sacrifice than the farmers and had a strong service tradition. The three sons of the Friends all became regular army officers before the war, and of these, Colonel George Friend was killed.[74] Captain Irvine Friend M.C. commanded the Thanet troop of the East Kent Yeomanry[75] and survived the war. Captain Aubrey Hatfeild M.C., son of the one presented at Court, served in the Royal Canadian Mounted Police before the war and in the Royal Flying Corps during it,[76] and his brother, army Captain C.E. Hatfeild, was killed in September 1918. Major Percy Powell-Cotton was in the Militia 1890–1907.[77]

Hospitals were opened by the gentry or rich farmers to nurse the huge casualties; there was a VAD hospital at Nethercourt, and a 36-bed other ranks hospital at Quex Park, Mrs Powell-Cotton's name being brought to the Secretary of State for War for her services.[78] Major Powell-Cotton was Red Cross transport officer for East Kent, military member of all the local war emergency committees and set up the Local Defence Volunteers (precursor of the Home Guard), and his name too was brought to the Secretary of State.[79]

Destroyer shells or bombs fell on the rural districts of St Peter's, Broadstairs, Kingsgate, Dumpton, Manston, Westgate, Westwood, Lydden, St Nicholas, Birchington and Sarre, and the first Zeppelin bomb was dropped on Nethercourt farm on 17 May 1915, but no casualties were reported among the farming community, nor any special damage.[80]

There were no more than two sales annually advertised during the war, and no indication whether they were caused by it, with the exception of the sale of Messrs Philpott's 120-cow dairy herd at Manston, given up in 1918 as "prices were too low, foodstuffs and labour too scarce and wages too high." They had had a contract with Ramsgate Council under the Food Controller, but they did not go out of farming altogether.[81] Farmers were concerned about fixed prices and rising wages imposed by the government from 1916. A leader in the *Isle of Thanet Gazette* in January 1917 considered the former unfairly restricted the farmers' profits (this perhaps reflected not only farming opinion but that of those who could have found more food available to buy if higher prices had restricted demand).[82] Anxiety about prices and wages – then standing at 33/- for a 48/54 hour week – was expressed at the inaugural meeting of the Thanet Branch of the NFU at the Birchington Institute (behind today's Forbuoys shop in the Square) on Tuesday 28 May 1918. At this memorable turning-point 60 attended, H.T. Willett was elected chairman and W.J. Gardner secretary; the meeting was convened by the latter and presided over by Major Percy Powell-Cotton.[83]

Yet despite their difficulties (about which see section on farming practices below for more detail) the Thanet farmers almost certainly made good money during the war, like British farmers in general.[84] On the other hand the Thanet towns suffered considerable damage from enemy action, flight of better-off residents, and loss of holiday trade, as well as greater liability to military service, which aroused a certain urban resentment against the farmers that lingered on in some quarters into the 1930's, when the author became aware of it. The farmers themselves tended to maintain that the war had been a terrible time when they had barely managed to stay afloat, and Eric Quested, who started farming in 1919, always loyally supported this view. Such little clear information as is available locally does indicate that there was money in farming circles. The prices fetched by the Philpott's cows in 1918 are not known, but at a sale at Manston Court in November 1917 two cows each fetched 53 guineas and they averaged £40, and the horses 110 guineas, three horses reaching 122, 128 and 142 guineas respectively. The total proceeds were about £4,000.[85]

Small-holders, small poultry farmers and market gardeners were another story, and some were definitely forced out of business by the call-up, apart from having a lower safety margin in adversity. (See p 188). There was a sharp fall in the number of holdings under 50 acres between 1911 and 1918, and particularly in those under 5 acres. (Table 19).

The gentry too suffered more from the war economically as well as in terms of military service: rents were frozen and their share in the net return of agriculture in 1918 nationally was estimated by a reliable authority at 87% of 1913–14, in comparison with 115% for the farmer and 98% for the worker.[86] Probably in response to these harder times the Friends started farming three of their formerly tenanted small farms during the war: West Northdown, Omer and Holly, as well as their home farm. E.S. Linington managed them all for them.[87]

General position of the farm workers

In East Kent generally the wage rates of ordinary labourers were 15/- pw from 1898 to 1903, when they began to rise to 16/-, and in 1914 rose to 17/-.[88] But in Thanet, according to a Parliamentary Commission report, they are said to have been 17/- for all farm workers in 1905, including horsemen, cattlemen and shepherds. Horsemen were often given £4 extra at Michaelmas.[89] (See p 175). If this was true a rapid change to a more differentiated wage scale must have taken place within the next 8 years.

From 1911 until war broke out Bar Sackett was paying his ordinary labourers 16/- a week, with 4d an hour overtime and £4 bonus at harvest, but he gave no harvest supper. He employed 40–45 men, with only 10 cottages on or near the farm, so many of the men had to walk varying distances to work. Two lived in King Street, Margate, one at the Haine crossroads, the latter got home at 9 pm in summer and had to leave for work at 4.45 am. The thatcher lived at Westwood and rode to work on a tricycle. Two married waggoners who lived on the farm were paid £2 a week each, and had free cottages with free coal, potatoes and broccoli (of inferior grades). Bar also had 10-score hogs killed twice a year, and each waggoner was given half one, which he pickled. All but the waggoners paid 3/- a week rent for their cottages, but had free potatoes and broccoli too, and coal at the wholesale price Bar paid for large deliveries for the whole farm. All the farm cottages had about ¼ acre garden, allotments in a field being provided for those with too small gardens. All the cottages were two-bedroomed, the waggoners' ones alone had sittingrooms. They had earth privies, cold water taps in the kitchen and paraffin lamps. Each waggoner living on the farm had to board three bachelors (covenanted yearly servants), who slept in loft rooms over the cottages, reached by an outside stair.

The waggoner was paid £1 a week for each of these boarders, who endured "awful" conditions, no heating in their bedrooms and no washing facilities but basins of cold water in an outhouse. At Woodchurch the yearly servants at this time slept in a large unheated room over the granary reached by an outside stair.

These yearly servants, who were the fourth waggoner, the third waggoner (who lodged in a cottage close to, but not on the farm), the waggoners' mates and the groom, were paid £14–£18 each at Michaelmas; during the year they received only overtime money, but could get an advance occasionally for sound reason. The only way they could break their contract and leave was by joining the army or navy, and once in a while a naval petty officer would come to Bar to "get a man's character". There did not seem to be any instance of a man joining the army in 1911–1914 (was this a survival of the old amphibian tradition?). In keeping with their antique conditions the yearly servants were allowed an antique recreation: on Good Fridays they went by tradition to a field in Shallows Farm (off the St Peter's Road, Margate) to have fist fights, and the police turned a blind eye.

The head cowman was paid £1 a week, the second and third cowmen 18/-, the milk roundsman £1 and the foreman £1/2/-, he also had a better house with three bedrooms. The head cowman was given a pint of beer before dinner daily and 1/- for each calf born alive; the foreman's total benefits were rather mysterious.

Bar Sackett had no married yearly servants,[90] but they remained numerous enough for the special long-service award class for them to be continued in the ploughing matches until the war. (See p 190). An extant contract between O.E. Stone, farmer of Brooksend, and Troward Cowell, waggoner of Gore End, Birchington, from Michaelmas 1904 to Michaelmas 1905 provides an example of their conditions then. T. Cowell was to receive "a weekly wage of seventeen shillings, and four pounds for all extra work throughout the year. Two pence a journey for taking out corn outside Birchington. One penny per acre for mowing for beer for self and mate, payable after mowing. Working hours from 6 am till 7 pm. Three pence per acre for sharpening knives and doing all mowing required."[91] (The knives were reaper knives).

Another waggoner who was paid at least part of his wages annually was Edwin Hudson at Great Brooksend farm. After getting this annual payment he and his wife would go to Canterbury to buy Oxford striped shirting, and she would sew shirts for all the large family.[92] It looks as if married yearly servants at this time received their pay in a reverse manner to single ones: main wages weekly, and overtime and extras yearly.

Women were not employed at East Northdown then, except in the house, and this seems to have been general in Thanet,[93] and throughout the Southern counties by 1900. The Friends were unusual in having their head cowman's wife as dairywoman.[94]

The married men living in the farm cottages at East Northdown "seemed to be reasonably comfortable" provided they did not have many children or their children had flown. The head cowman had about six, most of them married, and his eldest son, the milk roundsman, ended up with 14,[95] but these seem to have been exceptions. The two married waggoners, who only had two or three each, used to go out on Sundays with their families "dressed up to the nines" and walk down to Margate Marine Parade to enjoy the whelk stalls etc. One of them wore a bowler hat on these occasions.

Fat pork was eaten daily for breakfast by the waggoners, and the rest of the men's diet is thought[96] to have been on par with that reported for Kent by the Parliamentary Committee enquiring into the conditions of agricultural labourers in 1905: "Breakfast, white bread and cheese, sometimes porridge or bread and milk. Dinner: bacon or pork, hot tea, pudding, bread and cheese.

Tea: bread and butter, cake, tea. Supper: bread, butter and cheese. Meat other than pork would be bought for Sundays."[97] The tradition of pig keeping by labourers seems to have died out in Thanet with the Napoleonic period, but pork was the cheapest meat, so the menus here were probably the same, with vegetables from the cottage gardens as well.

The relative comfort of the waggoners is suggested by the fact that when a thatched cottage in Acol, inhabited by one of Val Smith's, burnt down in 1893, the insurance company paid out £85 to replace his effects.[98] Horses and waggoners seem to have been the most treasured items on the farms, yet even a favoured waggoner could sometimes fall into disgrace. Once all of Bar's waggoners and their mates came back drunk (except for two who were teetotal) from delivering wheat to the mill in Ramsgate. One fell off his horse and broke his leg, and two young ones chased the cowmen's teenage daughters round the stackyard. The lead horses came into the yard on their own, and the head waggoner was sacked on the spot.

It seems the men did drink rather more than their masters: the head cowman at East Northdown came home singing from the Wheatsheaf nightly, but was always up sharp at 5.30 and Bar seemed satisfied with his work, the daily pint of beer at lunchtime perhaps being given to stop him going to the Wheatsheaf then. His wife took in washing, which she and her daughters did in tubs in their cramped kitchen, squatting on the floor.[99]

Those who became unemployed through sickness or accident must still at first have faced great hardship or the workhouse. There was still much poverty in the towns: the Ramsgate and Margate soup kitchens started in 1849 were still going strong up to the mid-1920's. An appeal for clothing and boots to help the ill-clad Margate elementary school children was made in the press in 1907.[100] Later that year Margate Councillor Fishwick urged that a district nurse should be appointed, as one child in nine died in its first year, "and only recently one in five."[101] – which had been worse than the St Peter's figures much earlier (see p 143).

But the introduction of small state pensions in 1909 for people over 70 at last lifted the shadow of the workhouse from the elderly farm worker who managed to reach that age. Workhouse conditions had in any case become more humane, and in 1905 none of the 514 inmates who were not in the infirmary (200) or in hospitals (71) were any longer made to work, though there was a "general feeling" amongst the Board of Guardians that some of them should.[102] Charity continued to be at least intermittently generous. Queen Victoria's Diamond Jubilee was marked by meals for the labouring class at Cleve Court farm (G.M. Goodson, farmer and auctioneer), Minster Court, the Champion farm at Sarre (for 60), St Nicholas Court, Monkton Court, and Birchington Hall (Mrs Grey). (It was on the site of the Birchill estate).[103] At St Peter's all the labourers' children and people over 60 were taken in a huge procession of waggons and brakes and given "a splendid tea" and a medal and 1/- each.[104] Later, in 1915, a subscription of £34/8/3½ was raised for the widow of a Thorne farm labourer killed by a falling tree.[105]

1,323 Thanet names are recorded on the war memorials and rolls of honour as having died on active service in World War One, plus 40 civilians and five who perished in the Allied intervention in the Russian civil war of 1919–20.[106] There may even have been more than that, and it is certain that a significant proportion of the servicemen who died must have come from the families of agricultural workers, particularly in the villages. Amongst many, one may note Private Garlinge, son of a worker on Monkton

Road farm, who won the DCM and was killed,[107] Private Steed of Bromstone farm who won the MM and was recommended for the DCM,[108] George Kemp, foreman at Woodchurch farm 1914–1934, who had three sons in the forces and lost one.[109] One of the early casualties was 18-year-old ex-farm worker Herbert Woodland of Acol, lost with HMS Hawke in October 1914;[110] one of the last 19-year-old William Halliday from East Northdown farm (whose father was pigman there), killed towards the end of October 1918 after only enlisting on 23 May 1918.[111] Fourteen of Bar Sackett's men had enlisted by March 1915,[112] but the response varied somewhat from place to place, though Thanet was little affected by the great draft evasion movement centred on Folkestone and Hythe which was uncovered in 1916–17.[113]

Little local information is available about the impact of the rises in wages and prices during the war. The Corn Production Act of 1917 for the first time in British history laid down a minimum agricultural wage of 25/-, with subsequent annual rises by Act of Parliament until 1921, but it was reported from Kent that those with young families probably lost more by rising prices than they gained from higher wages. Conversely those with grown children who could earn must have benefitted.[114] The work of the Food Controllers in Thanet was praised on the whole but at Birchington in July 1918 prices had run out of control and the poor could not afford them.[115]

A handful of farmers kept the fading harvest supper tradition alive through the war. Ben Offen of Cheeseman's farm, Thos. Jarman of Acol farm and ? Setterfield of Acol Hill farm clubbed together to give one at the Acorn Inn, Birchington, though by 1918 "no joints could be provided", but only "some food".[116]

"After the long-drawn hideous nightmare of over four years . . ." as the *Kentish Gazette* editor without exaggeration put it, the Armistice was marked by processions of wounded soldiers through the flag-decked towns, the churches decorated with flowers and kept open all day, and coloured lights dropped from planes over Minster and St Nicholas. It was very different from 1814, for the suffering had been so much greater. Apart from entertainment of children at Quex Park, and a childrens' party at Minster organized by farmer C.F. Kennett in mid-January 1919[117] there were no specifically rural festivities: the patriarchal era was ending, and the mood was not jubilant.

Soon after the farmers formed the NFU branch, some of the men began to take an interest in the NUAW. Some at East Northdown joined towards the end of the war[118] but no branch was officially set up till 1919.[119]

Farming practices

As Tables 18 and 19 show, there was a rise in the number of holdings to 375 in 1901, which might be considered still in the trough of depression, but thereafter began a steady fall that has continued to the latest figures available in 1988. So John Mockett's forecast of partition of holdings, made in 1835,[120] worked itself out, and was followed by another tide of engrossment, mightier than any seen before. The fall in holding numbers in the 1900's may reflect somewhat improved prosperity of the successful farmers, but equally suggests decreased interest in farming in the population. The number of farms over 300 acres did not vary much to 1945, nor the general pattern of farm size. Though hops enjoyed a brief comeback around 1899–1901 and remained profitable on a few farms in Minster and Monkton, livestock was the main support in the years of low corn prices. Working agricultural horses, with a few breeding mares, stayed at nearly 900 to 1911, and cows and heifers in milk or in calf, reached their highest yet decennial maximum then. Sheep declined but recovered their numbers again by 1911, pigs increased over the late 19th century and almost regained their 1867 figure. Poultry were not mentioned in the agricultural returns, even though their numbers had clearly risen. There were 250 Minorcas at Drapers farm in 1904. (See note 149).

Markedly less wheat and barley was grown than in the previous period, and only a few farmers as yet grew broccoli besides Bar Sackett. It was very labour intensive apart from requiring fresh know-how. Fodder crops showed a steady increase as to be expected, but nut trees disappeared from the agricultural returns by 1901, when only onions were added to them. By 1916 nine kinds of table vegetables were shown, but in the pre-World War One returns broccoli were concealed under the heading "other green crops". Tables 21 and 23 show the acreage of the principal crops and livestock numbers.

Around 1901 there was a rise in the amount of fallow, and the returns of that year show a fall of over 1,000 acres in the amount of land under crops and grass. This seems to have been due to the abandonment of the poor high land in the centre of the island, where the aerodrome and the Woodchurch ridge houses, stables and kennels etc. now are. Low returns from this thin soil led to plans to create extensive housing estates from Nash Lane, to Lydden to Pouces: Vincent Farm estate, Kent Park estates (later Queensdown Estate) on the Woodchurch ridge, Manston or Alexandra Park Estate on the site of Pouces Farm and the later aerodrome. Around 1900 agents of Messrs. Payne and Thorp came to Margate to inaugurate these schemes, but the take-up was slow, and they had created nothing more than the settlements at Flete and Lydden by 1916, when a large number of plots which had been sold but never built on were bought up by the War Office to make Manston airfield.

One of Payne and Thorp's agents, Alfred Fife, a young Scot, took over Vincent's farm as the estate agency business did not prosper. He may have been the second or third of the group of enterprising Scots who came to Thanet before or soon after the First World War.[121] The first may have been Bill Craig Smith, who took Chamber's Wall and Downbarton farms in the late 1880's or early 90's, bringing all his live and deadstock by train from Scotland. On arrival at Birchington station the cattle were driven on foot to their new home, and Mrs Smith milked the cows in Birchington Square.[122]

Some of the abandoned land, failing to be bought for building, appears to have been converted back to sheep-walk by 1911,[123] when the area under crops and grass had risen again by 771.5 acres, despite urban development and the construction of the four golf courses – the North Foreland, St Augustine's, Westgate and Birchington and Hengrove or Margate. This last was the largest, 150 acres, opened in 1901. The four courses together took over 300 acres.[124]

Apart from market gardens and small pig or poultry farms, all farms were mixed, even those with a good deal of fruit or hops in the Minster-Monkton sheltered zone. Many upland farmers rented marshland and kept sheep; Bar Sackett did not, but in other respects probably farmed in a typical manner, though some younger and better educated men would have been more progressive. Bar was 70 in 1914 and probably educated at the National School at St Peter's. At the height of his operations (c 1900 – 1904) he with his two sons occupied four farms: East Northdown with Yorkshire farm as one unit, Chilton and Woodchurch. He sold Chilton and bought Reading Street farm in 1904, and sold Reading

Street in 1911.[125] He was a true entrepreneur – "everything he touched turned to money" – and patriarch, and like all capable farmers, patrolled his land constantly, driving himself in a trap, in wet weather holding in one hand a huge heavy trap umbrella, covering the whole vehicle. Later his grandson held it for him.

Wheat and barley were his main crops, with mangolds, lucerne and clover for the stock, and forty acres of broccoli, grown after potatoes or wheat, in 1911–14. At Woodchurch in 1910 white turnips (4 acres), tares (8), red clover (3) and peas (14) were also grown, so these crops may have featured at East Northdown as well.[126] Fertilizer was mainly good farmyard manure, but Bar used a patent barley manure from Mockett and Thorp, corn factors of Margate, as a top dressing for his barley in spring, and put nitrate of soda on his cauliflower and broccoli. Superphosphates were introduced into Thanet in this period: a prize was given by Odam's Manure & Chemical Co for samples of roots grown with their brand from the 1907 ploughing match on.[127]

There were about 50 "home-bred" cows, mostly Shorthorn type, and one Shorthorn bull (not pedigree) at East Northdown in 1911–1914. A cow was expected to give 600 gallons per lactation, if not was sold fat to Hancock the butcher in Charlotte Square, Margate. There were "about 20 steers" fattening in the yard at any one time, and a breeding herd of "40" Large White sows; the porkers were sold at 10 score to Knightons in Margate Market Place. Fowls were kept in large runs with morello cherry trees growing in them, with thatched, earth-floored wooden houses for roosting, laying and shelter. One section was purposely kept tremendously dusty, to the delight of the hens, which could enjoy dust baths all year round. The droppings were removed from beneath the perches at intervals, but otherwise the houses were never cleaned. If the ratio of birds to run size was right, the hens kept remarkably healthy, especially if given fresh lawn mowings and green weeds such as dandelion and sowthistle.[128] Milk, eggs and cherries were sold in Cliftonville by three milk roundsmen operating three milk chariots drawn by cobs. In 1912 milk was sold for 2d a pint from these open-back chariots, each with two 17-gallon churns in front.[129]

Bar kept four teams of four horses and three odd horses at East Northdown. Stock at Woodchurch, and Reading Street were similar, though fewer, and at Reading Street, where there was a small pond, there were a pair of geese, eight ducks and two drakes as well.[130]

Wooden turnwrest ploughs were still used for some operations as well as Davey Sleep iron ploughs, which had replaced the old double-furrowed iron ploughs by 1911.[131] There was a 3½ hp. Detroit paraffin engine, with chaff-cutting and root-pulping attachments. Possibly during the war Bar acquired several types of potato implements: a Gooch prime potato sorter, a Ransome digger and a Pierce sprayer.[132]

All the produce except the brassicas was sold locally, and as many as eight pair-horse waggons would take the wheat to Hudson's steam mills in Ramsgate and the barley to Cobb's brewery in Margate. The cauliflowers and broccoli were sent to Covent Garden by train, packed 3½ – 4 dozen to a "Cornish" crate, (a kind of tall basket with a lid), 32 crates to a pair-horse waggon. Sometimes eight pair-horse waggons and two small carts drawn by cobs as well would proceed down to the old Margate Sands station (where Dreamland now is). The stately processions of waggons with their fine black horses were quite impressive,[133] and no doubt similar processions made their way with produce from all the big farms in Thanet.

Railway charges remained a thorn in the flesh of the farmers. In 1893 charges were raised to an average of 30/- a ton, leading to a nationwide protest by farmers, and the re-establishment of a hoy company in Thanet, plying from Margate to London. Farmers attended the foundation meetings in Margate and Broadstairs, and at the latter a Mr Nicholas said the new charges would raise the carriage of his broccoli alone by £100, and with turnips etc. by £160. The railway companies reduced their charges again fairly soon, but the hoy company declared a 10% dividend the following year and remained in operation until 1914, although it is not known if farmers or corn merchants made any use of it.[134]

Later, in 1905, the rates were again said to be much too high, being then as follows: Small parcels of fruit and market garden produce irrespective of distance went at a reduced rate of 4d for 20lbs and 1d for each 5lbs more up to 3cwt. From Margate, larger quantities of broccoli and vegetables went at 12/9d per ton for 3 cwt to 1 ton, and 13/9d for 1–2 tons; fruit at varying rates 17/2d–28/11d. From Ramsgate town and harbour stations broccoli and vegetables paid the same as Margate, fruit 16/9d–28/2d. From Birchington prices were more diverse: vegetables 9/8d–16/9d, fruit 16/9d–28/2d. From Minster, vegetables 10/–17/2d, fruit 17/2d–28/11d. Potatoes went for 10/2d–17/9d from Ramsgate and 10/2d–17/1d from Minster. These charges were the subject of an official enquiry.[135] D.J. Hall considered them still much too high in 1910,[136] but the subsequent position is not known. Bar Sackett evidently found them tolerable enough.

Until 1918 farm implements in Thanet continued basically the same as in the previous period, with the exception of the potato devices. The stationary oil engine, described as the major innovation of 1890–1900,[137] could not be found in any Thanet farm sale announcement until after the First World War, although specimens must have been installed here much earlier. Threshing was universally done by steam, with locally-hired machines. In 1893 the Thanet Steam Machinery Department at Dent-de-Lion was supplying them,[138] but seems not to have lasted long. Oliver & Addis, agricultural merchants of Eaton Road, Margate, were doing much threshing locally until after the war.[139] In the 1890's the threshing was still often not done straight off as in later times, but a month here and a month there. Val Smith was threshing in March 1893.[140] Later, in 1911–1914, Bar Sackett had his done in three weeks.[141] The increasing power of the machines probably enabled the process to be speeded up, but no local details are available. Steam ploughs, cultivators and road rollers were also hired out by these firms. Some farmers owned their own threshing machines, as well as steam engines as in earlier times – when W.H. Pettman left Sackett's Hill farm in 1905 he sold 8 horses, 2 cows, a Clayton and Shuttleworth thresher and "a 4 hp portable steam engine by MARSHALL & SONS" (capitals sic) – evidently a gem.[142]

It seems that the main thrust of advance was in the field of improved and pedigree livestock and cleaner milk production. Traditional dairying as at East Northdown was hardly hygienic: the cows wintered in a cow stable where they were also milked, and the head cowman was "always covered in cow dung and looked as if he did not wash much"; he was not expected to. He had been 27 years with Bar by 1914.[143] The milk used in farmhouses seems not usually to have been boiled at any date, then or later, and at East Northdown was fetched from the dairy in uncovered jugs.[144]

Bigger milk producers like G.K. Burge (Hengrove and later Dent-de-Lion) were much more advanced before the 19th century had ended. "A practical demonstration of sterilizing milk" was held at Dent-de-Lion on 10 May 1897,[145] all his milk being sold sterilized from then on.[146] Presumably it was a kind of pasteurization. Burge moved to Dent-de-Lion when A.S. Padley sold out there in 1895, and although he held a sale of all the live and dead stock at Hengrove the following year[147] he continued to farm the land (600 acres in the two farms) and run the dairy there until 1899, when the dairy passed to F.J. Mason.[148] The dairies at both Dent-de-Lion and Hengrove were said to be "kept with the strictest cleanliness and good order, with all the latest modern appliances for cooling, separating, churning and management." Burge "even had both farms connected to the mains of the Margate waterworks, to ensure clean water for the cows to drink," and the cowsheds were "spacious, well-drained and well-ventilated". The 70 short-horns were under the supervision of E.L. Dixson MRCVS, Thanet's current qualified professional vet. Mason continued to use Dixson's services and presumably ran the Hengrove dairy on Burge's lines.[149] There was even some TT (tuberculin tested) milk on sale in Margate as early as 1912, but no details are available.[150]

From sometime in this period, as herd sizes rose, the practice of wintering cows in partially-covered straw-filled yards became commoner. It was started at Woodchurch, for instance, during the war, probably to save labour. Part of the barn there was used as shelter for the cows in the main yard, which previously had been used for bullocks, a new yard having been made some years earlier for the young stock.[151] The winter yarding practice was being advocated in the Kent NFU Journal in 1927,[152] which shows Thanet in a progressive light.

Considerable use of corrugated iron roofing was made at this time: at Woodchurch it was used to re-roof many buildings, and even the four-roomed worker's bungalow built in the 1870's.[153]

The Collard flock of Romney Marsh sheep, founded in 1867, was possibly the first Thanet flock to be registered with a breed society, in 1897 by F. de B. Collard.[154] The movement continued during the war: in October 1915 G.K. Burge sold his shorthorns to make way for pedigree stock,[155] and H.T. Willett was selling pedigree sheep (Kent and Southdowns) from Sarre Court in 1916.[156]

Val Smith's son H.A. started his own breed of Thanet Down sheep in 1912, by crossing Kent ewes with Southdown rams. Later by use of Suffolk rams it became more of a Suffolk-Southdown cross. It provided a neat carcass of mutton larger than the South-down and well let down in the breach, with excellent fleeces. The breed continued successfully in the family until they gave up livestock in the 1970's.[157]

From the late 19th century to the mid-1920's Thanet was briefly a centre of horse breeding. Between 1897 and 1907 Val Smith was in partnership with Sir William Ingram (who owned the *Illustrated London News* and lived at Rowena Court, Westgate) to breed racehorses at Monkton Court. They had 36 there at one period; horses were bred and broken in at Monkton, then sent to Newbury for training at two years. These animals and those of the Down-barton Stud Co, at St Nicholas (Captain S.M. Smith) and the carthorses bred by H.T. Willett at Monkton Parsonage farm as well as F. de B. Collard at Minster Abbey won prizes at the East Kent agricultural shows and East Kent horse shows.[158] The war slightly boosted the breeding of carthorses: 45 mares were being covered in 1916, and 48 in 1918. (See Table 21).

Though the Thanet farmers did not have to sacrifice very many of their sons, they may have lost a good many of their beloved carthorses, taken to pull Army waggons and the heavy guns for the Western Front. Agricultural horse numbers stood at 898 in 1901, were still 888 in 1911 but fell to 641 in 1916, and as breeding mares were included in the totals, not all these would have been working (Table 21). A team of Bar Sackett's was requisitioned in the field four days after war broke out in 1914 by a Major Harris, R.E.K.Y., whose name was mud in the family thereafter. The fall in horse numbers over all England was only 12.4%,[159] but the working life of a horse on heavy farm duties in Thanet, on the larger farms at least, was only about 7–8 years (from about 4 to about 11 years old), after which they were sold or switched to light work, such as hoeing row crops, or on very affluent farms even put out to grass.[160] So some 50% of the horses on large farms would normally have left work over a four year period anyway, and it is uncertain how far the decline in numbers was due to the army and how far to replacement difficulties. Research in the horse breeding areas would be needed to solve this problem, but the 9.4% rise in numbers by 1918 suggested that local breeding had stemmed the fall. Other livestock fell by marked percentages too, though fattening steers seem to have increased in the first two years and pig-breeding began to recover in the last two. (Horses on loan to farmers from the War Agricultural Committee were not included).

Arable production held up well, and fruit likewise, with official encouragement,[161] though the area under crops and grass fell slightly by 1916, and dropped by no less than 1,798 acres between 1916 and 1918 (Table 17), for which the only explanation seems to be abandonment, sale of land for building and its requisitioning for the aerodrome and the railway from it to Minnis Bay. In June 1917 the Thanet sub-committee of the Kent War Agricultural Committee started up, the secretary was Charles Taylor, but the

Table 13: Livestock decline in World War One[162]

	Cart-horses	Other horses	Cows & heifers	Other cattle	Ewes	Other sheep	Sows	Other pigs
A. 1911=100								
1916	72.2	61	87	111	78	86	73.2	86.1
B. 1916=100								
1918	79	82	91.2	99	73	94	111.7	77

astute and energetic corn merchant W.J. Gardner supervised the ploughing orders and labour supply and issued advice from his home in Birchington.[163] In July it was announced that 1,700 acres of grassland should be ploughed up in Thanet over that in cultivation in 1915,[164] but in fact only 644 acres of grass had been brought under the plough by November 1918.[165] W.J. Gardner took over cultivation of the grassland or wasteland on the Woodchurch ridge, part of the Hengrove golf links and some at least of the central building estate land not taken by the aerodrome. The poor land in the centre of the island seems to have been abandoned in face of labour and horse shortages, even if not taken for the aerodrome, and in the face of official opposition too. Abandonment was also attributed to the attempt to develop housing estates in central rural Thanet. A.E.G. Solly of Manston told the Canterbury Farmers' Club that land had gone out of cultivation because "it had been sold over and over again till they did not know who it belonged to".[166]

Protests were made at the ploughing up policy at the inaugural NFU rally at Maidstone in July 1918,[167] but the struggle to get this land ploughed up continued until the winding up of the KWAC in 1921. By 31 December 1918 69 compulsory ploughing orders had been issued in Thanet, but the total ploughed up still stood at only 777 acres and 1,164 acres remained to be done. Thanet had the fourth lowest scheduled acreage for ploughing up, the second lowest number of compulsory orders, but the lowest compliance rate in East Kent.[168] When the KWAC came to an end early in 1921 W.J. Gardner was still farming 238 acres for it: 75 acres on the Vincent Park estate, 20 acres on the Queensdown estate, 97 acres on the Alexandra Park estate and 46 acres on the Hengrove golf links, which had re-opened on about 100 acres soon after the Armistice.[169] The agricultural returns for 1921 showed a further fall in the area under crops and grass to 19,784½ acres (Table 17), and in the 1920's most of the area of the Woodchurch ridge, almost from Cheeseman's farm to the Hengrove golf links, was unused rough grass, increasingly occupied by small-holders and a few private houses.[170]

Some of the hardest labour shortage stories came from 1915 and 1916, especially after the start of conscription in March 1916: for instance only one married waggoner to help the farmer on a 100-acre farm with four horses at Monkton in December 1916.[171] In February 1916 the KWAC reported that in Thanet it was almost impossible to get skilled labour,[172] but soldiers were at work on Thanet farms by April that year and continued to be available for the rest of the war – presumably men not fit for the front.[173] The employment of farmers' own womenfolk was mentioned in March, and working women on farms in Birchington were reported as a novelty in May.[174] Female labour was mainly used for the harvest in Minster,[175] and the Vicar's wife, Mrs Molyneaux, began keeping a register of women wanting land work.[176] In September many Minster and Monkton women and children were hopping, "no amateur labour" being needed.[177] Many hoppers had probably always been local; back in September 1897 waggons were taking them from Birchington to Monkton between 5 and 6 am.[178] From June 1917 by arrangement with the War Office no more Thanet men in full-time agricultural employment were to be called up,[179] but a few were still taken after that. As late as 11 May 1918 a cowman and milk roundsman of a Minster farmer with 100 cows in milk and 328 acres and a cowman from Monkton were given exemption only till 6 August and ordered to the army immediately if substitutes could be found.[180] In any case the June 1917 agreement did not apply to small-holders, but only to workers. The impression gained from the press and what one heard in the inter-war years was that those with social clout, once they had let their single men go, generally managed to hold onto their married men, whilst the small-holders, market gardeners and some agrarian tradesmen were more harshly treated by the Military Tribunals, whose hand fell somewhat unevenly at times. The Thanet Rural Military Tribunal included several farmers (William Broadley, A.E.G. Solly etc.),[181] It is not known what the children of these Tribunal members did in the war, but the heir of the chairman of the East Kent Appeals Tribunal, the 4th Lord Harris of Belmont, won the M.C. on the Western Front.[182]

As stated, fourteen single men had enlisted from East Northdown by March 1915 (one can imagine Bar Sackett urging them to), but a Monkton farmer admitted that not one of his 22 hands were serving in April 1916, yet was allowed exemption for a waggoner.[183] In March 1916 a married Garlinge poultry farmer of 36 was refused exemption.[184] In July 1916 a 26-year-old market gardener with four brothers in the army had his appeal against conscription dismissed[185] and in November a married Minster pig-farmer of 29 the same.[186] In July 1917 a Birchington smallholder, married and category B2, was given only two months' exemption,[187] and in June a Garlinge wheelwright, implement maker and repairer, all of whose 22 employees had enlisted, was given only three months' exemption for his only son of 33, and the military representative on the tribunal objected to that.[188] A St Nicholas market gardener was given only two months to wind up his business in June 1918.[189] There was a desperate demand for men to sustain the war, and the value and efficiency of the respective agricultural enterprises must rightly have influenced the tribunals, but in the light of the foregoing cases one does wonder that a single head gardener looking after three acres of land "of a Margate lady" was not brought before a tribunal till September 1917 and then given three months' exemption.[190]

Not till June 1918 was it reported that one or two farmers, notably at Birchington, were using Land Army women[191] and they were also mentioned at Minster in September.[192] In mid-June the editor of the Isle of Thanet Gazette expressed the view that "it may be that Thanet has not suffered by the withdrawal of labour so much as some other districts, but it is affected", and advised the use of women, school-boys and part-time harvest labour.[193]

W.J. Gardner and his Thanet sub-committee of the KWAC were very active, lending horses at 12/- a day,[194] organizing the sharing of horse and knapsack potato sprayers using sulphate of copper (against "wart disease"),[195] hiring out a steam plough,[196] arranging the supply of seed wheat[197] and artificial manures (superphosphates, basic slag and sulphate of ammonia),[198] and by October, hiring out the first tractors, at 20/- per acre, soon raised to 26/-.[199] Threshing machines and teams of threshers were also hired out, at £3 per day, the team consisting of a driver, feeder and five women,[200] (no mention if they were W.L.A.)

Chemical, mechanized farming received an impetus from the war. When the fixed price for oats was announced in December 1916, the Government made this conditional on the use of artificial manures to the value of at least 25/- per acre.[201] The Thanet Sub-

Committee of the KWAC furthered their use, as noted. Within a couple of months of W.J. Gardner's offering of tractors for hire, a demonstration of a Wallis Junior was held at Monkton Road farm, Birchington, (A.W. Miller) to a large audience,[202] and in June 1918 Percy Mosely of West Bay Garage, Westgate, was taking orders for Fordsons at £250 plus delivery charges,[203] to be followed in three weeks by Oliver & Addis of Margate.[204] John Brockman claimed to have been the first Thanet farmer to purchase one and drove it himself.[205] The first tractors had been in use on British farms in 1902,[206] so Thanet was (characteristically in its post-18th century guise) quite conservative in experimenting with them. Widespread adoption was not to come for another 20 years, but the unreliability of the early tractors was the main retarding factor.

The Ploughing Match

In 1894 the last match before the abandonment was marked by excellent ploughing, and instead of a dinner by an exceptionally "sumptuous" lunch supplied by the West End Restaurant, Margate, in G.K. Burge's barn at Dent-de-Lion, decorated with bunting and a large quantity of chrysanthemums. There were a reduced number of toasts, but the whole afternoon was spent in speeches and songs by the farmers. The Society was said to be flourishing,[207] but the match was not held again for nine years.

It was restarted in 1903 on the initiative of Gerald Powell-Cotton (brother of Percy), who with two wealthy Thanet businessmen, F.M. Cobb and H.H. Marks, acted as financial guarantors, the farmers being afraid to risk their money. In the event the match paid for itself,[208] and thereafter the farmers themselves took responsibility for it again, running it successfully until the war put an end to it in 1914. In these years it was businesslike and low-key, though Lord Decies gave out the prizes in 1904.

A dinner was held only in the first year, in the Birchington public hall (apparently where the church hall now is), at which the M.P. James Lowther spoke, but "the waiters were making so much noise clearing the tables that he could not be heard" – evidently the acoustics were poor. There was only one toast, to the King and Royal Family.[209] A substantial lunch was provided in a barn at each match: the farmers sat at trestle tables and could have unlimited helpings for (2/6d?) – from great joints of beef, pork and lamb, with hot potatoes, all kinds of pickles, cheese and biscuits and cask beer. The competitors were given a pork pie each after the match,[210] which may have been a new departure or might have been started in the 1888 – 1894 incarnation of the match.

Though the social side was quiet, the matches, usually held in November, were strong on agricultural skills and were said to attract large crowds, but no estimate of numbers was ever given and the reporting became increasingly brief towards 1914. The number of ploughs entered was not large, the lowest being 36 in 1910 and the highest 45 in 1912.

There were the usual classes for 4,3 and 2-horse Kent or iron ploughs, the Kent ones being reduced to one class in 1912. The first prize for the four horse iron plough class was always £2, but at first the champion got £3, reduced to £1 in 1906 and raised again to £2 in 1910. There were also prizes for the best stable management, the best 4-horse team, sheep rearing and wintering (three flock-size classes in each of these categories at first and five by 1907), cowmen's work (two classes from 1907), and stacking and thatching (three classes for each by 1907). In 1903 and 1904 the old prizes for raising children without parish relief returned, Stephen Shonk being rewarded in 1903 for raising 12 out of 20 children. But this class was dropped after 1904, for it was evidently felt that large families were not to be encouraged now. Both married and single yearly servants were rewarded; one of the former had done 26 years in 1903.

Heralding things to come, the number of classes for the farmers themselves grew larger. As well as red and white wheat, barley and white and black oats, a malting barley class was introduced in 1911. By 1905 there were 16 root classes, but six had no entries, so they were reduced, and from 1910 there were prizes for four fields and six collections of roots. A typical prize-winning collection included kohl-rabi, wurzels, swedes, white turnips, "white" carrots, cabbage and thousand-headed kale.

The Committee and guests of honour sat in a waggon, from which the prizes were distributed on the field.[211]

This period was a chastening one for Thanet farmers, which saw them at perhaps their lowest ebb in recent times. Comparisons with anything before the Napoleonic wars are difficult to make yet, but there is obviously a great difference between the farmers of the 1830's quaffing good wine with titled men at the ploughing match dinners, and the farmers of 1903 – 1914 at the ploughing match barn lunches. The fortunes of Thanet itself played a part in this, and perhaps to some extent perceptions of what was fitting in a farmer's lifestyle; it would be interesting, if it could be done, to analyse the real economic position of individuals at various times. Whatever the exact situation in the early 20th century, the war of 1914 – 1918 for all its tragedy brought the farming industry back into the public eye and gave it an improved income, which those who were able to remain in it were to retain with relatively brief interludes until the latest times.

Chapter Nine: From the Armistice to Victory in 1945

General Position of the farmers

Thanet branch supported the 13-point programme of the Kent County NFU in December 1918, which ran as follows: 1) Raise the status of agriculture so that fair wages can be paid 2) Security of tenure 3) Decent cottages and clubs and institutions for men and women 4) Revision of local tax and rating 5) Revision and reduction of tithe rent charges and abolition of manorial rights 6) Revision of railway and canal charges 7) More facilities for agricultural education and research 8) Nationalization of all trunk roads 9) Revision of trespass and game laws 10) Better credit facilities and state aid of up to ¾ value of property at reasonable interest for farmers to buy their holdings 11) A central market in London 12) Regulation of foreign supplies 13) Measures to stop bad cultivation of land and development of agriculture to the utmost. Although the Conservative M.P. Norman Craig was sympathetic only to items 6, 8, 11 and 12, all but 6, the second part of 10 and 11 had been largely achieved in one way or another by 1939, mainly as a result of the resurgent German threat.[1] This was a period of great agrarian progress, as well as of the great crisis of 1931 which Thanet weathered better than many places.

1919 and 1920 saw steadily rising prices, nationally reaching three times 1911–1913 by September 1920, so that "no farmer could help making profits".[2] Therefore it was not hard times but the dammed-up need for personal changes which produced the spate of sales in 1919, when there were eleven, starting from April.[3] In April 1919 wheat at Canterbury market was 71/11, barley 61/6 and oats 44/1 per quarter,[4] but the Ramsgate food committee in May fixed milk prices at 2/4d per gallon and 3½d per pint,[5] showing that dairying were doing less well than corn. By January 1920 wheat at Canterbury market was 75/6, good malting barley 125–130/- and good black oats 64–65/-.[6] Discontent over milk prices led five leading Thanet farmers (H.T. Willett, Captain J.I.H. Friend, H.A. Smith, E.S. Linington and Ernest Philpott) to dispute the flat rate price with representatives of the NFU Central Milk Committee at Ashford in June 1919 – apparently without result.[7]

The Kent NFU again held protest rallies at Maidstone against prices and wages in June 1919 and January 1921.[8] Worry about high wages was expressed again by the farmers in February 1920,[9] but price control over meat and fat stock was abandoned in December 1919, and on dairy products in February 1920, so there was no protest rally that year. But during the winter of 1920/21 prices drifted down, falling precipitately from spring 1921, especially after the repeal of the Corn Production Act in August 1921 removed price support for corn, "so that no farmer could avoid making losses." The fall continued until autumn 1922, and by the end of 1922 price levels nationally were 157% of 1911–13, and cereal prices barely 33% above it, barley and potatoes being at times below.[10]

Yet regular annual Thanet NFU dinners from January 1920 took the place of the old ploughing match ones stopped after 1893, a sign that better times had returned. In 1920 at the St George's Hotel, Cliftonville, they had Whitstable oysters, two soups, sole, mutton and roast pheasant, though a rather meagre dessert assortment of creme caramel, fruit compote and Welsh rarebit.[11] In January 1921 the visiting County chairman called Thanet "a land flowing with milk and honey"; by the 1922 dinner at the Bungalow Hotel, Birchington (a pleasant but less grand setting) he thought "there was still plenty of milk, but he was a little doubtful about the honey!" However, 80 farmers were present then and there were at least six toasts.[12] In October that year at J.W. Smith & Sons annual sale the 58 non-pedigree Friesians averaged £37/3/6 (even up to 9th calvers), and a bull calf fetched 50 guineas – described as good business for the times.[13]

From authumn 1922 there was a period of price stability, though the return to the Gold Standard in 1924 started a further slow decline. 118 farmers attended the 1923 dinner;[14] the 1924 one was not reported, but in 1925, when 72 attended, Mr T. Hume, a visitor from the Canterbury branch, remarked that the Thanet members did not look depressed, the barley was a help to them, and the visitors.[15] In the early 1920's Thanet barley had suddenly become world famous, with the first in a series of championships being won in 1921 (see p 222), and consequent benefits for its sale. Meanwhile the towns continued to blossom as holiday resorts and fashionable places of residence, needing plenty of milk, eggs, vegetables and meat. In 1926 the Kent County Agricultural Show was held in Margate.

By 1927 average national prices were 144% of 1911–13, but this did not all go against the farmer: feed prices including oil cake fell in 1926 to 25% over 1911–13. Animal feed prices remained generally below average, so livestock husbandry was likely to be more profitable than cereal at this point.[16] Captain Friend in his speech to the 1927 N.F.U. dinner guests at the St George's said that Thanet farmers ought to thank God they lived in a district which practically had not a bad acre. Anyone who chose to work on it could make an honest living. The dinner included a musical programme "with special artistes".[17]

At the 1928 dinner at the Beresford Hotel, Birchington (another very good hotel), Captain Hatfeild said that agriculture had gone from bad to worse since the last year's event, but the Kent County Vice-chairman, J. Hillier French, when replying to the visitors' toast, said there were very few farmers with cheerful faces, "and one has to come to Thanet to find them."[18] In 1929, when the Great Depression had already begun, Captain Friend told the assembly at the Granville Hotel, Ramsgate, that "Thanet farmers were in the land of Goschen", and a solid silver tea service and tray were presented to W.J. Gardner for his great services as secretary to the local branch.[19]

Only in 1930 was there at last no suggestion in the speeches at least that Thanet was blessed. Eric Quested in the first speech at the dinner complained that agriculture had statutory obligations to the worker but no security of markets, and called for an import board, with guaranteed prices for the farmer and the development of a cartel system to share the market between the Empire, home farmers and foreign countries. E.S. Linington called on the government to support agriculture, which was the country's second line of defence after the navy.[20] It is plain from all the speeches of the inter-war period that Thanet farmers as a whole were solidly behind Churchill's thought on foreign policy. The 1931 dinner took place as usual, and was "as thoroughly convivial as any that have been held under the auspices of the" (Thanet) "branch". E.S. Linington strongly criticized the Labour government's Agricultural Marketing and Land Utilization Bills, but said that if he could see a single ray of hope he would support any party, socialist, conservative or liberal, which would help agriculture – strong words from a Thanet farmer. Eric Quested called attention, as he had the previous year, to the efforts being made in France, Italy and Germany to help farmers there, and said that he had written to the leader of the Conservative party, who had replied that he would guarantee a price for wheat if returned to power. The ever-cheerful Captain Friend pointed out that Thanet farmers were lucky to have an outlet for their milk, as he had heard of one getting 9d a gallon.[21] In fact, the Thanet farmers were getting 1/6d a gallon until 1 April 1931, when it dropped to 1/2d.[22]

The steady fall in agricultural prices since 1924 had quickened from 1929: 144% over 1913 in 1929, 134 in 1930, 120 in 1931.[23] Yet in the summer of that year H.A. Smith, then chairman of the Thanet NFU, was interviewed for the *Kent Messenger* and asked if Thanet farmers were paying their way. "He looked dubious when it was suggested that farmers were doing comparitively well in his district, but agreed that they were weathering the storm better than some, probably because of their adaptability and the advantages of the local market. 'The land here is farmed well', he said."[24]

By the winter things were worse. That was the only time before he retired when the author can remember that her father was really short of money. Her headmistresses had to be given two successive sacks of potatoes, as well as (if memory serves) cauli-flowers, as earnest that her private school fees would eventually be paid. The car was partly laid up, and she was taken to school in the milk lorry, which was parked a discreet distance from the school gates. But within a few months the fees were paid and the car in full use again. Eric Quested was in easier circumstances than many smaller farmers, having 250 acres, only one child and a wife with some money of her own, but his case was certainly not exceptional. Most of the larger farmers had probably always enjoyed some extra-agricultural benefits. Some had wives with keen business talents, which the author's mother lacked, and the smaller farmers did not feel the onus to send their children to private schools. When William Broadley of St Nicholas Court died in November 1932, he left £14,832,[25] evidently felt to be noteworthy since it was reported in the local paper.

Yet the situation remained serious for some years, and was particularly hard for those starting up. H.M. Steed (son of P.W.) returned from managing a 1000 acre farm in Kenya in 1933 and took over Drapers' farm: his daughter recalls her mother telling her that the family lived basically on soup of veal bones (cheap or free) and vegetables for a few years.[26]

The ploughing match was cancelled in 1931 and not held again until 1946, and the NFU dinner disappeared until 1937. In the winter of 1932–33 livestock prices collapsed, but malting barley at least covered its costs, so Thanet was again lucky. Then having reached 112% of 1911–13 in 1932 and 107 in 1933, prices began to rally and had returned to 133% of 1913 in 1938. Recovery came with a turn of the tide that was in retrospect dramatic. The devaluation of sterling and the progressive application of duties on food imports by the National government of 1931 checked the crisis; the Labour government's agricultural legislation that had so much incensed E.S. Linington was repealed, and the Wheat Quota Act of 1932 began 40 years of government assistance for farmers, later continued by the E.U. Hitler's advent to power in 1933 set the seal on the new policy and meant that the farmers could now rely on government support, even if for some years it was not nearly as much as they wanted. (Thus, when barley prices collapsed in 1938 due to over-production, the subsidy was doubled). The second Marketing Act of 1933 led to the successful establishment of the Milk Marketing Board (1933) and the Potato Marketing Board (1934), and the less successful Pig Marketing Board (1933). The Hop Marketing Board, of importance to only a few farmers here, had been set up in 1931 under the first Act.[27]

The farmers were even largely relieved of the tithe redemption problem. It was felt to be unfairly onerous in the early 1930's, when the Tithe Resistance Association flourished in Thanet,[28] and two local farmers were charged in court with non-payment – probably in a courageous deliberate defiance.[29] Under the Tithes Act of 1936 the arrears were paid by the government and collection passed to the Tithe Redemption Commission, the gradual rise in prices and incomes thereafter making the payments increasingly insignificant.[30]

No bankruptcies of Thanet farmers were reported in the press in the whole inter-war period, with the exception of that of a manager for the Cobb family at Thorne farm in 1935. This may have been an early example of the later widespread business practice of farming to lose money for taxation purposes, for this farm had consistently made a loss since 1922.[31] From 1920 to 1931 there were no more than five sales a year at most, and in 1931 there were only four: Shuart (due to the death of Mrs Margaret Smith), Cheeseman's, Whitehall farm near Ramsgate and Hazelden farm,

Minster – the last two quite small. Street farm, Birchington, was being sold for building, apparently derelict already, for no live or dead stock was advertised.[32] After 1931 auction sales almost disappeared; farms were changing hands by valuation, and the smaller ones were going for building or being absorbed by larger units.[33] Drapers' farm changed hands in 1922 for valuation of £2,695/11/4 with live and dead stock, and again in 1933 with ten more acres for £769/3/4 without live and dead stock.[34] On the whole, the sales picture confirms that given by the NFU dinners.

There may or may not be some significance in the high subscription arrears of the Thanet NFU; in 1926 its arrears were the third highest in the county, but it raised £440 for the new Margate hospital fund, having promised only 200 guineas.[35] In 1933 the arrears were the highest in Kent[36] and in 1938 the second highest.[37] There were only 25 paid-up members in 1928, and 16 in 1931, but these included a few small farmers, and many who did not actually belong to the Union must have come to the dinners, or the reported number of attenders could never have been so high. By 1935 there were 34 fully paid up members, with ten in arrears;[38] the number in January 1939 was said to be "40–50".[39]

The Canterbury NFU branch restarted its dinners in 1934, but Thanet not till 1937. The larger farmers could probably have afforded it before then, and the postponement may have been due to the smaller farmers and for tactical reasons, for the return of agriculture to government interest had inaugurated an era of fierce bargaining between Westminster and the farmers' organizations which has lasted until the present. Over 250 people (including women for the first time) attended the relaunched dinner in 1937, with a dance as well – a radical new departure. According to the local newspaper report "From the signal success of the function and the happy, carefree atmosphere the many visitors might be excused for imagining the farming industry to be at the height of a prosperity boom." But the speakers were full of gloom. The chairman of the local branch, Lt.Col. A.G. Tapp, stated that prices were now 129% over 1914 and labour costs 210% higher – a worrying situation.[40] There was "a record attendance" at the 1938 dinner and dance.[41]

At the 1939 dinner dance, again with nearly 250 present, the M.P. and all the Thanet mayors or council chairmen came as usual, and C.J. Elgar, one of the judges in the farm competition (see p 199) and chairman of the Ash NFU branch, said in his speech, "I cannot imagine farms better farmed" – "I consider Thanet jolly well farmed".[42]

The improved status of the farmers came against the first, ominous signs of Margate and Ramsgate's decline in the late 1930's. It was noted at the 1937 NFU dinner that the first was attracting too many day trippers.[43] Though Cliftonville, the smaller Thanet towns and parts of Ramsgate remained rather high-class, the Margate municipal orchestra had been considerably cut back by the eve of war, and there was an alarming recrudescence of unemployment in Margate and Ramsgate. In January 1939 a desperate mob was said to have fought day and night for the coal cargo of MS Aquiety when it ran aground on the Nayland Rock. Women were "knee-deep in the cold water", and children "still there at 2 am". There were 2,000 unemployed in Margate in September 1939.[44]

After the First World War Thanet farmers made their mark more and more in the wider world beyond the island. The establishment of the Milk Marketing Board owed much in SE England to the efforts of Eric Quested. Of the origins of his support for it he himself would tell the following story: his milk retailer told him most convincingly that he was losing money badly and forced to cut his price to the farmer. Shortly afterwards another farmer, a good friend of Eric's, was having an interview with his bank manager, when the latter was suddenly called out of the room, leaving a pile of documents on his desk. The farmer leapt to his feet and took a look: uppermost on the pile was a bank sheet showing that the retailer in question was making large profits.[45]

Eric Quested was chairman of the Kent Milk Recording Society 1928–1930, chairman of the Thanet NFU 1932–1934, and Kent representative on the NFU central milk and dairy produce committee 1928–1933, and as chairman of the Kent county milk committee in 1933 piloted the MMB through Kent, addressing many meetings and dealing with large numbers of concerned or even hostile farmers. Some considered the scheme far too generous to retailers, although no other East Kent farmer is on record as having gone so far as Messrs Nethersole and Champion of Chartham, who gave up their dairy and gave away their milk free in protest.[46] From 1933 to 1938 Eric was chairman of the SE Regional Committee of the Board, and from 1938–1970 MMB member for the SE Region (see p 206–7, p 239).

H.T. Willett J.P. (1865–1985) was a Thanet livestock breeder (see p 223) who served long years on the re-organized elected local government bodies. He was 40 years on the Thanet Board of Guardians and the Thanet Rural District Council set up in 1894, became chairman of the Thanet and District Guardians Committee established when the Board was taken over by the Kent County Council in 1930, and when the Thanet Rural District Council was merged in the Eastry Rural District Council in 1934 he served on that too. He took a special interest in the farms then attached to all the homes and institutions in the district, and before the war personally supervised the 9-acre farm at Manston Childrens' Home.[47]

H.A. Smith J.P. (1882–1979), son of Val, was a leading local cattle and sheep breeder (see p 224, 257) who was in the prime of his long life and to the fore in many aspects of the farming community in this period. He was chairman of the Kent Milk Recording Society 1924–26 and appointed to attend a national milk conference on behalf of Kent in 1928;[48] in the same year he was on the committee of the Kent bull show and sale. He served on many local, county and national NFU committees, being chairman of the Thanet branch 1930–32, served at least two stints on the Kent Agricultural Wages Committee[49] and was chairman of the Canterbury Farmers' Club in 1944.[50] He was also a J.P. and on the Thanet Rural District Council and Eastry Rural District Council, and joined the Stour river board in 1932.[51]

The premier all-round farmer of the mid-war period was E.S. Linington. Amongst his achievements, he was vice-chairman of the East Kent Milk Producers' Association in 1919, winner of the NFU all-Kent arable farm competition in 1928 and 1929, the first East Kent chairman of the Kent County NFU 1930–32, and five years chairman of the Kent NFU Insurance Committee, laying the foundations for the great success of NFU insurance in the county. He was a member of Margate borough council from 1927 to his death in 1946, Mayor in 1935, Alderman in 1936, deputy Mayor 1942–46 and a J.P. (See p 222).[52]

Other farmers served in many capacities in local affairs. For example C.F. Kennett of Minster was an Overseer of the Poor for 35 years, and a member of Thanet Rural District Council and the Board of Guardians for 25, a school manager at Minster for about 35 and a member of Minster parish council from its inauguration in 1894 to 1929.[53] Henry Terry of Ozengell Grange was another farmer who went into urban government, and was Mayor of Ramsgate 1930–1931.[54]

The world of county and national affairs, marketing boards and

NFU dinners belonged to the bigger farmers, that of the smaller ones could be very different. Some smaller farmers, like the then Major Arthur Tapp M.C. in his first farm at Drapers', were young men of good education, but new to agriculture, making a prudent start. (So far as is known, he was the first Thanet farmer ever to have attended a University).[55] Some began with little land or education but entrepreneurial gifts, like Bar Sackett or Augustus Brockman, and some made their way up over two generations, like the Philpotts, where the father Richard moved from a small farm at Haine to Manston Court, and his son Ernest died in the occupation of eight farms.[56] But most small farmers were, traditionally, trapped in a hard lot without any advantages. The plight of the small-holder was pin-pointed during a dispute over wages in the Isle of Thanet Gazette in 1920, when a W. Stone wrote from Rugby that some of his schoolfriends "have worked seven days a week on smallholdings at Garlinge all their lives and never made more than a living: they have not enough land."[57] Not surprisingly, the smallest holdings ebbed away: the number under 5 acres fell by 30 in 1918–1931, and by 18 1931–1941, those of 5–50 acres fell by 35 and 19 in the same periods. Yet the better prospects for farming led to some revival of small holdings from the middle 1930's and through the war (for instance on the Queensdown estate/ Woodchurch ridge), though this did not reverse the fall in total numbers till after 1941. (Table 19).

Numbers of farms of other sizes did not change much in this period, though there was a rise of 7 in the 50–100 acre group between 1931–1941. An indication of the ideal Kent farm size in those years comes from a Wye College farm management survey for 1944, which showed the average profit for a unit under 100 acres to be 4.8% of capital invested, for 101–250 acres 10.1%, for 251–400 acres 17.2%, and over 400 acres 10.8%.[58]

Soon after the 1914–18 war a significant infusion of fresh blood entered the Thanet farmers' ranks. Several more Scottish families arrived, of whom the best known now are the Lamonts, Montgomerys and Robertsons. Archibald Montgomery started at Nash Court in 1921 and moved to the larger Thorne farm in 1935. The Lamont brothers, James and John, joined him in partnership at Nash Court at first, and then James took it on and John took Manston Green. Five grandchildren of Archibald Montgomery and several descendants of the Lamonts and Robertsons were still farming or otherwise connected with agriculture in Thanet in 1993.[59] Lieut. Colonel Tapp, who was rising up in the Territorial

Army, far-sightedly moved to St Nicholas Court in 1933, further from the expanding towns and nearer to the marshes. Four of his seven children and two of his grandchildren became farmers in Thanet later. Another newcomer was P.W. Steed from East Kent, who took California farm in 1918 and East Northdown when Captain Friend left it in 1937, and also contributed a number of descendants to farming here from his family of seven sons and four daughters.[60] Edwin Baxter, of Thanet origins but with a business background, opened a branch of the family sausage factory at Sarre in 1921 and became a successful farmer as well, absorbing all the Sarre farms by his death in 1944.[61] Some left the district: C.F. Kennett moved to Woodnesborough in 1929, and none of his 14 children seem to have farmed in Thanet. (This was perhaps the record farming family of the time, and they were all alive in 1945).[62] In the early part of the war Thanet acquired its first Jewish farmer, the popular Bill Tabbush of Sephardic descent, who took Vincent farm.

The gentry continued to fare less well than the farmers through the inter-war years, for low rents continued. The rent of Elmwood farm, Broadstairs, was £225 for 113 acres in 1935 (£2 per acre)[63] and this was normal.[64] The Powell-Cottons put part of their Thanet estate (Haine, Monkton Road, Flete and Chalkhole farms) on sale in 1919 but only the last reached its reserve, the rest being withdrawn.[65] This family survived, but there were spates of freehold estate sales in East Kent, particularly in the late 1920's.[66] In 1919 the Friends, and in 1924 the surviving son of Mrs Maud Hatfeild of Hartsdown became farmers, but the aura of their former gentry status continued to invest them, and they were in demand as speakers at dinners, givers of prizes at ploughing matches and so on. Mrs Maud Hatfeild herself made history by becoming a county magistrate in 1920[67] and Mayor of Margate in 1926. As noted earlier, the owners of the small estates at Bromstone, Dane Court, Cleve Court, Callis Court etc. never seem to have been particularly associated with the farming community; they rented out their home farms and did not have other tenants.

Throughout this period the living standards of the farmers rose noticeably, and many now acquired conveniences that had only been available to the gentry, townspeople and a few farmers before 1914. By the mid-twenties probably all larger farmers had bought cars and had a telephone installed, although Val Smith preferred to drive a horse and trap to the end of his life. Eric Quested replaced his trap drawn by Nigger, a black cob, with a Morris

Oxford 11.9 open top costing £380 early in 1923. Motors meant that the dusty rural chalk roads were no longer acceptable, and following complaints and petitions Thanet Rural District Council had most of them tarred.[68] The first telephones had been connected to gentry houses in 1890,[69] but in 1919 the Post Office refused to install them in Monkton, St Nicholas and Sarre, though it later relented.[70] The telephone came to Woodchurch farm in 1925 – an upright model with the receiver hanging beside it.

Progress was made in the supply of mains water, enabling more bathrooms to be installed. For instance Margate Corporation agreed to supply water from its mains to Sarre in 1926,[71] but many farms were and still are without mains sewerage, although modern cesspools are now able to cope with bath water, unlike some of the earlier ones. Heating was by open fires, or the convenient but tricky Valor paraffin stoves, which emitted thick greasy black smoke if the wicks were not assiduously trimmed and changed. In the kitchen at Woodchurch there was a sulky coal-burning range, but some farmers' wives persuaded their husbands to install Rayburns or Agas, or made money from poultry and bought their own. At Woodchurch, farmer and worker families alike lugged pails of hot water to metal "hip-baths", until in 1933 the sewer from Manston aerodrome was connected to the farm on Eric Quested's initiative, and the bathroom came to the farmhouse with a more modern coke-burning stove to heat the water. The bathroom was a triumph of ingenuity, designed by James Graham, the clever Scots manager of Quex Estates, and built by the estate workers including the versatile young Walter Millstead, without the need for any outside help. But many smaller farms had no bathrooms till much later, and the war impeded this kind of development. When Callis Court farm was sold in 1943, the farmhouse had only four rooms, a kitchen, scullery and WC, although the dairy was modern and the farm was quite near Broadstairs. In 1941 the holdings on the Woodchurch ridge (by necessity) and Shottendane farm (by choice) still drew their water from wells.[72]

Although electrical appliances "for farm and home" were on display at the Kent Agricultural Show in 1936,[73] in 1941 only 36 of 116 Thanet farms and nurseries over 5 acres in size had electric light, and 22 power.[74] Lighting in farmhouses was still most often by oil lamps, perched at strategic spots in the kitchen, in halls and passages and on a ledge over the stairs. In the bedrooms candles reigned, and in the main living rooms petrol lamps, which were pumped up with air and burned with a strong, white light. In the

1920's the radio or "wireless" became universal in all the bigger farms, and in the 1930's most but the very poor small-holdings had it.

The approach of war in 1939 was met rather stoically, without the patriotic glee which had greeted 1914; there was a tendency in some quarters to overestimate the probable horrors, rather than under-estimate as 25 years before. This was probably not true of the farmers, but the private school attended by the author staged a positively histrionic evacuation by car to West Wales the day after war was declared, leaving at 6 am and expecting the dive bombers overhead at any minute.

John Furley Spanton, son of George and Fanny Spanton of Great Cliffsend farm, was killed in a plane accident whilst an instructor in the Fleet Air Arm in May 1939, but it is not certain that any Thanet farmer's son lost his life in the forces actually during the Second World War. Richard Stone, son of Mr and Mrs P. Stone who retired from Upper Gore End farm during the war, was reported missing in Libya in 1942,[75] but his name is not on Birchington war memorial. As he had emigrated and joined the South African army in 1939 and efforts to trace descendants of the family have so far failed, the question remains open.

One of the war heroes had an indirect link with Thanet: Squadron Leader Daniel Hatfeild Maltby, a grandson of Mrs Maud Hatfeild, won the DFC and DSO for his part in the bombing of the Mohne and Eider dams, to prevent Nazi atomic bomb development, and was soon afterwards killed on another mission.[76]

A number of members of the Thanet agrarian community are known to have served with some distinction. Lt Col Tapp retired from the Territorials in 1936, and rejoined the army as Major in 1939. Between 1940 and 1945 he set up and commanded the 3rd Maritime Regiment RA, responsible for the defence of merchant ships, and retired in 1945 with the rank of Colonel. The TD with three bars was added to his MC, and in the late 1950's the OBE.[77] Christopher Powell-Cotton joined the army at the outbreak of war fresh from Cambridge, and was commissioned in the Buffs. After a brief interruption when he was appointed to the Colonial Administration in Uganda, he was released again into the King's African Rifles, and served with them in East Africa, Somalia, Ethiopia, Ceylon, India and Burma, winning the MC as a company commander in Burma in 1945. His sister Antoinette was nursing in Central London for almost the whole war, and right through the

Blitz, in a first-aid post in 1940–41, then as a student nurse and SRN until 1945.[78]

Michael Smith, son of H.A., who also had been a Territorial, was commissioned in 1939, served in France, then was Captain ADC to two General Officers commanding Malta (Scobell and Deak), and then transport officer for a brigade HQ. He was mentioned in despatches in the Aegean Islands campaign and taken prisoner.[79] Walter Baxter, grandson of Edwin, was in the Hon. Artillery Company before the war, commissioned in 1939, and served in Burma from 1940, whence he walked 350 miles back to India to avoid capture by the Japanese, although suffering with a wound and hepatitis. Later he was ADC to General Slim and returned to Burma as a military secretary to the Commander 4 Corps.[80]

A little information is also available about some others. Douglas Ledger, of the Elms farm, Sarre, was captured in Crete but appears to have survived.[81] Douglas Fasham, son of R.W.J. Fasham of Flete farm, was a Lieutenant with the RE in Assam in 1944, though he was not a farmer himself but chief engineering assistant to Crayford UDC.[82] A son of Lewis Harrison of Callis Court farm reached the rank of Lt Col but nothing is known of his military career.[83] Robert Tapp was just old enough to serve in the Fleet Air Arm in 1944–46.[84] Not much is known of the war records of any farmers' daughters, except that the author served in the ATS in England, Northern Ireland, Italy and post-war Vienna. A farmer's wife, Mrs Betty Tyrrel, served in the Land Army, and a farmer's granddaughter, Ruth Paine, made a versatile war effort in the Land Army and as a part-time firewoman, and at the end of the war in the Wrens.[85]

Farmers at home played a more dramatic role than in 1914–18. A civilian hero of the war was Ray Fasham, brother of Douglas, who pulled an airman from a blazing plane which crashed in the garden at Flete farm, in August 1940, and drove the burned man and another who escaped to Margate hospital in his father's car. The author was told that he could never forget the screams of another airman whom he could not manage to rescue. For this action Ray was awarded a certificate and two guineas by the Society for the Protection of Life from Fire.[86] Captain, then Major Hatfeild of Hengrove (who was a Territorial between the wars), commanded No 3 platoon of the Home Guard set up in 1940; later Captain Pearce of Ebbsfleet commanded the Minster platoon and Lieut. G.G. Baxter of Sarre, brother of Edwin, the Sarre one.[87]

Many of the farmers were enlisted by the War Office in 1940 to form part of a clandestine national resistance movement against the Germans if they invaded. Three young men, Norman Steed of Grove farm, Manston, R.F. Linington and John Montgomery were made sergeants in charge of three units, of seven men each, under Lieut. (later Captain) W.G. Gardner, son of W.J., the seed and corn merchant of Birchington. W.G. was selected because his occupation would allow him to travel about and pass information. They trained in deep secrecy through the war till they were disbanded with the Home Guard in 1944. On one occasion they took part in a competition against other units in Wiltshire (probably near Coleshill, the national H.Q. of the British Resistance), which they won, and were given a mug as a prize. Bridges were mined at Sarre and Plucksgutter amongst other places, and arms were hidden at various sites, a cache being discovered after the war at Quex Park. Other arms were stored at the home of W.G. Gardner, some not being located again until after his death in 1985. Woodchurch was considered as a hiding place, but Eric Quested was busy with the Milk Marketing Board and had forgotten about the hidden chamber in the chalk under the sitting-room. The self-denying secrecy observed by the units can be judged by the fact that he was given the impression that the whole scheme was a rather half-baked idea confined to the Montgomery brothers and one or two others, whereas in fact it was official and indeed had a Churchillian touch to it. Only if men showed some interest in joining were they told more of the truth, and the secret was very well kept until long after the war ended.[88]

According to the Isle of Thanet Gazette, 283 high explosive bombs, 203 incendiaries, 4 parachute mines, 2 oil bombs, 1 phosphorous bomb, 8 fire pots, 2 V1 and one V2 fell on the rural areas of Thanet, by far the greatest number on Minster parish and Manston.[89] The farmers suffered no personal casualties, but the farm workers did. (See p 214–5). Several farms received damage, for instance Kemp's Corner, where one night in 1940 Mrs Kemp had to run out in her nightie carrying her baby daughter to the Anderson shelter in the garden, to find it full of passing airmen! At Nash farm, then a small-holding belonging to Kent County Council, the KCC Agricultural Committee paid out £140/-/5d in repairs.[90] Animal casualties are not known, but included a number of sheep which climbed the Northern sea wall and set off a land mine.[91]

RAF or allied planes crashed at various places besides Flete, and German ones at Goodman's farm, Manston, Monkton, Hengrove,

Sackett's Hill, Shuart marshes, near Great Brooksend farm, at Vincent, and probably other places too.[92] Some crews were taken prisoner, others did not survive to be captured.

It is well-known that agricultural production and food distribution were far better managed in the Second World War than in the First. The Ministries of Agriculture and Food drew on the pioneer initiatives of the First in this respect, and developed plans laid down in Whitehall in the 1930's. Thanet farmers played a fine part in the struggle for greater output. The Kent War Agricultural Executive in Maidstone under Lord Cornwallis was much more highly organized than in 1916–18. Norman Steed was a member of the agricultural machinery sub-committee and Eric Quested of the milk sub-committee and the technical and general purposes committee. Archibald Montgomery was chairman of the local Thanet sub-committee, of which Norman Steed and others were also members. Brian Egerton was secretary to Lord Northbourne, the East Kent sub-committee chairman, and also acted as Thanet labour officer from his home in Birchington. Eric Quested did much work for the Milk Marketing Board during the war, serving on several committees. As a member of the grass drying committee he was responsible for the profitable running of the Board's plant at Shipley, near Billingshurst, Sussex, in these years.[93]

During the "phoney war" period till May 1940 things went on in Thanet much as usual, but the next years brought stresses, offset by the government's concern to keep output up. British farmers' net incomes are calculated by an official war historian to have risen to 303% of 1937–39 by 1943–44, and to have been 229% of 1937–39 in 1944–45, because of poor yields nationally in that year.[94] Net farm incomes rose much faster than other incomes in the war,[95] and there were complaints about the 100% excess profits tax at the Thanet NFU meeting on 2 February 1942.[96]

Yet it could have been far otherwise in the peninsula of Kent. On Saturday afternoon 3 August 1940 there was an urgent meeting of dairy farmers at the Fountain Hotel, Canterbury, under NFU auspices, to discuss evacuation of herds and a sale of animals at Reading, to save them from the possible battle zone. E.S. Linington wanted to stay in Thanet with his young stock, for testing, and H.A. Smith and Eric Quested started negotiating to buy small grass farms in West Kent to which to move their cattle.[97] As it became clear that the RAF were winning the Battle of Britain these plans were dropped, but H.M. Steed did evacuate his herd to Herefordshire, where he farmed for the next ten years as well as keeping his Thanet farms. The evacuation of herd, Steed family and a cowman and his family was planned and executed within a week. Col. Tapp also sent his milking herd to Monmouth for the duration of the war, but kept St Nicholas Court going too.[98]

The bargaining between the government and the farmers seemed to grow more intense in the middle years of the war. There was great dissatisfaction in the Southeast with the MMB price structure changes in 1942, introducing a flat pool price for all areas. Eric Quested, supporting his electors, threatened in a speech to a mass meeting of milk producers in Maidstone in February that the region could easily revert to arable if milk production was uneconomic.[99] A further over-flowing NFU indignation meeting was held early in March, at which the small farmers particularly were opposed to the wheat and potato prices, and it was left to J. Hillier French, the County vice-chairman, alone to say that it would be better that they should all go broke than that the Germans won the Battle of the Atlantic.[100] Another mass meeting of milk producers addressed by Eric Quested was held on 3 October about the government decision to stop payments for special services (ie winter milk production in the SE) whilst allowing retailers to sell at the former prices, thus effectively passing the premium to them.[101] Matters seemed to come to a head in December 1943, when Kent NFU called for the replacement of the Minister of Agriculture, R.S. Hudson, on grounds that government intervention was reducing prices and subsidies and benefitting the consumer and not the farmer.[102] Yet in the three way struggle between farmers, retailers and government the farmers came out well, and the Mayor of Maidstone was not contradicted when he stated at the January 1944 Kent County NFU AGM that agriculture, formerly the Cinderella of the nation, "had been at the Prince's ball having a good time" for the past two years.[103] The same process had been at work with the farmers as with the farm workers (see p 215) – increased security and good bargaining cards made them determined to hold and better their gains.

A number of farmers helped the victory celebrations by providing meadows for the teas and sports (for instance, Alderman E.S. Linington, Mr and Mrs Dilnot at Acol, and A. Friend of Sheriff's Court provided his barn),[104] but practically all the festivities were organized by town and village committees on which farmers sometimes served, but were not mentioned by name in the press reports. Compared to 1815, the events were arranged on a far wider and more democratic basis, and were geared towards the children as much as adults. The general atmosphere seems to have been more like 1814–15 than 1918.

A last glimpse inside the farmhouses is afforded by the furniture at Manston Court sale in October 1945 (one of the last occasions when furniture was listed in a farm sale announcement): oak and walnut bedsteads, box spring and other mattresses, feather beds, bedroom suites, a Put-U-Up settee, an antique chest of drawers, a Hepplewhite style drawing room suite, an "up-right grand piano" by Collard and Collard, dining, fireside and easy chairs, oak extending, drawleaf and other tables, Axminster and Wilton carpets, Pye and Alba "wireless sets", oil paintings and other pictures, clocks, dinner and tea services, glass, plate and cutlery."[105] The furniture at Woodchurch farm then was roughly similar, no feather bed, no Put-U-Up either, no Hepplewhite style reproductions and no antique chest of drawers, but a fine big dining table of polished mahogany and a long mahogany sideboard, both from East Northdown farm, and an antique desk. When Marion and Val Smith died in 1941, within weeks of one another, amongst the items that they left was a silver rose bowl, a candelabra and a billiard table.[106]

General position of the farmworkers

The NUAW officially opened branches in St Peter's, and Minster in 1919, followed by a separate Northdown branch in 1920, but the Minster branch had closed by 1921 and all the Thanet branches had disappeared again in 1922.[107] Their failure seems to have been caused basically by the crisis of poverty into which the farm workers were now again plunged. As a well-known social historian has pointed out, rural union membership seemed to be dependant on good wages, which induced a feeling of security and reduced the fear of annoying the farmers[108] – although there is no record that the formation of the union branches met with any adverse reaction from the latter in Thanet in these years.

During the rising prices of 1919 and 1920 wages too rose fast, but apparently not enough to prevent a worsening of the farm workers' position. In June 1920 wages locally stood at 43/6d for a 50 hour week and with overtime often reached 60/-,[109] but in February 1921 the Agricultural Wages Board refused a demand from the NUAW for 46/-.[110] The farm workers' cause was taken up in a veiled way by a reporter of the *Isle of Thanet Gazette*, who once even mentioned, some weeks after the event, an open air (probably Union) meeting held somewhere in Thanet in support of higher pay.[111] A certain Charles Pantling wrote letters to the *Gazette*, insisting in January 1921 that the farm labourers "all say they were better off thirty years ago. Last week one said he brought up seven children on 16/- a week, but wouldn't like the job now."[112]

From February 1921 when prices began to fall, agricultural wages were repeatedly cut too; in July 1921 Kent Farmers' Union demanded reduction to 40/-.[113] The replacement of the Central Wages Board by voluntary County Conciliation Committees under the Corn Production (Repeal) Act of August 1921 left no real central control.[114] In February 1922 Canterbury NFU branch proposed 31/6d for May – October, but suggested that the better-off farmers could pay more.[115] According to Ministry of Agriculture figures the UK average was 28/- by the close of 1922,[116] and if Eric Quested's memory was correct (he was unsure) he was paying 28/- here at that time. It still varied from farm to farm, for instance an indignant letter to the Isle of Thanet Gazette in July 1922 said some were getting 30/- for a 54–60 hour week, but some less.[117]

We have a partial range of basic prices at the Margate International Stores, and other cheap Thanet stores, for the summer of 1921. (See table 14).

In January 1922 the price of a 4-lb loaf had fallen to 10d at the International Stores,[118] and Minster Coal Club was selling coal at 30/- a ton to its members.[119] Combined with their home-grown vegetables, and milk and possibly potatoes or cauliflowers at reduced prices or free, with coal at wholesale price, farm workers who could get into Margate would not have gone very hungry at this time, but most were dependent on almost certainly dearer local shops or still costlier visiting food vans, and the uncertainty of the wage and price situation must have made things worse.

The author's mother, a town girl, was dismayed at the poverty of the farm workers in the early years after her marriage in September 1919, but thought those in Thanet were not nearly so badly off as those over in East Kent. She would say later that it was very distressing to see them on Saturdays, when the farmers made their weekly trips into Canterbury by trap, train, or car and crowds of farm workers' wives pushed their prams long distances into the city to hunt for cheap goods. She used furtively to hide a pound note in particularly pathetic-looking prams whilst the owners were in a shop. Although she may sometimes have been mistaken, she

Table 14 Some prices in cheapest stores, 1921

January 1921	4lb loaf (white)	1/4d
June 1921	Golden syrup	9½d
	Eggs	1/6d dozen
	Granulated sugar	7d a lb
	Corned beef	2/6d a tin
	Candles	1/5½d a lb
(ITG 18/6/1921,7A, E-H; 25/6,7A,B)		
August 1921	Bacon	2/8d lb
	Soap	13/6d 3 dozen cakes
	Lard	10d lb
	Margarine	10d lb
	Cheapest Tea	1/8d
	Cheese	1/4d lb
	Best steak	2/6d lb
	Butter	2/2d lb
(ITG 6/81921, 2, A, B,; 20/8, 2A, B)		
September 1921	Best pork sausages	1/8d lb (Terry's, Market Street, Margate.)
	Jam	1/9-1/11d lb
	Butter beans	3½d
	Sugar	6½d
September	Men's boots	13/11d
"sale prices"	Flannel shirts	9/-
	54″ blanket cloth	6/11d per yard
(ITG 10/9/1921, 9,A-B,E-H;17/9,2A-B)		

maintained that in those days you could always tell farm workers' families in Kent by their poverty, slightly different dress, and more "open-air" look. Her memory is borne out by an editorial in the *Isle of Thanet Gazette* in January 1923, referring to the acute depression in the rural areas of Kent, especially in the Weald and the Cranbrook area, where the number of bankruptcies and reduction in wages was particularly bad.[120]

Eric Quested reduced his cottage rents to 2/6 a week from 3/- for a while, and in 1920 and 1921 revived the old harvest suppers for his men and their wives. They were held in the granary: in 1921 they had joints of beef and pork, with trifle, custard and jellies, and he recalled long afterwards how delighted the men were at the joints of meat.[121] But in 1922 the suppers appear to have been stopped, and Ben Offen also stopped his suppers of much longer standing, "because things were getting better".[122]

For the rest of the 1920's prices stayed low and the partial restoration of central control over wages by the 1924 Agricultural Wages (Regulation) Act resulted in an average national rise to 31/5d in 1925, and to 34/9d in 1939.[123] Local wage figures are not available again until January 1937, when they were reported to be 210% higher than in 1914, or already about the 1939 national average.[124] Thanet farm workers' position had thus slowly improved and was better than that of their fellows in many parts of the country, yet it remained one of the lowest. The author even as a small child became uneasily conscious of the gap which separated her from the workers' children on our isolated farm in the 1920's and early 1930's. Her clothes were usually all new, theirs rarely so it seemed, and what remains firmest in memory are the feet: she had leather shoes in winter and leather sandals in summer, they had old-fashioned laced boots in winter and shabby black canvas plimsolls in summer. But their general appearance was vastly better than that of the London hop-pickers' children, glimpsed as we passed their camps on Sunday drives – and their boots were warmer than shoes – the author often had cold feet in winter – whilst the plimsolls basically differed only in shabbiness from the canvas shoes fashionable for summer both then and now. In those years farm workers still tugged their forelocks when they spoke to the farmer, and went to work in old but not ragged suits, with string tied round the trousers under the knee.

Some prices from 1926 show that their lives were bearable if not easy: cheese 1/1d lb, margarine 10d, plum jam 6½d, cocoa 6d ½lb, sausages 1/4d lb, women's shoes 10/- a pair.[125]

Education was still not thought by many people to be much needed for the farm worker. When it was proposed to set up a new Central School (providing education to 15 instead of the usual 14) at Manston in 1928, the Board of Guardians assent was required. Mrs Maud Hatfeild was for it, but A.E.G. Solly and J.H.A. Smith (Ambry Court, St Nicholas) were strongly opposed, as boys were needed on the land. The school was never started.[126] Perhaps it was natural for A.E.G. Solly J.P. to think as he did, for he himself was farming successfully at Preston farm with apparently only modest education, and had been chairman of the Board of Guardians, and of Margate Hospital Board and Thanet Rural District Council as well.[127]

Yet social mobility for the farm worker class was slowly

increasing even before 1930. By 1929 the children of Alfred Studham, who had worked for three generations of the Hatfeild family as a horseman at Hartsdown, had become respectively a farmer at Selling, nurserymen at Acol, and rating and valuation officer for Margate Corporation.[128] (One feels that these men's success could not fail to have met with encouragement from Mrs Maud Hatfeild).

By the later 1930's things were changing faster. All the workers at Woodchurch had bicycles, and even some of the wives, once the pram could be dispensed with. One elderly man held out against a bicycle for years. ("My legs be better nor them wheels in the wind." How right he was). Cars were bought by the bailiff and the head cowman, who had savings salvaged from his own small farm, given up in the Great Depression. Eric Quested started sending the workers' children to school in the farm car, driven by the bailiff, and arranged with the landlord, Major Powell-Cotton, to have bathrooms put into all the cottages well before the war. The two oast cottagers had to give up their third bedrooms for this purpose, but did so by choice, as they could use one of their two living-rooms for sleeping instead. The other cottages had bathrooms on the ground floor. A bedroom was hived off from the farmhouse to provide a third one for the cottage adjoining it (which had all been part of the farmhouse until 1914), and Major Powell-Cotton had two new three-bedroomed houses with bathrooms built for the bailiff and head cowman. By the end of 1939 wages were 40/- for specialists and 38/- for the rest.[129] But four roomed cottages were still common in Acol[130] and there were still three at Woodchurch, though one was always occupied by an elderly couple.

Further government legislation brought the landworker closer to, but still not equal to the urban one. A weekly half-holiday had been given on larger Thanet farms outside harvest before 1914,[131] and became obligatory, or overtime money in lieu, in 1924. A week's holiday was generally introduced in 1938, but Thanet was one of the areas where not more than three days could be taken consecutively, so the general farm holiday, always after harvest, was just a long weekend.[132] The Agricultural Unemployment Insurance Act 1936 at last relieved the farmworkers of applying for outdoor relief at the discretion of the Board of Guardians, but gave them a maximum of 30/- a week regardless of the number of children, and they could not draw full benefit until they had paid in for two years. Families had however become much smaller on average, and the maximum benefit was raised to 35/- in 1939.[133]

Unemployment in farm workers was in any case low: they were fleeing to other employment and with their generally good reputation were doing this so successfully that it was said at the 1938 NFU dinner that "there was the greatest difficulty in keeping good workers on the land."[134] In December 1939 the Thanet representatives on the Kent Wages Committee, H.A. Smith and A.J. Montgomery, were amongst those who wanted wages of 42/-, not the 40/- then fixed.[135]

In the villages especially the farm workers and their families were becoming absorbed into the new social life which was arising amidst the great expansion of the lower middle class and the better pay of the skilled workers. Between the wars all the villages acquired public halls, where organizations like the British Legion, the Womens' Institute, the Red Cross, youth organizations, sports and horticultural societies and so on could hold functions, attended by all classes. In 1935 electric light was offered to all the villages and accepted by all but Acol, which preferred to stick with gas for a while longer.[136] The old dark and dreary village life of the 19th century, illuminated only by chapels, churches, pubs and flickering gas had passed away. Yet country life still had its hazards – in the exceptionally cold winter of 1939–40 Minster, Monkton, Sarre and St Nicholas were cut off by snow drifts and the last two were without bread for three days.[137]

One of the most striking signs that a new age was beginning was the reporting in the press of the weddings of farm workers' daughters, sometimes dressed in full bridal regalia of long, white gowns with orange blossom chaplets and veils, attended by bridesmaids in pretty dresses. It was in keeping with the embarassment now felt by farm workers at their status that the father's occupation was never mentioned in these reports, and was only obvious when the address was such-and-such farm cottages.[138] Jokes about country yokels, Jews and black people featured in the Journal of the Kent NFU almost down to the war (some of them still seem funny, if you aren't one of them at least), and it was said by an Eastry Rural District councillor in 1938 that "agricultural wages were so low that" (farm) "men would not describe themselves as such. They were trying to get out of agriculture".[139]

This sad situation makes it harder to discover the part played by the farm workers' families in the Second World War than in the First. The total Thanet armed forces deaths in World War Two according to the war memorials were 357, or 26.9% of those of 1914–18. Yet in the villages the percentage was higher: St Nicholas

12 in World War One, 5 in World War Two (41% of the earlier war), and in Minster and Monkton combined 55 against 20 (36% of the earlier war).[140] It must be added that the village figures were probably more accurate than the town ones, which may have missed some casualties. 14 women and 140 men from Minster and 3 women and 38 men from Monkton served in the forces during the war;[141] only 10.2% of those who served from Minster and Monkton thus died. Figures from other rural parts are not available.

A number of young farm workers or farm workers' sons joined the forces as regulars before 1939; one such was Harry Hughes of Acol, a cowman before he enlisted in 1934, who as Sergeant won the MM in 1943.[142] Another was Arthur Smith of Acol who joined the RA at 18 about 1927, and was a Lieutenant by 1943.[143] Many farm men must have enlisted after war broke out, for the number of regular workers over 18 fell by 132 between 1939 and 1941. (Table 27). Amongst those who can be identified are Leading Stoker Herbert Harnett of Minster, a farm worker for four years who enlisted in 1941 and was mentioned in despatches,[144] and Ernest Fagg, originally a farm worker at Monkton, who was killed in Italy aged 19.[145] Three RAF aircrew Sergeants were reported missing: Norman Hood who had worked at Monkton Court, George Whitaker who had worked at Nether Hale farm and Ron Hogben, grandson of the bailiff at Hengrove.[146]

W.R. Lawrence, still at work at East Northdown in 1944 after 50 years, had five sons and two daughters in the forces and two sons in the Home Guard.[147] Mr and Mrs White of Acol Hill cottages had five sons, two daughters, five sons-or daughters-in-law and one granddaughter in the forces or doing war work in 1941.[148] Many local girls joined the Land Army, and one of these, Mollie Wanstall of Garlinge, was chosen to be the all-England representative of the Land Army at the victory service at St Paul's cathedral in May 1945.[149]

Some of the civilian rural casualties are mentioned in Humphreys' *Thanet at war*, but the newspapers record others not included in that book. As well as Ivy Impett of Foster's Folly, and Elizabeth and 11 year-old Dorothy Christian of Sarre, who were killed by bombs on 12 August 1940, and Alfred Jackson of Manston killed on 28th of that month,[150] two landworkers, James Woodcock and Arthur Impett, father-in-law of Ivy, were killed by a bomb whilst going to work in a lorry (apparently near Ramsgate) in March 1941.[151] Two other farm workers employed by William

Smith, at Great Brooksend farm, were severely injured by machinegun fire from a German plane in November 1942.[152]

Some farm workers kept on the land by government orders, or too young or too old to enlist, joined the Home Guard. In May 1940 the first platoon formed from St Nicholas, Monkton and Sarre consisted mainly of them – at this stage the whole Thanet Home Guard only had a few rifles, picks, shovels and one bomb![153] It was hard for men working long hours on farms to keep up the drills, even though some allowance was made for them; two from Woodchurch joined but eventually had to give it up.[154] Some others were too reluctant to do so officially, and were prosecuted for non-attendance (a horseman at Minster doing a 65-hour week was fined £2 in 1944 because he had not shown up for months).[155]

Though this might seem a harsh penalty, wages continued to rise throughout the war. The Agricultural Wages (Regulation) Amendment Bill of 1940 raised them to 48/- without guaranteeing farm prices, but although the Kent and Thanet NFU objected,[156] the county wage committees lost most of their power in 1942, and by 1945 according to Government statistics minimum wages were 99% higher than in 1937–1938, whilst retail prices were only 48% higher.[157] It was a clear gain, and a striking result was the swift re-emergence of the NUAW in Thanet and throughout Kent, where there had been only two branches left in 1930, and 7 in 1938. Minster and Ramsgate branches opened in 1943 when Kent basic wages were 69/- for 48-52 hours plus overtime, and by 1945 there were branches at Garlinge, Westwood and St Nicholas and district as well. The last must have included Monkton and Sarre and appeared between 1944 and 1945.[158]

It is fair to say that more of the discomforts of war were borne by the farm worker class than by the larger farmers. Few children from the villages were evacuated in 1940, and there was no schooling for those who stayed behind here for a year, until half-day school began again in June 1941, and full-day in February 1942.[159] Farmers' families could drive out for a meal in a restaurant or hotel, where there always seemed to be enough food, for so long as trips were made in the daytime – and not always in daytime – some excuse connected with the farm could always be found to account for the use of petrol – the basic private ration was abolished in 1941. Townspeople had the cheap government-organized "British restaurants", but the village and isolated farm people had to bear the rigours of the ration book, helped it is true by their gardens and farm perquisites, (which many farmers stepped up somewhat during the war), and the odd rabbit, domestic or wild. The NAUW and the NFU complained about the inadequate 1/2d meat ration for farm workers and the tiny cheese ration in January 1941,[160] but not till summer 1942 were a year-round special cheese ration and harvest rations introduced for them, and the famous "village meat-pie scheme" for tasty snacks to be baked for them without coupons by local butchers.[161] Farmers' families could buy good second-hand clothes through magazines such as "The Lady", but the workers' families only had the coupons, for local second-hand clothes shops (in those days usually grotty places) had vanished in 1940 and in any case were regarded with growing distaste. At least one farm worker's wife with three children to clothe went through all the cold winters of the war bare-legged: she was young and strong and would not be seen in thick stockings or in socks.

Many farmworkers over 65 continued working during the war, but this was probably as much a continuation of an immemorial custom of going on as long as possible, and enjoyment of the better wages, as war effort, for there were still 104 over 65 in 1948. (Table 28). Better health through better pay and conditions was no doubt another factor.

Farming practices

This was a period of all-round advance and quickening change, to which the war of 1939–45 overall gave as much stimulus as hindrance, so that the war years are best discussed as a continuation of the 1930's, rather than as a discontinuity as in 1914–18. The inter-war and war years were also a time when Thanet farming was more in the public eye than it had been perhaps since the 18th century.

Use of tractors was complete on the larger farms before the war, though the smaller ones relied mainly on the horse till the 1950's. There was a good deal of resistance to the tractor until pneumatic tyres replaced the steel spiked ones in 1933 and Harry Ferguson perfected the three-point linkage in 1934.[162] Ten tractors were sent by a machinery firm to demonstrate at the 1920 ploughing match at Woodchurch, but Eric Quested, who had started farming in his grandfather's tradition in 1919, would not allow them on his land, lest they compact it too much, so they had to perform at Cheeseman's farm next door. (He would laugh about this later to the end of his life). Three however entered a class in the match itself at Woodchurch, and a Garner won first and third prizes.[163] In 1921 Captain Friend had a Titan, "nearly as big as a threshing machine", which won first prize, and J.W. Smith and Son won second also with a Titan at the match that year.[164] But tractors then disappeared from the match until 1927, after which they entered annually. The leading farmers probably all had one or more by about 1930: in 1928 E.S. Linington's son R.F. won second prize in the class, which was won by Captain Hatfeild's man, and the third prize by R. Solly of Manston.[165] Both Fordson and Overtime tractors were sold at Updown and Haine farms in 1923,[166] four of unspecified make featured in the sale at Somali farm when the tenancy of Page and Son was given up in 1928,[167] and a Fordson appeared in a sale at Ozengell in 1929.[168] When Westwood farm was taken over by H.M. Steed in 1933, he acquired with it a half-share in a Fordson tractor, valued at £79/13/-.[169] Most larger dairy farms also had milk lorries or motor vans by 1931,[170] and the Page sale had included two Ford ton vans.

A South African farmers' delegation came to Thanet in 1927, but they ran late and were able to make only flying visits to the farms of J.W. Smith and Sons, H.T. Willett and E.S. Linington. They were particularly impressed with Willett's Friesians and Linington's horses at Dent-de-Lion.[171]

Then in 1930 the NFU summer tour was held in Kent, and the same three farms were visited. What they saw was the splendid swansong of traditional Thanet horse farming: "The farms of Mr Linington were notable for the merit of the crops, absence of weeds, and the skill with which the standard and cash crops were made to harmonize in the scheme upon which the twice champion farmer of Kent proceeds. I had heard of Mr Linington's farming, but here again, seeing was more impressive than verbal description could possibly be. A higher standard of uniformity in crops, especially cereals, broccoli and potatoes, and livestock, probably is not to be found anywhere. The fifteen farm horses paraded made a picture rarely seen, while the Dairy Shorthorns and young stock also elicited high praise." Photographs were taken of the farm and tea was served in a marquee on the lawn by Mrs Linington, her daughter, daughters-in-law and "a bevy of charming young ladies."[172] The other two farms were not reported on in this journal but cannot have been far behind in excellence.

E.S. Linington's tractor seems to have been kept in the background on this occasion, but within a few years he and his son went over to them. Eric Quested followed him in 1936 with most of the remaining larger farmers who had not done so already. At Woodchurch two and later three tractors replaced eight horses, but there and at Monkton Court, and probably elsewhere too, two horses and finally just one were kept for shimming (hoeing row crops) and odd jobs, and to gladden the hearts of a few men like George Christian, at Woodchurch, supremely loyal employees of the old school devoted to horses.[173] During the war horses made a slight comeback and the KWAEC pronounced in 1943 that there were "few farms which could not find work for one or two."[174] But carthorses declined in number by 21.5% in 1921–1931, by 34% in 1931–1939, and a further 31% in 1939–1945. (Table 21). The tractor and engine survey carried out with the 1941 agricultural returns showed 127 tractors on 116 Thanet farms and nurseries converting to field crops (those under 5 acres were not included). Most farms at this time had only one or two tractors, chiefly Fordsons of 20–30 hp; the Liningtons, Captain Hatfeild and H.A. Smith had three each, P.W. Steed and Edwin Baxter four each, and H.T. Willett six, but his were of very low horse-power.[175] Two earlier machinery surveys made in 1937 and 1939 have not survived.[176]. In 1945 there was still the appreciable number of 238 working cart-horses in Thanet. (See Table 21).

Implements specifically designed for tractors did not come in at once on most farms, and throughout the whole period there was a process of improvement and adaption of the older horse-drawn kinds, though the local implement-makers were fading away now. To take one simple example: Bar Sackett's wooden waggons at Woodchurch had wheels which could not lock underneath and were very difficult to turn, so in 1919 his grandson Eric had two new ones made by Goodban the carpenter of Garlinge for £24 each, and had the front wheels of two of the old waggons cut down and an extra axle put on them, so that he could use them for a while longer.[177]

The oil-fired engines which, nationally, were the great innovation of the 1890's began turning up in farm sales between 1919 and 1930, a Blackstone 6½ hp at Minster Abbey farm in 1928,[178] an 8 hp Blackstone at Haine and a 4½ hp petroleum engine at Grove farm, Manston in 1919.[179] There was also a gas fired National 8 hp engine at Drapers' farm in 1922.[180] An Ellington potato sorter and a Ransome digger also surfaced at the Minster Abbey sale. The 1941 agricultural returns showed 84 oil or petrol engines, 15 electric and four gas. (See p 231).

No sales inventories are available from large farms after 1932, but the process of modernization can be judged to a limited extent from three war-time and immediate post-war sales. At the Hillside small-holding at Woodchurch in 1943 a van mare, 40 Rhode Island Reds, a balance plough, a Howard potato plough and three pairs of zig-zag harrows were advertised.[181] In October 1945 at Grove farm Manston the following were on sale: a Howard 1-furrow balance plough, a 2-horse Davey Sleep cultivator, a 9-tine Martin cultivator, a tractor-drawn self-lift spring-time Martin cultivator, a 7-chep Suffolk drill, a Massey Harris 11-chep disk drill, a 1-horse Albion mower, a Hornby reaper and binder, and a 2½ hp Dunston oil engine. The tractors, livestock and best implements had evidently been sold separately, or were accompanying the farmer to a new holding. At Hopeville farm, St Peter's in the same month (evidently a complete retirement from business): 5 horses, 32 dairy cows, one bull, twelve followers, 90 pigs, 11 geese, 18 ducks, two Fordson tractors, tractor ploughs, cultivators, tractor disk harrows, self-binders, York and zig-zag harrows, hand seed drills, a corn-grinding mill and poultry equipment.[182]

Only the introduction of the most spectacular new machines ever found press mention. P.W. Steed was the first farmer in Kent to have a combine harvester, for the 1939 harvest; it was pulled by a tractor.[183] The Scots partners Archibald Montgomery and James Lamont, John Lamont and Alec Robertson seem to have been the next to acquire one or more (probably Canadian made and self-propelled), for they won first and second prizes in the combine and drier class barley at some unspecified competition in 1943, briefly reported in the press.[184] P.W. Steed also had an "automatic planting machine" in 1939,[185] probably for broccoli.

The reference to "cash" (catch) crops in the description of the Linington farms in 1932 draws attention to one of the most radical developments of the period. Catch cropping was started at an uncertain date on the larger farms, in the 1920's perhaps, and after the introduction of tractors was followed by the regular growing of three crops in two years. This was standard on larger farms during the war.[186] It encouraged the production of table vegetables: the area under them excluding broccoli/cauliflower more than doubled between 1931 and 1941, and doubled again by 1945 (Table 26).

Only examples from the cropping of a smaller farm are available for the 1920's and 1930's, by coincidence the same one for which the 1841–59 crop information was found. In the years of low corn

Table 15 Draper's farm

Crops on 53 acres: November 1922

	Acres	Rods	Perches
Wurtzel	11	0	36
Swedes	1	0	0
Cabbage after tares	1	0	20
Spring cabbage, 1 piece after potatoes and the other after maize	2	0	26
Broccoli after cabbage	3	1	8
Late mustard, after mustard cut off for cows	1	0	25
Lucerne in oats	5	2	0
Lucerne, cut 1921	5	0	4
Trefolium after barley	2	1	37
Rye after barley	1	0	26
Winter tares and oats, after barley and potatoes	2	3	38
White turnips after trefolium	3	0	30
Oat gratten (ie. stubble)	8	3	28
Barley gratten	4	3	0

In the garden 100 young gooseberry bushes
and 588 rhubarb crowns – 18 different
crop species in all.

Crops on 63 acres: October 1933 – after a different tenancy

	Acres	Rods	Perches
Marrow-stem kale	2	1	15
Wurtzel after early broccoli	2	1	30
White turnips, broccoli off	5	2	0
Maize	0	3	0
Barley gratten (in 3 places, 5 acres being burnt)	19	2	0
Lucerne ley	2	0	0
Broccoli plant bed	1	0	0
Wheat gratten	3	2	0
Late broccoli off	2	2	0
Oats and tares after oats and tares	1	2	0
Growing cauliflower	3	0	4
Growing broccoli	16	0	0
Lucerne seeds in oats (seeded)	3	2	0
Early trefolium (seeded)	6	2	0

No rhubarb or gooseberries – 12 different
crop species.

(Documents supplied by Jill Smith, daughter of H.M. Steed who took over Draper's
farm in 1933.)

prices this farm had gone over mostly to livestock and fodder crops, virtually abandoning corn, but the tenant of 1922–1933 had grown a substantial amount of broccoli and barley at least in the last year of his occupation, and probably before. (Table 15).

In 1922 the livestock on this farm were as follows: 6 sows (4 in-pig), 18 piglets and a Middle White boar; 81 hens, 47 pullets, 2 cocks, 9 cockerels and 4 guinea fowl; 27 cows, 4 in-calf heifers, 1 bull, 2 buds, 3 calves and an unspecified number of bullocks, which had apparently been sold previous to the sale; 4 cart horses, 5 milk chariot cobs and a vanner. Although there were ten fowl houses and three fowl shelters, the tenant did not keep as many fowls as he or his father had in 1904 (see p 179). Amongst the implements were a "Thanet nidget", Kent plough, potato plough and attachments, an 8 hp National gas engine, a Massey Harris binder, a Bamford mower and Bamford swathe turner.[187] When this farm was sold in 1933 the outgoing tenant took his livestock and implements with him, and no details are available.

From 1918 until the Second World War the area under crops and grass shrank by 2,565 acres, according to the agricultural returns, apparently mainly because of building, but it fell only by 148½ acres during the conflict (Table 17). At least 200 acres was added then, for Major Hatfeild took over the 150-acre Hengrove golf links, which was brought completely under cultivation this time and never returned to golf, and Victor Spain cultivated the land of Ramsgate civil airport (40 acres?).[188] One recalls that many and various odd pieces of wasteland or allotments were also brought under field cultivation, but no statistics are available. Aerial surveys may exist. The net loss was presumably due to the enlargement of Manston airport in the later stages of the war to accommodate bigger planes, and to the use of land for AA guns and anti-invasion defences – concrete "pill-boxes" and the like.

Wheat acreage fell and barley rose to 1939; by 1945 the wheat acreage was the lowest ever in the decennial figures – only 831 acres. Oats and fodder beans declined with the horses; cauliflower/broccoli rose steadily to 1945, likewise potatoes after a dip in the 1920's perhaps due to pests. Fruit growing held up well and hops continued on a small acreage. The amount of unmown permanent pasture fell by 781 acres 1931–41, then had risen again by 85 acres in 1945 (Tables 22 and 23), despite some pioneer cultivation of the marsh grassland during the war. (This was mainly on the Minster-Monkton side, but also done near St. Nicholas by the Tapp family). The techniques used to cultivate the marsh at this time are described by Garrad:[189] it was considered then that only one or two corn crops could be taken off it before reversion to grass because of the lack of organic matter, but yields were high: potatoes and sugarbeet 14+ tons per acre (35 tonnes per ha.), barley 1.8 tons (4.57 per ha.), wheat 1.6 (4+ per ha.)[190]

Thanet barley sprang to world fame when E. and C. Philpott of Manston won the world championship for British, foreign and colonial malting barley at the Brewers' Exhibition in 1921, also the Mark Lane Express Challenge cup for seed barley and first prize in the special county classes for Chevalier barley.[191] This barley was grown at Haine, but later the champion barley came from the North side of Thanet. Captain Friend won the barley world championship in 1923 and 1929,[192] E.S. Linington in 1932[193] and Cyril Watson at Somali farm in 1934.[194] Many other awards, silver cups and gold medals were also won by Thanet barley during this period.

After the first world championships in 1921 the Wellingborough, Northants, brewers G.A. Wolston and Bull began sending representatives here to buy barley, which thus secured a better price. In 1929 a Mr G. Bull said at the NFU dinner that Thanet barley was now better than Norfolk, though he had to buy less in 1929 and 1930.[195] The varieties in those years are not known, but later, when Messrs. Lamont and Montgomery won the Reserve Championships in 1943, it was with Plumage Archer.[196] H.A. Smith was growing Beaven's 1924 Plumage Archer type in 1935.[197]

In 1943 the KWAEC recommended Crown, Yeoman and Cote d'Or wheat to Thanet farmers, and a variety of oats: Hardy White, S 172 and S 147 winter oats, and Ayr Bounty, Eagle and Star for spring.[198] Whether farmers actually grew these varieties is not known!

In February 1932 E.S. Linington, a leading producer of the increasingly popular broccoli, was growing (in order of value) No. 1 & 2 Roscoff, Felthams, Sutton Satisfaction and Snow White, fertilizing them with 4–6 cwt bone and meat meal, 2–4 cwt kainit and 2–4 cwt sulphate of ammonia. He grew late varieties after catch crops of trefolium, rye and tares, or early potatoes and spring greens or possibly early broccoli. The early varieties were grown after bare fallow. After harvest the land was cultivated 3–4″ deep, and all weeds and stubble burnt; it was then dunged not too heavily and ploughed 7–8″ deep.[199] Four years earlier, in 1928, Eric Quested was growing the first three varieties mentioned by E.S. Linington, and Late June, Queens, Giants and Early Whites.

Autumn Protecting was tried in 1927 but dropped.[200] He was to stay with these kinds for many years. E.S. Linington won many awards for broccoli, and Eric Quested won two firsts in the Early Market Produce Show of the Royal Horticultural Society, both in 1935 and 1936.[201]

The Cornish crates for packing broccoli were still in use in 1919,[202] but later they became unobtainable and only mats were used until E.S. Linington started using a new kind of wooden-slatted crate in 1929, and Eric Quested and other growers followed him. Mats were continued only for the smaller heads. In 1931 E.S. Linington was already sending his broccoli by road to Covent Garden market, and again the others followed.[203] By 1936 there was said to be "a very large volume of nightly traffic to London with Thanet market-garden produce", and so many complaints of noise were made that the issue of licences to hauliers was stopped for a while.[204] By government intervention the railway rates were reduced from 100% to 66½% over pre-war in 1927,[205] but this did not apply to wheat and barley.[206] Road transport offered a saving in both time and money even for broccoli, but corn continued to be sent by rail until after World War II.

Potato trials sponsored by Wye College were held at Nash Court in 1923, followed by others. In 1923 the Scottish Farmers' strain did best, producing 14 tons 3 cwt of ware, 1.4 tons of seed, and only half a ton of chats.[207] The 1924 trials found Majestic and Up-to-Date to be winners. Fertilizers previously applied were as follows: 5 cwt of Krinit on wheat, sulphate of ammonia, 8 cwt of "complete artificial" and 20 tons of seaweed.[208]

Sugar beet trials in 1925 were disappointing,[209] but the cultivation of the crop was increased during the war (probably on government wishes), with 221 acres in 1941, and probably a peak in 1942 dropping to 91 acres in 1945. (Tables 23 and 24).[210]

Horse breeding declined soon after the First World War; the number of brood mares had fallen to 37 in 1921 and was no longer significant enough to be recorded separately in 1931. H.T. Willett won ten horse prizes, including eight firsts, at the East Kent Agricultural Show in 1920,[211] probably a high water mark, and both he and J.W. Smith & Son (Val and H.A.) won prizes at other East Kent shows and Lord Northbourne's colt show held for a few years in the early 1920's. The Smiths switched their attention entirely to cattle when Val retired and hot summers in that decade affected the grass.[212] H.T. Willett continued to gain some awards for cart-horses at the Kentish shows to 1937: second for a shire mare and foal and three thirds in 1936,[213] third and reserve for a carthorse in 1937.[214] After the merger of the East Kent show into the all-Kent one in 1936, competition became stiffer from areas with better grass, and big breeders from all over the Southeast soon started entering, so that Thanet horses no longer had much chance. But H.T. Willett still had one stallion in 1945, the year of his death.[215] (Table 21)

When G.H. Garrad, the Kent county agricultural advisory officer, visited Thanet in 1919 he described it as one of the three chief milk-producing districts in Kent, together with Bromley and Sevenoaks.[216] Dairying continued to produce some of the most obvious evidence of advance. G.K. Burge sold out in 1924, his herd having already been dispersed,[217] but the number of pedigree herds and model dairies rose, faster in the 1930's, the role of Wye College advisors probably being important. H.T. Willett had a large pedigree Friesian herd by 1920, when he sold 61 of them for a total of £9,747, the best cow, Monkton Bangle, fetching 450 guineas from a buyer from Wrexham.[218] His pedigree Friesian Monkton Martin was the first to give a 2,000 gallon lactation here in 1921,[219] and the following September he had another, when H.A. Smith's Manor Pants also gave 2,000 gallons. At this time most of the latter's cows were accepted as Foundation cows by the British Friesian Society or the Shorthorn Society upgrading register.[220] In 1926 he sold much of his Friesians to concentrate on Shorthorns.[221] By 1935 he had 40 pedigree Shorthorns and 320 upgrading, many of which were shortly to be eligible for entry in the herd book. His Kentish Honey Jean gave 2,000 gallons in three separate lactations and helped to win the Bledisloe Trophy for the Shorthorn team at the 1934 Dairy Show.[222] In 1945 he had 12 Dairy Shorthorns giving a total of 85½ gallons between them daily. He won many awards in the East Kent, Kent and Tunbridge Wells shows at this time, and must have had the finest-named bulls in Kent: such as Kentish Astrologer and Kentish Solomon.[223] H.T. Willett won the main class of the Kent Milk Recording Society (MRS) dairy herds competition in 1938.[224] Eric Quested had started a pedigree Dairy Shorthorn and upgrading herd by 1932,[225] and in the latter half of the 1930's started a pedigree Guernsey herd. This continued to be built up during the war, which did not greatly impede transactions.

As an example of war-time prices for a mixed group of cattle, when he sold his herd on 31 March 1944 (see next paragraph for explanation), 19 pedigree Guernsey cows fetched from £26–210 (average £74/10/-), three pedigree Shorthorns £48–56 and 33 non-pedigree or cross-bred cows and heifers, mostly served by pedigree bulls, £13–74 (average £25/12/-). Two pedigree Guernsey bulls made £36 and £85.[226] An earlier example of ordinary livestock prices comes from Westwood farm in 1933: two horses fetched £35 and 17 guineas, cows an average of £22 and a bull £13.[227]

Captain Friend was a pioneer of the systematic testing of cattle for tuberculosis (TT) in Thanet, commencing in 1919.[228] Useful cattle which tested positive for the infection were sold off to farmers not interested in the procedure. H.A. Smith was running a TT herd by 1926 (the Friesians he sold then were TT),[229] and in 1928 his herd was Grade A TT.[230] Even pedigree herds were not necessarily TT at this time (there is no record that H.T. Willett's were, for example) and only 10% of British milk was TT in 1945,[231] so Irvine Friend and H.A. Smith were leaders in this. Eric Quested, inheriting inferior, probably tubercular cattle in 1919 (the author had two very mild attacks of probably bovine tuberculosis in childhood), started TT in the middle 1930's. But positive reactions kept appearing in apparently healthy animals, so to eradicate it he sold his whole herd in 1944, starting afresh after the war in 1946 with new pedigree Guernseys from a strain provenly free and resistant. An entirely tuberculosis-free herd resulted. To avoid infection his new young stock were no longer run in summer on the marshes, as those of the old herd had been. It is likely that other farmers had to go to the same lengths to gain the same results, though the author is not informed about this.

Milk recording and clean milk were other parts of the upgrading process which became widespread. Captain Hatfeild won a challenge cup in the Kent MR Society clean milk competition in 1924,[232] Captain Friend, J.W. Smith & Son (HA) and two other less well known Thanet farmers won certificates in the similar competition at the Bath and West show at Maidstone in 1925, and J.W. Smith & Son won second prize in the Kent MRS competition in 1928.[233] By 1932 Eric Quested's cowmen were "all wearing clean white coats, aprons and caps" and strict hygiene was observed; he had upgraded his dairy and milking parlour,[234] and had new concrete ones completed in 1939, soon after war had started. When the Milk Marketing Board was established the campaign was on to make the generality of farmers and retailers follow better practices. It was reported in 1933 that there were 60 registered cow-keepers and purveyors of milk, 34 dairy farms and 36 retail dairies and milkshops in the Thanet area. 34 visits of inspection were made by the local authority sanitary inspectors and "several cowmen's attention drawn to the need for greater cleanliness".[235] In 1935, the year the Accredited Milk scheme was launched by the MMB, 35 dairy farms and 60 cowkeepers were reported, and "an increasing number" were "taking greater interest in cleanliness".[236] The TT scheme came into effect in 1938,[237] and a year later there were said to be 155 TT cattle in the Broadstairs area alone.[238] In those years there was a hope that great cleanliness and scrupulous testing would obviate the need for pasteurization, which was considered by many, including H.A. Smith and Eric Quested, to spoil the milk. But in the end it proved to be unavoidable.

Pig numbers rose steadily to 1939 (Table 21). A farmer applauded locally for his pigs in the late 1930's was Ernest Philpott, who in 1937 won the Thanet NFU farm competition for holdings with a minimum of 50 acres including fruit and market gardening. An elderly man[239] with 175 acres of pasture (150 marsh), 320 of arable, and 10 acres of fruit, he had not mechanized at all, having 10 horses, 128 cattle, 262 pigs (14 breeding sows) and about 600 poultry, kept intensively. His pigs were described as excellent, though the 800 stores he sold annually were "a bit too fat". His piggeries were model: central sheds with raised concrete corridors running the length, with open piggeries on each side, for sun or shelter according to weather. There were glazed half-pipe troughs, a central weighbridge and loading dock. One of the two other detached piggeries was on the Danish plan, and he had a "first-rate licensed slaughter-house not in use" at the time.[240] Not all pigs were kept in sties all year: H.A. Smith had good results running Large White sows free on the marshes in summer.[241] They would sometimes farrow out there and appear proudly with their piglets.[242]

Poultry keeping mushroomed after 1918 and had reached over 42,000 fowls in 1931, though ducks, reaching 2,387 in 1921, declined by 1931, following on serious losses.[243] Fowls were intensively kept in Thanet from an early date, but no details are available. Marjorie Smith, wife of H.A., started keeping White turkeys at Monkton Court in 1924, and laid the groundwork for her great White flock by developing special trapnests and pedigree saddles. She increased her numbers right through the war.[244] Although the agricultural returns indicate that she was probably the largest turkey breeder here by 1941, geese and turkeys increased everywhere in Thanet during the war, ducks barely changed and only fowls declined in the 1930's and plummetted in the war, especially the last four years. (Table 22).

Marjorie Smith was a pioneer Thanet woman in farming public life, being a member of the British Turkey Federation, and British representative at the World Poultry Congress in Rome in September 1933. There she exhibited one of her turkey hens, Jemima, which was given the run of the forum. In 1939 she represented Britain at the World Poultry Congress in Cleveland, Ohio. At that time she supplied Anthony Eden's Christmas turkeys on behalf of the BTF, and played a strong role in fighting unmarked turkey imports. Alan Smith's wife Norah at Nether Hale also kept fowls very successfully, even exporting some to India just after World War Two.[245]

Livestock numbers, especially pigs and sheep, fell drastically in the first two years of war, and far more than in 1914–16; but dairy cow and heifer numbers stabilized in the later years of the war, and the number of followers and bulls had more than made up their losses by 1945. It seems that it was the smallest farmers and cow-keepers who accounted for most of the dairy cattle decline; the larger farmers were able to maintain their herd sizes. The number of breeding ewes was never so great in the inter-war years sampled as it had been before the First World War, for reasons unknown, although sheep were always important, not only for breeding on the marsh but for winter folding on the uplands and winter fattening on the marsh. The fall in ewes in 1941–45 was also much less than the fall in 1916–18, and pigs increased again, although not nearly making good their previous fall. Factors other than shortage of labour and feed were at work. The winter of 1939–40 was the severest in Thanet between at least 1894–95 and 1993 (worse than 1962–63), and of the remaining five winters of the war four brought frost and snow. Thanet had not experienced so much hard weather since the 19th century. This told on the sheep; the marsh cultivation would have been a concomitant not a cause of sheep decline. In 1940 Eric Quested, for instance, was moved by heavy losses to give up his sheep, which like many upland farmers he had fattened with bullocks on the marsh in the inter-war years.[246] (His bullocks, saved in 1940 by the great efforts of his looker,* were continued till 1943, when his marshes were given up for good). Pigs suffered from the evacuation of the towns

---

* Lookers were men living in the villages near the marsh who looked after the upland farmers' livestock there – a responsible job.

Table 16

Livestock numbers 1939–1945 (see Table 21)						
	Cows and heifers	Other cattle	Ewes	Other sheep	Sows	Other pigs
1939 = 100						
1941	86.6	79.5	76.9	77.5	59.2	70.4
1941 = 100						
1945	99	122.8	83.9	62.3	121	125
Poultry numbers	*1939–1945*	*1939 = 100*				
	Fowls	Ducks	Geese	Turkeys		
1945						
	51.1	98	200.9	161.3		

in 1940; no swill from the holiday trade either, and many small pig-keepers were forced to give up.[247]

Labour, already presenting a problem in 1939, must have become a greater worry in the early years of the war to some farmers. It depended partly on their alacrity in getting their men registered exempt from call-up, and smaller farmers unable to provide as many perquisites as larger ones, and less adept at dealing with officialdom, were probably the ones to lose most, as young men grabbed the chance to escape from the land or were simply eager to enlist. Most farm-workers were registered exempt, although those under 21 were threatened with conscription at one point. Although the labour force over 18 fell by 14.9% from 1939–41, it rose again 15.2% 1941–45 and was actually three higher in June 1945 than in June 1939. Moreover the numbers under 18 remained steady and there were 103 Land Army girls as well in 1945, plus a big rise in both male and female casual workers. (Table 28). The increased productivity of the war years was achieved nationally more by increased labour than by increased machinery, and it looks as if Thanet was perhaps not an exception. Nearly 2 million hp of tractors and combines, mostly American, were added to British farms between January 1940 and January 1942,[248] but early in 1943 farmers were asked to buy less machinery, as a result of sinkings of merchant ships.[249] Nevertheless it is a tribute to Norman Steed's work on the KWAEC machinery sub-committee that Eric Quested could not recall any great difficulties over tractors and other implements except over one tractor in 1943. It was announced in November 1942 that men in subsidiary agricultural occupations – pigmen, poultry farmers, nurserymen, fruit workers etc. – could expect to be called up,[250] but there is no Thanet information about this. The frantic manhunts of the First World War were not repeated.

New methods were being tried against pests and diseases, but farmers were still more at their mercy than in later times. Foot and mouth disease struck in what then seemed a haphazard manner, for instance all the young stock and sheep were lost at Monkton Court in 1923[251] and several other Thanet farms were hit at various times. The loss was great, as insurance had not yet started, the restrictions on cattle movement were tiresome and the great pyres of burning carcasses a grim sight and smell.[252] Swine fever was also a problem, especially because the many small keepers in the interwar, and even war years, found it hard to observe the movement restrictions and notifications, and there were a number of summonses against them.

Spraying against pests, started with potatoes during the First World War, was further developed in the 1920's. As early as 1922 and 1923 trial spraying of the noxious weed Devil's Cabbage (*Lepidium Draba*) (see p 124) was organized at Cheeseman's and four other farms by G.H. Garrad. In 1922 they tried 32 lbs of copper sulphate in 80 gallons of water to the acre,[253] and in 1923 in addition 2 cwt of sulphate of ammonia in 60 gallons of water, and 14 lbs of copper sulphate mixed with 56 lbs of sulphate of ammonia in 70 gallons of water. All three mixtures proved "fairly" effective.[254]

Not till 1942 did the first effective pesticides reach Thanet.[255] The author remembers her amazement on arriving home on leave in 1943 to find the flies had gone. They had been the immemorial scourge of farms, growing worse no doubt as livestock numbers rose in the 19th century. Lice and bugs had probably been eliminated from decent farm homes in the 18th century, fleas were kept at bay with derris powders like Keatings since the late 19th, but right down into World War Two every farm food table had a fly-catcher hanging over it, black with flies soon after it was hung in warm weather. Their nuisance in the milking parlour and dairy was even greater. It seemed a miracle that DDT had abolished them, but the downside we were yet to see.

Thanet had never suffered unduly from rabbits, and these became useful again in the war, not only for food. Before the end of 1941 rabbit and mole skins were wanted urgently for export[256] and a farm worker was fined £2 for poaching them near Cleve Court in 1945.[257]

Innovations in marketing were another feature of this period. The Isle of Thanet & District Market Growers Association was founded before 1920, when its name was changed to the East Kent & District Market Gardeners & Wholesalers Association at its AGM in Sandwich. It seemed to be flourishing, but later faded away, and probably Thanet growers did not participate much in it.[258] The KWAEC revived it in 1941 as the Sandwich and District Growers' Association; Archibald Montgomery and Norman Steed were amongst the directors. This time it was very effective, and amongst other things had supplied nearly 300 tons of vegetables for preserving by a government-financed plant at Birchington by March 1942.[259] In 1934 H.A. Smith, Eric Quested and others formed the Thanet Farmers' Dairies, opening shops in Margate and Cliftonville to sell dairy products and full cream ice-cream. Although moderately successful, it ended with the outbreak of war.

The Ploughing Match

The ploughing match was revived in 1920 by the NFU and operated successfully until the Depression. It was run on the same lines as before 1914, with lunch in a barn or granary for the farmers and their guests; there was no special dinner because of the NFU one. Classes were similar to the pre-war ones, but the single and married yearly servant class was stopped after 1921. There were rather more special prizes for farm produce donated by companies. Prizes were still given from a waggon; the Mayor of the local town and usually the MP were present, and large numbers of visitors if it was near a town. There was no wooden plough class after 1913.

A feature of this phase of the match was the greater attention given to the competitors. For the first time they were given a supper, a few days afterwards, as well as the pork pies for lunch at the match.[260] In 1921 £100 was distributed in prizes, and every unsuccessful ploughman was given 2/6d.[261] This seems to have been kept up, and much jocularity and banter seems to have been the fashion at the prize-giving.[262] It was still the great annual holiday for the farm workers, who could be seen with their families in their hundreds, if not thousands, "early in the morning, wending their way along the rural roads of Thanet", on foot.[263] Traditionally, they did walk all the way, seen off by the farmer and his family, but by 1929 the buses were coming to their help. They aimed to leave from Woodchurch farm soon after sunrise that year for the match at Sarre, but were delayed by domestic emergencies. Then the cry went up that the leaders of the stream of people-from the Shottendane valley farms were in sight striding along the Shottendane road, and the Woodchurch people set off in haste. They all walked to Birchington, where those who most wanted managed to get the bus. Maybe there was a special excursion rate, on what was probably a single-decker, hard-seated, open-top "charabanc". Some walked all the way to Sarre, and even the whole way back. The 1930 match at Northdown was easier, they went down to Westbrook and took the cheap and frequent trams, and there was no send-off as it was so simple. The competitors with the horses left the farm well before daylight, the horses a splendid sight with braided tails and manes and gleaming brasses. They had been partly got ready the evening before, and rested at least the previous day.[264]

Entries seemed much as pre-1914: 42 in 1927, 45 in 1928.[265] The fashion for Suffolk horses in the late 1920's brought a special judge, A.W. Kidner, from that county in 1930. He praised the local specimens, but said they did not have enough work: three would be enough to pull a Thanet plough. Identical remarks had been made in the 1860's, but this match at East Northdown was the last in the old tradition, and a tractor-drawn plough won the Reserve Championship.[266]

Writing of the 1930 ploughing match emphasizes the very great changes which took place between then and 1945, once the troubles of the Depression were over. These changes were as great in every way as those between 1870 and 1890, and came faster. For a while at least, when P.W. Steed bought the first local combine harvester in 1939, and others followed him, Thanet may again have been in the forefront of agricultural innovation.

The 1941–1943 national farm survey, carried out here by the KWAEC in 1941–1942 strikingly revealed the good fortune and good skills of the Thanet farmers. It divided the land into three categories: good, fair and bad. Of 116 farms and nurseries included (those under 5 acres were omitted), 73 (62.9%) had 100% good land. A further 8 (6.8%) had at least 70% good land, and a further 10 (8.6%) at least 50% good. The rest of the land was described as fair, except only for Lower Gore End farm (now built over) which had entirely bad soil. 93 farms (80.1%) were graded A for satisfactory or excellent management; of the 23 graded B all were thought to be doing their best in difficult circumstances, and there were no cases for take-over by the Committee.[267]

Chapter 10: From Victory to Glut to Where? 1945–1993. With a postscript to early 1996

General position of the farmers 1945–1973. A "Golden Age"?

Victory over Germany in 1945 found British farmers in a seemingly victorious position in the nation too. Yet 1945 was another historic national watershed, marking the end of Britain's great power status, already relatively weaker since 1918. The post-war Labour government, absorbed in state socialist reforms and winding-up the empire after five years of wartime office, had no energy or vision to pursue the enormous possibilities then for uniting Western Europe virtually on British terms, with our prestige there at an all-time high. The country and perhaps in particular many British farmers were to pay a price for this, but subsequent governments too spurned Europe for the will-o'-the-wisp of control over the Commonwealth and a continuing world role. Britain was psychologically fettered by its past successes, and what remained of our trade and investments after the war was still largely trans-oceanic. Yet in the 1960's Conservative and Labour governments in turn were forced to retract national pretensions and look towards Europe: only too late did Macmillan try to enter the European Community in 1962 and Wilson again in 1967, both to be snubbed. Edward Heath finally gained entry in 1972, on far from optimum terms; by then British trade was increasingly orientated towards Europe.

Meanwhile all this was masked by the post-war "Golden Age" of rapid growth of output in all sectors of the national economy, combined with pretty full utilization of capital and labour and a certain amount of redistribution of income, which lasted more or less till 1973. The age of mass consumption arrived, and the prosperity of the British rose beyond all past experience. Thanet farmers, like British farmers in general, shared in the benefits, and agricultural policy was not nationally contentious until the late 1960's, although the farmers everywhere were far from always satisfied.

The first two post-war years were difficult and more uncomfortable in some ways than the war itself, with shortage of fuel and food diverted to the half-starving Continent. Rationing became stricter for a while, and hotel restaurants in Thanet had to turn away all customers on occasion, something unheard of in the war. At the same time Stalin, like Hitler before him, became a powerful "ally" of British farmers as the Cold War developed.

Our farmers were urged to go all out, and the wartime system was replaced by the 1947 Agricultural Act, which provided an elaborate system of guaranteed prices and deficiency payments with generous subsidies for fertilizers (especially nitrates and phosphates) and new farm buildings. The County Agricultural Executive Committees were put on a new footing to help the farmers implement the scientific and technical recommendations of the government-funded National Agricultural Advisory Service. At the same time the government set limits to the production of certain items in order not to glut the market, and enforced some import controls. There was a remarkable rapport between the NFU chief James Turner and the Labour Minister of Agriculture, Tom Williams.[1] Eric Quested would rather shame-facedly vouchsafe long afterwards that Williams was the best agriculture minister of his working career, and he was not alone in this opinion amongst Thanet farmers, Conservative though they normally were.

The first post-war Thanet NFU dinner, held in February 1946 at the Cliftonville Hotel, managed to circumvent the food shortage, and was "a great affair, boasting much of the glitter and brilliance that characterized the function in the earlier part of the decade," in the words of the Isle of Thanet Gazette reporter. "Evening dress was predominant amongst the large company, and outwardly there were few signs of lean times." "The only note of austerity was introduced by the farmers themselves, in speeches reflecting their anxiety over the national food shortage."[2] The dinners continued in this way, and there were 300 at the St George's in February 1950.[3] After the mid-1950's the dinners were less and less reported in the press, but there were still 250 at one in February 1969.[4] The ploughing match, that other barometer of Thanet farming life, was also re-started in 1946 and by contrast greatly publicized, indicating a "golden age" indeed until the late 1960's at least (see p 267).

At the 1946 dinner the new Principal of Wye College, Duncan Skilbeck, just back from five years overseas, was one of the chief speakers, and apparently felt something like Rip van Winkel. He described how he had been "most forcibly struck by the extraordinary renewal of the farming industry." He had found the changes in the countryside "greater than he had ever imagined." "The interest now shown through farmers' discussion groups in their approach to technical problems represented a complete change of outlook and was nothing short of a revolution."[5] The farmers had been caught up in the third, scientific-technological wave of the Agricultural Revolution, which had begun in a small way around the turn of the century, and now came in far faster than had the crop revolution starting in the 16th century and the livestock breed and mechanical revolution starting in the 18th.

Subsequent governments continued broadly similar policies, with less generosity to the farmers after the peak of their importance had passed. This probably happened in 1953, when food de-rationing began in Britain and the death of Stalin brought the end of the Korean war and the worst fears of another world war. Under the Conservative governments of 1951–1964 and the first two years of the Wilson government to 1966 farmers' incomes nationally continued to rise with only intermittent checks, from £297 million in 1954 to £442 million in 1966.[6] But between 1953 and 1955 guaranteed prices were cut for surplus commodities.[7] Thanet as always must have been amongst the best-off areas, but by 1955 the chairman of the local NFU branch, R.F. Linington, stated in his dinner speech that "farming now had to consider which way it was going".[8] At the 1956 price review feeling ran so high that the Kent branch NFU sent up a resolution against it, for the first time since 1943, but the 1957 Agriculture Act was thought an NFU success. The government promised not to reduce the total value of guarantees by more than $2\frac{1}{2}$% a year and to allow in full for changes in costs, but in return the NFU gave up the privilege of demanding special price reviews in emergencies. There was a relaxation of some controls and a shift from price support towards production grants. The 1958 and 1960 reviews were especially hotly contested,[10] and between 1958 and 1960 farm prices nationally fell short of costs by over £85 million.[11]

But support continued, though the Labour government of 1964

modified the system of deficiency payments and improvement grants of the Macmillan government. Later there were attempts at market sharing with other governments and more stress on grants to raise productivity. The Agriculture Act of 1967 allocated £40 million to the farmers for grants for the next five years, these were directed towards amalgamation but did not make much progress.[12] Then in the last years of Wilson and under the Conservative government of Heath farm prices, especially for corn, put on another spurt, as the government sought to shift support for agriculture towards the market in preparation for entering the EC.[13] It was at this point that agricultural policy could be argued to have departed from the best interest of the farmers as a whole, for what had been reasonable progress in easing farming down towards the needs of the time was replaced by a headlong boost to it, with speeded amalgamation of holdings. Actual net farm incomes nationally at current prices after depreciation rose 37% from 1966–67 to 1971–72.[14] Much of this was taken by inflation, but figures quoted by the NFU indicated a rise 19% over the inflation rate between 1968 and 1974, when farming income rose from £455 million in 1968 to £796 million in 1974, at current prices,[15] a rise including inflation of 74%.

The prosperity of the larger Thanet farmers, like that of the rest of Thanet and the country, was there for all to see in these years. Electricity was laid on to a number of farms after the war, and brought changes as phenomenal as had DDT. It is hard for people now to realize how magic was the transformation from the toil with smoky lamps and stoves and open fires – though many outlying farms did not get power, or not a good supply, for some time. Little Cliffsend had none till 1973, and at Nether Hale the supply collapsed during Peter and Jill Smith's first dinner party of their married life in 1960. A few farms were not connected until later than 1973. But domestic appliances and cars in many farms multiplied and grew larger, houses were improved and holidays taken to a widening range of places. Probably the greatest Thanet farmer traveller of all time was R.F. Linington, who went practically world-wide, and even to Antarctica in 1968. His slide shows of his travels were received with much interest by the local NFU and other audiences.[16] But others too travelled far, building on an old tradition here, for even the conservative old farmer John Mockett had gone to Norfolk, Hampshire, Berkshire, Devon and Northern France. (He also went yearly to London,[17] like Bar Sackett). Many children of the bigger farmers were sent to public schools, sometimes famous ones, whereas local private and grammar schools had been more the norm before the war. This was partly enforced due to the eleven-plus exam and disappearance of local private schools, farmers wanting as always to do their best for their off-spring. Attendance at agricultural college soon became universal and essential for those wishing to farm, and Colonel Tapp's farmer sons followed their father to University. Since then others including Philip Smith have also taken University degrees, Wye College being their usual choice.

Eric Quested is known to have been paying surtax in 1966–67 and 1967–68, and it is unlikely that he was the only Thanet farmer to do so, or only in those years. Yet 1968 by contrast was disastrous for broccoli, early potatoes and corn, and he paid no tax on the farm; others must have been in the same position.[18]

Increasingly the farmers bought their land: the owned acreage was 8,310 acres in 1971, as against 4,985 in 1921, (Table 15). By way of example, Colonel Tapp bought St Nicholas Court farm in 1947.[19] Many tenant farmers bought land whilst continuing to occupy rented land: thus R.F. Linington, though mainly a tenant, bought Chambers' Wall and Bartletts in 1948,[20] and a smaller tenant farmer, the late W. Tabbush of Vincent farm, bought Little Cliff's End sometime before 1958, when he sold it to H.M. Steed.[21]

Land prices soared. In May 1947 Ozengell Grange fetched £11,000 for 159.6 acres (£68.9 per acre), and Chilton £8,250 for 111.9 acres (£73.7 per acre).[22] In 1948 Downbarton fetched £25,500 for 275 acres (£92.7 per acre) and Chambers' Wall £26,000 for 278.75 acres (£93 per acre).[23] By 1960 marshland was fetching from £5–£625 per acre, depending on the state of drainage, and upland above the marsh £500 per acre.[24] In 1974 the price of a good 200-acre farm in West Kent was £1,000 per acre[25] and the better land must have been worth more here.

The rise in the size of holdings which started in the 1930's continued apace. The smaller farmers were disappearing fast, giving up their land to building or amalgamation: the number of holdings fell from 193 in 1951 to 96 in 1971. (Table 18). By 1947 the optimum farm size was already over 400 acres, judging from a report in the *Kent Farmer* that year.

After the war urban Thanet's prosperity was more or less restored in a somewhat different way, again providing a useful market for dairy and livestock farmers. Westgate and Birchington never quite recovered their pre-war cachet – partly because of the deterioration of some of their beaches – but with Cliftonville,

Returns on capital invested per acre in Kent, excluding land value, 1947[26]	
Up to 100 acres	Nil
101–250	5¼%
Over 250 acres	13¼%
Over 400 acres	13¾%

Broadstairs and parts of Ramsgate again became fairly moneyed residential areas. The middle classes soon began to go further afield for their holidays, and most of the private schools either did not return or closed in the 1960's, but the people coming to Margate and Ramsgate were ever more, as the welfare state, full employment and high wages liberated city dwellers who could never afford proper holidays earlier. The USAF presence at Manston till 1958 also helped the local economy.

A striking feature of the "Golden Age" was the unprecedently high performance of Thanet farmers on the regional and national stage. The work of John Montgomery of Thorne farm at NFU headquarters touched the lives of all farmers in the land, since he served on many HQ committees, being on six by 1948.[27] It was in the President's advisory committee, the general purposes committee and the economic and taxation committee that he played the greatest part, and in particular in the national Price Review Committee of which he was a member for many years between 1948 and 1968. He attended a vast number of meetings and functions throughout the country at the invitation of NFU and other farming organizations, to explain NFU policies. In the late 1960's he was a member of the "Little Neddy Committee" (NEDC) to advise the government.[28] The OBE he was awarded in 1972 was well-deserved.

Robert Montgomery, his brother, was chairman of the NFU HQ potatoes and vegetables committee in 1947 and 1948, serving on these committees for a number of years, and he was a member of the Potato Marketing Board from 1955–1962.[29] H.A. Smith was on the Kent Rivers' Board till 1968, completing thirty six years service from 1932, which included the critical time of the 1953 sea floods,[30] when he was chairman (1947–1957). H.M. Steed was a member of the panel of arbitrators of the Land Tribunal from 1960.[31] N.H. Steed and Robert Montgomery served on the KAEC under Lord Northbourne after the war, and N.H. Steed remained for some years on the smaller re-organized East Kent committee under Hugh Finn from 1959. For this and other services to agriculture N.H. Steed was awarded the MBE in 1967.[32] (See p 206, 259). Eric Quested was the only Thanet man to stay on the KAEC until its closure in 1972, being on the milk production sub-committee of the main Maidstone committee continuously from 1939 to 1972.[33]

He was MMB member for the SE Region for 32 years from 1938 until his retirement in 1970, being returned unopposed in all elections but one, when the rival candidate lost his deposit. After the war he served on several Board committees and attended conferences and studied conditions in most West European countries on behalf of the Board. In 1948 he went to Denmark with the then chairman Ben Hinds to study artificial insemination, and when on their return the Board introduced it in England, he set up the Whiligh A.I. centre and sub-centres in the SE region. In 1953 and 1959 he was part of small study delegations from the Board which travelled widely in the US and Canada, and he became chairman of the working party set up to introduce US style bulk collection of milk in this country, being responsible for the procedure established for testing farm vats. He was also chairman of the Board's dairy equipment committee. When the MMB took over the country milk recording societies and regionalized them, he took an active part in this too. Amongst non-Board committees he was on the Dairying Industry Standards committee of the British Standards' Institute 1950–1972, and on the Rural Electrification Advisory Committee 1945–1970. On the political side of his work, he fought in several notable battles with the government or the Board itself on behalf of milk producers of the nation or region. One recalls how in 1966 (at the age of 70) he fought the Board to rescind the high levy imposed on the SE region to compensate the Western milk manufacturing regions for transport. (This came about because the Board members from the Western regions outnumbered and outvoted those from the East and Southeast). After unsuccessful representations to the Minister of Agriculture Tom Peart – the only person empowered to give orders to the Board – he took his case to the House of Lords, which ruled in favour of it. (Unfortunately Lord Scarman, a relative of H.A. Smith and present resident of Monkton, was one of the five judges involved who dissented from the judgement)! Eric Quested was given the MBE in 1972.[34]

Women farmers in Thanet also began to come more into their own in these years. Some may have farmed independently since the remotest times; widows had probably done so in the Middle

Ages and certainly did in the 17th century (see pps 31 and 54), and both widows and spinsters are known to have done so since the 19th (see p 138). Yet they had always been excluded from all the local farming clubs, associations, lunches and till 1937 dinners, even after town or gentry women had become magistrates and mayors. During the war two senior farmers' wives, Marjorie Smith and Mrs E. Willett, had managed to infiltrate the NFU, being paid up members from 1941[35] on an apparently temporary or unofficial basis. In 1943 the widow of a big farmer near Faversham, Mrs O. Honeyball, was admitted to the Canterbury Farmers' Club, so there was probably a general forward movement then, but the resistance was evidently stiff.[36] In February 1945 Marjorie Smith was poultry delegate to the County NFU, in May on the sub-committee to draw up a scheme for a regional organization of poultry producers, and in July on the commercial egg production sub-committee, again all apparently on a semi-official basis.[37] In September 1945 her name was put forward as suitable to serve on the HQ county poultry advisory committee, and she was co-opted onto the table poultry sub-committee of this early in 1947, apparently still as an outsider.[38] Meanwhile she was already officially on the management committee of the British Turkey Federation![39] In 1958 at last women were officially admitted to Thanet NFU: Jill Steed (daughter of H.M. and soon to be wife of Peter Smith), Margaret Smith (widow of Andrew Craig Smith) and Jean Steed (widow of Ron Steed) joined in that year.[40] Mary Tyrrel was the first woman to join the ploughing match committee in 1967.[41]

At the end of the "Golden Age" farmers' wives or widows began to become J.P.'s. Elizabeth Montgomery, who had been a magistrate in Somerset before her marriage to John, was transferred to the Bench here, and served from 1955 to 1969, when the couple moved to Somerset. Muriel Spanton (widow of Eric) was a magistrate from 1963 to 1982, Mary Montgomery (wife of Robert) from 1964 to 1973, and Ann Linington became one in 1971.[42]

Christopher Powell-Cotton became a magistrate on his return from Africa, and a number of the larger farmers were also J.P.'s: for instance H.A. Smith, who continued until a late age, H.M. Steed, R.F. Linington and N.H. Steed. But farmers' involvement in the higher echelons of local government seems to have lessened after the war. Many were active on parish councils (Eric Spanton for instance was five times chairman of Minster parish council before his sadly early death in 1961),[43] but in the later years of the Eastry Rural District Council they were not so prominent, and there were no more urban mayors or councillors from farming or gentry circles.

General position of the farmers 1972–1993: in the EC

When Edward Heath signed the Treaty of Rome in 1972 British farming was drawn into the European Common Agricultural Policy, designed mainly to help the small farmers in many parts of the continent to adapt to the intensification of methods already long prevalent in Britain, in order to remove the threat of hunger for good. It had no special relevance to British needs, and with various unfavourable aspects of the deal imposed on Britain was the price of late entry. Farmers were henceforth maintained by subsidies and higher agricultural prices, with minimum intervention prices at which the government must buy and in some cases store, if there was no market for the produce.[44] Decimalization too encouraged rocketing prices throughout the economy from 1974, from which farmers particularly benefitted, and the successive devaluations of the green £ helped British food exports till sterling's recovery in 1980 tended to make it more of a barrier. Thereafter too the number of restrictions and exacting standards to which farmers have had to conform greatly increased, sometimes due to the zeal of British civil servants in implementing EC general directives, rather than to the latter themselves.[45]

The effect was to step up the stresses and, at first, the already massive pressures on British farmers to produce more by more intensive methods. They had supplied only about 40% of the nation's food in 1939, but by 1983 they were producing 62.1% of a greater total for a population some six million larger (imports being to a high degree luxuries), and 78.1% of produce that could be produced in this country.[46] According to an academic survey, output on British general crop farms rose 10.8% between 1975 and 1984,[47] but it could not last. Nationally, output prices rose rapidly in real terms from the middle 1970's to the early 1980's, but then began to trend down and were lower in real terms in 1988 than in 1984. In 1989 and 1990 they rose again but did not keep pace with input prices; since then to 1993 the trend seemed to be on the whole down. Not surprisingly, technological changes seemed increasingly to generate cost savings rather than output increases, and output on British general crop farms in total rose only another 2.06% in 1985–90.[48]

Government statistics published some six years or more retrospectively showed farm business income for the whole UK at current prices reaching a peak in 1976, and thereafter trending down with fluctuations till a new peak was reached in 1984.[49] Thanet farmers shared in the prosperity within the inflation; since 1972 they seem to have been well up the field as ever in increasing efficiency and output. Government statistics available to 1986 show that large, owner-occupied cropping farms were by far the most profitable type,[50] and though only something over half the acreage may have been owner occupied in 1993, much of Thanet was clearly at an advantage. But smaller farmers continued to go out of business, and the fall of only 35 in the number of farms here between 1971 and 1988 compared to a fall of 97 in the previous twenty years (see Table 18) may be due to the larger size of the units being combined or passing out of agricultural use.

The best measure available of the prosperity of Thanet's surviving farms is the price of land, despite the large measure of general inflation this has contained. Prices peaked in 1982–83 at over £3,000 per acre,[51] after doubling in the previous six to seven years. Elmwood farm, Reading Street, (not prime land) had fetched £1,113 an acre in 1976.[52] By 1986 prices were more uncertain. In that year 153 Grade 1 acres at Gore Street were put up for auction at £3,100, but finding no buyer[53] were later sold for "close to" £2,450 per acre, though Hoo farmstead and land totalling 179.6 acres reached £3,062 an acre (perhaps because of the value of farmhouses as residential property).[54] In December 1988 46.8 Grade 1 acres at Upper Hale made "near their asking price of £2,350 per acre."[55] Ebbsfleet farm with 534 acres (175 Grade 1, 359 grade II) fetched £2,420 per acre in 1989,[56] but after sale was partly let and partly derelict till 1994, awaiting conversion to a golf course. Land prices in Thanet were in June 1993 roughly around £2,000 an acre, against a national average of about £1,500.[57]

British farm exports and farm incomes nationally were helped by the devaluation of sterling in October 1992 and the attendant 20% devaluation of the green pound, according to statements on the radio by NFU national spokesmen, but Thanet vegetable crops faced considerable difficulties from competition. Even the larger Thanet farmers faced many problems, in view of their high inputs, the tremendous demands of the bureaucracy, the new ruthlessness of financial institutions, the stranglehold of supermarkets on consumer and seller alike and the growing tide of vegetable and fruit imports, on which the British government imposed no quality controls, whilst strict ones were exacted from the British grower. Another factor against the farmer was the incredible pretentiousness of British consumers, who had long ago forgotten about patriotism and the more affluent of whom, or even the not-so-affluent, now required greengrocery of all kinds from anywhere in the world out of the normal local seasons. Yet Thanet continued to provide a livelihood for farms of varying size, and it was said by some, though opinions differed, that the smaller farmer might now be in a better position than the larger: though he could gain less, he had less at risk. Be that as it may, a younger farmer of 300 acres decided in 1992 that the only way he could continue was by paying off his seven workers, and growing mostly corn, doing all the work himself with some help from contractors.

Farming's relative share in the national market was falling. According to government statistics, the proportion of consumer expenditure spent on food fell from around 23% in the early 1960's to 12.7% in 1986, and whilst supermarkets flourished, the Marketing Boards weakened or disappeared. The farm gate retailing of specialist high quality products, successful in some parts of the country, was not prominent here, with some interesting exceptions (see p 264, 266). There had only been a few farm vegetable shops in Thanet, and an attempt to open one met with planning refusal for some time in at least one case. Thanet people wanting organic produce found only one heroic very small holding willing to experiment with this market, so far as is publicly known. There were no attempts to run entertainment farms for the public, like for example Farming World at Boughton under Blean.

There seemed to be a consensus locally and nationally that stress was now a serious factor in modern farming. The *Farmers Weekly* for 20 November 1992 ran two pages on "the heavy burden of farming", featuring an interview with a farming stress consultant, Mrs Jenny Cornelius of Sandwich. Typical causes in her opinion were government interference, isolation, work overload, and the pressure of keeping pace with new technology. But most of her nationwide clientele came from the smaller farmers of the North and West, who did not yet farm like businessmen, which they did here. Moreover a national survey of 501 farmers carried out for the *Farmers Weekly* by Professor Cary Cooper of Manchester University and reported in the same pages also found that farmers in the South of England were not amongst the worst affected.[59]

Nevertheless, in March 1993 farmers' suicide hotlines were opened in parts of Kent,[60] indicating a shocking situation, and although local farmers were coping better than many, many seemed hassled as they never were before. But a good season for corn in 1993 brought greater cheerfulness.

Another obvious casualty of intensification was the lively community life of the Thanet farmers. The splendid ploughing match declined rapidly from the late 1960's and ceased to exist after 1973. Although it may partly have collapsed under its own weight, (see p 268), the Young Farmers' Club wasted away about the same time. The first club in Kent started in 1925,[61] but the Thanet one appeared late. Begun in 1949 by the NFU, with the active involvement of Peter Linington (son of R.F.)[62] and others – his future wife Miss Ann Walker became secretary in 1953 – the Thanet branch had 24 members in 1950 and throve until the late sixties. In 1968 two members, Michael Hancock and Arthur Slate, gained the Silver Badge for seven or more proficiency tests,[63] but in 1972 there were only six members, all over 25,[64] and it closed in 1982.[65] The falling numbers of farmers were the basic reason and the fact that they were rather banded in age groups, so that at that time there was a dearth of young people.[66] Needless to say, there was a far greater dearth of them in 1993.

The NFU branch also suffered, and although membership may have more or less held up, attendances at meetings were said to be normally very low.[67] There were 99 paid-up members in 1953,[68] 66 in 1979 (including Invicta Airways),[69] and 62 in 1988 with 13 at the AGM.[70] Only 185 were at the dinner dance at the St George's in 1976, and 85 of these were guests of the chairman, Peter Smith, who brought them to make the event pay, as ticket prices had been set too low.[71] It was said to be a very enjoyable evening, but it is not recorded that any civic dignitaries were present as in former days.[72] (See p 246). After that it went quickly downhill, but about 1980 was "revived" "from a low ebb".[73] It then struggled on, and in 1993 was said to be rather lacklustre and attended by no more than 30–40 from Thanet and the same number from the Ash branch, with which Thanet was paired in 1971.[74] Visits by local MP's still occurred, and the Euro MP Christopher Jackson occasionally spoke at NFU meetings both local and county, as at Sandwich in December 1992 to Thanet and Ash branches. The pairing of these two branches in 1972 seemed to mark a turning-point. After that both shared the same permanent professional secretary working from Ash, and held some meetings jointly, some separately. That a loss of identity was involved in this change must have been in the mind of the late John Ash (Updown farm), who declared that he would resign if a merger came about.[75] In the event it was not a complete merger and he continued to serve the branch, but it did emphasize the decline of the Thanet farm community. In 1993 the author was told that the local branch had far less importance than it used to have, as the bigger farmers had links with the NFU at higher levels, and this was part of a nation-wide pattern. Yet Thanet farmers continued keenly to support the Canterbury Farmers' Club, 11 of them becoming chairman of it between 1943 and 1994.

Despite everything Thanet farmers continued to work for the wider agricultural community, although nobody now had the time to spare that a John Montgomery or Eric Quested could devote to extra-farm business. Robert Montgomery junior was invited onto the Potato Marketing Board in 1983 and became vice-chairman. Peter Smith was on the NFU HQ potato committee for some fourteen years, and had been on the County committee for over 33 years by 1993, probably a record. Peter Dyas served on the HQ peas and processed vegetables committee from 1983–1993. Many other Thanet farmers had served and continued to serve on the County committees. David Steed headed the successful resistance to Thanet being made a nitrate restricted zone in 1989, and was invited onto the NFU National Nitrate Committee in 1991. (See p 270). Mary Tyrrel served on the Kent County Agricultural Show livestock and agriculture committee from the 1970's, became its Goat Steward in 1979 and was elected to its Council in 1993. As down the centuries, farmers continued to be on the Stour-Wantsum river board in its various manifestations. In 1993 Martin Tapp was chairman of the current River Stour (Kent) Inland Drainage Board, of which Peter Dyas had been a member since 1972. Martin Tapp was also on the Flood Defence Committee.

There were still three J.P.'s from farming circles: Ann Linington, Jean Spanton, and Tessa Tapp. Michael Smith succeeded his father and retired in 1988, and the male farmers now seemed to have disengaged from this role under pressure of work. They were particularly vulnerable in it too; the author was told that all the male farmer J.P.'s suffered one or more severe farm fires in the 1960's and 1970's which were suspected of being started as revenge against them.[76]

The social position and influence of the larger farmers remained high, but useful as their talents would have been there, they were

too busy for any part in local government except at a parish level.
They were now less formally involved in local administration than
at any time since the Middle Ages. Before the 20th century, they
had taken little part in urban affairs, but were always powerful in
rural ones; then followed the fleeting phenomenon of high farmer
profile in town and rural councils, which waned after World War
Two. Since 1974 the inter-war "balance of power" had been
reversed, with Thanet District Council taking over rural Thanet,
much of which had become in atmosphere increasingly a semi-
rural, semi-industrial suburb, with factories here and there and
farm buildings themselves often looking like factories, whilst many
farmhouses and cottages were now occupied by townspeople.
Between February 1988 and 1 June 1993 there were some 112
applications for planning permission for non-agricultural developments in rural Thanet, mostly for dwelling houses, riding stables
and industrial buildings, but also for golf-courses, petrol filling
stations, hotels, roads, and caravan parks. Some of these only were
refused, yet inland, west of Haine and Nash Lane, the traditional
wide vistas of open fields largely remained, though shrinking in
places.[77]

The headlong decline of urban Thanet as a resort and residential
area since the late 1960's did not fail to influence the nature of its
local government and contributed to these changes. At some point
urban and rural Thanet drew apart in the public eye in a new way.
The author was told that the Thanet NFU decided to ban local
government personages from its dinners a generation ago, after a
Mayor disgusted the company at one "with stories hardly fit for
a sergeants' mess". The chairmen of Thanet District Council
appear never to have been invited to an NFU dinner, these having
long since become informal and restricted to agricultural guests of
honour or an MP or MEP. Contacts between farmers and Thanet
District Council now seemed mainly to take the form of consultations between the NFU and the paid officials of the Council, who
were a power in the land. From being major employers of labour
and filling a unique position in the island's hierarchy, farmers had
now in town-dominated Thanet become virtually one amongst the
various groups of businessmen, and one which employed comparatively little labour. In 1988 at least 180 people were in regular
fulltime agricultural employment and 77 in regular part-time; these
numbers may really have been somewhat higher but had declined
by 1993. (See Table 29. Thanet farmers also relied much on seasonal labour, but as noted in Table 29, this is not adequately

reported in the agricultural returns). In 1993, of the six largest employers in Thanet, Canterbury & District Health Authority employed 1,600 on the island, Hornby Hobbies at Westwood 600, Carradon Heating 150, Steelcase Strathmore 150, Navico 150, British Telecom 120 and Thanet District Council 110.[78]

Farming here seems not to have been immune to the bad press which it nationally tended to acquire in the 1970's, when a breach began to open between the intensive methods which the farmers were being taught and given strong financial incentives to pursue, and the growing perception of environmentalists that these were or might become damaging in many directions. As everywhere in the arable zones, farming's image in Thanet suffered from the straw and stubble burning which became standard practice then, by occasional instances of people being caught or claiming to have been caught in chemical spray drift and by animal lovers' campaigns against battery fowls – although the public eagerly consumed cheap chicken and eggs. After the end of the ploughing matches urban people here generally had little contact with farmers and were thus more prone to believe the worst.

Back in 1972 Thanet farmers complained that they had been snubbed by not being invited to a Common Market conference at Ramsgate organized by Neville Hudson,[79] and in 1975 a local businessman and Thanet councillor, alarmed by the decline of tourism, accused the farmers in a letter to the press of spoiling the island's views by cutting down all the trees and hedges. R.A. Robertson of Downbarton farm sprang to their defence by pointing out that most of these had been destroyed centuries before, as indeed they had. (But see p 273).[80] In 1984 David Steed, then chairman of Thanet NFU, reported that they were working hard to improve their public image,[81] and there were other references in the Kent NFU journal to this problem and to the need to pay attention to relations with the TDC. The end of straw and stubble burning, greater care with chemical sprays since the 1970's and improved weather forecasting which helped the farmer avoid drift, even the disappearance of battery fowls in Thanet probably all helped. Yet in late 1992 the author heard a well-known urban person (not connected with TDC) in a lecture to a local civic society accuse the farmers of ruining the soil of parts of upland Thanet with their deep cultivators. Such attacks would have been inconceivable in earlier times, when basic farming methods were not in question – even though deep cultivators of a sort were used from the second quarter of the nineteenth century – and when a significant proportion of the Thanet population depended on farming for a livelihood.

The nature of landowning changed greatly. Some of the Oxbridge colleges continued to own land here, the Conyngham family still had some, the Powell-Cotton estate remained, and some was owned by large financial institutions, but the farmers themselves were the largest landowning class, though possessing 57% of the land in 1984 against a national figure of 70% in farmers' hands in 1985.[82] The former small landowners at Dumpton Park, Dane Court, Cleve Court, etc, either sold out for development or let their homes long since. Our one surviving resident gentry family, the Powell-Cottons, farmed most of their land themselves after 1970 through their farm manager, Anthony Curwen having succeeded his father John in this post, and the Liningtons were now their sole tenants. The estate was run as a trust, and the family heirs were businessmen in other parts of England. A new social pattern had emerged in the Thanet agrarian community. Christopher Powell-Cotton CMG, MBE, MC, a former member of the Colonial Service and minister in the Ugandan government in the latter days of the Empire, and his sister Antoinette, were the last resident standard bearers of the old gentry class.

Although rent control under the 1948 act was abolished in 1958, rents nationally had on the whole risen less than farm incomes.[83] The tenant security act of 1946, even though modified, and the taxation system discouraged the letting of land to farm, and with the high investments required made it hard for new blood to enter the industry; this was the position in Thanet no less than nationally.

The farm workers' position 1945–1993

In this period their distinctive local Thanet condition merged in the general one of all British farm workers: perhaps it was the end of their history. With steadily rising nationally imposed wages and a strong NUAW, their standard of living rose in the "Golden Age" with that of the rest of the nation, though it remained behind that of the skilled industrial workers. The NHS and the welfare state in their early happy years brought them enormous, sudden benefit, which does not need detailing here. Wages reached 100/- a week in 1950. At Woodchurch at least they still got cheap milk and only paid 3/6d a week rent in 1968, whilst two who lived in council houses had their rent subsidized.[84] Other perquisites like cheap coal had been dropped as wages rose. Seven days consecutive holiday was started soon after the war, and raised to two weeks in 1948.[85] Many farmers laid on a coach to take their workers and families to ploughing matches and the Kent agricultural show; this started at Woodchurch not very long after the war.

In the 1950's the single men began buying motorcycles, and in the 1960's most farm employees acquired cars. After the car, the goal for many, especially on the isolated farms, was a council house, which enabled a man to seek work outside agriculture, and even if he stayed in it, put his wife in easy reach of shops and work whilst he drove to the farm. As many council houses were built by all the urban councils from the late 1940's to the '60's,[86] this dream was realized in some cases.

Electrification and other improvements reached many farm cottages, but came only gradually to outlying ones – Plumstead farm, occupied by a bailiff, was perhaps the last one in Thanet to get electricity in 1991.

Educational opportunities did not improve as fast as material ones, but two girls from Woodchurch passed the eleven or thirteen plus exams in the 1950's,[87] and over the years two young people from Nether Hale farm workers' families, and the son of a Polish refugee employed at Spratling Court went to University.[88] This must have been paralleled on other farms, and the raising of the school leaving age to 16 in 1973 brought a full secondary education and attendant opportunities in theory at least to all.

Some upward and outward mobility for the farm workers themselves also existed in the "Golden Age", for instance when Eric Quested retired in 1970 his head cowman Leslie Furlong became head cowman at Wye College farm until his own retirement in 1985, and Bill Christian, another long-term Woodchurch employee, got a good job with the Gas Board.

Since then the Thanet farm worker had suffered like many others from intensification. Many farm workers, like many farmers, were driven from their chosen calling, not all found equally congenial or better paid work. Jobs were far fewer, though as ever good workers were not always easy to find. In much fewer numbers and with a consequently weakened union the farm workers were still somewhat less well favoured than those exercising comparable skill and responsibility in other industries as far as wages were concerned. On the other hand, farm cottages were now generally as good as council houses, quite often with central heating, and practically free at £1.50 a week, as long as the job lasted. According to the Rural, Agricultural and Allied Workers' section of the TGWU, fewer than 1% of all British farm workers owned their own homes in 1991. But industrial workers too were dwindling, and in the conditions of the time the lack of a mortgage might be a blessing.

The farmers' interest now seemed to lie in employing more part-time and casual labour and using contractors, which was not in the interest of the workers or of the rural community as a whole. Amongst other issues where farm workers' and farmers' financial advantages were currently at variance was the Council Tax, in 1993 under debate between the two unions. (The rates had been covered by a Union agreement and the Community Charge was also paid by employers in nearly all cases in this area).

A further cloud on the horizon was a recent decision by the Agricultural Wages Board to introduce flexible working, with no formal days off and an average of 39 hours work per week in every three week period. This was opposed by the union and not popular with men with families.

In order to encourage skilled entrants to agriculture, the Kent Apprenticeship scheme for farm workers was fully launched in 1993. But the skills of 80% of those employed in Thanet agriculture up to management level were already being improved by the courses run by the East Kent Training Group, a charitable trust which took over the task from the Agricultural Training Board around 1980. Roger Hobcraft, manager of Cleve Court farm, became chairman in 1990, and most Thanet farmers were involved. The trust was financially self-supporting with 70 members, all courses being paid for by attenders or employers.

Interestingly, the position of the agricultural workers' union had changed twice since the Second World War. The post-war years of strength were succeeded by a weaker period due to the workers' prosperity: amalgamation with the TGWU in 1976, thought by some local members to be a mistake, came about partly because young agricultural workers were joining less, as well as falling possible membership. Some existing members too preferred to leave and buy into a pension. However, the difficulties of that time were now said to be past, and the Union not to be doing badly locally. This was considered due to the harsher climate in agri-culture and lack of off-farm opportunities, unlike the situation in

earlier times when cold economic winds led to mass desertion of
the Union in the 1870's and 1920's.

Amongst cases being taken up by the Union in 1993 were those
concerning rent levels for former tied cottages occupied by former
employees of a farmer owner who had reduced his workforce and
wanted to let his property at an economic rate. Most of the union's
work however now lay with the considerable body of part-time or
seasonal workers, mostly female, who in 1993 were not entitled in
law to any statutory benefits, but who might have depended on
such jobs for years. The Union saw them as a new constituency, as
the full-time workers ebbed away,[89] (and the 1994 law extending
benefits to part-timers hardly eliminated their need of Union back-
up).

The general picture of the farm workers' life nationally seemed
hardly jollier in 1993 than the farmers' – less so perhaps, for they
did not have the farmers' bonus of good years. There were reports
of increased suicides amongst the workers too, in their case said to
be caused more by loneliness and lack of workmates with whom
to talk over family problems.

Farming practices 1945–1993

The "Golden Age" until the nineteen seventies saw the apogee of
Thanet mixed farming. The use of herbicides made most of the
island's fields immaculately weed-free again, as perhaps they had
not been since the mid-18th century – although even in the early
1960's one sometimes saw a weedy field. At the same time most of
the soil was probably in all-time peak condition, for it was receiving
both plenty of subsidized artificial fertilizer and abundant good
farmyard manure – though little horse manure after 1960.

In 1954 G.H. Garrad published one of the most detailed descriptions of Thanet farming, as of the year 1950.[90] It was the first such
since 1846. He picked out R.F. Linington as a prime example,
noting that he "followed no fixed rotation but a flexible one, based
on early potatoes planted about the middle of January and lifted
about the middle of June, followed by broccoli, kale, mangolds,
green maize or oat and tare silage for his dairy herd, followed by
two or three corn crops (barley or wheat) in succession. He usually
sows 30 or 40 acres of Plumage Archer barley in December and
the rest as early in the spring as he can sow in good condition. As

elsewhere some farmers are better than others but the standard of farming in Thanet is still definitely high. The farms are rather larger than in most parts of Kent." A common rotation of crops is 1) early potatoes 2) broccoli 3) barley 4) barley 5) lucerne for 3, 4 or more years 6) wheat."[91]

The following year, 1951, R.F. Linington won the silver challenge cup value 100 guineas for the best managed mixed farm in Kent, two to two and a half crops per year being taken from most of the arable. The quality and condition of his cattle were very good and the pigs "were in very good condition and full of bloom." The judges liked "the method of maintenance of soil fertility and noted that full use was made of old buildings."[92]

Another brief picture of the Linington farms comes to us from 1965: by then 338 owned acres at St Nicholas and 568 between Birchington and Margate in the main site. There was a concentration on four crops: 190 acres of cauliflowers, 95 acres of early potatoes, 450 acres of cereals, (wheat and barley), 110 Ayrshire cows in two herds, and a full-time workforce of 45.[93]

At Monkton Court in 1967 the crops on 960.5 acres showed wide variety, as did the livestock: peas (for canning) 154 acres, wheat 41, barley 77, oats 63, peas for harvesting green 37, corncobs 14, maize 7, wurtzels 6, broccoli 84, lucerne 9, grass seed $67\frac{1}{2}$, grass 624, orchards 6, sugar beet seed 24, savoy cabbage 6, kale 25, brussels sprouts 6; 485 Thanet Down sheep, 250 dairy Shorthorns (1963 figures) and 150,000–160,000 turkeys of all ages. 40 men and 18 women were permanently employed, the latter mostly on the turkeys.[94]

A slightly different kind of farming was done by the Montgomery family whose main base was at Thorne farm: in 1952 on about 800 acres on several farms they grew early potatoes, grass seeds, broccoli and cabbage, with a small acreage of cherries and a larger one of special stock strawberries on a farm outside Thanet. Very few livestock had been kept on their farms since the war.[95]

Eric Quested, a smaller farmer, had 300 acres by the mid-1960's, and grew wheat, barley, potatoes, broccoli/cauliflower and fodder crops, had a herd of 80–100 Guernseys and employed 9 full-time men in 1970, with an efficient bailiff, Bert Kemp, on whom he had relied much over the years. He normally grew three crops in two years in his latter years.[96]

Yet another type of enterprise was run on one of H.M. Steed's farms at Chilton: this was primarily a market-garden unit with 150 acres of barley fertilized by a pig herd of 15 sows and a boar and their progeny.[97]

Barley remained Thanet's most outstanding crop in the "Golden Age", and R.F. Linington won the championship at the Brewer's Exhibition in 1949, 1950, 1951 and 1960, came second at the Royal Agricultural Winter Fair in Toronto in 1961, and won prizes in various lesser competitions. This was with Plumage Archer, later in the 1960's they used Proctor.[98] H.A. Smith was growing Proctor Union and Zephyr barley, and Condor oats in 1967;[99] few oats were grown after the farm horses went, and Condor where they were.

Cappelle wheats were introduced here probably not long after East Anglia, and were widespread in the 1960's. J.P. Ash won first and J. Redwood of Fulham farm, Garlinge second in the Home Counties' eliminating competition for milling wheat in 1957.[100]

There was a drop in vegetable growing in the 1950's for some reason but they increased very much in the 1960's and reached 1,434.25 acres in 1971. (Table 26). In general the whole period since the war had seen a marked swing to wheat, early potatoes, broccoli-cauliflower and other vegetables. Peter Smith has records of cauliflower-broccoli varieties he has grown since before 1960, but little is said to have been saved in most farmers' records about varieties. Eric Quested was growing Home Guard, Ulster Chieftain, Majestic and Comet potatoes in 1968, obtaining Comet seed direct from Scotland in 1970.[101] Jill Smith grew Comet, Ulster Prince and Premier in the 1960's at Little Cliff's End farm. Up to the early 1950's the Liningtons were growing the following broc-coli/cauliflower varieties: Late Feltham Satisfaction, Queen's, White Beauty, Snow White, Superb, Early White and Autogiant. In 1963 they were growing the first three in the previous list, with Reading Giant, Roscoff 1–5, Extra Early Roscoff and Late Enterprise.[102] By 1968 new Australian varieties had come in, and in that year Eric Quested was growing Treveau 3 and 4 and Late June broccoli from his own seed, and from bought seed St David's Seal, Whitehead Mayfayre, 2910 Early Whitehead, Markanta, Late Enterprise and Midsummer, and the following cauliflower: White Acre, Novo Mother (sic) and Decimo from bought seed. He bought Enterprise, and St David's Seal (2910 plants) from R.F. Linington and Captain Hatfield as well. In 1970 he grew Barrier Reef, Novo and Decimo cauliflower from his own seed, Late Autumn and Kangaroo from plants bought from John Ash, and the following 11 varieties of broccoli: 9803, Treveau 4, Markanta,

St David's Seal, Annato, Mayflower and Late Enterprise from his own seed, Thanet, Manston, Summer Snow and June Heading from plants bought from Reginald Tyrrel.[103] Thanet and Manston were presumably developed locally.

There was a problem with containers for packing broccoli-cauliflower. When wholesalers stopped supplying returnable boxes most Thanet growers used orange boxes till Peter Linington developed his own returnable bushel crates (made by a Canterbury firm at 5/- each) in 1963–64.[104] H.M. Steed persuaded Kent Vegetable Co-operative (see p 259) to use returnables,[105] and most larger concerns did so. Smaller and older farmers may have stayed with the orange boxes; Eric Quested was still using them in 1968.[106]

Amongst the various pests attacking potatoes were Colorado beetle, against which Kent County Council sent spraying teams from summer 1947 to the end of 1956.[107] Virus mosaic disease was a serious problem affecting 75% of Thanet broccoli fields in 1949–50, but was defeated by spray control of aphids which carried it.[108]

Seed growing began to take on in this period, the Montgomerys and Lamonts leading the way. Early in 1961 two of their farms (Thorne and Manston Green) featured in a farm walk in connection with International Seed Year, on which the Aberystwyth herbage varieties of Kent wild white clover were featured.[109]

More of the leading innovators followed P.W. Steed and the Thanet Scots and bought combines and grain-drying plants towards the end or soon after the war. Already in September 1945 N.H. Steed addressed a discussion meeting of the Canterbury NFU on the subject of combines. By this time H.M. Steed had an Allis Chalmers combine and dryer and his brother Ronald a Marshall one at East Northdown.[110] In 1945 Ronald Steed invented a device to pick up lodged corn with this combine, which had not proved able to do so satisfactorily. With the aid of H.J. Richards, chief engineer of H.S. Tett & Co of Faversham, he had his machine equipped with straight spring tines on a pick-up reel, rotating through the fingers of the knife-bar, in place of the standard sails.[111] Later models of combine were adapted by all manufacturers in this way. This farmer was quite an inventor, and his farm and workshops contained "many and ingenious devices", but his life ended too early in a tragic road accident.[112] R.F. Linington bought a combine in 1946, which arrived in boxes from Canada to be assembled on the farm.[113] At Monkton Court there were two Allis Chalmers combines at this time.[114] The bulk of the farmers did not buy combines and dryers till the 1950's; Eric Quested bought a Massey Harris in 1953, "because all the farmers are getting them now." This brand was the general favourite; with it was installed at Woodchurch a Kennedy & Kemp's corn-drying plant, with a Penny & Porter's corn winnowgrader.[115]

In 1954 Colonel Tapp's farm was cited amongst others outside Thanet as an example of good practice in grain drying and storage. He used compressed wooden panels on angle iron for the sides of bins built on a concrete floor raised some 8 feet above ground level in a Dutch barn. The bins held some 300 tons of barley and cost about £750 to construct. Mobile tankers could be driven underneath to be gravity filled through a hole in the bin. Colonel Tapp had had an orthodox high temperature grain dryer for some time, but had recently constructed a 10-hold in-sack dryer, using hot air from the furnace of the orthodox dryer. By using sleepers and material available on the farm, the cost did not exceed £10.[116]

Some mechanized broccoli planters were in use by 1950[117] and in 1960 Peter Smith patented a U-shaped detachable platform to fit round a tractor to carry 120 one-bushel packing boxes. It weighed 12–15 cwt empty and could be detached in five minutes. As the tractor moved through the field the cutters could hurl the broccoli onto this platform, where other workers packed them immediately, thus saving a good deal of time. The prototype of this device was first invented by Peter's father-in-law H.M. Steed at Updown.[118]

Tractors increased greatly in number on the larger farms, less so, though with rising horsepower, on 250–300 acre holdings. Eric Quested had four from post-war to 1970, Massey Harris or Ferguson, with one horse until George Christian retired in the late 1960's, but at Monkton Court there were 26 tractors by 1973, with one horse.[119] Some hiring of machinery through contractors had started in the 1960's: in 1968 Eric Quested hired a Ford tractor dung loader from Invicta Motor Works, Canterbury.[120]

Garrad noted that the use of seaweed as fertilizer had almost ceased in 1950 because of labour costs,[121] and the Council were obliged to collect and dump it.[122] However by the following year there was considered "to be a fortune in it", 40 licences had been issued to collectors and many more were asking for them.[123] No more mention has been found of this and nobody now can remember anything about it. By 1968 the beaches were piled with rotting weed with which even the Council seemed unable to cope.[124] Increasingly it was washed up mixed with plastic and other garbage, which littered Thanet's shores, making it impossible to use, in any case.

The only scraps of information about the type of artificial fertilizer used comes from Woodchurch. Eric Quested normally applied 2 cwt additional potash to his broccoli "to make them frost resistant." In 1968 he was putting "GP2 Patullo Higgs" on his cauliflower, "Main Crop potato manure", nitrate of chalk, sulphate of ammonia, nitrate of potash and Fison's Topgro 9C on other crops. He also applied shoddy, sugar beet pulp and well-rotted dung from his own stock.[125]

Pesticide spraying appeared to have become prophylactic by the 1960's, probably from the 1950's. In 1968 at Woodchurch early potatoes were sprayed with carbyne, wheat with M25, barley with an unidentified substance and the broccoli plant bed with metasystox,[126] all apparently as a routine precaution. Devil's Cabbage (*Lepidium draba*), still rampant in 1950, was amongst the noxious weeds brought under control in this period by chemical sprays.

In Garrad's 1950 survey he no longer assigned Thanet to a leading position among Kent milk producing areas as he had in 1919, but he noted the importance of milk supplied to summer visitors and boarding schools.[127] This last period of Thanet dairy farming was characterized by high efficiency and cleanliness, as the many small unhygienic businesses of the 1930's were eliminated or improved by the combined effects of the war, amalgamation of farms and the MMB and KWAEC/KAEC. Eric Quested enjoyed his Woodchurch pedigree Guernsey herd from 1946 to 1970. He claimed it was one of the first six entirely TB free herds in Kent, and with H.A. Smith's, one of a small number of brucellosis-free ones in the whole of the UK. It ran at about 80–100 head from 1950–1970. After electricity was installed in 1946, a new all-electric dairy with the most modern equipment of the day was built, with a Frigidaire condensing unit for the cooler, a sterilizing room and electric fans. An Alpha Laval bucket plant milking machine followed not long after. The whole area around the dairy and milking parlour was concreted and kept clean too. He was probably one of the first, if not the first, in Thanet to have this kind of equipment, which became standard in all the better farms in this period. He was also a local pioneer with de-horning, which originally dismayed his vet, but brought a much better life to the cows. The boss cow and the hierarchy of lesser bosses under her (see Ill.) were reduced to the ranks, and all the bullying disappeared. On winter nights all cows cuddled together for warmth under the lodges, whereas before the dominant few had denied the use of the lodges to most of them. Eric's bulls tended to be pets and get too fat! They were superseded by artificial insemination in the mid-1950's. This was fairly early, but bulk tank collection of milk started in Thanet rather late, in 1968, the first tank at Woodchurch costing £685.[128]

In May 1970 the Woodchurch herd consisted of 70 cows, 24 heifers and 15 calves. 8 cows and 8 calves considered inferior were disposed of,[129] and when the residual herd of 62 cows, 28 heifers and 7 calves was sold on his retirement in November 1970, 13 cows were classified as Very Good, 19 Good and the rest Average – not outstanding but a decent herd for a busy MMB member with poor grass. The prices fetched were judged to be below the real value – the best cow went for £155, average for served cows and heifers £71, total £5,653,[130] and the Inland Revenue made him a refund on this account.[131] But Guernseys, with their exceedingly rich milk, were going out of fashion.

Other herds in Thanet were larger: as mentioned R.F. Linington had 110 in two herds in 1965, and H.A. Smith had 159 pedigree T.T. Shorthorns in 1963, with 84 young stock and 8 bulls, for he did his own breeding. Some Red and White Friesian blood had been introduced by A.I. by 1972, when the herd was slightly smaller at 100 cows, and was brucellosis-accredited too.[132] Nobody in Thanet found it worth-while to be very ambitious with cattle-breeding, there was not the grass. Garrad noted in 1950 that lucerne was the commonest hay crop,[133] and that because of the poor summer grass, much reliance had to be placed on green fodder silage crops. Many farmers made silage in these years (it started here during the Second World War), but Eric Quested and some others only made a grudging experiment with it and abandoned it with distaste.

Sheep declined more in number after the war than during it: only 1,456 breeding ewes in 1951. After getting back to 3,402 in 1961 (Table 21), they ebbed away rapidly to 565 in 1971. H.A. Smith continued with his interesting Thanet Downs, and was possibly the last farmer keeping sheep in 1971. In 1967 there were 485 Thanet Downs and in 1973 the flock was described as 3/4 Suffolk, 1/8 Southdown and 1/8 Kent. There were then five family lines of 60 ewes each, all twins were retained for breeding, and that year 35 flock rams were to be sold at Ashford at 18 months. H.A. Smith told the journalist making this report that the most they fetched had been 47 guineas, but they never failed to find buyers. Henley Homewood, a commercial flock master on 500 acres at Charing, was then a regular buyer, and "his only fear was that the breed may disappear."[134]

Pigs rose in number to 642 breeding sows in 1951, fell to 452 by 1961, and were almost the same in 1971: 453 sows and gilts, 11 boars and 2,932 other pigs in that year's returns. (Table 21). H.M. Steed's pig unit at Chilton farm (see p 253) attracted attention in 1961. Old cowsheds and stables had been converted by farm labour at a total cost of £2,000 into two pig houses, each with an open yard attached, in which the sows and boar wintered. In winter individual feeding of the breeding stock was up to 7lb per day of a mixture of 2/3 barley, 1/3 wheat plus minerals. During the summer the sows and boar ran out on ley and were fed nuts at 5lbs per head on the ground. About 200 baconers were sold annually. A separate rearing and fattening building was equipped with three modified Ruakura-type pens designed by Norman Snell, which proved most efficient. The sow had access to an exercising and feeding run through doors at the end of the creep. The piglets stayed two or three weeks in this house, the light in the creep being gradually raised, so that they were hardened off by the time they went to the fattening pens. Selected Large White/Landrace gilts were kept for breeding, and the fat pigs were sold at 6–7 months. They reached a maximum of 6lbs meal per day.[135]

Laying fowl flocks returned to about pre-war levels by 1951, and reached over 23,000 in 1961, but never regained the all-time high of 1931. In 1961 there were over 10,000 broilers as well in Margate parish, but it is not known who kept them. Broadstairs was another area with a large number of intensively kept fowls. In the decennial figures examined, geese dwindled after their 1945 peak of 436 and ducks after their 1951 one of 2,211. Intensive fowl keeping much reduced between the 1987 and 1988 agricultural censuses. (Table 22).

By far the largest and most spectacular poultry enterprise in Thanet was Mrs Marjorie Smith's white turkey flock at Monkton Court, continued by her son Michael after she retired. The 1961 returns showed it at 21,328, (Table 22) and in 1967 a maximum of about 150,000 were hatched. Most were sold day-old, but 20,000 were kept for selection for breeding. Three breeds were kept by this time: Broad-breasted Bronze, Broad-breasted White and River Rest. There was a breeding flock of 3–4,000, and birds of all shapes and sizes were available for the table throughout the year, ranging from 45lb Broad-breasted White dimple stags (MCF.1 line cross) to 9½lb hens (MCF.3 line cross). In the post-war period the special trap-nests and pedigree saddles which Marjorie had pioneered came into general use, and in the early 1950's she also pioneered turkey incubators and special food for day-old turkey poults. From 1952 the extremely broad White strain was eliminated by AI to produce the final Hybrid White, by mating high-laying White hens to very broad White stags and mating the female offspring again to Broad stags. Even in cold weather a 92–94% fertility rate resulted, whereas with the broad strains the best was 35% before AI. The breeding was based on selection of families of excellent siblings.

After a study tour in the US Michael Smith introduced pole barns on the American model, in which turkeys were kept for final fattening from 13 weeks old till killing at 26 weeks. These barns (150ft × 44ft, 7ft6″ at the eves rising to 10ft6″) were put up by a man and a boy, six barns to the acre, with simple materials (hemlock wooden framework on fir poles, wire netting and felt roofs). Western Turkeybators were used for hatching, with a 39,000 egg total capacity, and the poults were brooded for 8 weeks in farm-made brooders, glass wool lined, with hardboard tops. The cold store, immersion freezer and dressing line were all home-built from surplus stock.[136]

Marketing changes continued in the "Golden Age". Already before the war pedigree stock were sold at Reading or directly between breeders, and as time passed only increasingly inferior animals were sent to Sandwich or Canterbury markets. Sandwich market closed in 1974. Tollemaches of Ipswich supplanted Wolston & Bull as the chief buyer of malting barley (in the late 1940's?). The Marketing Boards were in their heyday for milk, pigs and potatoes, and co-operative marketing of broccoli/cauliflowers and other vegetables, which started during the war, now developed further. The Sandwich and District Growers seemed to be on its last legs in 1947, when its turnover had fallen from £14,543 to £4,815 in a year, and it was decided only to fulfil existing contracts.[137] But it revived and H.A. Smith joined it in 1954, marketing his broccoli through it; later Michael Smith was a director. By 1972 it had 250 members, a turnover of about £900,000 and cold store capacity for 3,000 tons. Two thirds of the turnover was accounted for by fruit from East Kent, but a number of Thanet farmers used it for their vegetables.[138]

In the early 1960's Norman Steed did a great deal of work setting up the Kent Vegetable Co-operative, which was launched in 1964. The first Board had Hugh Finn as chairman, Norman Steed as

Vice-chairman, and Colonel Tapp, Richard Tapp and H.M. Steed amongst the directors. Initially 1,205 acres of crops with an estimated net return of £149,254 were marketed through it.[139] There was no report of any Thanet farmers joining sheep, pig, poultry or egg co-operatives as in West Kent.

Road transport completely replaced rail in this period. During the war there had been some broccoli/cauliflower trains to the North of England arranged by Fridays of Canterbury who had connections in Liverpool,[140] but after the war they all went by road again. In October 1959 an attempt was made on the initiative of W.J. Gardner & Co (W.G. Gardner) to send cauliflower to Lincolnshire on a special train. 6,000 sacks were loaded with 300 tons of heads, the equivalent then of 30 lorry loads, but loading took five days and the experiment seems not to have been repeated.[141] Probably it was in the autumn of 1952 that there was excitement one morning at Woodchurch farm when Tollemaches sent a fleet of eight lorries (not large by modern standards) unannounced to take all the barley, then still held in sacks, straight to Ipswich by road. Very hard work ensued to get it all loaded within the time demanded. The farm had been expecting lorries to take it to the trains over a period of days, but the age of leisurely ways and managerial insouciance was ending.

The immense post-war changes which came to Thanet farming actually began with the marshes at the height of the "Golden Age". From 1 February 1953 a near hurricane North wind blew for 36 hours. It stopped an unusually high tide from ebbing, and during the night brought another tide in on top of it: an 8'8" surge on top of a high tide. The old farmhouses shook that night as never in memory; and the sea breached the Northern sea wall (13 feet above sea level) in two places, covering the Thanet-Chatham railway line across the marshes, and sending long arms inland as far as Great Brooksend farm and Sarre. Along the Birchington-Westgate coast the sea looked like a boiling mass, covering the promenades, with waves breaking over the roads above them where they dipped, and spray constantly hurtling over the tops of the cliffs. Six percent of Thanet farmland was flooded,[142] but the techniques and government money were available to put things right. The Northern sea wall was rebuilt and raised to 19 feet, and within two years almost 50% of the whole marsh drainage network had been completely overhauled, mostly between the Northern sea wall and Sarre. 75–100% of the costs were paid by the Government for approved schemes, in which farmers and the Kent River

Authority worked together. Farmers cleared internal dykes (ditches) of silt and weed trapping the sea water, and wooden dams and pumps were installed by the River Authority where an internal ditch opened into the arterial system or went into a neighbour's land. Drainage was not restored through the Northern sea wall until 1955.[143]

An analysis of the marsh soil by S.W.T. Solly, the provincial soil advisory chemist, in the early 1940's showed that it had plenty of lime, an unusually high potash content and phosphate well above normal.[144] Once well-drained, the return from cropping it was above that of livestock at this time. By March 1954 W.A. Sayer of Cleve Court farm had drained 30 acres of Minster marshes, that had not been affected by the sea. He had widened and deepened the dykes (ditches), laid tile or pipe drains across the land at 22 yard intervals, sealed the dykes and pumped the water out.[145] Government grants were available for drainage work independently of the funds allotted for restoration after the floods, so whereas in 1840 at least 92% of the marsh in the Wantsum/Stour area, both on the Thanet and mainland sides, had been under grass, by 1958 this had fallen to about 52% and by 1966 to 37%.[146] All the marsh was eventually drained in this way, although farmers who were very fond of livestock, like H.A. Smith, were amongst the last to drain completely. Work was begun on tile draining the last 150 acres at Monkton Court in 1972, at an average cost of £20 per acre after grant.[147]

Great impetus was given by the effective draining of the marsh to the contract growing of crops for seed, including clover, mangolds, radish, rape, tick beans, wheat and coltsfoot, rye and timothy grass.[148] This also made considerable progress on the upland. No questions about growing for seed were included in the agricultural returns to 1988, so it is impossible to tell the full extent of it, but many farmers grew some. David Steed of Spratling Court farm, who farms in the Manston area, went over to an all-seed rotation in 1972, growing wheat, triticali, peas, rape, sugar-beet and grasses for this. In 1976 he won the Maris Huntsman award for a 3-ton yield over a given acreage, and in 1978 the Nickerson's Cereal Husbandry National Competition for the best cereal system in Great Britain.[149]

Livestock ebbed away from Thanet, as the Western parts of Britain with better grass alone could saturate the market. By way of example, national milk production rose 110 million gallons between 1958 and 1962 and liquid consumption only by 22 million gallons.[150] Gradually all the Thanet farmers gave up their dairy herds. The Montgomerys had led the way in this during or soon after the war (see p 252). Alan Smith at Nether Hale gave up his cows in 1962, and Eric Quested on retirement in 1970. At Monkton Court all the stock were given up after Michael's son Philip (BSc HMS MSc) took over in 1976, even the turkeys in 1985. There were only 684 cows in milk or in calf in Thanet in 1971, and none by 1981, though there was some move into beef cattle, with 166 breeding cows and heifers by 1984. But milk production continued at Zeila Farm from Mary Tyrrel's herd of pedigree goats. Sheep likewise were down to 546 breeding ewes in 1971, but later made a come-back through the Smith family of Nether Hale. Only pigs were still almost as numerous as ever in 1984, often kept in small-holdings, but they have since all vanished. (Table 21). Intensive poultry keeping was reduced five-fold between 1987 and 1988. (Table 22).

Basic farming practices also changed. From the 1970's much less ploughing was done, weeds being destroyed by herbicides instead, and straw and stubble burnt. Not long after the war H.A. Smith's brother Larry had brought back the idea of minimal cultivation from India, where he had managed large farms, and so it was introduced at Monkton Court even as early as that on a limited scale. This regime was also introduced from the US and became more or less nation-wide, together with the use of deep cultivators before early potatoes by some farmers. During that period the only organic matter being returned to much of Thanet farmland was the ploughed in residues of vegetable crops and various crops grown for seed. Intensive farming at that time could take on a destructive aspect. For instance, even in the late 1960's Eric Quested, who had always tended and planted trees and appreciated Nature, ploughed up an historic right-of-way, and decimated an attractive, ancient hedge, on the advice of ADAS, in order to gain or improve at most two acres with grant aid. Similar things happened elsewhere, but greatly more damage was done by Dutch elm disease, which destroyed a large percentage of our rural trees here from the mid-1960's.

By 1993 there had been changes in a reverse direction. Straw burning seemed to have ceased largely in the 1980's – Monkton Court gave it up on the marsh in 1985 and in 1990 on the upland – and a ban on stubble burning was enacted by the government from 1992. So ploughing after corn with lesser use of herbicides returned, except where farmers wanted to prepare the ground as quickly as possible for a fresh crop. Good practice now called for the use of pesticides only when pests appeared, on the grounds of cost reduction, as well as incidentally reducing possible health hazards.[151] Some local farmers had planted quite a few trees by 1993, and much more successfully than Thanet District Council. Looking further ahead, Michael Linington of Sackett's Hill Nursery was working on biological pest control. Since 1989 Wye College staff had been collaborating with Thanet District Council to find a way to compost seaweed for fertilizer, but problems remained with this.[152] In 1992 weed was laid directly onto the fields by Quex Park Estates and at Geoffrey Philpott's Elmwood farm. Quex stopped it, but at Elmwood and three other farms, none large, it continued in 1996 – from 20 to 40 tons an acre.

Another change in agricultural practice was the widespread use of irrigation, which came in with the drainage of the marshes and the greater "water-consciousness" of recent years of fluctuating rainfall and ever-growing urban and country demand. All farmers with land on the marsh now had irrigation licences to extract water from dykes. Farmers also constructed reservoirs on the marsh, just as many of the old farm ponds and small concreted farm reservoirs had been filled in (as at Woodchurch). Some upland farmers also irrigated with mains water, and there was at least one upland reservoir at Thorne, quite early, and others later.

The following information about 1992–3 practices on Thanet farms was offered by the farmers and does not represent a systematic enquiry:-

At Nether Hale the Smith family had a licence to abstract 20 million gallons a year from dykes on about 80 acres of marsh. They also had another 14 million gallons or so from two new reservoirs on the marsh on their main farm at Nether Hale, and stored mains water in two reservoirs (one half a million gallons, one 50,000) in their two other upland farms. In 1991 the Smiths acquired a state of the art soil moisture monitoring and irrigation advisory service run by A. & P. Hill Fruit, the European agents for Neutron Probe Services, which precisely measured soil moisture content to below rooting depth and the rate of use by crops – something impossible to do by guesstimation. The Smith's equipment – also seen on other farms – was a Wright Rain 350m. hosereel raingun and six lines carrying 15–20 sprinklers each, and a system of portable pipes with which most of the irrigation done. Irrigation usually started in late April on spring-heading cauliflowers (broccoli were now known as cauliflower too), and on early potatoes in May (worth over £250 a ton).

The above farm had 350 acres of cauliflower, 30 acres of spring and winter cabbages, and 140 acres of early potatoes, rotated with 180 acres of winter wheat. The breeding flock of 1,200 ewes utilized crop residue and grazed rye drilled after wheat. The ewes, lambed under cover at Nether Hale about Christmas-time, provided manure both from the fold and direct onto the fields, though most of them were not in Thanet for most of the year. The cauliflower was cut from August to June with a break in January and February – over 120 different varieties were grown.[153] Potatoes were lifted by machine in some seasons: in 1990 a Grimme potato harvester was used and in 1992 a Standen new proto-type performed excellently with earlier varieties.[154] This family was the first locally to use a soil-separator with a potato harvester, and the first to make large-scale use of plastic covering for field crops here.

Peter Linington and his son David had 450 acres of cauliflowers, 600 acres of wheat and barley and 120 acres of early potatoes. They fattened 100 bullocks each winter and their dung went on the land. 28 tractors were used (mostly 80 hp but three of 45) and 33 regular workers employed. They did not use a sub-soiler or potato harvester but had a roteria. Minimum cultivation with herbicides was done after potatoes before cauliflower to save time, but after other crops ploughing was done. Pesticides were used only when pests appeared,[155] and herbicides to a minimum, the land being triple hoed after ploughing.

As well as the Nether Hale sheep, Quex Park Estates farm had Thanet's one breeding beef herd, and Zeila farm its herd of pedigree Anglo-Nubian and British Saanen goats, Mary Tyrrel's original new venture. She sold the milk to health food suppliers and Westons (a Margate dairy), and kid meat to ethnic restaurants, later to Howlett's Zoo. On the other farms no livestock were kept, but the small piggeries had been replaced since 1984 by (mostly small) stables for riding horses scattered over the island, and so some horse manure was going onto the land again.

At Monkton Court the regime was almost unrecognizable from H.A. Smith's day. Wheat, barley, early, middle and late potatoes, oil seed rape and peas were grown. Only four regular workers were employed and there were six tractors (1 of 180 hp, 1 of 125, 2 of 100, and 2 of 45). The principal other machinery was as follows:

1 New Holland 20′ cut combine.

1 self-propelled 20 m sprayer.
1 self-propelled 12 m sprayer.
1 Grimme potato harvester.
2 row diggers (Bagger or Bulker).
1 4 m roteria.
1 6 m springtime cultivator.
1 5 m heavy disc.
2 sets 6 m rolls.
1 5-teg subsoiler 14"–15" depth.
2 350 m long irrigation reels.
2 fork lifts.
Various 5-furrow ploughs.

Of 1,050 acres on the farm, 982 were cropped (the remainder made up of woodland, roads, dykes and a 7-acre reservoir completed in 1992). 126 acres were left fallow under the 1992 set aside scheme, according to which it could only be mowed twice but might be ploughed after 1 July 1993. The whole farm was ploughed every year. The five main buildings on the farm were 1) an original hop oast used for storage of small tools, foreman's office and spray store. 2) a building 150' × 200' put up to winter dairy cows, now used to store equipment and boxed potatoes. 3) a building 150' × 150' put up to store corn, now used to hold some corn and rape seed but mainly for artificial fertilizers, tractors, other equipment and a workshop. It had on-floor drying and could take up to 1,400 tons of corn on the floor if required. 4) a corn store to take 1,700 tons. It also contained 3 large silos to hold the corn prior to it passing through the cleaner, before placing on the floor that had under-floor ducting for cold air ventilation. Outside there were two silos to take 320 tons, and a diesel corn-drying plant. 5) a building 50' × 120' to hold seed potatoes, under strip lighting in winter, and refrigerated. The following artificial fertilizers were applied annually: on the marsh 150 tons of nitrogen and 10 tons of phosphate, on the upland 10 tons of nitrate of potash, and 151520 fertilizer on potatoes.[156]

The largest area in the occupation of one family that Thanet had ever known was now farmed by the Tapp brothers and nephew at St Nicholas, over 2,000 acres in all. By 1984 Thanet had six holdings of between 741 and 1,235 acres (300–500 ha), but the agricultural returns to 1988, their last publicly available date at the time of writing, did not require mention of holdings over 500 ha, so the Tapp acreage had not gone on official record to that time. In 1980, when they had already 1,750 acres, they were growing 900 acres of milling wheat, 200 acres of potatoes, 70 acres of spring greens, 60 acres of sweet corn, and 40 acres of over-wintered onions.[157] In 1979 perhaps the eight largest silos in Thanet, holding 2,000 tonnes, were erected at St Nicholas Court,[158] and in 1989 a packing house of about 40,000 square feet. The Tapps were also pioneers here in an interesting kind of diversification when they began baking bread from their own wholemeal flour in 1979. Thousands of pounds were spent on building and equipping a suitable mill, and the baking team even entered the Guinness Book of Records in 1986 when they baked a batch of loaves and delivered them to the local bakery at the record speed of 41 minutes 13 seconds. It is sad that this enterprise was crushed by the large bakers, who were preferred by the supermarkets.[159]

Amongst the smaller farmers, William Friend now occupied the remaining 140 acres of his grandfather's land at East Northdown, with 180 acres near Deal and 30 at Manston. As well as cauliflower, other vegetables and corn he had a flower nursery at East Northdown, and employed a total of 15 on all the holdings.[160]

Probably the smallest full-time arable farmer was David Spanton, who took over the 40-acre Kent County Council smallholding at Nash farm in 1986, and now occupied 130 acres, 60 of them under green vegetables, with potatoes and corn as well and a farm shop. He worked flat-out himself, a cauliflower mobile planter and potato planter enabling him to manage with two more or less full-time workers (one in the shop). He considered that a farm this size could only survive in Thanet, and that if absolutely forced he could exist on 50 acres and the shop.[161]

In 1993 co-operation between the farmers had still not gone very far. Kent Veg sold more than £15 million worth of produce in 1989 and had 59 members in Kent, with sophisticated facilities for grading, pre-grading and temperature control, including refrigerated trucks. The management had "all the latest methods of communication, including fax". Richard Tapp had been chairman since 1982,[162] but both it and Sandwich Growers were no longer farmer-owned. Most large Thanet cauliflower growers still sold their produce individually through a wide range of outlets, changing daily according to prices – a far cry from the old reliance on one Covent Garden firm. Most Thanet vegetables, however marketed, went to wholesale markets in London or further afield, currently having most of the London market for winter cauliflowers.

Corn-growing appeared to be protected as yet by the subsidies, and brought good returns nationally in 1993, but Thanet farmers expressed concern about vegetables, particularly cauliflower. On the initiative of Peter Linington some had formed a seed group for the production of their own new strains of this crop. Some expressed the view that they needed to join or form a new marketing co-operative through which to gain access to supermarkets, but there seemed to be some reluctance about this, and back in 1988 the late Martin Jackson, then NFU secretary for Thanet and Ash, diagnosed Thanet's unwillingness to co-operate as a weakness of the place.[163] Comparison with the quite different attitudes in Cornwall, an area in other ways something similar, suggests that possibly Thanet farmers had simply lacked the critical mass to sustain much co-operative effort. Yet it had taken the crisis of 1931 to launch the once successful Milk Marketing Board in England. The relative absence of co-operation here in 1993 must mean that Thanet agriculture was surviving well enough without it.

The ploughing match

This was restarted with great enthusiasm in 1946 at Woodchurch farm, with 54 entries (including 12 horse-ploughs), and went rapidly from strength to strength.[164] By the 1950's it had become something like a small agricultural show, and the largest event of its kind in the Southeast. Garrad reported it to be the biggest match in Kent in 1952 when there were 114 entries at Hengrove farm, including ten horse ploughs.[165] But the peak had already been reached in 1951, when there were 124 entries at Edwin Baxter's farms at Sarre.[166] This was the historic maximum number of entries, before or since. By 1956 when the "Hundredth Ploughing Match" was held, at Woodchurch farm again (it was actually the 78th, but was thought to be the hundredth) catalogue entries were only 96, although it was claimed that with late entries there had been 100. But the estimated 7–8,000 spectators were the most ever to appear at any match.[167] In 1959 the last solitary horse plough was entered, and after the horses went the public's interest slowly waned too, though entries and attendances were still high until the late 1960's.

In 1951 the match featured a horse show with nine classes (three agricultural), a parade of the West Street foxhounds, and 31 trade exhibitors, displaying farm machinery and equipment. These numbers were kept up till the late 1960's – except for the agricultural horses – and from 1963 sheepdog trials were featured too.

An impressive amount of silver cups were donated to be won annually: 36 by 1960, 39 by 1971, by which time there were 11 other special prizes as well.[168] Eric Quested's long mahogany sideboard at Woodchurch was loaded with silver cups from end to end, and some other farmers' must have been even more so. A fair number of cups also went to the ploughmen.

From 1946 there was a dinner after the match, often held at the Beresford Hotel, Birchington until it was shut down in 1966.[169] So until 1972 there were two Thanet agricultural dinners yearly, though the ploughing match one was seldom reported in the press. A supper for the farm worker participants and wives was held from 1946, and upgraded to a dinner at the Nayland Rock Hotel from 1951,[170] a concert party being added in 1957, when it was held at the Bungalow Hotel, Birchington. But this was not very popular and was stopped again.[171] The pork pies for their lunch at the match – with two pints of beer – were "splendid and really big, from Scott's in Margate market place" in Jack Hulk's recollection.

Another innovation from 1950 was the enormously popular Women's Section, with many classes for homecrafts, eggs, fruit, etc, and childrens' activities. There were 758 entries in 1956, and still 561 in 1968. It had its own President and Committee, Mrs May Tapp, wife of the Colonel, being President for a long time, and there were several cups for farm workers' wives or daughters' entries alone, as well as open cups.

Thatching was dropped from the competitions in 1956, showing the near-universal use of combines, but there were always classes for long service, and good work by cowmen, shepherds and until 1960 horsemen. The classes for farmers' produce included silage by 1956 and herbage seeds from 1963 (grasses and clover).[172]

When Eric Quested ended a 5-year stint as chairman in 1960, the ploughing match committee had £100 in hand,[173] but by the early 1970's it was in financial straits. Public attendance at matches had greatly fallen, and the farmers themselves were losing interest in them, with 55 ploughs entered in 1971[174] and 30 in 1972.[175] Falling numbers of farmers meant that a few large ones were increasingly taking all the prizes and competing in ever smaller groups.

The chairman, A.C. Tyrrel, and the committee tried to keep it going by turning it back into a plain ploughing match in 1972, without the displays and exhibits. A mini-match on these lines was

held at Somali farm on an appallingly muddy day in 1972,[176] and
again on a much better day at Woodchurch in 1973, with a pony
gymkhana as well,[177] just a mini-match had been tried at Minster
in 1875 when the match was failing then. But after 1973 as after
1875 the attempt to continue foundered against most of the
farmers' unwillingness. (See p 157). The womens' section was
ended after 1972, not without indignant protests, and the farm
workers too, by all accounts ever heard, enjoyed the match to the
end and were sorry to see it go.[178]

An accident of prophetic ill-omen occurred at the 1973 match:
the Thanet champion, Maurice Pratt from David Steed's Spratling
Court farm, had part of his left hand crushed when the reversing
mechanism of his tractor failed four furrow ends from home, and
he had to operate it by hand. Yet he kept on to win, and was taken
to Margate hospital to be treated afterwards.[179] No accident to any
participant, let alone a champion, had ever been reported in the
press from any of the other 94 Thanet ploughing matches, and
Maurice was the last Thanet champion, as it seems, that there was
ever to be.

Something of the heart seemed to go out of the farming community with the passing of the ploughing match. The East Kent
Match by contrast continues to this day; its historian, Julia Small,
attributed this to its having "never ceased to adhere to its earliest
principle: that the day of the Ploughing Match is the workers'
day."[180] But to be fair, the larger size of its catchment area has also
helped.

By February 1996 Ministry of Agriculture publications showed
that the position of British farmers improved a great deal from the
summer of 1993. The average net income of general cropping
farms rose as follows:[181]

	1992–93	Thousand £ 1993–94	Provisional rise in total UK farming income 1995
Large farms	51.4	63	
Medium farms	17.4	22.9	25.6% (21.5% deflated by RPI)
Small farms	9.9	13.4	

Nothing has happened to suggest that Thanet can have been an exception. Farmland prices here fell to £1,500–£800 by July 1994, but were back to £2,000–£1,500 by July 1995.[182] By early September 1995 they were somewhat higher, when 216 acres of high-grade land at Ebbsfleet fetched £570,000.[183]

The reasons for this appear to have been mainly the increased cereal prices and increased arable area payments for cereals, the last nationally £2 million in 1992, £393 million in 1993 and provisionally estimated at £543 million in 1994.[184] More wheat was consequently grown in Thanet in 1994 and 1995, and less oilseed rape, for which area payments were reduced 16% after the 1994 harvest. Cauliflowers and potatoes continued to cover a large acreage here, and the total value of British horticultural produce rose 5% in 1994 because price rises offset a fall in total quantity.[185] Most recently the cold winter of 1995–96 brought higher cauliflower prices as well as frost losses. Set aside payments were another factor, and also the 25% depreciation of the UK pound since Britain's withdrawal from the Exchange Rate Mechanism in autumn 1992, which raised the sterling value of EU farm subsidies by a similar amount.[186] Locally in Thanet land prices were probably also stimulated by the purchase of 10 acres of farmland by Thanet District Council for around £100,000 per acre in September 1995, in order to set up a business park to secure Euromoney.[187] Farmers here must therefore be keeping an eye on government handouts almost as much as on the weather and the markets, and some of them must be hoping eventually to sell their land for business developments. But the new world food deficiency now looming bodes well for future demand.

Thanet farmers too have continued to show their enterprise. The new nitrate restrictions have been confined to a relatively small area around Minster. The cauliflower seed group has made its public debut as Trinity Growers co-operative and there is a new marketing firm, Wantsum Produce Ltd, selling cauliflower partly to the Continent, as well as in this country – a radical new move. Geoffrey Philpott of Elmwood farm is chairman of the first and director of the second.[188] Edward Spanton of Way farm won first prize in the Lincolnshire Seed Growers Association national seed wheat competition in the summer of 1995.[189] TDC's £1 million land purchase was from a farmer owner.

The forward movement in British agriculture is now more than ever confirmed as being towards low-input sustainability, often involving very high technology, though with a slowly growing organic sector. High chemical-input intensive farming is today's conservatism. Although Thanet farmers are obviously at varying points on this spectrum, it may be true to say that like most British farmers they are on the whole rather more toward the conservative end. Thanet's intensive cultivations with relatively low organic input on most farms have undoubtedly had an effect on the soil (see Conclusion for further discussion). Should a widespread nitrate restriction regime be enforced the cauliflower may have to be abandoned and other changes made, but that is in the future. With the information yet available it looks as if the two great progressive peaks in the history of Thanet agriculture remain the ecclesiastical manorial cultivation of the High Middle Ages, and the perhaps Low Countries-inspired techniques of the 17th and 18th centuries. Many parts of Britain could not boast of such highs, and even at other times Thanet farmers seem to have maintained a generally impressive level of efficiency by the prevailing standards of each era, as far back as any detailed reports go.

Conclusion

Environmental losses and gains since 1800

The agrarian community once encompassed the whole Isle of Thanet and is still an integral part of it: in taking final stock of the environmental changes we should look once again at the whole, with particular attention to aspects closely linked to farming.

Since the first modern census of 1801 Thanet's population has risen from 5,048 to over 123,000, with a growing number of factories, a large airfield and a highly productive if slowly shrinking agricultural area; a population and economy unimaginable at the earlier date. The length, and quality of many aspects of human life has risen greatly, though with alarming backsliding recently for certain groups both in town and country.

We have gained, too, many attractive gardens: there are certainly far more flowers and ornamental trees here than ever before, not a half of the present strains or even species of garden plant being in England at the opening of the 19th century. Before 1914 most farmhouse gardens did not contain many flowers – though a few even had greenhouses – and the famous cottage gardens in places like Minster had only a limited range.[1] Except for the small town middle class and the gentry, gardens generally meant vegetables if they were to be found at all in 1800.

The tree position is harder to assess. Upland Thanet was mostly bare and wind-swept in John Lewis' day, but Minster certainly had far more trees than now in the mid-18th century. Yet Thanet as a whole may actually have more now than in the mid-19th century. Many of the 4,305 trees listed in Minster in 1760 (see p 55) were sold by the Conyngham family for timber,[2] and some trees may have been cut for firewood in the years of the labourers' great poverty.[3]

Though no relevant Thanet rural photos can be found, some of the Wye area show decidedly fewer trees in 1850 than now,[4] and it was said in 1872 that "Thanet has no trees worthy of the name except in a few scattered localities."[5] After that they increased a little in the towns. Many have been lost since 1945 by building over estates such as Dumpton Park and Dane Court, farming hamlets like Northdown and Dumpton, or the large gardens of late 19th century houses like Queen Bertha's school in Birchington. Drought, disease and hurricanes have wrought havoc too, but in recent years a fair amount of planting has been done, and there is greater public interest. The farmers' record has been mixed. Whilst many have preserved and some planted trees and even hedges, and some have collaborated with the Farming and Wildlife Advisory Group, the small wood called Minster Rough has been almost grubbed out, and many miles of hedgerows on the marshes (admittedly, mostly recent in origin). If any place not far from trees is left undisturbed a few decades it reverts to wood, though builders generally get it in the end. Meanwhile Thanet District Council optimistically plans community woodland in the dry Shottendane valley. If rainfall holds, the tree future may not be unhopeful, but if it continues to dwindle Mediterranean species may be needed.

The most trees now are often in places where there were few or none 250 years ago. For example, Quex Park plantations were laid down in the early 19th century (and replanting of hurricane damage is well under way). The Whiteness Bay – George Hill – Convent Road area, described as bleak and bare in Lord Holland's time, now has many trees.

Trees and flowers aside we have largely spoiled the beautiful island of 1800, although on several fronts the tide of public policy has just turned against pollution and destruction. Of necessity, Thanet's farmland is now less attractive than of yore. Gone is the long-stalked corn rippling gracefully in the wind like water, replaced by the firm short stalks withstanding wind and rain, and "endless" brassicas. Gone are the picturesque sheaves and stacks, most of the animals, and the blossoms of the old fodder crops like clover and trefolium.

With the agricultural beauty has gone much of the individuality of our island. The Thanet rural dialect has all but passed into history, but deserves mention as part of the psychological environment. Down into the Second World War it survived vigorously in the farms and villages as a distinct accent (intonation and pronounciation), though with only a few special words left. How far it may have differed from that in other parts of East Kent is unsure, but it was unlike the Canterbury accent in having brisker cadences. Even by the 1930's the Thanet towns had largely gone over to standard Southern English, the so-called "tortured vowel" speech already then common to Outer London and many towns in the Southeast. Sadly, after 1945 the old rural accent soon became thought uncouth, and people who spoke it beautifully changed their way of talking to standard Southern (sometimes called Estuary) English. This has now swallowed Thanet, though with increasing education BBC English gains ground. Before the First World War the island identity was much stronger – Bar Sackett's household for instance always called the rest of East Kent "over the river", and one still heard this expression very occasionally until after 1945. Now we can only imagine the attitude of Thanet people in 1800 to the rest of the county, but it is likely that they had a greater feeling of separateness from it.

Thanet had no maritime sewage problem in 1800 when almost everyone must have used earth privies, but from the 1860's to the 1890's it was acute in the towns. The Victorian sewage systems with short sea outfalls then worked adequately until they were overwhelmed by the population rise after the Second World War. By 1990 many beaches had much deteriorated, as shown by bacteria counts and the replacement of seaweed (*Fucus*) by carpets of mussels (*Mytilus edulis*) on many chalk rocks. Crabs and other small marine beach life also disappeared in places and the water became murkier.[6] The new sewage works opened in 1995 have already brought marked improvement, and in August 1993 English Nature declared the whole Thanet coast no 7 of 27 Sensitive Marine Zones, though the designation was not statutory and the scheme is still at a consultative stage.[7] Some old unmapped outfalls apparently remain to be eliminated, and the Botany Bay and Joss Bay works remove only solids and do not treat the liquid. They thus pump out to sea heavy metals, organo-chlorides from household cleaners and nitrates leached from soil, nor can these be removed totally even by the modern plants.

Local fishermen have expressed suspicion that the above are harming the North Sea fish,[8] which are already internationally known to be seriously depleted by over-fishing. Both local fisheries officers and fishermen alike seem rather reluctant to talk about catches.

Whales are known to have beached sometimes on the Kent and Thanet coasts since the Middle Ages; the recent rise in strandings or near-strandings, often dead or sick, has been ascribed by the

Seawatch Foundation to the creatures' hunger and confusion in the ever more barren and engine-roar filled North Sea, which they may pass on their migrations.[9]

Polecats, stoats, weasels, badgers and otters vanished long since. Foxes have adapted, and are now settled in many urban areas of Thanet, but studies elsewhere show that the lives of town foxes are generally shorter and hungrier than those of their forebears who ate rabbits, partridges, leverets, poultry and maybe even lamb! Rabbits, decimated by myxamatosis in the late 1950's, are back in small numbers, many resistant to the now endemic disease.

Coursing was done here since the Middle Ages. The Harriers left here in 1915 as hares had become fairly few in Eastern Thanet by then,[10] but there were still plenty in the central parts in the mid-1930's and H.A. Smith, a coursing enthusiast, said he had to place wiring round his crops against them in 1933 at Monkton.[11] But in the late 1930's they were sometimes said to be "really short" there.[12] Eric Quested and some other farmers detested coursing, and though it started again after the war, shortage of hares and perhaps changing opinion ended it finally in the 1960's. In the spring of 1988 the author saw what must have been one of the last Thanet hares in a field between Flete and Lydden.

The number of birds has dropped dramatically since 1939, and may have been falling in the 19th century. If 50 nightingales could easily be heard on an evening's walk in Thanet in 1817 (though was this an exaggeration?), it was thought remarkable that they sang at Northdown and Minster in 1900.[13] When Eric Quested and his young wife first lived at Woodchurch in 1919 swallows nested in the front porch of the farmhouse, the front door not being opened on their account, but within a few years they had gone. Most farms had barn owls down to 1939,[14] and at Woodchurch we had a colony of tree sparrows (*Passer montanus*) in the old fir trees in front of the house. The dawn chorus from our secluded garden and orchard – as from so many large gardens in the towns now built over – exceeded anything to be heard anywhere in Thanet now, despite a few cats. Tree sparrows and barn owls have gone, and there are few thrushes left anywhere now; it was their plentiful song mingled with the many blackbirds which gave the pre-war dawn choruses their lost splendour.

Until the late 1940's several hundreds of rooks and jackdaws used to fly out from Quex Park to Woodchurch and other farms daily to feed in the fields. There were other rookeries elsewhere in Thanet. The farmers loathed them, and still dislike them, though a nest count in early spring 1993 indicated a maximum of 25 pairs of rooks in Quex Park and very few jackdaws. There were similar rookeries only at Cleve and Monkton, and jackdaws in Monkton church tower. By 1996 the rooks had appreciably increased, though there seemed fewer at Cleve. It may be noted that the great rook and jackdaw population explosion must have come after Quex plantations were made in the early 19th century, though they probably nested more in farms before that.

Partridges are now rare; they have been seen in places such as Nether Hale where they were bred some years ago, and in 1993 in the then abandoned farmland at Ebbsfleet. Larks amazingly survive in much fewer numbers than of old in various places, and the set-aside helps them.

Everywhere in Thanet on land only the toughest species of birds remain in numbers: seagulls, sparrows, starlings, collared doves, urban pigeons, and magpies (the last rare before 1939) and blessedly the resilient blackbirds, though they too and the sparrows are dwindling. Their worst enemies apart from developers are magpies, no longer kept down by gamekeepers and partridge-shooting farmers, and multiplying inordinantly.

A striking exception to the gloom is Pegwell Bay, now a protected nature reserve, a Site of Special Scientific Interest and a UN Ramsar Site. Here come internationally important populations of migrants, including the fairly rare turnstones (*Arenaria Interpres*), known in Thanet since the 19th century.

Nature itself played a part in the above losses, through elm disease and the harder winters from 1938 to 1986–87, but in the main it is our whole civilization which has destroyed the beasts and birds – and certainly not the farmers alone. Migrant thrushes for instance have been decimated by "sportsmen" in Latin Europe, and there are more cats. Yet agricultural practices have contributed. Partridges, larks and hares have been victims of the double and treble cropping which began in the 1930's. The NFU reported more than 8,087 rooks killed in their campaigns against them in Kent, in 1948,[15] but they did not need to continue these for long, for rook numbers fell 68% in the county between 1949 and 1975, due to chemical seed dressing, Dutch elm disease destroying their roosts, and more efficient harvesting methods.[16] Examination of 194 dead wild birds and mammals by the Ministry of Agriculture and Fisheries in 1982 found 85 poisoned by farm chemicals (organophosphates, carbamate compounds and miscellaneous compounds, also strychnine), 80 with cause of death unestablished, 20 due to disease and 9 to trauma.[17]

The marshes used to be moist pastures, divided into small sections by a network of channels supporting plant, bird and reptilian life. Drainage on the Thanet side of the Stour had changed the smaller dykes by the mid-1980's to deep ditches full of reeds, and sometimes thickets and even a few trees, which were splendid cover for wildlife, but the farmers since have been bulldozing these and efficiently turning the marshes into a replica of the bare fields of upland Thanet. Once all trees and bushes are gone and only the deeper channels remain, well-dredged, there does not seem to be much wildlife, except seagulls after ploughing and a few swans and coots or moorhens on the Reculver side, occasionally a mallard, more rarely a heron. In winter about 50 swans gather in one or two groups on the marsh, and in Spring disperse. In the post-war years, before the full draining of the marshes began, there were some three times as many, and a higher percentage of immature birds.

As striking as the loss of wildlife have been the changes to the ground water, soil and air. In 1933 Woodchurch farm began to receive its water from a previously untapped aquifer via a new pumping station on the Birchington–Manston road.[18] Farming in those days used chemical fertilizers in small quantities compared to today, and in the opinion of all who drank it this water was unsurpassed for purity and taste, but by 1970 its taste had markedly worsened. By 1989 Ministry of Agriculture and Fisheries investigations found that nitrate concentrations in Thanet boreholes frequently exceeded the EC limit of 50mg per litre.[19] Talk of including Thanet in the nitrogen restriction zones began in the mid-'80's, but the NFU was opposed.[20] In 1990 it was reported that the secretary and members of the Thanet NFU had worked very hard to keep the initial restriction zone out.[21] They succeeded, and Thanet water had to be diluted with water brought from West Kent by a new pipeline at considerable cost, whilst at the Lord of the Manor borehole, where nitrate concentrations of 60 mg plus were regularly reported, a nitrate removal plant was installed at the end of 1991 at the cost of £2 million.[22] The cost of pipeline and plant passed to the water rates. Given the abundance of water in other parts of England, and the government's need to make the NFU accept nitrogen restrictions over a larger area in East Anglia, its decision to abandon the small region of the already affected Thanet aquifers seemed rational. The farmers fought the nitrogen restriction proposals to maintain their high output through heavy

applications of chemical fertilisers, especially needed for cauliflowers after the decline of livestock farming here, and were acting
no differently from farmers in other arable districts. In 1994–1995
they resisted a new attempt by the government to make Thanet a
nitrogen restriction zone, yielding only a small area round Minster,
as noted at the end of Chapter 10. The NFU bases its opposition
on the fact that the World Health Organization sets a limit of only
100 mg of nitrate per litre of drinking water, but the EC limits
are based on the not well-understood links between nitrates and
cancer as well as the rare "blue baby syndrome". It is a classic
clash of legitimate interests.

   Apart from Hall and Russell's investigation of two sites at
Minster in 1911,[23] no scientific analyses of the Thanet farm soils or
of their depths have been published, those made for individual
farmers being their business secret. William Marshall, an impartial
observer, described Thanet in his report published in 1818 as "the
deepest soiled, most valuable passage of chalk hill in this island"
(ie Britain).[24] He had described it in more detail in the 1790's:
"Even on the lesser margins of the swells, and on some of the
flatter parts of the area, the soil is from 18″–2′ deep. Even on
the very summits of the central and western heights there is
10″–14″ of free culturable soil. On the uppermost stages of the
more broken heights, towards the NE margin, the soil is thinner
and more flinty. But I know of no tract, of equal extent, with so
large a proportion of good and so inconsiderable a share of bad
land" (either in the Yorkshire Wolds, the Wiltshire Downs, Dorset,
Hampshire, Sussex, Surrey or Kent, he went on to write).[25] Marshall's descriptions have sometimes been misquoted, with claims
that he reported the soil on the heights generally to be 2′ deep, but
the above is the correct version. Hall and Russell found depths of
2′–4′ over chalk on low land at Minster.[26]

   Soil scientists investigated about 4 m of brickearth over Thanet
Beds and Upper Chalk exposed on Pegwell Bay cliff face, and
found it to date from approximately 3,000 BC; it was part of the
pre-Neolithic Thanet forest soil mantle. One section was overlaid
with 1–2 m of silty hillwash containing Neolithic flint flakes,
showing that erosion began with the first slash-and-burn agriculture,[27] as would be expected. Whatever may have been the
depth of the pre-Neolithic mantle on the higher chalk land, a great
deal of soil must have been lost by Marshall's time. Yet we know
that the depredations of earlier, more primitive farmers were
partly offset, not only by periods of depopulation, but by the

strenuous manuring of the 17th and 18th centuries. This strenuous manuring continued to the mid-20th century, but farming practices since have generally reversed its healing trend, raising the threat of humus depletion bringing accelerated erosion in its train. A local farmer told the author that over 20 years ago walking from his own family's well-manured land onto his neighbours' which received no dung "was like stepping off a good carpet onto lino".

Dr Paul Burnham of Wye College Department of Agriculture, Horticulture and the Environment wrote on 31 July 1992 that the Thanet soil is mostly "very dependent on a reasonable humus content to maintain structure. If the humus content falls below about 3%, the tilth 'slakes' under heavy rain, leading to capping and soil erosion. Continuous arable, especially growing crops like broccoli which may require the ground to be partly bare to summer rainstorms – like the one a fortnight ago which led to 2″ of rain in one night in Thanet – will lead to increasing soil erosion, which happened, for example, near Cliffsend. In places the soil had to be scraped from the roads. The evidence we have from similar soils in other parts of East Kent is that some arable top-soils are already below the danger level in respect of humus content, and that large areas are approaching the 3% danger level".

In a letter in 1996 Dr Burnham referred to investigations by one of his postgraduate students for a successful PhD in soil science. These revealed erosion on a ridge and down the axis of dry valleys in Thanet. On the lower slopes the soil was found to have deepened by redeposition of some of the eroded soil. 80 cm of soil was found deposited as colluvium at a beach edge, further soil having presumably been washed out to sea. No conspicuous rill or gully system was found, but one incipient gully was noticed after a rainstorm.[28]

Reports of soil loss have come from Thanet Archeological Trust. At Lord of the Manor 20 cm of topsoil was found where ploughing unearthed Saxon skeletons probably buried about 60 cm deep, and many other instances of depletion since prehistoric times.[29] But Paul Bennett of Canterbury Archeological Trust reported 1′–3′ of topsoil along the Thanet Way between Mount Pleasant and Monkton roundabout.[30] The areas of Thanet Beds soil remain deep – 12′ near Zeila farm, Garlinge, and more in some parts of Thanet.[31] In general the English Nature estimate of 1′–4′ over most of the chalk cited on page one may still hold good – though for how long? At the time of writing drought seems a menace as well as rainstorms, low humus content not helping in either. The ban on straw and stubble burning is positive for humus, but herbage seed growing, restorative to the soil and quite prevalent until a few years ago, now is little practised. Where manure is applied, by a few farmers only, it is not available in the quantities of the livestock farming days, and seaweed is only used by a very few in 1996. The circumstantial evidence is overwhelming that the humus content of much of the Thanet soil, built up by centuries of careful manuring, has been greatly reduced in the past generation. This must be well known to the farmers.

The deterioration of Thanet air is noticeable to older residents. Forty or fifty years ago one was immediately struck by its great purity on alighting from the London train. It is still much better than London's, and in certain wind directions (notably due northerly) almost as good as ever. But outpourings from the heavy industrial zones across the Channel reach us now, and as soon as one emerges from the station, if not even before, one is liable to be met by a blast of car exhaust. In still weather, luckily infrequent here, the fumes linger heavily in town streets and country roads alike. This is potentially the most serious of our environmental problems, contributing to the greenhouse effect, to acid rain and to human disease. Fifty years ago it was unimaginable that today whole regions of Britain, even sometimes including Thanet, would be described by the Meteorological Office as having "poor air quality" in certain weather conditions.[32] The compulsory fitting of catalytic convertors on new cars from 1993 will take time to make an impact here, where most cars are bought secondhand, and many are old. Judging by the strength of the fumes, a considerable number here also escape an MOT. Legislation since 1993, and particularly the Environment Act of 20 July 1995 suggest that we may just have seen the tide turn against air pollution, but there is still far to go as the nation is largely car-dependent and often car-adoring.

Not all the loss has been regrettable: few would lament the disappearance of flies, *Lepidium Draba* and other weeds nearly as bad. In 1921, for example, mention was made of the "enormous damage done by Devil's Cabbage to corn in Thanet", "suffocating the corn crop and robbing it of food and water."[33] In those days farmers would say that the only way to kill it was to build a manure heap on it two years running. It is improbable that it could have been overcome so soon without modern chemical sprays; G.H. Garrad's copper-sulphate of ammonia mixture could only keep it more or less at bay, and even now it lurks on many a verge or neglected patch, waiting to make a come-back.

Summing Up

So in our mind's eye we have looked at Thanet and its farming community over some 8,000 years. What will the future hold? Will our own highest yet population peak end in some catastrophe, as the Roman peak ended in the Jutish invasion and the 14th century one in the Black Death? In a few hundred years will there still be prosperous white farmers here, as for so long in the past? Or will they have given way to pigmented-skinned, perhaps subsistence farmers? Will the island be covered over with buildings and roads, or will it be a forest again? Or will ever-rising temperatures and melting icecaps have put it under the sea?

Of one thing we can be sure. We have inherited a tract of splendid soil, famed for nearly 2,000 years at least, which in the uncertain future may be badly needed, if not to feed this nation then to seize export opportunities. Most of Thanet's beauty has gone, most of the wildlife, and most of the busy rural community, but we still have most of the best of this kind land. Let us keep it as long as we can. Faced with great enough need or hope of gain, any owners might want to sell their farmland for building and roads. So our land should surely be preserved by strict planning laws, by keeping the farmers in good business and encouraging the maintenance of soil fertility. If it cannot be profitably farmed, it would be better under sports fields, woodland, common land for riding and walking, even the more damaging golf courses, from which it could be more or less restored to production if required. If much more of the best Thanet land is preventably and irrevocably lost, it will be, in terms which a materialist or agnostic could use, short-sighted vandalism, and in the language of those who see a greater dimension to life, a crime against our ancestors and our descendants, and the Providence that gave it to us.

Appendix

Material for further research

Amongst many possible topics for further research some arouse particular curiosity. One is the medieval agarian history of the St Augustine's lands, regarding which Anne Oakley, senior research archivist at Canterbury Cathedral, wrote to the author on 12 July 1993:-

"I think the real reason why no-one has used the St Augustine's records is that they are scattered all over the place. A few are here" (in the Cathedral archives); "some are among the records of the Court of Augmentations in the Public Record Office; others may be in the royal collections. Some are published . . . but much is 'lost' in the sense that it has never been brought together on paper. It would be an interesting exercise for someone."[33] So far as is known nobody has begun work on this topic to the date of publication.

One would love to know more, too, about the probable Low Country source of the remarkably high farming standards of the 17th century. Parish registers might indicate movement of immigrants to Thanet from Sandwich. The names are now known of 2,447 Protestant refugees who were in Sandwich at some time between 1561 and 1601. Most of them hailed from the Westkwartier of the Netherlands (today's Southern Netherlands and Flemish Belgium). Many did not stay long but many remained, and their descendants may be discerned in later Thanet farmers' surnames – for instance in the 19th century Mayhew (Mahieu) family of Nethercourt and Sevenscore? (See p 131 Chapter 7). Some few refugees were Walloon or French, as Mahieu illustrates.

Migration from the Continent obviously took place earlier too. The Queke family at Birchington may have had Flemish origins, for the Elizabethan immigrants at Sandwich included a Queeke and a Queecke. (M.F. Backhouse, "The Flemish and Walloon communities at Sandwich in the reign of Elizabeth I 1561–1601", University of Southampton PhD thesis 1992, 3 vols, for the complete list of names). Moreover, the amazing new information about the 1688 revolution recently discovered in the Dutch archives suggests that the answer might not be found in English sources alone.

There is room for an MA, at least, on all East Kent agriculture from 1760 to, possibly, 1848, to carry on where Dennis Baker left off, and perhaps look more closely at general arable techniques than at hops. This should throw light on the reality or not of Thanet's supposed pre-eminence and its decline.

A much more exact evaluation of Thanet's relative position in the nation's agricultural advance in each period is needed, and could perhaps be the subject of an article by an experienced agricultural historian. This involves the speed of dissemination of change over the whole country over the years, which might possibly make an interesting larger study.

Another topic far from local suggested by our material is the relations between the farming organizations and the government, which are normally left out of agrarian histories, but form a vital thread in recent political life.

From 1726 onwards the newspapers provide the basis for essays, diplomas, perhaps even theses on many aspects of East Kent if not solely Thanet history, which too should be able to supplement and improve on this book.

Addition to 2nd Edition

Many Thanet wills, leases and sale deeds involving farms are now more conveniently catalogued and available for inspection at the new East Kent Archives at Whitfield, near Dover. Some more are held at the University of Reading, and the Royal Bethlehem Hospital at Wickham, Surrey, has much material on the history of Garlinge Farm from the early 17th century to 1926, and Cliffsend Farm from 1702 to after World War II. All these give opportunities for research into local land prices and rents, and family histories and finances as well as landlord-tenant relations and farming methods. Whitfield also has the archive of the Staple, near Ash, auctioneer Charles Petley, with many reports on 20th century Thanet farms. I am grateful to Dr. Dawn Crouch for telling me about the Bethlehem archives.

Tables 17–29 based on agricultural returns; PRO
MAF 68/1329, 1899, 2469, 2754, 2868, 3030, 3570, 3981, 4129, 4240, 4351, 4728, 5228, 5907, 6061, 6112
Note: Figures under different headings in the agricultural returns do not always correlate exactly.

Table 17

	Acres Owned	*Acres Rented*	*Total Crops and Grass* (Including Fallow, excluding Rough Grazing)	*Total Area*	Rough Grazing
1891	1,904 ½	20,752 ¾	22,657 ¼		
1901	4,473.25	17,142 ½	21,615 ¾		
1911	2,543 ½	19,843	22,386 ½		
1916	2,244 ¼	19,991	22,235 ¼		
1918	1,697	18,740 ¼	20,437 ¼		
1921	4,985	14,799 ¼	19,784 ¼		
1931	na		18,318		
1941	na		17,872 ¼		183.25
1945	na		17,724		232.25
1951	na		17,700 ¼		262
1961	na		17,765 ¼ (sic)		146.5
1971	8,310 ¼ (sic)	8,689 (sic)	16,706 ¼	16,995 ½ (sic)	135
1984	9,335.7 (3,778.1 ha)	6,935.9 (2,806.9 ha)	14,534 (5,881.8 ha)	16,271.7 (6,585 ha)	97 (39.3 ha)
1988	7,097 (2,872.2 ha)	5,765 (2,333.4 ha)	11,556.5 (4,676.8 ha)	12,863 (5,205.6 ha)	113.9 (46.1 ha)

(The 1988 returns appear to be incomplete)

Table 18 No. of Holdings

	Occupiers of Land	Keepers of Stock Only	Rented	Owned	Mixed	1–300 Acres Not Farmed For Business
1867	172	29	na	na	na	
1881	319	23	na	na	na	
1891*	325	7	233	73	19	
1901	375					56
			Rented or Mainly Rented			
1911	334		265			
1916	301					
1918	292					
1921	270		205			
1931	220					
1941	193					
1945	219					
1951	193					
1961	142					
1971	96 (36 Part-time)					
1984	75 (33 Part-time)	*Nil Crops and Grass*				
1988	61	2				

* From 1885 through 1921 the returns show holdings not occupiers.

Table 19 Size of Holdings (acres)

a: owned   b: rented — (Lacking wholly or partly uncompleted returns)

	1–5 (Under 5)	5–50	50–100 (a: owned)	100–150 (b: rented)	150–300	300+	500–700	700–1000	1000+	Rough Grazing
	a b	a b	a b	a b	a b	a b				
1911	31 86	27 96	12	65		1 16				
1916		93	113	34	21	23	16			
1918		87	111	28	23	23	16			
	a b	a b	a b	a b	a b	a b				
1921	7 56	25 77	9 19	4 17	3 15	3 3				
1931	57	76	23	19	24	14				
	1–5					*300–500*				
1941	39	57	31	18	27	9	2	2		6
	Under 5					*300–400*	*400–700*	*700–1000*	*1000+*	
1948 (1945 na)	40	68	27	17	22	6	5	2	1	
						300–500	*500–700*	*700–1000*	*1000+*	
1951	47	71	24	14	22	10	6	1	1	2
1961	35	42	16	11	18	12	4	3	1	
1971	26	22	7	3	12	12	4	6	1	
	Under 2ha (4.94 a)	*2–20ha (under 49.4 a)*	*20–40ha (under 98.8 a)*	*40–100ha (under 247 a)*	*100–200ha (under 494 a)*	*200–300ha (under 741 a)*	*300–500ha (under 1235.5 a)*			*Nil Crops and Grass*
1984	13	24	3	11	11	6	6			
1988	23	9	2	8	11	4	5			2

Table 20 Holdings under 50 acres

	ST PETER'S		ST LAWRENCE (Incl. Ramsgate)		MINSTER		ST JOHN'S		THE 7 OTHER PARISHES	
	Under 5	5–50	Under 5	5–50	Under 5	5–50	Under 5	5–50	Under 5	5–50
1911	32	24	24	32	19	16	15	14	27	37
1916	23	22	22	26	18	14	10	10	20	41
1918	23	25	19	29	15	13	10	4	20	40
1921	21	18	10	27	11	16	3	2	16	39
1931	13	14	10	20	14	13	3	2	17	26
							Incl. all Margate Borough*		*Less Birchington & Westgate etc**	
	Under 2ha	2–20ha	Under 2ha	2–20ha	Under 2ha	2–20ha	Under 2ha	2–20ha	Under 2ha	2–20ha
1941	10	10	10	13	5	13	11	15	3	6
1948	8	14	11	16	7	12	9	20	5	6
(1945 na)							*Includes Acol*			
1951	9	15	13	17	7	11	10	19	8	9
1961	8	5	7	8	5	7	9	13	6	9
1971	4	3	4	5	6	6	8	4	4	4
1984	1	10	1	6	3	2	5	3	3	3
1988	8	1	3	2	4	3	5	2	3	1

* From 1941 St John's, Northdown, Garlinge, Birchington are all included under Margate. Acol included in Margate from 1984.

Table 21 Livestock 1901–1939

	1901	1911	1916	1918	1921	1931	1939
Agricultural horses including brood mares	898	888	641	655	675	530	345
Mares being covered that year			45	48	37		
Agricultural stallions			2	5	4	3	2
Unbroken horses	104	81	113	64	51	6	19
Other horses		137	360	292	138	104	40
Dairy cows and in-calf heifers	1,480	1,905	1,654	1,507	1,689	1,904	1,951
Bulls					53	66	58
Other cattle	967	1,343	1,509	1,488	1,022	1,292	1,296
Ewes	4,644	5,738	4,468	3,231	3,930	3,991	3,999
Gimmers							1,206
Rams					136	194	147
Lambs under 1 year	4,356	} 14,605	} 11,746	3,557	4,117	4,633	4,402
Other sheep over 1 year	7,747			7,449	3,813	3,169	2,715
Sows	283	395	289	323	377	477	457
Boars					43	47	38
Other pigs	1,785	3,129	2,693	2,050	2,598	3,527	3,405

Table 21 Contd. Livestock 1941–1988

	1941	1945	1951	1961	1971	1984	1988
Agricultural horses	294	238	111				
Agricultural stallions	2	1					
Unbroken horses	12						
Other horses	16	16					
Dairy cows and in-calf heifers	1,694	1,661	1,575	1,671	684	43	
Bulls	59	48	57	29		2	
Other cattle	1,018	1,323	1,325	1,498	910	42	
Ewes	3,079	2,584	1,456	3,402	546		408
Ginmers	715	715	828	1,473	102		178
Rams	148	103	53	157	107		39
Lambs under 1 year	3,130	2,541	1,919	4,518	935		
Other sheep over 1 year	2,624	765	2,624	1,113	193		639
Sows and in-pig gilts	271	328	642	461	453		18
Boars	30	34	54	39	16		3
Other pigs	2,394	2,994	4,418	3,507	2,932		8
Total sheep						1,015	
Total Pigs						3,077	
Breeding beef cows and heifers							20
Other beef cattle					66	150	128

Table 22 Poultry

	Fowls		Ducks	Geese	Turkeys		Broilers, Table	Broilers, Other
1921	20,539		2,387	210	69			
1931	42,074		1,723	191	289			667
	Over 6 mths	*Under 6 mths*						
1939	15,302	18,729	962	217	230			
1941	14,677	10,697	796	213	123			
1945	7,443	9,980	943	436	371			
1951	14,791	19,603	2,211	229	1,545			
	Hens & Pullets for eggs	*Breeding Hens and Cocks*			*Turkey Hens*	*Others*		
1961	12,558	10,640	84	76	21,328		9,950	
1971	19,250	208	86	32	3,458	12,600	50	
1984	Poultry	12,708						

(Acol 768, Margate Borough 899, Broadstairs/St Peters 10,705, Minster 134, Monkton/Sarre 27, Ramsgate/St Lawrence 175)

1987	Fowls	11,406

(Margate Borough incl Acol 2188, Broadstairs/St P 8620, Minster 89, Monkton/Sarre 111. Ramsgate/St L 410)

	Ducks	34
	Geese	42
	Turkeys	–
1988	Poultry	2,057

(Margate Borough 1,922)

Table 23 Major Crops (acres excluding fractions)

	1901	1911	1916	1918	1921	1931
Wheat	1,644	2,432	2,982	3,436	2,521	1,178
Barley	3,481	2,888	2,619	2,581	2,736	3,337
Oats	1,860	2,159	2,381	2,154	1,880	1,086
Potatoes	734	660	583	1,050	1,031	758
Lucerne	1,691	1,420	1,830	849	865	924
Hops	119	78	37	13	31	16
Permanent pasture, mown	603	1,061	1,379	991	678	1,062
Permanent pasture, not mown	5,336	4,134	6,205	5,233	5,245	5,273
Clover, sanfoin and other rotated fodder crops, mown	293	834	884	682	1,055	731
Clover, sanfoin and other rotated fodder crops, not mown	1,261	110	222	169	92	–
Fallow	573	208	109	76	202	275
Other green crops incl. broccolli and cauliflowers	304	502	451	483	444	268
Peas (fodder and table)	598	418	71	95	97	46
Beans (fodder and table)	78	135				
Mangolds	1,380	965	825	853	700	770
Turnips/swedes	722	737	568	600	623	224
Fodder cabbage						350
Cauliflower/broccolli						
(incl. fractions)	n.a.	n.a.	182.5	194¼	229½	690.75
(Less fractions)			180	192	228	687

Table 24 Major Crops 1941–1971 (acres excluding fractions)

	1941	1945	1951	1961	1971
Wheat	1,991	831	2,045	2,181	3,677
Barley	3,139	3,446	2,906	3,107	2,281
Oats	962	796	715	333	426
Potatoes early	564	1,110	1,602	1,586	2,083
2nd early main crop	584	383	586	674	533
Lucerne	677	n.a.	675	328	104
Hops	16	20	21	10	25
Flax	64	53	–	–	–
Vetches & tares	362	111	62	–	–
Fodder cabbage & kohl rabi	49	Includes kale 964	248	14	68
Fallow	196	267	341	445	827
Clover, sanfoin, etc, mown	418	Includes lucerne: 1,224 Excludes lucerne, includes mown	–	910	
Clover, sanfoin, etc, not mown	89	150 and unmown:	1,146	602	
Cauliflower/broccoli	824	1,166	883	Winter 1,247 Incl Kale: / Summer: 543	994 / 1,052
Permanent pasture, mown	885	490	423	545	}1,412
Permanent pasture, not mown	4,492	4,577	3,768	3,289	}1,412
Mangolds	416	458	342	115	20
Turnip/swedes	180	67	47	85	8
Kale	342	n.a.	n.a.	299	n.a.
Sugar beet	221	90	91	170	114
Fodder Peas	73	36			
Fodder Beans	51	63			

Table 25 Major Crops Acres (ha)

	1984 (ha)		1988 (ha)	
Wheat	6,759	(2735.4)	4333	(1753.6)
Barley	1,093	(442.5)	805.8	(326.1)
Potatoes	2,887	(1,168.4)	1781.6	(721)
Cauliflower	1,212.7	(490.8)	1353	(547.8)
Hops	10		–	
Grass 1984 or later			297	(120.5)
Other			558.2	(225.9)
Oilseed Rape	339	(137.3)	785	(317.7)
Peas harvested dry	364	(147.4)	633	(256.2)
All stock feeding crops except maize	993	(402.1)	117.8	(47.7)
Fallow			334.3	(135.3)

Woods and Plantations

| 1891 | 26 acres (Birchington & St Peter's only. Absence of Minster may be a mistake) |
| 1988 | 22.2 acres (9 ha) (Minster and Margate borough only) |

Table 26 Table Vegetables & Fruit (acres including fractions) (Not Cauliflower/Broccoli)

	SMALL FRUIT	ORCHARD FRUIT	ORCHARD & SOFT FRUIT	MARKET GARDENS	NURSERY GARDENS	UNDER GLASS
1881	n.a.	210.25		153	9	
1891	219.25	128.		199.25	4.5	
1901	201.5	244.25		Vegetables Incomplete	1901–1931 n.a.	
1911	209.75	288.25		400.25 (1)		
1916	208.25	332.25		298.5 (2)		
1918	161.	367.75				
1921	296.5	220.5		306.25		
	SOFT FRUIT ONLY	*ORCHARDS & SOFT FRUIT UNDER*			*Flowers, Bulbs and Hardy Nursery Stock*	
1931	65.5	482.75		297.75	21.5	
1941	36.75	504.5		611.5 (3)	25.5	
1945	25.5	485.5		1,254.5		
		ORCHARDS	*ORCHARD & SOFT FRUIT*			
1951	69.25	477.75	33.5	1,086.5	44.25	
1961	25.25	269.	5.5	613.75	8.75	
		TREEFRUIT (NON COMMERCIAL)				*UNDER GLASS*
1971	3.	95.75		1,434.25 (4)	6.75	2.75
1984	13. (5.3ha)	8.6 (3.5ha)		1,522. (616ha)	9.3 (3.8ha)	2.7 (1.1ha)

Includes

(1) Carrots, Cabbage, Onion, Celery, Rhubarb, Brussel Sprouts. Cabbage includes fodder and table. Peas and Beans excluded.
(2) Same as (1) but excludes fodder cabbage.
(3) Includes Peas, Cabbage, Savoys, Brussel Sprouts, Carrots, Parsnips, Turnips, Onions, Swedes, Broad, Runner and French Beans, Celery, Lettuce, Calabrace, Kale, Beetroot, Tomatoes (under glass and in open), Rhubarb.
(4) Excludes Kale, otherwise same as (3).

Table 27 Table Vegetables and Fruit (including fractions)
Includes Brussel Sprouts, Cabbage, Parsnips, Beetroot, Carrots, Peas (dry),
Swedes, Onions, Broad, Runner & French Beans, Lettuce, Calabrace, Kale,
Tomatoes and "Other"

1987	1,977.5 acres (800.3 ha)
1988 (incomplete)	1,574 acres (637 ha)

Table 28 Labour 1921–1971

Regular Workers

Year	Male 21+/20+	Male (younger)	Male 65+	Female (main)	Female (younger)	Land Army
1921	856 (21+)	164 (21–)		52		
1931	863	117 (21–)		56		
1939	828	63 (18+)		37	68 (18–)	
1941	708	51 (18+)		45	67 (18–)	
1945	766	128 (21–)		156		103
1948	873	80 (21–)	104	163	51 (18–)	24
1951	803	117 (21–)	74	88	34 (18–)	–
1961	578 (20+)	28		38	46	

Casual Workers

Year	Male 21+/20+	Male 21–/20–	Female	(POW)
1921	126 (21+)	14 (21–)	90	
1931	125	5	94	
1939	100	18	83	
1941	83	20	175	
1945	129	19	388	POW 3
1948	172	18	308	–
1951	98	6	189	
1961	*Part-time* 20+ 41	20– –	68	

Not Directly Employed Casual Workers

Year	Male 21+/20+	Male 21–/20–	Female
1921	–	–	–
1931	–	–	–
1939	–	–	–
1941	–	–	–
1945	6	–	5
1961	*Seasonal or Temporary* 20+ 71	20– 20	F 340

1971

Farmers, Partners and Directors

Whole-time	Part-time
81	32

Family

Whole-time		Part-time	
M	F	M	F
19	8	2	11

Hired Workers

Regular whole-time		Regular part-time	
M	F	M	F
381	13	33	78

Seasonal or Casual Workers

M	F
37	496

Table 29 Labour 1984–1988

	Farmers Whole/ Part-time	Spouses	Other Partners & Directors Whole/Part-time	Spouses	Salaried Managers	Whole-time Family		Part-time Family		Hired Whole-time Workers		Part-time		Casual		YTS
						M	F	M	F	M	F	M	F	M	F	
1984	52/8	22	9/20	3	16	4	1	2	3	286	9	31	93	55	161	1
1988	40/9	16	8/13	–	10	2	–	1	3	174	6	13	64	43	116	2

The date of the agricultural returns was not the peak season for casual labour

Notes

Chapter One

1. Fordham S.J. and R.G. Green, *Soils of Kent. Soil Survey Bulletin No 9* Harpenden, 1980, fig 7. English Nature Report file ref: TR/35–4, pp 3–5 (unpublished).
2. Paper given by Dr Street, environmental assessment specialist for Kent County Council, at Council for the Protection of Rural England Water Conference at Wye College, 19/7/1991.
3. Lamb, H.H., *Climate, past, present and future*, London, 1977, 2/367.
4. A recession of 2½–3 miles at Reculver was postulated with some evidence by C.L. So, "Early coast recession at Reculver", *AC* 86/93–98.
5. Information from David Perkins and Nigel MacPherson-Grant. Lamb op cit 2/373.
6. Hawkes, C.F.C. *Pytheas: Europe and the Greek Explorers*, 8th J.L. Myers Memorial Lecture, Oxford, 1975, revised and amplified, with 10 maps.
7. Collected works of the following: Diodorus Siculus tr C.H. Oldfather, London 1933, 3/155; Strabo tr. H.L. Jones, London, 1917–1932, 2/255; Polybius tr E.S. Shuckburgh, London 1889, 3/57, 34/5, 10. C.F.C. Hawkes inclines to think that Pytheas went through the Wantsum and meant the South Foreland by Kantion Corner, but this does not square with the mouth of the Rhine being opposite it. He was possibly not aware that the Continent is occasionally visible from the North Foreland and more often from Ramsgate.
8. Information from David Perkins and Nigel MacPherson-Grant; Thanet Archeological Unit (Trust), *Gateway Island*, 3–37.
9. Salway, P. *Roman Britain*, Oxford 1981, 544–599.
10. *De Bello Gallico* V/1, 2; Mercer R. (ed), *Farming practice in British prehistory*, Edinburgh, 1981, 9.
11. Strabo tr Hamilton and Falconer, London, 1854, V chapter 4.
12. Salway, 824.
13. Frere, S. *Britannia. A history of Roman Britain*, London, 1987, 98, 339.
14. Stevenson translation, British Library ref 202.e.21.
15. Everitt J., *Continuity and colonization*, Leicester, 1986, 104.
16. Though Golding thought that Solinus must mean the Isle of Wight Caius Julius Solinus, *Collectanea rerum memorabilium*, tr Arthur Golding, London, 1587, repr Gainsville, Tennessee 1955, with introduction by George Kish, Ch 33.

17. Diodurus Siculus wrote that British tin was taken in horse panniers across Gaul to the Rhone, thence by water to Masilia (Marseilles) and Narbo (a Roman colony). (Oldfather tr 3/157, 203). Very small quantities of corn could have taken the same route in theory.

18. Waddelove A.C. & E. "Archeology and research into sea level during the Roman era: towards a methodology based on the highest astronomical tide". *Britannia* 1990. 31/253–266.

19. Information given by David Perkins; Lamb 1977, 2/374.

20. Wallenberg J.K. *Kentish place names.* Uppsala, 1934, 43; Everitt, 107.

21. Jones M.E. & P.J. Casey, "The Gallic Chronicle restored: a chronology for the Anglo-Saxon invasions and the end of Roman Britain", *Britannia*, 1988, 19/397. Naturally some disagree – J. Campbell (ed) *The Anglo-Saxons*, London 1991, 38, for example.

22. Myers, J.N.L. *The English settlements*, Oxford 1986, 37–39; AHEW 1.2, 423–424; Reaney, P.H. "Place names and early settlement in Kent", *AC* 76/59 and Everitt, 161 seem to disagree.

23. Reaney, 62, 63, 67; Everitt, 114.

24. Everitt, 114.

25. AHEW 1.2, 423–424; Drewett, P., D. Rudling and M. Gardiner, *The Southeast to AD 1000*, London, 1988, 257.

26. Drewett et al 257, 275; Yorke, B.A.E., "Joint kingship in Kent c 560–785", *AC* 1983, 99/11, 12.

27. Witney, K.P. *The kingdom of Kent*, London, 1982, 26, 236; Drewett et al, 280.

28. Drewett et al, 280; Thanet Archeological Unit (Trust), *Gateway Island*, 44.

29. Drewett et al, 273; AHEW 1.2, 262.

30. *Gateway Island*, 48, 51.

31. D.R.J. Perkins, "The site of the church of St Giles, Sarre", *AC* 105/291–7.

32. "Residens sub dive", Venerable Bede, *Baedae opera historica*, with English translation by J.E. King, London, 1930, 1/109.

33. Stanley, Canon A.P., *Historical memorials of Canterbury*, London, third ed 1912, 29.

34. Rev Christopher Donaldson, a former Birchington vicar, quoted in *Thanet Extra* 4/3/1988.

35. Venerable Bede, op cit 1/111, para 9.

36. John Lewis, *The History and Antiquities as well Ecclesiastical as Civil of the Isle of Tenet, in Kent.* 2nd ed London 1736, 83.

37. Bede, op cit, 1/109.

38. Witney, K.P. 1982, 67 and in "The Period of Mercian rule in Kent and a Charter of 811", *AC* 1987, 103/104–109.

39. E.G. Quested (EGQ), R. Quested (RQ).

40. Rollason, D.W., "The date of the parish boundary of Minster in Thanet", *AC* 1979, 95/7–17.

41. Rollason, D.W., *The Mildreth legend*, Leicester, 1982, 11.

42. Birch, W. de Gray, *Cartolarium Saxonicum*, (CS) London, 1885 Vol 1 no 35; Rollason 1982, 34; Brooks, N. *The early history of the church of Canterbury*, Leicester, 1984, 183.

43. Rollason 1982, 35.

44. Drewett et al 314–315.

45. Brooks, 183; Rollason 1982, 47–50.
46. Birch, CS 42 and 44; Witney K.P. "The Kentish royal saints: an enquiry into the facts behind the legends", *AC* 1984, 101/9–10.
47. Rollason 1982, 47–50; Brooks, 183.
48. An earlier speculation of Witney, 1982, 142; Hopkins, P.D., *Minster-in-Thanet*, Thanet, 1985, 8.
49. Rollason 1982, 10; 1979, 14–15, 17.
50. Brooks, 285.
51. Birch, CS nos 1/177, 189; Brooks 366, note 63; Everitt note 15 to chapter 8; Wallenberg, 21–22; Witney 1984, 14.
52. Newman, J. *North East and East Kent*, London, 1976, 389. Part of Pevsner N. (ed) The Buildings of England series.
53. Kilburne, R. *A topographie or survey of the County of Kent*, London, 1659, 193.
54. 1982, note p 203.
55. "Monasterio" – Birch CS no 1/177.
56. Birch, CS 1/35, 40, 41, 42, 44, 86, 88, 96, 141, 149, 150, 177, 189, 846.
57. Birch, CS 1/40.
58. Birch, CS 1/141.
59. Darby, H.D. and Eila M.J. Campbell, (ed) *The Domesday geography of Southeast England*, Cambridge, 1962, 494.
60. Witney 1982, 191.
61. Witney K.P. "The woodland economy of Kent, 1066–1348", Ag HR 1990, 38/1, 20–39.
62. Birch, CS nos 1/149, 150, 188.
63. Ibid, nos 1/177, 189.
64. 1736 ed, 65, document 11.
65. CS no 1/77.
66. Opinion of Dr Ann Williams, lecturer in medieval history, University of London, given to the author at Institute of Historical Research in 1990.
67. Lewis, 1736, 26; Hasted, Edward, *The history and topographical survey of the county of Kent*, Canterbury, 1797–1801, (folio edition), 4/305 mentions but does not venture a date.
68. Witney 1987, 88.
69. Witney 1982, 179; 1984, 1–14.
70. Birch, CS no 1/45; Du Boulay, F.R.H., *The lordship of Canterbury*, London, 1966, 20, 23, 383.
71. Witney 1982, 69, 149.
72. Information from David Perkins.
73. Lamb 1977, 2/374.
74. AHEW 1.2, 74.
75. Drewett et al, 330.
76. AHEW 1.2, 497.
77. Witney 1990, 25.
78. Stenton, F.E. *Anglo-Saxon England*, 3rd edition Oxford, 1971, 206–208, 231; Witney 1987, 88, etc.
79. Witney 1982, 225; Darby & Campbell, 486.
80. *Domesday Book for Kent*, tr Philip Morgan, Chichester, 1983, first page of index of places. (There are no page numbers). He cites J.E.A. Joliffe, "The

origin of the Hundred in Kent", in J.G. Edwards, V.H. Galbraith, and E.F. Jacobs (eds) *Historical essays in honour of James Tait*, London, 1933, 155–168.

81. Brooks 30, 150; Drewett et al, 322.
82. Brooks, 30, 150, 204, 282; Rollason D.W., "The translation and miracles of St Mildred", *Medieval Studies*, 1988, 48/160, notes 16, 30, 37; Witney 1987, 88, 92, 93; Drewett et al, 322.
83. Brooks, 205, 206.
84. Drewett et al, 259.
85. Kerridge, E., *The agricultural revolution*, London, 1967, 54, 219. Nor does he mention Thanet in his latest book, *The Open Fields*, London, 1992.
86. Tithe maps in Canterbury Cathedral archives; microfilm copies at Kent County archives of those too damaged to examine in the original.
87. AHEW 2/324–325.
88. Brooks, 285; Birch, CS Nos. 780, 784, 791.
89. Brooks, 285.
90. Hasted, folio edition, 4/308.
91. Detsicas A. (ed) *Collectanea historica*, Maidstone, 1981, 679.
92. Brooks, 285.
93. Hasted, 1800 edition, Canterbury, 10/332, 359, 380.
94. Also a payment to the Manor of Blean, for reasons unknown, possibly for renting marshland – Barrett, J.P., *A history of the ville of Birchington*, Margate, 1893, 157.
95. John Gillingham, "Thegns and Knights in eleventh century England", *Transactions of the Royal Historical Society Sixth Series*, V/129–153. Alan Everitt, *Continuity and colonization: the evolution of Kentish settlement*, Leicester, 1986, 173–177

Chapter Two

1. Douglas, David C., *William the Conqueror*, London, 1977, 205.
2. Witney, K.P., "The development of the Kentish marshes in the aftermath of the Norman conquest", *AC* 1989, 107/32.
3. Douglas, op cit, 347, mentions but does not specify which districts; his appears to be the best documented modern work on the Conqueror.
4. Morgan, Philip, *Domesday Book*, Vol 1, Kent, 3.7, 7.8, Domesday Monachorum tr VCHK 3/255 mentions St Giles and its 7d payment.
5. AHEW 2/82.
6. Witney, *Kingdom of Kent*, Appendix C; VCHK 3/259.
7. Witney, "Mercian rule in Kent", 104–109.
8. AHEW I.2/499.
9. Lewis, John, *History* 1736 ed, 11.
10. Darby, H.C., *Domesday England*, London, 1977, 175–178.
11. Drewett, *Southeast to AD 1000*, 341.
12. Brandon, P. and B. Short, *The Southeast from AD 1000*, London and New York, 1990, 32.
13. Stenton, *Anglo-Saxon England*, 470–472; AHEW 2/49–50 confirms.

14. AHEW 2/971.
15. Ballard, A. *The Domesday inquest*, 2nd ed London, 1923, 89, 154.
16. AHEW 2/10, 11.
17. Nash, A. "The Domesday population of Southern England", *Southern History* 1988, 10/8–10.
18. Davis, A.H. *William Thorne's chronicle of St Augustine's Abbey, Canterbury*, Oxford, 1934, 64.
19. Mockett, John., *John Mockett's journal, with observations on agriculture*, Canterbury, 1836, 9; David D. Scurrell, *The parish church of St John the Baptist in Thanet* (leaflet), 2.
20. Davis, op cit, 68.
21. Cotton, C. *The history and antiquities of the church and parish of St Lawrence*, London and Ramsgate, 1895, 22–23; P.J. Hills, *The parish church of St Peter in Thanet*, Gainsborough, 1970, 28; Scurrell, op cit 2.
22. Kent Archaelogical Society Records, vol 15, Ashford, 1986, cxxv.
23. Jenkins, P. "The church of All Saints' at Shuart", in A. Detsicas (ed) *Collectanea Historica*, Maidstone, 1981, 147–154.
24. Information given by the vicar; anon, *Guide to the parish church of St Nicholas-at-Wade with Sarre*.
25. Walker, A.T., *A guide to the parish church of All Saints in Birchington*, Thanet, 1967, 5.
26. Gilham, J.C. (ed) and P.D. Hopkins, *The parish church of St Mary the Virgin in Minster in Thanet*, Thanet, 1987, 8; anon, *A short guide to St Mary Magdalen, Monkton*.
27. Smith, R.A.L., *Canterbury Cathedral Priory. A study in monastic administration*, Cambridge, 1943, 113.
28. Du Boulay, F.R.H., *Lordship*, 197.
29. Lewis, *History*, 1736, 39.
30. Du Boulay, *Lordship*, 80, 382.
31. Philipott, Thomas, *Villare Cantianum, or Kent surveyed and illustrated . . .* London, 1659, 351.
32. Kent Archaeological Society Records, 15/205.
33. Davis, 586, 622.
34. Reaney, "Place names and early settlement in Kent", 68; Everitt, 91; Turner, G.E. and H.E. Salter, *The Black Book of St Augustine's*, British Academy Records of Social and Economic History vols 2 and 3, London, 1915, 427.
35. Mate, Mavis, "Pastoral farming in Southeast England in the 15th century", *EcHR* 2nd series, 1987, 40/4, 525. Christchurch's "marsh manor of Lydden in Thanet" which she describes is obviously the marsh Lydden Valley midway between Sandwich and Deal. The real Thanet Lydden is and was a good three miles from the marsh, in the heart of the then St Augustine's dominated Eastern half of Thanet, and there is no other suggestion that it ever belonged to Christchurch or even was a manor. Likewise in "Property investment by Christchurch Priory 1250–1400", *Journal of British Studies*, 33/8–9, she writes of a tide mill at Lydden in the Isle of Thanet, which would be impossible.
36. Du Boulay, *Lordship* . . . 118, 266, 383.

37. Smith, Ann., "Regional differences in crop production in medieval Kent", *AC* 78/149.
38. Davis, 682.
39. KA U 438 M7/1.
40. Hills, P.J. *Dane Court, St Peter's in Thanet*, Gainsborough, 1972, 2, 3, 109; Hasted 1800 (ed), 10/280, 283, 299, 300, 305, 336, 341, 359, 378, 380, 381, 382.
41. Melling, Elizabeth, *Some Kentish houses*, Kentish Sources V, 2. For Thorne manor and chapel, Lewis 1736, 34; Davis lxiv.
42. Du Boulay, *Lordship*, 98.
43. Ibid, 182.
44. Thirsk, Joan, AHEW 4/62.
45. Du Boulay, cited in AHEW 2/621.
46. Thirsk, "The Open Fields", *Past and Present*, 1964, 3–25; also in AHEW 4/1–15.
47. Baker, Dennis., *Agriculture, prices and marketing, with special reference to the hop industry in N.E. Kent 1680–1760*, New York, 1985, 22.
48. Witney, "The Kentish royal saints", 31.
49. In a letter to the author dated 2.10.1991.
50. Smith, R.A.L., 114; du Boulay, *Lorship*, 197.
51. Mate, Mavis, "The farming out of manors; evidence from Canterbury Cathedral Priory", *JMH* 1983, 9/331–332.
52. Rowles, W., *The Kentish Chronologer and Index*, London and Maidstone, 1807, 41.
53. Du Boulay, *Lordship . . .*, 181.
54. Bolton, J.L., *The medieval English economy 1150–1500*, London, 1980, 25–26.
55. Davis, xli-xlii, xlvii-xlviii, 259, 432–434.
56. Land, John, *A parish history of St Nicholas-at-Wade and Sarre*, Thanet, 1990, 4–5.
57. Cave Brown, J. (ed) A topographic pamphlet of the British Archeological Association, title page missing, 19th century, 298–302. (Library of Institute of Historical Research, University of London).
58. Davis, xlii, 432–434. Dom D. Prangnell, *The chronicle of William of Byholte* (1310–1320), Ramsgate, nd.
59. Mate, "The farming out of manors . . .", 335–336; R.A.L. Smith, op cit, 114.
60. Du Boulay, Lordship . . . 197.
61. Smith, R.A.L., 133. Unpublished research by J. Burgon Bickersteth needs to be evaluated.
62. AHEW 2/321. R.A.L. Smith gives higher figures.
63. Smith, Ann, 149.
64. AHEW 2/319; R.A.L. Smith, 40–41.
65. Du Boulay, *Lordship . . .*, 131, 132, 207; AHEW 2/322.
66. Gras, N.B.S. *The evolution of the English corn market from the 12th–18th century*, London, 1915, 293.
67. Davis, 276–279. K.M.E. Murray, *The constitutional history of the Cinque Ports*, Manchester, 1935, 50, 53, 241, 242 etc.
68. Du Boulay, *Lordship . . .*, 134.
69. Davis, 208; Eileen Bowler, "A study of the works of the Sewer Com-

missioners", in Detsicas (ed) *Studies in modern Kentish history*, Maidstone, 1983, 29–48.

70. Davis, 208.
71. Du Boulay, *Lordship* . . ., 211
72. Murray, K.M.E. 23, 45.
73. Du Boulay, *Lordship* . . ., 209; R.A.L. Smith, 140, 152.
74. Smith, R.A.L., 148, 150, 159, 162.
75. Du Boulay, *Lordship* . . ., 215.
76. Smith, R.A.L., 146.
77. Ibid, 124, 133.
78. Du Boulay, *Lordship* . . ., 106.
79. Kent Archaeological Society Records, 15/282, 336.
80. Smith, R.A.L., 177, 122.
81. Davis, lxiv.
82. Ibid, xliii, lxiv.
83. Du Boulay, *Lordship* . . ., 118.
84. Davis, 403–405. Word definitions from *Oxford English Dictionary*.
85. Brandon and Short, op cit, 72.
86. Ibid, 72; M. Bailey, "The rabbit and the medieval East Anglian economy", *Ag HR* 36/1, 1; J. Sheail, "Rabbits and agriculture in post-medieval England", *J Hist Geog* 1978, 4/4, 354.
87. Chalklin, C.W. "The Kent lay subsidy roll of 1334–1335" in *Kent Archaeological Society Records* 18, Ashford, 1964, 71–76, map facing pp 1–2.
88. E.W. Parkin, "The ancient Cinque Port of Sandwich", *AC* 100 (1984)/191. K.W. Hardman, "Stonar and the Wantsum channel", *AC* 53/41–54, *AC* 65/37–49.
89. Chalklin, "The Kent lay subsidy . . ." 63.
90. Barnwell, P.S., *Southern History* 16/4. Newman, *Northeast and East Kent*, 64.
91. Chalklin, "Kent lay subsidy . . ."; Barnwell, 12–15; Du Boulay, *Lordship*, 181.
92. Brandon and Short, 70–72, map 73.
93. Unpublished researches by J. Burgon Bickersteth.
94. Kent Archaeological Society Records, 15/72, 341, etc.
95. Chalklin, "The Kent lay subsidy roll . . ."
96. Hasted, folio edition, 4/229.
97. Rowles, 42–45.
98. Ibid, 66.
99. Smith, R.A.L., 125–127.
100. Lamb, 1977, 2/449–452. But this view is contested by David Farmer in AHEW 3/439–440.
101. Mate, Mavis, "Agrarian economy after the Black Death: the manors of Canterbury Cathedral Priory 1348–1391", *EcHR* 2nd series, 1985, 37/3, 345; R.A.L. Smith, 125–127, gives years as 1327, 1348, 1363, 1369 and 1386.
102. Mate, Mavis, "High prices in early 14th century England", *EcHR* 1975, 28/1, 12.
103. Lamb, 1977, 2/454–456; R.S. Gottfried, *The Black Death*, London, 1983, chapter one.
104. Mate, "Agrarian economy" . . ., 354; R.A.L. Smith, 125–127. Researches

by J. Burgon Bickersteth found a catastrophic fall in sown area at Monkton by 1371, but this has not been mentioned by Smith or Mate.

105. *Kentish Register* June 1795, 204 claims that these were laid down by Parliament in 1378, but the *Statutes of the Realm* vol 2 does not show this; Vol 1/307 gives the statute of 1349 which confirmed "those customary for the previous five or six years".

106. Du Boulay, *Lordship* . . ., 197.

107. Mate, "Pastoral farming . . .", 353.

108. KA Conynghan archive U438 RTR 329/8.

109. Unpublished researches by J. Burgon Bickersteth.

110. Thanet Archeological Trust, *Gateway Island*, 58.

111. Jenkins, F. "The church of All Saints at Shuart", in A. Detsicas (ed) *Collectanea Historica*, 152.

112. Barrett, J.P., 18, 20; A.T. Walker, *The Ville of Birchington, its history and bygones*, new edition, Thanet 1991, 172–174.

113. Davis, 565–578.

114. Ibid, xlv.

115. Flaherty, W.E., "The Great Rebellion in Kent in 1381". *AC* 1860, 3/65–71, is still much the best source for the events in Thanet. Andrew Prescott's University of London, 1984, PhD thesis, "The judicial records of the 1381 rising", quotes Flaherty and adds only that Medmenham was a coroner.

116. Mate, "The farming out of manors . . .", 337–340.

117. Smith, R.A.L., 193.

118. Mate, "The farming out of manors . . .", 337–340.

119. AHEW 3/690; R.A.L. Smith, 127 note 2, 200 says some only got 13/4d.

120. Du Boulay, *Lordship* . . ., 197, 223–224.

121. Smith, R.A.L., 200.

122. Mate, "Pastoral farming . . .", 524, 525.

123. Carlin, Mary., "Christchurch Priory and its lands from the beginning of the Priorate of Thomas Chillenden to the Dissolution", Oxford B. Litt, 1970, 102, 112, 126, 195.

124. KA Conyngham archive U438 RTR 329/8.

125. Gras, 293.

126. Du Boulay, *Lordship* . . ., 197; AHEW 3/133, table 2.14.

127. Lamb, 2/456, 457, 458–459; Farmer in AHEW 3/439–440.

128. KA U438 329/8 Lambeth file 79430, copy of PRO Class 1 Bundle 25. no 20 – a court case. For the 1190's one, Richard Holt, *Mills of Medieval England*, Oxford 1988, 174.

129. Hasted 1800, 10/229.

130. Smith, R.A.L., 142 note 42, citing Cal. Charter Rolls 25–26 Henry III, 79–80; Hasted folio ed 4/309.

131. AHEW 3/335.

132. Harvey, I.M.W., *Jack Cade's rebellion of 1450*, Oxford 1991, 5, note, quoting E357/8 Kent and Middlesex, documents on the property of traitors, outlaws, felons and fugitives.

133. *Statutes of the Realm*, 2/338, 23 Henry VI.

134. *Kentish Register*, June 1795, 204. These figures are more plausible than those of the *Statutes of the Realm*, which contain such oddities as 4/ld (sic)

for clothes for a common male servant in husbandry and 4/- (sic) for a woman's clothes.

135. Latin text of the agreement in Lewis, *History*, 1736, Appendix 35; translation in VCHK 3/349.
136. Gray, H.L., *English field systems*, London, 1959, 299.
137. Smith, R.A.L., 204; article by C. Cotton in unidentified journal mentioned in A.T. Walker MS notes for the cloaks. Royal fish included whales, sturgeons etc.
138. Barrett, 20.
139. Hills, *Parish church of St Peter . . .*, 59.
140. Rowles, 46.
141. Cotton, 96.
142. Scurrell, 2, 4.
143. Burke, J. *Jowitt's dictionary of English law*, London, 2nd ed 1976, 132, 721.
144. Barrett, 18, 20, 21, 22.
145. Newman in Pevsner series, op cit, 163.
146. Scurrell, 2.
147. Lewis, 1736, 115.
148. Murray, 23, 44, 45, 46, 50, 54, 55, 241; Cotton, 2; Gore End is said to have joined Dover under Edward I (1272–1307) by Barrett, 17–18, but Murray does not confirm.
149. Kilburne, R., *A topographie*, 356; Murray, 44, note 2; frontispiece map.
150. Cooper, W.D. "Jack Cade's followers in Kent", *AC* 7/233–271.
151. See note 132.
152. *The Descripcion of Engelonde*, edited Caxton, first ed 1480.

Chapter Three

1. Hasted 1800, 10/249. The *Statutes of the Realm* 2/525–586 show it was not a direct Act of Parliament as he says, but must have been enacted by one of the Commissioners of Sewers, who in 1472 (12 Edward IV) were appointed in all parts of the realm with powers to ordain and execute statutes and ordinances. Henry VII continued this policy.
2. KA Conyngham archive RTR 329/8.
3. Du Boulay, F.R.H. (ed) *Documents illustrative of medieval Kentish society*, Kent Archaeological Society Records vol 18, Ashford, 1964, 266.
4. KA Conyngham archive U438 RTR 329/7.
5. Barrett, 44.
6. Brandon & Short, 135–137.
7. Sherlock, D. "The account of George Nycholl for St Augustine's 1552–1553", *AC* 99/29.
8. Quex Park terrier 1774.
9. Baker, A.R.H. and R.A. Butlin, *Studies of field systems in the British Isles*, Cambridge, 1973, 80.
10. AHEW 4/246; Clark, P., *English provincial society from Reformation to Revolution*, Hassock, 1977, 6.
11. AHEW 5/294.

12. KA U86 96 N. 172.
13. Baker, Dennis., *Agriculture, prices and marketing, with special reference to the hop industry in N.E. Kent 1680–1760*, New York, 1985, 1/21.
14. Baker, A.R.H., "Some early Kentish estate maps", *AC* 77/177.
15. Chalklin, C.W., *Seventeenth century Kent*, London, 2nd ed, 1978, 20.
16. Barrett, 33.
17. Holinshed, Raphael, *Chronicles of England, Scotland and Ireland*, Vol 1, London, 1577. Continued to 1586 by John Hooker, London 1586, reprint 1801, 294–295, 343.
18. Philipott, Thomas., *Villare Cantianum, or Kent surveyed and illustrated*, London, 1659, 386.
19. Rowles, 28.
20. Hasted 1800, 10/274.
21. Lewis, 1736, 69; Barrett, 53–54; Rowles 49, 50, 55.
22. Barrett, 53, 54, 55, 76, 104.
23. KA Conyngham archive U438 RTR 329/7.
24. Lewis 1736, Appendix 4–5, 12.
25. Lewis 1736, 43–44; Barrett, 27; Rowles shows no Knights of the Shire from here after 1332.
26. Coleman, D.C., "The economy of Kent under the later Stuarts", University of London PhD thesis 1951, 410; Barrett, 132–133, 136, 143.
27. AHEW 4/xxxi.
28. By the late 16th century many gentry were using their parks profitably for grazing cattle. AHEW 4/641. Oliver Rackham, *Ancient woodlands of England: the woods of SE Essex*, Rochford, 1986, 19. Thirsk, letter to author dated 10.8.1993.
29. KA U438 M7/1.
30. Zell, M., "Early Tudor J.P.'s at work", *AC* 93/131–132; Lewis 1736, 39–40.
31. Zell, 131–132.
32. Lambarde, W., *A perambulation of Kent*, London, 1576, reprint, Chatham, 1826, 25, says Sir Richard Crispe; Barrett 54 indicates it must have been Sir Henry.
33. KA U438, Conyngham archive.
34. Baker, Dennis., 6.
35. Barrett, 55, 66–72.
36. Black, J.R., *The reign of Elizabeth*, Oxford history of England series, Oxford, 1959, 213.
37. Walker, 85–86.
38. Barrett, 24–25, 89–90.
39. Hasted 1800, 10/241.
40. Davies, Richard., paper on "Lollardy and locality" given at the Royal Historical Society one-day conference on Christian life in the later Middle Ages on 15 September 1990 at the Institute of Historical Research, University of London.
41. Thomson, J.A.F., *The later Lollards, 1414–1520*, Oxford, 1965, 172, 183, 184, 185, 188, 189; Hudson, Anne., *The premature revolution*, Oxford, 1988, 121, 134, 136, 450.
42. Clark, 48.
43. Davis, J.F., *Heresy and Reformation in the Southeast of England 1520–1559*.

Royal Historical Society Studies in History series, London, 1983, 83–84, 91–94, 102–103, 107.
44. Davis, 125–126. Alchorne was probably churchwarden of All Saints Birch-ington, as there was one of that name at that time – Alfred Walker, MS notes.
45. Clark, 48, 59, 63; Ingram Hill, Derek., *The Six Preachers of Canterbury Cathedral 1541–1982*, Ramsgate, 1982, 13, 16, 18; Hogben, B.M., "Preaching and Reformation in Henrician Kent", *AC* 100/172, 177.
46. Clark, 163; Barrett, chapter 8.
47. Clark, 38, 48, 59, 174–175, 177, 323.
48. Barrett, 57, gives details for Birchington, which collected £23/6/8d towards fitting out a ship at Dover.
49. Bird, J.E., *The story of Broadstairs*, Broadstairs, 1974, 39. See note 160.
50. Barrett, 95–98, 102–104. For the 1643 rising, Geo. Hornby, seminar at Institute of Historical Research 6 June 1995.
51. Hopkins, 18–19; Barrett, chapters 12–14; Clark, 369.
52. Barrett, chapter 13.
53. Timpson, Rev. Thomas, *The Church history of Kent*, London. 1859, 200.
54. Barrett, 140, 147–148; KA NFQ, "Notes on Kent Meeting Houses by John Elgar"; KA QSB; Walker, 51–52.
55. Barrett, 119–122.
56. Transcript of St Mary's Minster churchwarden's book, 1630–1636.
57. Hasted 1800, 10/222, 249–250; Lewis 1736, 42; Philipott, 384.
58. Dobson, M., "Marsh fevers: the geography of malaria in England", *Journal of Historical Geography*, 1980, 6/384–386, cited by Alan Armstrong, *Farm-workers: a social and economic history 1770–1980*, London, 1988, 38–39.
59. MacDougall, P., "Malaria: its influence on a North Kent community", *AC* 95/255–264.
60. John S. Moore, "Canterbury visitations and the demography of mid-Tudor Kent", *Southern History* 15/36–85.
61. Lambarde, 27; Moore, op cit.
62. Walker, 172–174; Hussey, A., "Visitations of the Archdeacon of Canter-bury", *AC* 25/13; RQ. An archeological dig found large quantities of fowl and human bones – *Gateway Island*, 61. The church ruin was there till after the dig in 1981.
63. Barrett, 46–47, 58, 71, 141. His estimates of the total population seem too high and he does not explain how he arrived at them.
64. Coleman thesis, 386, 410.
65. Barrett, 132–133.
66. Chalkin, C.W., "The Compton census of 1676", in *A 17th century miscel-lany*, Kent Archeological Society records vol 17, 153–172.
67. AHEW 4/598. For the 40/60 ratio, note 66
68. AHEW 4, fig 473 shows no markets in Thanet 1500–1650. Holinshed neither in 1st nor 2nd editions reported any markets or fairs in Thanet, though he listed many in East Kent, including a market at Reculver.
69. Hasted 1800, 10/321.
70. Kilburne, 154, 196, 215.
71. Hasted 1800, 10/324. *KG* 16/10/1798, 1. Corn was sold at the Fountain Inn.
72. Hasted folio ed 4/302.

73. Hopkins, 18.
74. Jordan, W.K., "Social institutions in Kent 1480–1660", *AC* 75/160/161.
75. Lewis 1736, 57; Seymour, Charles, *A new survey of the county of Kent*, Canterbury, 1776, 606, 636–637.
76. Clark, 201.
77. Chalklin, *Seventeenth century Kent*, 219.
78. Hasted folio ed 4/302.
79. Parker, R. *The schools of St Nicholas-at-Wade 1640–1957*, Canterbury, 1957, and Anneli Jones, "The changing face of St Nicholas-at-Wade", 24.
80. Hasted folio ed 4/297.
81. Marcus, G.J., *A naval history of England*, London, 1961, 1/32.
82. Navy Records Society, Vol 123, 28.
83. Ibid vol. 8, xxi, xxii, 153, 292, 312. Oppenheim M., *The Administration of the Royal Navy 1509–1660*, London, 1896, 69. etc.
84. Albion, R.G., *Forests and seapower*, Canterbury, 1926, 111.
85. *The Laboryeuse Journey and Serche of John Leylande for Englandes antiquities . . .*, London, 2nd ed. 1596. np.
86. Barrett, 52–53.
87. Holinshed, 1st ed 1577, 53, 343.
88. Camden, William. *Britannia*, 2nd ed tr by Philemon Holland, London, 1610, 339.
89. Evelyn, John., *Diary*, ed E.S. de Beer, Oxford, 1955, 3/611.
90. Evelyn, 3/615.
91. Fiennes, Celia., *Through England on a side-saddle in the time of William and Mary*, with introduction by Hon. Mrs Griffiths, London, 1888, 105.
92. Hopkins, 25, photocopy of the tree survey in KA U438 T83.
93. Land, 14; information from Jill Smith, and David Fuller.
94. AHEW 4/736; Parken, E.W. "Durlock Grange, Minster-in-Thanet", *AC* 77/82–91.
95. Mingay G.E., *English landed society in the 18th century*, London, 1963, 239.
96. AHEW 4/736; Parken article.
97. Mr Goodwin, the present owner, showed the author round in 1988; the author was born and grew up in the house.
98. Newman in the Pevsner series 435.
99. AHEW 4/737; Parken article; author's recollections of Woodchurch. KA AC831 U442 E43.
100. Jacqueline Bower, "The Kent yeoman in the 17th century", *AC* 114/158. Hopkins, 21–22.
101. Bird, 53, citing KA PRC/326.
102. Du Boulay, *Lordship*, 230.
103. Walker, MS notes.
104. *Statutes of the Realm* 2/586. Barrett, 44.
105. Putnam, B, "The earliest form of Lambarde's Eirenarche: a Kent wage assessment of 1563", *English history review*, XLI/260–273.
106. Barrett 63, 125.
107. AHEW 4/737.
108. Mockett, John, *John Mockett's journal, with observations on agriculture*, Canterbury, 1836, 26.
109. Baker, Dennis., 1/160.

110. Ibid, 153–163.
111. Barrett, 132–133.
112. Sic, Coleman thesis, 386.
113. Sic, Chalklin, *Seventeenth century Kent*, 255.
114. Harrington, D. (ed) *The Kent hearth tax enrollment assessment*, Kent Family History Society, Canterbury, 1983, Hundred of Ringslow lists.
115. Barrett, 70–71, 128–131; Walker, 72.
116. Land, 35, 36.
117. Clark, P., "The migrant in Kentish towns 1580–1640", in P. Clark and P. Slack (ed) *Crisis and order in English towns*, London, 1972, 137, 147.
118. Kerridge, E., *The agricultural revolution*, London, 1967, 181, 344, 345, 347, 348.
119. Lewis 1736, 17.
120. Lewis 1736, 15, 25; he states the same in the 1723 ed.
121. Chalklin, *Seventeenth century Kent*, 96.
122. Kerridge, 219.
123. AHEW 4/126, 512–513; information from David Ormerod.
124. Baker, Dennis., 241.
125. Young, Arthur., *Annals of Agriculture*, London, 1781, 5/38, Dennis Baker, 212.
126. Baker, Dennis., 130, 212, 255.
127. Coles Finch, W., *Watermills and windmills. A historical survey of their rise, decline and fall as portrayed by those of Kent*, London, 1933, 134, 165. I am indebted to Alan Kay for a copy of Symondson's map, of which the original is in the Bodleian. AHEW 2/930.
128. Barrett, 73.
129. Information supplied by Jacqueline Bower, from the probate papers of Jane Cantis, widow of Monkton, KA PRC20/13/485.
130. Baker, Dennis., 224, quoting Camden Society publications, old series CXXX, 1862, 109.
131. Lukehurst, Clare, "The Stour marshes: a study of agricultural change 1840–1966", University of London PhD thesis, 1977, 44, quoting Dugdale, W. *The history of embanking and drayning of divers fenns and marshes, both in foreign parts and in this kingdom, and of improvements thereby*, London, 1662, 36–59, also Camden, *Britannia*, London 1695 ed, 201.
132. Baker, Dennis, 388–389.
133. Ibid, 359.
134. Ibid, 348–351, 359, 450.
135. Ibid, 347.
136. Ibid, 212.
137. KA Conyngham archive U438 RTR 329/7. Chalklin, *Seventeenth century Kent*, 61.
138. Cotton, 222, 231.
139. Barrett, 136.
140. Chalklin, *Seventeenth century Kent*, 58.
141. Bower, 158. Baker, Dennis, 665.
142. Transcript of St Mary's, Minster, churchwarden's book.
143. Barrett, 44.
144. Lewis 1736, 124.

145. J.M. Gibson, "The 1566 survey of the Kent coast", *AC* 112/348 – the house numbers may refer to a much larger area than the fishing villages of Margate, Broadstairs and Ramsgate.
146. Gras, 293.
147. "Document in the Public Record Office copied by R.A. Coats in 1939", Margate library ref. 060.198.L 3392.
148. Coleman thesis, 226.
149. Baker, Dennis, 149–150; AHEW 5.1, 307.
150. Information from Jill Smith.
151. Brandon and Short, 167.
152. VCHK 3/429. Theo Barker in Alan Armstrong (ed) *The economy of Kent 1640–1914*, Maidstone, 1995, 132.
153. Barrett, 127.
154. Andrews, J.H., "The Thanet seaports 1650–1750", *AC* 66/38.
155. Baker, Dennis, 665; Samuel Pepys, *Diary*, London, 1949 ed 1/121–122.
156. Andrews, 38–44.
157. AHEW 5.2/506, 532, 578.
158. Gardiner, Dorothy, *Historic haven*, Derby, 1954, 174; Boys, William., *Collections for the History of Sandwich*, np 1792, 740–747; Bentwich, Helen C., *History of Sandwich in Kent*, Deal, 1971, 37.
159. AHEW 5.1/297.
Note 49 continued. Articles by J.R. Scott *AC* 11/390, J. McGurk *AC* 70/71–90.

Chapter Four

1. John Lewis, *History*, 11.
2. Ibid, 26.
3. Ibid, 42.
4. Ibid, 144. Barrett, 144.
5. Lewis, 25.
6. Ibid, 11.
7. Ibid, 42.
8. Ibid, 32.
9. Ibid, 39–40.
10. Ibid, 70.
11. Ibid, 33–35.
12. Ibid, 24.
13. Ibid, 25.
14. 1723 ed, 9.
15. 1736 ed, 33.
16. Ibid, 178.
17. 1723 ed, 15.
18. 1736 ed, 79.
19. Ibid, 13.
20. Ibid, 15.
21. Ibid, 73.
22. Ibid, 15.

23. Ibid, 17.
24. Ibid, 21.
25. Ibid, 16.
26. Ibid, 13.
27. 1736 ed plates 3–5.
28. Dennis Baker, 212.
29. Ibid.
30. Lewis 1736 ed, 15.
31. Ibid, 16.
32. Ibid, 17.
33. Ibid, 16.
34. Ibid, 21; AHEW 5.2/584.
35. Lewis 1736 ed, 25.
36. Ibid, 24.
37. Ibid, 18.
38. Ibid, map facing p 2.
39. Dennis Baker, 325.
40. J. Harris, *The history of Kent*, np, 1719, 314.
41. Daniel Defoe, *A Tour through the whole Island of Great Britain*, London, 1927 reprint of 1727, 1/119–120.
42. Hopkins, 21.
43. KP 9–13/4/1725–26, 4.
44. AHEW 5.1/307.
45. J.H. Andrews, 37–44.
46. E. Waterman, "Some new evidence on wage assessments in the 18th century", EcHR XLIII, 1928, 405–407. This writer considers the wages quoted by J.L. & B. Hammond, *Village Labourer* 144, from the *Gentlemen's Magazine* 1732, to be incorrect.
47. Charles Seymour, *A new Survey of the County of Kent*, Canterbury, 1776, 557.
48. Pridden MS.
49. Ibid. Until after World War II the date was still legible on the bridge itself, which was replaced by a flat concrete one suitable for farm machinery in the early 1980's. It stood on the old curve of the main road, which was straightened with a new bridge before the 1872 ordnance survey map was made.
50. Pridden MS has a clear drawing dated 1777 and copy of the bridge plaque with date 1757; Hasted 1800 10/165 says 1759.
51. Anon, *A short description of the Isle of Thanet*, Margate, 1796, 95.
52. R.E. Hunter, *A short account of the Isle of Thanet*, Ramsgate, 1st ed 1799, 5; P.H. Panton, "Turnpike roads in the Canterbury area", *AC* 102/171–191.
53. Lewis lists them all: 1736 ed 72–73, 155–159, 172–173, 188.
54. KG 4–7/1/1775, 4.
55. Anon, *A Description of the Isle of Thanet and particularly of the Town of Margate*, London, 1763, 14.
56. GE Mingay, *English landed society in the 18th century*, London, 1963, 255, citing Arthur Young's *General view of the Agriculture of Essex*, 1802, 123–4.

57. KA U 438, M7, Account book of John Bridges, which also gives some autobiography.
58. AHEW 4/461.
59. Lewis, 1736 ed, 35–38.
60. *A description of the Isle of Thanet . . .*, 1763, 9. One wonders if this was an exaggeration to assure visitors that they would be able to communicate with the natives, but on the other hand these may have been bilingual, like many lowland Scots and English dialect speakers today.
61. Dr R Pococke, *Travels through England*, London, Camden Society 1889, ed J.D. Cartwright, 2/86, 88.
62. Harris, 314.
63. Hasted 1800, 10/326–327; 1799, 4/228.
64. Anon, *The Kentish Traveller's Companion*, Canterbury, 1779, 186.
65. R.E. Hunter, 1st ed 1799, 8.
66. Mockett, 2, 50.
67. Dennis Baker, 360.
68. Kerridge, 344–348; Dennis Baker, 168, 360.
69. KA U 1438 E 31/1. Minster manor's total rent was £1348/2/9d in 1743, but it was larger than in 1599.
70. Anon, *The Thanet guide*, circa 1850, 41.
71. *Museum Rusticum et Commerciale*, 1766, 1/109, 113.
72. Pococke, 88.
73. *Museum Rusticum . . .* 1/112.
74. Hopkins, 21.
75. Dennis Baker, Table 19.
76. R Dossie, *Memoirs of Agriculture and other oeconomical Acts.* (Letters to the Royal Society), London, 1764, 1771, 1782 1/7, 2/343–353, 3/139–147, 447, 449. Mockett, 46.
77. Information from William Friend. ITG 6/5/1939, 13C.
78. *Museum Rusticum . . .* 1/110, 111, 260–265.
79. Arthur Young, *A Tour through the Eastern Counties of England*, vol 3, London, 1771, 96–110.
80. Dennis Baker, 347.
81. Ibid, 258.
82. *The Kentish Traveller's Companion*, 186.
83. Anon, *The New Margate Guide*, 1831, 108.
84. Dennis Baker, 44.
85. John Broad, "The cattle plague in 18th century England", *Ag HR* 31, 104.
86. Mockett, 317; R.W. Butcher, *The new illustrated British flora*, London, 1961, 274.
87. Barrett, 156; Walker 86.
88. K 4/7/1891, 8D, quoting *Canterbury Journal*, 29/1/1771. Comment by G.E. Mingay, in letter to the author.
89. *Description of the Isle of Thanet*, 8.
90. Dennis Baker, 609.
91. KP 27–31 August 1726, 4, offered 5/- for a butcher's lad, farmers were vaguer in KP 19–20/10, 4, and 26–29/10, 4.
92. KG 12–15/2/1783, 1.
93. KG 16–19/8/1775, 1.

94. R Grant, *A short account of the rise and progress of Methodism in the village of St Nicholas . . . 1822–1908*, Margate, 1908, 1–2, ITG 20/5/1922, 3F.
95. KG 23/11/1792, 1.
96. John Boys, *A general view of the agriculture of Kent*, London, 1796, 185.
97. Mockett, op cit, 1–2.
98. Young, *Tour through the Eastern Counties*, 3/106, 109.
99. PP 1833, vi, 266, John Cramp's evidence.
100. For example it has been very evident amongst the new middle-class Chinese in Hong Kong in the last two generations, particularly amongst males.
101. David Grigg, *English agriculture A historical perspective*, Oxford, 1989, 5.
102. D. Davies, *The Case of the Labourers' in Husbandry*, London, 1795, 31; Sir Frederick Morton Eden, Bart, *The State of the Poor*, London, 1797, 1/554.
103. AHEW 5.2, 664–665; Parken, op cit, 82–91.
104. KG 30/9/1775, 1.
105. AHEW 6/963; the author could not find the reference in Cobbett but in *Rural Rides*, ed G.D.H. and M. Cole, London, 1930, 1/276 he inveighed at an "upstart" mahogany table in a Reigate farmhouse on 20 October, 1825, recalling when that farmer had used only oak furniture, which he considered much more suitable.
106. University of Reading archives, KEN 6/7/1.
107. KG 27/5/1856, 6D. Ann Hughes, *Diary of a farmer's wife 1796–1797*, Penguin, 1980, 31, 134, gives some examples of flower wine recipes.
108. C. Greenwood, *The Epitome of Kent*, London, 1838, 325.
109. Cotton, 203.
110. Newman in Pevsner series, 425.
111. Ibid, 392.
112. Ibid, 364, 435.
113. Hasted 1800, 10/257.
114. VCHK 1/487–488.
115. Hasted 1800, 10/257; Rowles, 60.
116. *Description of the Isle of Thanet*, 27–28; Barrett, 143.
117. Barrett, 159, and see Note 118.
118. Information from Christopher Powell-Cotton; Barrett, op cit, 160–161: R.F. Jessup, "The Follies of Kingsgate", *AC* 71/1–13, but the last two state erroneously that John Powell was Paymaster-General.
119. *Observations on the coasts of Hampshire, Sussex and Kent, relative chiefly to Picturesque Beauty, made in the summer of the year 1774*, np 1804, 99.
120. Hasted, 1800, 10/220.
121. *Short Description of the Isle of Thanet*, 1796, 5.
122. Hasted, 1800, 10/232.
123. Ibid, 1800, 10/322.
124. Seymour, 558.
125. *Kidd's Picturesque Companion to the Isle of Thanet*, Margate, (1847?) 147–148. But in 1837 William Benge found few interesting shells on the Thanet coast – *Diaries of Frederick William Benge*, Broadstairs, 1994, 37.
126. Hasted, 1800, 10/378.
127. L. Fussell, *A journey round the coast of Kent*, London, 1818, 119.
128. Anon, *The New Margate Guide*, 1816, 24.

129. *Thanet Magazine*, 1817, 29.
130. Barrett, 149, 156, 176.
131. William Marshall, *Rural Economy of the Southern Counties*, London, 1798, 2/7.
132. *Rural Rides*, 1/230.
133. *New Margate Guide* 1816, 24.
134. Hasted, 1800, 10/356.
135. *Kentish Traveller's Companion*, 1779, 189.
136. *Short Description of Thanet*, 1796, 59.
137. *Description of the Isle of Thanet*, 1763, 17.
138. Hopkins, 30, quoting *Thanet Itinerary*, 1825.
139. E.W. Brayley, *Delineations, history and topography of the Isle of Thanet and the Cinque Ports*, London, 1812, 1, facing 23.

Chapter Five

1. AHEW 6/96, 98–100. *Kentish Register* June 1795, 234. Mockett, 35.
2. KG 16/10/1804, 4. Barrett, 156, mentions army camps at Birchington in 1795 and 1799.
3. KA RU 1231 E 11.
4. Boys, John, *A general view of the agriculture of Kent*, 3rd edition, London, 1805, 35.
5. PP 1833, V, 258, John Cramp's evidence to the Parliamentary Committee on Agriculture.
6. Ibid.
7. KG 19/11/1830, 3C.
8. KA U 438 M7 1–2.
9. Mockett, 298.
10. KA U 438 M7 1–2.
11. Thompson, E.J. *Robert Bridges*, Oxford, 1944, 1,2. Stanford D.E. (ed) *Correspondence of Robert Bridges*, Newark, London and Toronto, 1983, 81.
12. The median age has now dropped again due to the fashionable use of cars and disdain for exercise amongst many women.
13. KA U438 M7 1–2.
14. Thompson 1–2; Stanford 81.
15. Mockett, 215
16. KG 25/4/1843, 3C.
17. They were not used at Cleve Court mansion.
18. KG 11/5/1804, 1.
19. Barrett, 169.
20. KG 16/10/1804, 4. Boys, 1st ed, London, 1794, 32.
21. KA U438 M7 1–2; Mockett, 72.
22. KG 31/5/1811, 1.
23. Mockett, 33, 53.
24. Bloomfield, P. *Kentish sources X: Kent and the Napoleonic Wars*, Gloucester 1987, 157.
25. KA U1453 0 28/11. Margate Museum Newsletter 1/3, p 7 *Sic*.

26. PRO IR23/35, 36.
27. AHEW 6/646–655.
28. Barrett, 152, 167.
29. Boys, 2nd edition, London, 1796, 165.
30. Mockett 36, 57.
31. Marshall, William, *The rural economy of the Southern counties*, vol 2, London, 1798, 24.
32. *Thanet Magazine*, 1817, 162.
33. Pococke, 88.
34. The reason for the decline in St Nicholas is not known, but could be investigated.
35. Barrett, 154–155.
36. Mockett, 36.
37. *Lloyds' Evening Post*, II/536, quoted by Dobson, C.R. *Masters and journeymen: a prehistory of industrial relations 1717–1800*, London, 1980, 117; mentioned by Alan Armstrong, *Farm workers: a social and economic history 1770–1980*, London, 1988, 573. Another account in *Kentish Register*, November 1795, 435 gives a trifle more information.
38. Mockett, 36.
39. Davies, D. *The case of the labourers in husbandry*, London, 1795, 31.
40. Fussell, G.E. *From Tolpuddle to TUC: a century of farm labourers' politics*, Slough, 1948, chapter one.
41. As mentioned on p 97, Boys' account is rather complacent and obviously favours the farmers.
42. Boys, 1st ed, London, 1794, 24–25; 2nd ed 1796, 163; 3rd ed 1805, 192–193.
43. Walker, MS notes from Birchington parish archives.
44. Boys 1796, 165.
45. Ibid, 30.
46. 1805 ed, 33. Barrett 167.
47. AHEW 6/355–810.
48. KA U438 M7 1–2.
49. PP 1836 VIII ii, 8.
50. Boys 1796, 39; 1805 ed 45. Margate and Ramsgate were not quoted separately from St John's and St Lawrence as they were not yet separate parishes.
51. Mockett, 108.
52. Walker, 78–81.
53. Barrett, 169.
54. Hume, R. "Educational provision for the Kent poor 1660–1811", *Southern History*, 4, 1982, map p 125 excludes St John's, Sarre and Monkton, but Sarre and Monkton were within walking distance of St Nicholas or Minster schools.
55. Land, 30.
56. Pointer MS. Quoted by Walker, 187.
57. AHEW 6/702.
58. Boys 1st ed 1794, 22–23.
59. KG 15/11/1811, 4. Wellard's was a Deal firm (Boys 1796, 47).
60. KG 11/9/1815, 4.
61. Hunter, R.E. *A short account of the Isle of Thanet*, Ramsgate, 1799, 78.
62. Fussell, G.E., *The farmer's tools*, London, 1952, 64, 68.

63. Blith, Walter, *The English improver improved*, 3rd ed London 1652 201.
64. Marshall, 1798, 2/43–44.
65. Quoted in Fussell 1952, 37.
66. *Tour of the East of England*, 3/98–99.
67. Hall A.D. and E.J. Russell, *A pilgrimage of British farming*, London, 1911, 22.
68. His descriptions of the plough in 1794 ed 21–22; 1796, 45–46.
69. Boys 1796, 98.
70. *Thanet Magazine*, 1817, 240.
71. Marshall, William, *The Review and Abstract of the County Reports to the Board of Agriculture*, York, 1818, 5/440.
72. Marshall, 1798, 12, 28–31.
73. Marshall, 1798, 19, 26, 27.
74. Ibid, 14–15.
75. Boys, 1794, 1, 16, 17, 25, 30.
76. Mockett, 46.
77. Boys, 1794, 28–29, 31.
78. Marshall, 1798, 39–40, 43–44.
79. Ibid, 156.
80. Ibid, 11. Boys, 1796, 147.
81. Marshall, 1798, 35–36. Boys, 1794, 20.
82. Marshall, 1798, 35.
83. Boys, 1796, 156–159.
84. Mockett, 320–323.
85. PRO HO 67/4, 1801.
86. Notes written on the 1774 Quex Park terrier.
87. 1799, 4/310.
88. See Monkton assessment and map, Canterbury Cathedral Archives.
89. St Peters and St Johns tithe assessments and maps, Canterbury Cathedral Archives.
90. Walker, MS notes from Birchington parish archives.
91. Joan Champion's document.
92. KG 5/7/1814, 3.
93. Barrett, 173–174.
94. Mockett, 72.
95. KG 15/9/1815, 4.
96. Walker, 31.

Chapter Six

1. KG 14/2/1815, 4.
2. AHEW 6/975. *KG* 10/5, 30/7, 23/8 1822 etc.
3. KG 7/3/1815, 4.
4. Quoted by G.E. Mingay, (ed) *The agricultural state of the kingdom in 1816*, Bath, 1970, 123.
5. KA, Conyngham MS U438 M7, 1–2.
6. KG 22/2/1822, 4C.

7. Hopkins, 29.
8. KG 1/10/1822,1; 15/10/1822, 1.
9. AHEW 6/975, PP 1833 Vi 266.
10. KA AC 831 U442 E43.
11. KA Powell-Cotton MS U1063 T68/9.
12. Mockett, 176.
13. Quex Park terrier 1834, appendix with map of farm and house, no date. Woodchurch and Cheeseman's farms were sold by auction to John Powell Powell of Quex in 1837 – KG 20/6/1837 2A.
14. PP 1833 Vi, 254–255, 266, 268.
15. PP 1836 VIII ii, 6–15.
16. KG 29/9/1835, 3E.
17. KG 5/7/1836, 3D.
18. KG 14/8/1838, 3E.
19. Mockett, 177.
20. Ibid, 176–177.
21. KG 29/5/1837, 2C; 12/9, 2F.
22. KG 14/2/1837, 2A.
23. Ibid.
24. PP 1833, Vi, 259.
25. Mockett, 211.
26. PP 1833 Vi 255, 269.
27. It is possible to distinguish individual occupiers and owners of land with a high degree of probability from the tithe assessments, but absolute certainty is impossible as the census clerks' notebooks are faded or illegible in large parts and missing for Acol and Sarre. They do not show occupations in all cases and richer inhabitants seem often to have made a point of being away from home for the census. Microfilm in Margate Library.
28. The father died in 1842 – KG 1/3/1842, 3C – also Minster tithe assessment for that year. Tombstone in St Johns churchyard, close to the path.
29. Clare Lukehurst, 117, mentions a James White with "almost 1000 acres on the marsh", which I could not account for. "James White" had 426 acres (excluding rods and perches) in entirely arable lots, the rest being pasture or mixed lots. In all the assessments only 7.3.36 acres occupied by Henry Collard at Monkton are described as marsh ploughland; the marsh was still as Lukehurst's thesis shows practically all pasture, with some "salts" (salt marsh).
30. PP 1833, Population of Great Britain, Enumeration Abstract, 1/260.
31. PP 1833 Vi 257.
32. Mockett, 84; VCHK 1/487–488 for a full history.
33. Mockett, 108, 134.
34. Barrett, 169.
35. William Champion's diary, 5, 8. William (1820–1894) was Thomas' eldest son.
36. KG 4/3/1845, 3D.
37. KG 3/7/1838, 3D.
38. William Champion, 3.
39. PP 1801, Census enumeration 1800, 1/147, 157; PP 1812, 1811 Population

of Great Britain Enumeration Abstract, 138; PP 1822, 1821 ditto, 138; PP 1833, 1831 ditto, 1/260; PP 1843, 1841 Census Enumeration, 128.

40. Mingay, *The agricultural state* . . . 123, 138.
41. Mockett, 85, 89, 90, 94–95, 132.
42. Pointer MS. Quoted in Walker 1991, 166, 167.
43. Quex letters, Charlotte Powell – Charles Deare 10/12/1830.
44. Mockett, 327–328.
45. Fussell, *Farmers' tools* . . . 152–153, 160–162.
46. *Thanet Magazine* 1817, 240.
47. Account by G.H. Garrad in the 1956 Isle of Thanet ploughing match catalogue; KG 12/12/1854, 4E. Boys, 3rd ed 1805, 56–59.
48. Mockett, 131–132.
49. Cobbett, *Rural Rides*, I/233–234.
50. PP 1825 XIX, 386–387; Mockett, 89–90, 92.
51. Hobsbawm E. and George Rudé, *Captain Swing*, London, 1969, chapters 4 and 5; Charlesworth, A. *Social protest in a rural society: the spatial diffusion of the Captain Swing disturbances of 1830–31*, Cambridge, 1979, 26, 44 etc. (Historical Geography Research Series No 1).
52. KG 8/10/1830, 3D.
53. KG 8/10/1830, 4B.
54. KG 2/11/1830, 4B.
55. Quex letters: Charlotte Powell – Charles Deare 30/11/1830; 10/12/1830.
56. Hobsbawm and Rude, 100. T. Garrett was farming at Nethercourt in 1836.
57. KG 9/11/1830, 4D; 12/11, 4C.
58. KG 19/11/1830,, 4B.
59. KG 26/11/1830, 4D.
60. Sic, letter to Charles Deare, Quex letters.
61. KG 24/12/1830, 4C, D.
62. According to PRO HO 52/8, K. Cobb letter of 28/11/1830 and TS 11/3413, cited in M. Dutt, "The agricultural labourers' revolt in Kent, Surrey and Sussex", University of London PhD thesis 1967, 177–178. But these documents have vanished from the PRO now.
63. KG 26/11/1830, 4D.
64. KG 26/11/1830, 4D; 30/11, 4D.
65. Dutt thesis, 177–178; the *Times* 29/11/1830, 3A.
66. Quex letters: Charlotte Powell – Charles Deare 10/12/1830.
67. KG 30/11/1830, 4D.
68. Quex letters: Charlotte Powell – Charles Deare 10/12/1830.
69. KG 23/11/1830, 4C.
70. KG 30/11/1830, 4C.
71. Hobsbawm and Rude, *Swing* . . . 248–149; KG 9/11/1830, 4D; 12/11, 4C.
72. A.T. Walker, MS notes from Birchington parish archives.
73. Mockett, 298. For descriptions of life in the Minster workhouse, see Hopkins, 32–34, and Joyce C. Gilham, *The Isle of Thanet Union workhouse, Minster-in-Thanet*, Thanet, 1991.
74. He said "neglected" parishes, but obviously meant mismanaged. PP 1836, VIII ii, 8.
75. PP 1833 V i, 263, 264.
76. PP 1836 VIII ii, 8.

77. Buckland, George, "On the farming of Kent", JRASE 6, (1845), 261.
78. PP 1843 XII (510), 172–173.
79. Ibid, 192.
80. Ibid 172–173.
81. Quex letters: Charlotte Powell – Charles Deare 10/12/1830.
82. William Champion 1839, 7; 1844, 15.
83. KG 30/4/1844, 3D.
84. KG 16/12/1794, 1; 18/6/1811, 4; 2/6/1815, 4.
85. KG 26/7/1842, 3D.
86. KG 24/11/1868, 7D, ploughing match dinner speech by the Rev. Sickle-more, reminding George Hannam he joined the Association 34 years ago.
87. KG 13/12/1836, 4B, C.
88. Whoever presided at the dinner was called the chairman on that occasion, but was not necessarily an office-holder.
89. KG 13/12/1836 4B.
90. KG 25/11/1870, 8C.
91. Julia Small, *The East Kent Ploughing Match Association: Ploughing matches from 1840*, Canterbury, 1979, 5, 7, 8 etc.
92. Not given in 1836, but in 1839 – KG 10/12/1839, 4A.
93. KG 13/12/1836, 4B, for the complete account of the match.
94. See Small, *East Kent Ploughing Match*, 3.
95. Francis Cobb, *Memoir of the late F.C. Cobb of Margate, compiled from his letters and journals*, Maidstone, 1835, 56.
96. KG 11/12/1838, 3C.
97. KG 13/12/1842, 3C.
98. KG 12/12/1843, 3C; 10/12/1844, 3B.
99. KG 9/12/1845, 3C.
100. KG 8/10/1846, 3C.
101. KG 8/12/1840, 2F, 3A.
102. KG 26/7/1842, 3D.
103. KA, Cobb papers, U 1453, Z52/15, FLD 1–18 has the 1844 application form.
104. Ibid, list of subscribers and regulations.
105. Mockett, 231.
106. William Champion.
107. William Champion 13. KG 16/5/1843, 3C.
108. William Champion, 3.
109. PP 1833 Vi, 256; 1836 VIII ii, 12.
110. William Champion, 6, 9.
111. Ibid, 7.
112. Ibid, 10 etc., 14. They hired from Holman from 1845.
113. Ibid, 15.
114. Ibid, 7, 9.
115. KG 10/12/1830, 4C. He produced his enormous carrots at the ploughing match dinner two years running, and the second year announced he was going to feed nothing else.
116. Whyman, John, "Three weeks holiday in Ramsgate in 1829", *AC* 96 (1980) 185–225, 192 especially.
117. Butcher, R.W. *The new illustrated British flora*, London, 1961, 286.

118. G.H. Garrad, *A survey of the agriculture of Kent*, London, 1954, 71; Hanbury, F.J. and E.S. Marshall, *Flora of Kent*, London, 1899, 41–42; K 6/7/1901, 8D; EGQ.
119. *Thanet Magazine*, 1817, 162.
120. Walker, 1991, 85–86.
121. KG 8/10/1839, 3D.
122. William Champion, 9.
123. KG 8/10/1839, 3D.
124. KG 14/12/1841, 3A; 13/12/1842, 3A.
125. "Tradesmen" meant thatchers, carpenters, harness-makers, bricklayers, blacksmiths etc. Their charges had been reduced, in St Peter's at least, to 3/- a day for carpenters, bricklayers and thatchers in 1820 – Mockett, 89.
126. KG 25/4/1843, 3C; 16/5, 3CD.
127. William Champion, 3.
128. As it was before the enlargements of 1989–1990.
129. KG 21/6/1842, 3D; 25/6/1844, 3B; 24/6/1845, 3C.
130. Mockett, 309–316.
131. See note 77.
132. EGQ.
133. PP 1833 vi, 256.
134. Mockett, 319. Buckland, 259, 260, 302.
135. PP 1833 Vi, 256; 1836 VIII ii, 7.
136. KG 6/2/1844, 2A.
137. University of Reading archives KEN 4.12, 4.19.
138. KG 6/2/1844, 3C.
139. Coles Finch, 138–140, 242, 243, 246, 260.
140. Buckland, 260

Chapter Seven

1. KG 11/5/1847, 4E.
2. KG 10/7/1849, 4E.
3. KG 7/1/1851, 3G.
4. KG 11/12/1849, 2F.
5. KG 29/1/1850, 2F, G.
6. KG 5/3/1850, 5D.
7. KG 1846, passim. William Champion, 14.
8. KG 8/1/1850, 3F; 11/6, 2C, 3G; 30/7, 2B; 17/8, 2B; 3/9, 2A; 24/9, 2D.
9. KG 28/11/1865, 6A.
10. KG 23/11/1869, 6C.
11. KG 16/10/1875, 8E.
12. KG 25/12/1860, 3C.
13. KG 7/9/1869, 5G.
14. KG 10/3/1868, 5F.
15. KG 9/7/1878, 5F.
16. KG 11/1/1880, 5F; 12/7, 5G.
17. KG 13/1/1885, 5F.

18. KG 25/10/1887, 5G; 10/1/1888, 5G.
19. Lukehurst, 234.
20. Groves, R. "A great depression in Kentish hops?", *Cantium* 3/3, 57–76.
21. K 8/1/1887, 8C.
22. KG 3/1/1884, 2E; K 12/9/1885, 6B.
23. K 12/9/1885, 6B.
24. KG 9/10/1885, 1C; 19/10, 1C; 23/10, 1C.
25. *Kelly's Isle of Thanet Directory 1885–1886*, 85–90. K 3/1/1885, 2E.
26. K 9/3/1881, 8A, 8B.
27. *Royal Commission on the Agricultural Depression, Assistant Commissioners' reports*, PP 1881, XVI, 25.
28. K 23/10/1886, 4B.
29. K 5/11/1887, 8F.
30. K 29/8/1891, 8D.
31. K 12/9/1891, 4A; 26/9, 4B; 17/10, 4A; 10/10, 4B.
32. K 30/5/1891, 8B.
33. Ploughing match speeches, KG 23/11/1858, 7C; KG 22/11/1859, 5C.
34. PP 1882, XV i, 376.
35. K 12/4/1884, 8E.
36. KG 27/9/1890, 4B.
37. K 8/1/1887, 5B.
38. K 22/4/1882, 3C.
39. In the 1891 census yearly servants were boarded in the farmhouse at St Nicholas Court, Ambry Court, Nether Hale, Woodchurch, Cheeseman's and Nash, amongst other farms. Microfilms of Census, Margate library.
40. K 9/5/1874, 4A.
41. K 5/10/1872. 1C.
42. K 17/9/1881, 4B.
43. KG 29/5/1860, 1C. The rectory at Langley, W. Kent, had one in 1793 – N. Yates, R. Hume and F. Hastings, *Religion and society in Kent 1640–1914*, Maidstone 1993, 30. There were probably a number in Margate by 1864, for Dr Fred Chambers' report on the sanitary conditions that year mentioned "common cesspool systems" emptying into the King Street stream which served as the town sewer and ran into the "stinking harbour giving off a fearful fume at low tide" – KG 16/2/1864, 6C. This was likely one of the reasons Margate was becoming less fashionable.
44. KG 21/6/1870, 6D.
45. Marion Smith's diary.
46. K 26/8/1871, 5D.
47. K 4/5/1872, 5C.
48. VCHK 2/488.
49. K 12/10/1872, 3B.
50. KG 12/7/1887, 5C.
51. K 7/1/1888, 8F. He had a fall.
52. K 17/3/1871, 5D.
53. KG 6/7/1847, 2F.
54. KG 6/7/1847, 4B reports the 11th annual show.
55. KG 10/1/1865, 6D.
56. Second one appointed in 1859 – KG 6/12/1859, 6B.

57. KG 27/3/1866, 8D.
58. p 3.
59. KG 11/8/1867, 1D.
60. K 1/10/1886, 5C.
61. Grigg, D. *English agriculture: a historical perspective.* Oxford 1989, 111.
62. Peter Linington heard this from his father and other senior farmers.
63. Ambrose Collard was paying this for 216 acres of upland and 43 of marsh at Gore Street farm when the owner offered it for sale in May 1860. – KG 29/5/1860, 1E.
64. *Kelly's Isle of Thanet Directory* 1885–1886, 85. Evershed, H. *The farming of Kent, Sussex and Surrey,* London, 1871, 55.
65. Vol 2, 142, 169, 178, 188.
66. Watson's Corn Merchants account book.
67. KG 27/11/1860, 3D.
68. K 6/2/1892, 5G.
69. KG 19/6/1849, 3B. For the one-off dinner for the award-winning farm-workers in 1862, KG 25/11/1862 6D.
70. KG 25/12/1860, 3C.
71. Ploughing match speech, KG 1/12/1863, 6B.
72. PP 1868–1869 XIII, Appendix Part II, 54.
73. K 14/9/1872, 8D.
74. TA 24/8/1872, 3F.
75. K 14/9/1872, 8E.
76. ITG 13/2/1937, 11E, diamond wedding of the Paynes of Sholden.
77. KG 19/7/1864, 8B.
78. Judging from remarks by Alfred Simmons at his rally, K 31/8/1872, 3D, E.
79. PP 1868–1869 XIII, Appendix Part II, 54, Vicar of St Nicholas report.
80. K 26/11/1878, 3B. The Fleece was another early name for the Canterbury Farmers' Club, which met at the Fleece Inn in the High Street – Garrad, G.H *A survey of the agriculture of Kent,* London, 1954, 190.
81. K 2/11/1878, 2C; 19/11, 5C; PP 1900 LXXXII Cd 346, 44, 48.
82. K 6/10/1883, 6F.
83. K 5/11/1887, 8F.
84. K 7/10/1892, 4C.
85. KG 11/12/1849, 3A, B.
86. KG 1/12/1863, 6B, C.
87. KG 22/11/1859, 6F; 25/12/1860, 3B.
88. KG 14/12/1852, 2F.
89. KG editorial 9/5/1865, 3D.
90. KG 23/11/1869, 6D.
91. KG 25/12/1860, 3C.
92. KG 1/12/1863, 6B.
93. KG 27/6/1865, 6E.
94. KG 1/12/1863, 6C for instance.
95. K 25/11/1870, 8A.
96. Orwin C.S. and E.H. Witham, *The history of British agriculture 1846–1914,* 2nd ed Newton Abbot 1971, 326.
97. Eric Quested could not recall seeing any in the 20th century.
98. Hasted 1800, 10/310.

99. KA U442 E 43.
100. His name is on a plaque on the front of the farmhouse, with the date.
101. 1871 Acol census return. The author remembers them clearly from the 1920's and early 1930's, and the land where they stood is still marked by a tree and partly uncultivated.
102. 1871 Minster census return.
103. K 8/4/1876 8C says there were now four. EGQ remembers being told this bungalow was there when his grandfather and uncle took over the tenancy in 1895. It had a wooden roof then, later replaced with corrugated iron, which it kept till 1970.
104. K 3/11/1857, 4C, 6B; 22/11/1859, 6C; 28/11/1865, 6B.
105. Yates N., "The major Kentish towns in the religious census of 1851" *AC* 100, 408, 418.
106. Based on Hodgson, John, *Observations in reference to duration of life amongst the Clergy of England and Wales and (in an appendix) amongst the children of clergymen, and also amongst children and married persons of the Labouring Classes of the Parish of St Peter's in the Isle of Thanet*, London, 1865, 42, 43. Hodgson made the first actuarial tables for these two classes of people, and was a founder and first Secretary of the Clergy Mutual Assistance Society. Yates, Hume and Hastings, 224.
107. Ibid, 28, 42, 43.
108. K 31/8/1872, 3D, E, but *Kebles* editor condemned the Union.
109. K 14/9/1872, 8D, E. *TA* 14/9/1872, 3E.
110. Orwin and Witham, op cit 232.
111. K 16/11/1872, 3D.
112. K 16/5/1874, 2B.
113. K 3/5/1879, 5C.
114. TA 18/7/1872, 3C.
115. K 28/9/1889, 8 F-E.
116. *Kelly's Isle of Thanet Directory 1885–1886*, 46.
117. KA U438 E42, valuation report for the Marquis of Conyngham.
118. K 23/1/1886, 8B; 30/1, 8E; 13/2, 8F; 24/1/1891, 8D.
119. KG 30/1/1866, 6E. He opted to return to Collard.
120. KG 29/3/1864, 6D.
121. K 1/10/1892, 8B.
122. PP 1868–1869 XIII, 6–11, reports of Commissioners.
123. Ibid, Appendix Part II, 54.
124. K 14/11/1881, 8A.
125. Orwin and Witham, op cit 292; Alan Armstrong in the *Cambridge Social history of Britain 1750–1950*, 1/132–133. Evershed, 54.
126. Opinion of G.E. Mingay.
127. KG 22/1/1861, 5B.
128. Pointer MS.
129. But he was immersed in learning how his grandfather farmed and in the East Kent Yeomanry.
130. KG 11/7/1865, 5D.
131. KG 11/1/1859, 6E.
132. Pointer MS.
133. KG 17/6/1862, 5C.

134. K 1/10/1887, 8 F-G.
135. KG 10/12/1850, 3B. Schedule C was based on rent.
136. KG 11/12/1849, 2F.
137. KG 12/12/1854, 4E.
138. KG 25/12/1860, 3B.
139. KG 26/11/1867, 3A.
140. KG 2/11/1869, 1C.
141. Julia Small, *The East Kent Ploughing Match Association: ploughing matches from 1840*, Canterbury, 1979, 9.
142. KG 10/7/1860, whole of p 6; 25/12/1860, 3C.
143. KG 26/11/1861, 6A.
144. K 24/8/1872, 3E.
145. KG 27/11/1866, 8A.
146. KG 26/11/1867, 3A.
147. K 15/11/1873, 3A.
148. K 24/11/1888, 8C.
149. KG 28/11/1865, 6A; 24/11/1868, 7B.
150. KG 23/11/1869, 6C; K 25/11/1870, 8A. Evershed, 54.
151. *Kelly's Isle of Thanet Directory 1885–1886*, 85–90.
152. K 2/10/1875, 4A.
153. K 15/9/1877, 4B; 29/9, 8C.
154. K 28/4/1871, 6A.
155. K 10/10/1891, 4B.
156. K 2/10/1875, 4B.
157. KG 1/12/1863, 6D.
158. K 29/11/1884, 8D.
159. K 11/3/1876, 5B.
160. KG 16/1/1866, 1 C-D.
161. Friends' House archives, records of Michael Yoakley's charity, crop diary of John Clelan Bennett, ref. 748/5/3. Evershed, 53.
162. KG 22/ 11/1859, 5C.
163. Evershed, 51.
164. KG 28/11/1865, 6D.
165. Coles Finch 174, 260.
166. K 3/10/1874, 4B.
167. Evershed, 51.
168. K 12/10/1878, 4B.
169. K 28/6/1881, 1C.
170. KG 2/1/1866, 5C; 6/3, 5E; 27/3, 8E. "Days of humiliation" were held in London churches but not reported in Thanet. A.E. Constant MRCVS was the vet – *Kelly's Directory of Kent*, 1866.
171. K 5/4/1879, 2B.
172. K 23/10/1880, 2C.
173. K 2/9/1882, 8C.
174. Dennis Baker, 665.
175. KG 23/11/1858, 7D.
176. EGQ.
177. K 22/9/1888, 8F; 21/4,5C.
178. EGQ, RQ.

179. K 23/9/1882, 8E.
180. K 30/9/1882, 8D.
181. Information from William Friend.
182. EGQ. *Kent Post Office Directory 1883–1884.* The pair were still too insignificant to feature in the 1870 directory, the only earlier one extant.
183. TA 11/6/1870, 2; 18/6, 3. Evershed, 55.
184. 1871 census, St Peter's return. Baxter, Wynne, *A Domesday Book of Kent,* Lewes, 1877, 42. The 15 acres later, before World War One, included an orchard, which was still there until fairly recently.
185. St Peter's return.
186. Watson's corn merchants account book.
187. EGQ.
188. Obituary, ITG 21/8/1942, 7D.
189. K 20/6/1891, 8D.
190. K 18/6/1892, 5B.
191. Meredith, C. "A study in mid-19th century Monkton, with special reference to the census returns of 1851, 1861 and 1871", University of Kent at Canterbury diploma in local history, 1983, 37 et seq.
192. KG 1/3/1864, 5B. See p. 50
193. All this information is taken from the *Kentish Gazette* and *Keble's Gazette.*
194. K 30/10/1875, 6E.
195. K 5/9/1874, 8E.
196. K 2/6/1870, 10D.
197. KG 25/12/1860, 3A,B; 22/1/1861, 5B. He had estates in Somerset, Hertfordshire and Oporto, and left £120,000.
198. K 1/12/1863, 6A; 22/11/1864, 6A; 27/11/1866, 8A; KCT Christmas Supplement, 1868.
199. K 16/9/1871, 8E.
200. KG 1/12/1863, 6A.
201. KG 10/12/1850, 3B.
202. K 15/11/1873, 3A.
203. In 1864 it was reported that "the higher class are deserting Ramsgate for Folkestone" (where the smart part of the town was further from the harbour) – KG 26/4/1864, 6D.
204. KG 23/11/1869, 6C.
205. K 16/11/1872, 3C.
206. KG 28/11/1865, 6C; KCG 18/11/1869, 3 A-D.
207. K 24/11/1888, 8C et seq.
208. K 23/11/1889, 8A.
209. K 22/11/1890, 8A.
210. K 21/11/1891, 8A.
211. K 6/2/1892, 8C.
212. K 19/11/1892, 5B.

Chapter Eight

1. William Champion's diary, 29.
2. K 11/11/1893, 7C.
3. K 9/9/1893 4A; 16/9/1893, 8B.
4. K 22/9/1894, 4B.
5. K 23/9/1893, 4A.
6. K 7/10/1893, 8E.
7. K 18/11/1893, 5D.
8. K 16/6/1893, 4A; 22/9, 4B; 29/9, 4A; 13/10, 4B.
9. K 1/10/1887, 8 F-G.
10. K 16/6/1894, 6A, B, C.
11. K 28/9/1895, 4C.
12. K 7/9/1895, 4C; 5/10, 4B.
13. K 28/9/1895, 4C.
14. K 7/9/1895, 4C.
15. K 14/9/1895, 4B,E.
16. K 7/9/1895, 4C. For Warren at St Nicholas, K *passim*.
17. K 16/11/1895, 2G. Information from G.E. Mingay and J.D. Sykes.
18. Minster parish census.
19. K 5/9/1896, 4C; 10/9, 4C; 19/9, 4C; 3/10, 4A; 10/10, 4 B-C.
20. K 10/10, 4B.
21. K 19/9, 4C.
22. EGQ; K 26/9, A, B; 10/10, 4 B, C; 17/10, 4B.
23. K 18/9/1897, 4A; 25/9, 4C; 2/10, 4A; 9/10, 4C.
24. Pointer MS. Quoted by Walker 1991, 165.
25. K 6/2/1897, 8E.
26. K 24/9/1898, 4B; 8/10, 4B; 15/10, 4A.
27. Whitehead, C, "A sketch of the agriculture of Kent", *Journal of the Royal Agricultural Society of England*, 2nd series, 10/449–451.
28. KG 25/6/1899, 2G; 24/9, 8F.
29. K 17/9/1904, 4 A-C; 24/9, 4A, B; 3/10, 4C; 15/10, 4A; 29/10,4A.
30. Sales catalogues with prices in author's possession formerly, now in KA at Ramsgate.
31. Valuation document formerly with author, now in KA Ramsgate.
32. Account book of Watson's corn merchants, agents for Liverpool, London and Globe Insurance Co., by courtesy of NFU branch, Ash and Thanet.
33. *Times*, 19/9/1910, 4A.
34. JKBNFU, February 1927, 54.
35. K 9/7/1898, 8A. Possibly for tax or inheritance reasons, many farming families became companies at this time.
36. K 6/7/1901, 8A-B, 8/7/1905, 8B.
37. RQ. K 23/7/1904, 8B.
38. K9/11/1895, 5E.
39. K 7/11/1896, 8C.
40. K 2/12/1905, 6E.
41. K 2/1/1909, 5E.
42. *Kelly's Isle of Thanet Directory*. K 3/10/1891, 8D.

43. Marion Smith's diary.
44. Bar's wife used to put "something out of a tin" into the privy to stop the smell (EGQ), but many households put ashes from their fires, which had the same effect, and rendered the contents innocuous enough to lay straight on the land (David Steed).
45. EGQ.
46. K 5/10/1895, 4C.
47. K 7/10/1905, 4C.
48. EGQ.
49. EGQ, RQ.
50. Mr Bennett, *Pride and Prejudice*, chapter 37.
51. K 13/10/1906, 5B.
52. Mingay, G.E. *The gentry: rise and fall of a ruling class*, London, 1971, 171. B.A. Holderness and M. Turner (eds), *Land, labour and agriculture 1700–1920*, London, 1991, 233, 237.
53. EGQ.
54. KA Conyngham archive U 1453 E39/93, sale of Thorne farm.
55. EGQ, William Friend.
56. K 30/12/1905, 6D, events of 1905.
57. ITG 28/8/1937, 7E.
58. ITG 30/8/1946, 5E, F, obituary of E.S. Linington.
59. The *Times*, 16/3/1900, 10 D-F for a general account of all the riots. TA ignores.
60. K 17/3/1900, 8G; Hansard's *Parliamentary debates* 4th series 80/926–930, 15/3/1900.
61. Obituary of Mr Maas ITG 31/3/1923, 5D. *Kelly's Isle of Thanet Directory*, 1898–99, 1900–01, 1905, 1923, 1933. In 1900 Henry Maas lived at 3, Sussex Avenue, Margate, a suitable home for a bakery partner. Perhaps his wife let lodgings, for in 1905 they had a lodging house at 13, Athelstan Road. The author remembers the Fort Road shop clearly. She was told the story several times over the years by family members. Later, aware of changing times, the family put out a version that Grandfather and Uncle had gone down to watch the sacking of the shop.
62. K 24/3/1900, 5G; TA 24/3/1900, 2G.
63. Hansard's *Parliamentary debates* 4th series, 81/691, 29/3/1900.
64. K 31/3/1900, 8G.
65. EGQ. Penny Ward has information about the attacks on German property in Margate.
66. ITG 16/10/1915, 8C.
67. ITG 28/10/1916, 8A.
68. ITG 11/5/1918, 6E.
69. ITG 2/3/1918, 5B.
70. ITG 12/5/1917, 5D.
71. Obituary of F. Swinford, ITG 22/10/1938, 7D.
72. ITG 18/11/1916, 6F.
73. ITG 12/1/1918, 7F.
74. Information from William Friend; EGQ.
75. "East Kent Yeoman", 1914–1915, 41. (A stencilled journal put out by the

first line regiment before they went to France, now in the Yeomanry
Museum at Croydon).

76. Information from Mary Tapp, nee Hatfeild.
77. ITG 26/10/1918, 4C. Information from Christopher Powell-Cotton.
78. ITG 10/7/1915, 2E; 10/6/1916, 5F; 9/2/1918, 8B etc.
79. Information from Christopher Powell-Cotton; ITG 28/9/1918, 6C.
80. EKT 4/12/1918, 3; 11/12/1918, 6D; 18/12/1918, 6C; 25/12/1918, 4 C,D.
81. TA 3/8/1918, 3A. P.W. Steed at Finglesham found the price of cattle feed
    rose 339.6% and cost of labour 177.6% between 1913–14 and 1917–18
    (document from Jill Smith).
82. ITG 20/1/1917, 5B.
83. JKFU June 1918, 153; ITG 1/6/1918, 2E.
84. See inter alia Dewey, P.E. "British farming profits and Government policy
    during the first World War", EcHR 1984, XXXVI/378–9, 386; A.G. Street,
    Farmers' Glory, London 1932, 142.
85. ITG 3/11/1917, 6C.
86. Orwin C.S. *Farming costs*, Oxford 1921, 111.
87. ITG 30/8/1946, 5 E-F, obituary of E.S. Linington.
88. PP 1919 IX i,51.
89. PP 1905, XCVII, 168.
90. EGQ for all the above. Waggoners seemed to get no special cash bonus.
91. This contract was fastened to a page of the Birchington and Westgate
    history exhibition in Birchington library in May 1992 by a person unknown,
    and is now in the Kent archives at Ramsgate.
92. Information from his grandson, William Hudson.
93. EGQ.
94. PP 1900 LXXXII, 54. For the Friends' dairywoman, information from Mrs
    J. Rootes in a talk to Margate Civic Society, 16/3/1994.
95. ITG 25/2/1944, 7D: war service of the family.
96. EGQ.
97. PP 1905 XCVII, 335, second report of Mr Wilson Fox.
98. Marion Smith's diary.
99. EGQ.
100. K 2/2/1907, 8G.
101. K 12/9/1907, 6A.
102. K 13/5/1905, 8F.
103. K 26/6/1897, 8 C-G.
104. Pointer MS.
105. ITG 27/2/1915, 5C.
106. Ransley MS.
107. ITG 22/7/1916, 8C.
108. ITG 2/12/1916, 8A; whether he got it or not is not known.
109. Information from Joyce Jordan; EGQ; ITG 5/12/1914, 3C.
110. ITG 24/10/1914, 8E.
111. ITG 30/10/1918, 4E.
112. ITG 11/3/1915, 2E.
113. See ITG 14/10/1916, 2 and other issues for the huge lists of evaders.
114. PP 1919 IX.1, Wages and conditions in agriculture II/127.
115. ITG 13/7/1918, 8D.

116. ITG 25/9/1915, 8F; 12/10/1918, 6C.
117. ITG 21/12/1918, 8D; 18/1/1919, 8F; KG 16/11/1918, 2C etc.
The Vicar of Westgate said in a sermon at a thanksgiving service in November that "From such a strain as we have been passing through, relief does not come as a swift rebound. We have suffered too much. . . ."
118. EGQ.
119. NUAW *Reports and balance sheets.*
120. Mockett, 176–177 See p 105.
121. ITG 11/6/1921, 5E, his obituary.
122. Tom Miller told A.T. Walker it was in 1888; ITG 18/1/1957, 3D, obituary of Andrew Craig Smith, suggests it was about 1890.
123. Memories of George Kemp, told to EGQ.
124. K 2/11/1901, 5A; information given by existing golf club secretaries.
125. K 4/10/1904, 4B; ITG 27/8/1911, 8E; EGQ.
126. Valuation of Woodchurch farm 1910, now in Kent archives at Ramsgate.
127. EGQ; K 16/11/1907, 5F etc.
128. EGQ; RQ from memories of similar hen-keeping at Woodchurch for the household.
129. EGQ.
130. EGQ; Reading Street farm sale catalogue 1911, now in Kent archives.
131. EGQ.
132. Sale at East Northdown after Bar's death, KG 29/8/1919, 2A; sale catalogue now in Kent archives at Ramsgate.
133. EGQ.
134. K 28/1/1893, 2A; 4/2/1893, 8C,D; 10/2/1894, 2A; ITG 6/7/1918, 5D.
135. PP 1904 LXXXIV, Report on railway rates, 22.
136. *Times* 15/9 1910, 4A; 19/9/1910, 4.
137. Whetham E.H. "The mechanization of British farming 1910–1945" *J.Ag.Ec.* 1970, 21/3,331.
138. K 4/11/1893, 4 C, D.
139. K 18/11/1893, 4D and many other advertisements over the years.
140. Marion Smith's diary.
141. EGQ.
142. K 29/9/1905, 4A.
143. EGQ; also his ploughing match long service award in K 14/11/1908, 8A.
144. EGQ; RQ.
145. K 1/1/1898, events of 1897.
146. K 29/5/1897, 4C, D.
147. K 10/10/1896, 4B.
148. K 25/11/1899, 5A.
149. *Margate Illustrated and Historical*, (1904?). It was usual for guides to copy material from earlier years. I am indebted to Ann Linington for this reference. K 25/11/1899, 5A. For Drapers hens, *Margate Illust.*, 91.
150. ITG 12/10/1912, 6C, Margate Medical Officer of Health's report.
151. EGQ. Family photos.
152. JKNFU January 1927, 17.
153. EGQ.
154. Report on the Minster Abbey farm sale, KG 6/10/1928, 7E.
155. ITG 20/10/1915, 1D.

156. ITG 4/10/1916, 5B.
157. Information from Michael Smith. *Farmers' Weekly* 31/8/1973, 61; 8/11/ 1935, 33.
158. Information from Michael Smith; ITG, K.
159. AHEW 8/210.
160. EGQ. Horses were earlier worked much longer – Boys, 1796, 157.
161. K 5/1/1918, 7F for instance.
162. Based on PRO MAF 68/2469, 2754, 2868.
163. ITG 23/6/1917, 2D; 30/6, 3B; 7/7, 3F.
164. ITG 14/7/1917, 3D.
165. JKFU November 1918, 94–95.
166. EGQ; KG 2/3/1918, 7 C, D.
167. JKFU July 1918, 9.
168. JKFU March 1919, 55.
169. ITG 26/1/1921, 8E; 13/12/1918, 1C.
170. RQ. There was some land farmed from Vincent farm between the golf links and the rough grass.
171. ITG 23/12/1916, 5G.
172. ITG 19/2/1916, 7E.
173. ITG 8/4/1916, 6E.
174. ITG 18/3/1916, 8A; 20/5, 5G.
175. ITG 12/8/1916, 6B.
176. ITG 15/7/1916, 5G.
177. ITG 9/9/1916, 6F.
178. K 11/9/1897, 8D.
179. ITG 30/6/1917, 3B.
180. ITG 11/5/1918, 6B.
181. ITG 6/5/1916, 4D etc.
182. ITG 6/5/1915, 4E etc. J. Martin Robinson, *Belmont. Debrett's Illustrated Peerage*, London, 1921. The Major Harris who commandeered horses for the REKY was thought by EGQ to be "a son of Lord Harris of Belmont," but Debrett 1864 and 1913, and Burke's *Peerage and Baronetage*, London, 1916, indicate only that he might possibly have been a first or second cousin of the 4th Lord, descended from a younger son of the 1st or 2nd Lord. Probably only a fairly senior man would have been given the unenviable horse task. The Major was clearly loathed by Thanet farmers on account of the horses; his local demonography featured his not having gone to France with the regiment, and various other allegations against his character.
183. ITG 8/4/1916, 6A, B.
184. ITG 11/3/1916, 3B.
185. ITG 29/7/1916, 4C.
186. ITG 18/11/1916, 5G.
187. ITG 7/7/1917, 3F.
188. ITG 30/6/1917, 2G.
189. ITG 22/6/1918, 6D.
190. ITG 1/9/1917, 6B. He was not said to be unfit.
191. ITG 22/6/1918, 6B.
192. ITG 21/9/1918, 6D.

193. ITG 15/6/1918, 5A. The Ramsgate mayor's daughter, Miss Childs, joined the Land Army, and a "gaily decorated" LA recruiting car visited the Thanet towns in June – EKT 19/6/1918, 4A.
194. ITG 6/10/1917, 3C.
195. ITG 23/6/1917, 6A; 30/6, 3B.
196. ITG 4/8/1917, 5E etc.
197. ITG 13/10/1917, 4B.
198. ITG 4/8/1917, 4C.
199. ITG 27/10/1917, 4F.
200. ITG 7/9/1918, 3C.
201. ITG 30/12/1916, 6D, meeting of agriculturists at Canterbury with the newly-appointed Government Controller of Cultivated Areas.
202. ITG 1/12/1917, 5A.
203. ITG 22/6/1918, 3E.
204. ITG 13/7/1918, 6D.
205. His obituary, ITG 13/1/1950, 5F.
206. Whetham, "Mechanization of British farming", 317.
207. K 17/11/1894, 6A.
208. K 21/11/1903, 8D.
209. K 21/11/1903, 8D.
210. EGQ.
211. K 21/11/1903, 8D; 19/11/1904, 5F; 17/11/1906, 6C; 16/11/1907, 5F; 14/11/1908, 8A; ITG 13/11/1909, 5F; 12/10/1910, 10A; 11/11/1911, 2A; 9/11/1912, 5F; 8/11/1913, 3E.

Chapter Nine

1. JKFU January 1919, 13; ITG 21/12/1918, 2B.
2. AHEW 8/142.
3. KG 12/4, 1E; 10/5, 1F; 17/5, 1E; 31/5, 1F; 28/6, 5A; 19/7, 2C, 9/8, 2A, 16/8, 2B; 23/8, 1G, 1919.
4. KM 5/4/1919, 4D.
5. ITG 3/5/1919, 4D.
6. KG 24/1/1920, 7B.
7. ITG 21/6/1919, 2E. Territorial officers were always called by their rank socially in the inter-war years, and before.
8. JKFU June 1919, 138; January 1921, 16.
9. ITG 7/2/1920, 6F.
10. AHEW 8/142, 143.
11. JKFU February 1920, 16.
12. JKFU February 1922, 53; ITG 21/1/1922, 6A.
13. ITG 28/10/1922, 6E.
14. ITG 1/12/1923, 5F – mentioned in the AGM report. AHEW 8/143.
15. ITG 7/2/1925, 11E.
16. AHEW 8/148.
17. ITG 22/1/1927, 7F.
18. ITG 28/1/1928, 6F.

19. JKBNFU February 1929, 62; ITG 2/2/1929, 7E.
20. JKBNFU February 1930, 52; ITG 1/2/1930, 13A.
21. KFJ February 1931, 63.
22. Minutes of Thanet branch NFU, April 1931.
23. AHEW 8/226, 230.
24. KM 4/7/1931, 13D and E.
25. ITG 18/2/1933, 7C.
26. Information from Jill Smith.
27. AHEW 8/226.
28. ITG 21/1/1933, 11B; 17/3/1934, 7F; 16/6/1935, 8D.
29. ITG 13/5/1933, 9F.
30. AHEW 8/263.
31. KA, Cobb papers, U 1453, E34/1.
32. ITG 19/9/1931, 6C; 26/9, 6A; 3/10, 6A, B; 17/10, 6A.
33. EGQ.
34. Documents supplied by Jill Smith.
35. JKBNFU December 1926, 193, 196.
36. KFJ 1933, 248.
37. KFJ 1938, 234.
38. Minutes of Thanet branch NFU.
39. KFJ 1939, 122, NFU County Chairman's speech.
40. ITG 6/2/1937, 6F, G.
41. KFJ March 1938, 122.
42. ITG 18/2/1939, 3A, B.
43. ITG 6/2/1937, 6G; 12/1/1940, 4B, too.
44. ITG 7/1/1939, 2 A–C with photo; 14/1, 9A; 30/9, 2A;
45. In later versions of this story it was an accountant not a bank manager, but it was in fact a bank manager. (RQ).
46. KG 14/4/1934, 3C, D.
47. Obituary, ITG 7/9/1945, 3C.
48. JKBNFU 1924, 8; ibid, 1928, 109.
49. KFJ 1932, 164; September, 1941, 65.
50. KG 21/1/1944, 4B.
51. Interview, ITG 1/1/1954, 6F; information from Michael Smith.
52. Obituary, ITG 30/8/1946, 5, E, F; KFJ August 1934, 80.
53. ITG 12/1/1945, 3B.
54. Obituary, ITG 22/1/1960, 4C.
55. So far as is known, he was the first Thanet farmer ever to have attended a University. He left his studies at King's College London to join the army in the First World War, winning the MC in Palestine. (Information from Rodney Tapp).
56. Obituary, ITG 11/2/1939, 7E.
57. ITG 20/11/1920, 7F.
58. KFJ 1946, 24.
59. Information from Mary Montgomery.
60. Information from Jill Smith and David Steed. ITG 28/8/1937, 7E.
61. Obituary, ITG 17/3/1944, 7C, D.
62. ITG 12/1/1945, 3B.
63. ITG 2/1/1935, 8A.

Notes

64. EGQ.
65. ITG 28/6/1919, 6D.
66. See *Kentish Gazette*.
67. ITG 1/1/1921, 9: events of 1920.
68. Eric Quested wrote to them complaining of the bad state of the Wood-church roads, and the "ladies of Monkton" sent them a petition for tarring – ITG 8/2/1919, 3E; 4/12/1920, 5B.
69. To Hartsdown and Dent-de-Lion, for example – ITG 13/12/1890, 8D.
70. ITG 27/9/1919, 9G.
71. KG 23/10/1926, 11G.
72. ITG 31/12/1943, 1A for Callis Court farm; for the wells, note 175 below.
73. KG 4/7/1936, 12F, G.
74. See note 175 below, these figures come from the 1941–42 farm survey.
75. Information from Muriel Spanton; ITG 31/7/1942, 5D.
76. ITG 11/6/1943, 40; 24/6, 2C.
77. Information from Richard Tapp.
78. Information supplied on request by Christopher Powell-Cotton.
79. Debrett's *People of Kent*; ITG 7/7/1944, 5E; information supplied on request by Michael Smith. He was in Colditz.
80. Information supplied by Michael Smith and on request by Walter Baxter.
81. ITG 19/2/1943, 5C.
82. ITG 15/12/1944, 5D.
83. ITG 16/11/1942, 11E.
84. Debrett, *People of Kent*.
85. Information from Betty Tyrrel and Ruth Ramsden née Paine.
86. ITG 30/8/1940, 5C.
87. ITG 9/6/1944, 5D. Our HG was the 6th Kent Bn (Thanet).
88. Information from Norman Steed, Ann Linington, Jill Smith. Lampe, D. *The last ditch*, London, 1968, 66, 97, 101, 102, 137, 163. Churchill expressed deep personal interest in the establishment of the organization, and was one of only two people to receive regular weekly reports on it.
89. ITG 13/10/1944, 5E; 1/12/1944, 6B.
90. Information from David Kemp; KA CC/MC 34, 1/15.
91. ITG 12/2/1943, 11C.
92. Humphreys, R. *Thanet at war*, Stroud, 1991, 59, 71, 73, 75, 107, 204; ITG 4/9/1942, 9C.
93. Information from Norman Steed; EGQ.
94. Murray, K.A.H. *Agriculture: the history of the Second World War UK civil series*, London, 1955, 289–291, 379.
95. Holderness, B.A. *British agriculture since 1945*, Manchester, 1984, 9.
96. Minutes of Thanet branch NFU.
97. KG 10/8/1940, 30; KFJ August 1940, 52; EGQ.
98. Information from Jill Smith; EGQ.
99. KFJ February 1942, 35. Speech at the Queen's Hall, Royal Star Hotel, Maidstone.
100. KG 7/3/1942, 3C.
101. KG 10/10/1942, 3E.
102. ITG 24/12/1943, 10B.
103. KFJ January 1944, 1.

104. ITG 24/8/1945, 5E; 5/10, 3D; 18/5, 5C.
105. EKT 20/10/1945, 1D.
106. Information from Jill Smith.
107. NUAW *Reports and balance sheets 1918–*.
108. Armstrong, Alan, *Farmworkers: a social and economic history 1770–1980*, London, 1988, 184.
109. ITG 26/6/1920, 9F.
110. KG 12/2/1921, 5E.
111. ITG 28/8/1920, 6E; 6/11, 6E; 1/1/1921, 6D.
112. ITG 13/11/1920, 7E; 22/1/1921, 3G, etc.
113. KG 7/7/1921, 2B.
114. AHEW 8/153.
115. KG 25/2/1922, 7E.
116. Alan Armstrong, *Farmworkers*, 180.
117. ITG 22/7/1922, 3C.
118. ITG 7/1/1922, 3D.
119. ITG 7/1/1922, 2E. Best kitchen nuts were 56/-: ITG 7/1/1922, 5A.
120. ITG 13/1/1923, 5C.
121. EGQ; ITG 11/9/1920, 3D; 3/9/1921, 4E.
122. EGQ.
123. Alan Armstrong, *Farmworkers*, 182–183.
124. ITG 6/2/1937, 6F.
125. ITG 9/1/1926, 9C; 18/9, 9A.
126. ITG 21/7/1928, 3C.
127. Obituary, ITG 31/3/1934, 15D. He had walked to school in Margate from Haine, then to school in Ramsgate from Manston, but no details are known.
128. ITG 12/10/1929, 4D, account of the Studhams' Golden Wedding.
129. ITG 8/12/1939, 2E.
130. ITG 6/9/1940, 4G.
131. EGQ.
132. Alan Armstrong, *Farmworkers*, 197; EGQ.
133. Alan Armstrong, ibid, 197; ITG 27/2/1937, 5C.
134. ITG 12/2/1938, 13E.
135. ITG 8/12/1939, 2E.
136. ITG 20/7/1935, 10E.
137. ITG 2/2/1940, 4G.
138. ITG 15/4/1939, 6D; 22/7, 5E; 15/12, 2B.
139. ITG 15/1/1938, 4F.
140. Ransley MS.
141. EKT 2/1/1946, 2D.
142. ITG 22/1/1943, 5C.
143. ITG 18/6/1943, 7D.
144. ITG 19/11/1943, 5E.
145. ITG 25/2/1944, 5B.
146. ITG 19/6/1942, 5E; 27/4/1945, 3F; 19/10/1945, 3D (refers to 1944).
147. ITG 25/2/1944, 7D.
148. ITG 14/11/1941, 7E.
149. ITG 18/5/1945, 5C.

150. Humphreys, 242.
151. ITG 7/3/1941, 11C.
152. ITG 6/11/1942, 6B.
153. ITG 2/6/1944, 2F, 5D.
154. EGQ.
155. ITG 30/6/1944, 3F,G.
156. KG 23/9/1940, 2D; ITG 5/7/1940, 4C.
157. Alan Armstrong, op cit, 213–214, quoting Ministry of Agriculture & Fisheries, *A century of Agricultural statistics*, HMSO 1968, 65.
158. Reports and balance sheets of NUAW 1918–.
159. ITG 31/5/1940, 7D; 7/6, 1 E-G; 27/9, 3A; 13/6/1941, 4D; 6/2/1942, 5E.
160. ITG 24/1/1941, 1D.
161. ITG 8/5/1942, 5E; 19/6, 4C; 25/9, 8D.
162. Grigg, *English agriculture*, 152.
163. ITG 6/11/1920, 7E; EGQ.
164. ITG 26/11/1921, 5G; information from Michael Smith; EGQ.
165. ITG 10/11/1928, 12D.
166. ITG 29/9/1923, 4A.
167. KG 22/9/1928, 1E.
168. KG 28/9/1929, 6C.
169. Information from Jill Smith.
170. EGQ.
171. JKBNFU August 1927, 40.
172. JKBNFU August 1930, 39.
173. EGQ.
174. ITG 9/4/1943, 9C.
175. PRO MAF 32/1016/320; 1020/325; 1031/324; 1032/236, 237; 1035/238; 1036/241, 327.
176. KFJ June 1939, 248, states that one was being made with the agricultural returns that year, and K.A.H. Murray, *Agriculture*, 56, mentions one made in 1937, but neither of these has been preserved at the PRO.
177. EGQ.
178. KG 22/9/1928, 6E.
179. KG 20/9/1919, 1B, 2C.
180. Jill Smith's documents on the tenancy.
181. ITG 26/3/1943, 7A.
182. ITG 5/10/1945, 4A.
183. Information from Jill Smith and Peter Linington; ITG 26/8/1939, 2A; PRO MAF 32/1031/324.
184. ITG 23/7/1943, 5B refers to a Canadian combine in use on barley at Birchington; ibid, 12/11/1943, 1E reports the award.
185. ITG 26/8/1939, 2A.
186. EGQ.
187. Jill Smith's documents, as used for Table 15.
188. ITG 11/9/1942, 11C; EGQ.
189. Garrad, 67–68.
190. Lukehurst, 57, quoting letter from S.W.T. Solly – Minister of Agriculture Tom Williams 18/11/1949.
191. ITG 5/11/1921, 6H.

192. ITG 10/11/1923, 6F; 9/11/1929, 10A.
193. Obituary, KFJ September 1946, 30.
194. Obituary, ITG 19/2/1945, 5C.
195. His speech at the dinner, ITG 2/2/1929, 7E; EGQ.
196. ITG 12/11/1943, 1E.
197. *Farmers Weekly* 8/11/1935, 33.
198. ITG 8/10/1943, 9 C–D.
199. E.S. Linington's talk at Borden Farm Institute, KFJ March 1932, 208; ITG 5/3/1932, 14D.
200. EGQ diary.
201. ITG 25/4/1936, 2B; information from Peter Linington.
202. Quested family photo.
203. KFJ March 1932, 208; ITG 5/3/1932, 14D; 16/6/1934, 12G; information from Peter Linington; RQ.
204. ITG 4/4/1936, 4B.
205. JKBNFU January 1927, 16.
206. Ibid, February 1929, 62.
207. JKFU January 1923, 18.
208. JKBNFU December 1924, 208–209.
209. Ibid, November 1925, 161.
210. See also ITG 5/6/1942, 7C.
211. ITG 17/7/1920, 7C, D.
212. Information from Michael Smith; EGQ.
213. ITG 11/7/1936, 2D, E.
214. ITG 17/7/1937, 7F.
215. The Agricultural Returns show one at Monkton, probably his.
216. JKFU September 1919, 54–56.
217. Only 5 cows and 2 registered shorthorn bulls remained – KG 20/9/1924, 1F.
218. ITG 11/9/1920, 3D.
219. ITG 24/12/1921, 6C.
220. JKFU September 1922, 77, 100.
221. KG 2/10/1926, 1D.
222. *Farmers Weekly*, 8/11/1935, 32.
223. ITG 15/6/1945, 6E; information from Michael Smith.
224. ITG 4/6/1938, 5E.
225. KFJ July 1932, 33, his paper to a milk conference in Sittingbourne, text in full.
226. EGQ documents; sale catalogue, all now in KA Ramsgate.
227. Jill Smith's documents.
228. Obituary, ITG 20/5/1955, 9D.
229. KG 2/10/1926, 1D.
230. JKBNFU October 1928, 131.
231. *Home Farmer*, June 1945, 7, speech by Sir Thomas Baxter, chairman of the Milk Marketing Board, *sic*. This does not mean that 90% of British cattle were infected, but a considerable number were. 49% of herds were tested by 1951 according to *The work of the Milk Marketing Board 1933–1955*, written and published by the M.M.B. in 1951, 30.
232. ITG 21/12/1924, 2D.
233. JKBNFU June 1925, 184; October 1928, 131.

234. KFJ July 1932, 33.
235. ITG 13/5/1933, 13F.
236. ITG 23/3/1935, 4E.
237. KFJ July 1938, 28.
238. ITG 8/7/1939, 11B.
239. He died in February 1939 – ITG 11/2/1939, 7E.
240. ITG 31/7/1937, 7C.
241. *Farmers Weekly*, 8/11/1935, 33.
242. Michael Smith, description of Monkton Court farm for visitors 1965.
243. The writer recalls stories of horrific Khaki Campbell duck losses.
244. Information from Michael Smith.
245. Ibid.
246. Alan Smith at Nether Hale and apparently the Montgomerys at Thorne also gave up sheep during the war.
247. Viz. Lord Cornwallis' speech to Kent County NFU AGM, KFJ January 1942, 13.
248. KFJ 1942, 1, Minister of Agriculture's New Year message.
249. KFJ January 1943, 8.
250. KFJ November 1942, 52.
251. Michael Smith, description of Monkton Court farm 1965.
252. EGQ.
253. JKFU April 1922, 124–126; May, 201.
254. JKFU April 1923, 138.
255. KFJ 1942 contains advertisements and instructions.
256. KFJ November 1941, 140.
257. ITG 9/2/1945, 6D.
258. ITG 15/5/1920, 3D.
259. Information supplied by Norman Steed. ITG 2/5/1941, 3D; 6/3/1942, 2 A, B.
260. EGQ. Ploughing match catalogues.
261. ITG 26/11/1921, 5G.
262. ITG 8/11/1924, 2B, for example.
263. ITG 5/11/1927, 8C.
264. The author, aged six, watched them leave with her father. She also has hazy memories of the mass walks to earlier matches going back to the 1926 one at Monkton Road. That year there was no racing for buses, and the Shottendane valley people met up with the Woodchurch ones for a get-together at the corner of Quex Park, and they walked together through Acol to Monkton Road, with the contingents from Garlinge and the Closes etc. too. Large numbers of people also walked out from the towns to all these early matches, and the post-1945 ones at Woodchurch.
265. ITG 5/11/1927, 8C; 10/11/1928, 12D.
266. ITG 8/11/1930, 8A.
267. PRO MAF 32/1016/320; 1020/325; 1031/324; 1032/236, 237; 1035/238; 1036/ 241, 327.

Chapter Ten

1. Holderness, 16.
2. ITG 22/2/1946, 6D etc.
3. ITG 24/2/1950, 3D.
4. KF 1969, 140.
5. ITG 22/2/1946, 6D.
6. H.A. Marks, *100 years of British food and farming. A statistical survey*, London, 1989, 145.
7. Holderness, 20.
8. ITG 25/2/1955, 3F.
9. KF 1956, 2.
10. Holderness, 20. Richard Howarth, *Farming for farmers? A critique of of agricultural support policy*, London, 2nd ed 1990, 12.
11. Holderness, 22.
12. Ibid, 23, 24.
13. Grigg, 24.
14. *Annual review of agriculture for 1972*, Cmnd 4928, table 13, p 30.
15. KF 1975, 225–226. Marks, 149.
16. Thanet NFU branch minutes, December 1968.
17. Mockett, 75, 155 etc.
18. Correspondence between EGQ and Fowles Accountants, Broadstairs, now in KA Ramsgate.
19. ITG 10/12/1976, 5 centre, his obituary.
20. Information from Peter Linington.
21. Information from Jill Smith.
22. Jill Smith's documents.
23. Peter Linington's documents.
24. Lukehurst, 293, from farmers' communications.
25. KF 1974, 22.
26. KF 1947, 60.
27. KF 1948, Feb, 14; July, 3.
28. KF 1969, 398.
29. Information from Mary Montgomery.
30. Information from Michael Smith and the Clerk to the River Stour (Kent) Inland Drainage Board.
31. His obituary, ITG 8/11/1967, 1; Thanet NFU branch minutes 6/4/1960.
32. Information from N.H. Steed; KF 1959, 229.
33. Letter from Hugh Finn – EGQ 11/8/1972, now in KA Ramsgate.
34. EGQ; also his letters and papers.
35. Thanet NFU branch minutes.
36. KG 27/2/1943, 3E.
37. Thanet NFU branch minutes 6/2/1945; KFJ May 1945, 55; July, 5.
38. KFJ September 1945, 28; March 1947, 36.
39. Information from Michael Smith.
40. Thanet NFU branch minutes February and October 1958.
41. Ploughing match catalogues.
42. Information from Ann Linington, Mary Montgomery and Muriel Spanton.

43. His obituary, ITG 5/1/1962, 5 C–D.
44. Holderness, chapter 3.
45. Local farmers' opinions. M. Tracy, *Agriculture in W. Europe*, 2nd ed. London, 1980, 312–313.
46. Grigg, 8.
47. Thirtle & Bottomley, "Total factor productivity in UK agriculture 1967–1990", *Journal of Ag. Economics* 1992, 43/3, 392.
48. Ibid, 392, 394.
49. *Annual review of agriculture for 1988*, Cm. 299, HMSO 1992, table 25, p 36. Farm business income is defined there as the return on the labour of farmers and spouses, non-principal partners and directors for their labour and management skills and all capital, own or borrowed, invested after allowing for depreciation. Marks, 149.
50. Ibid, table 30, p 42, table 31, p 43 etc. The term "large" is not defined in this publication and the agricultural census to 1988 only asked for farm size up to 500 ha.
51. Opinion of Jill Smith, James Linington and Peter Linington.
52. *Farmland market* no 6, July 1976, 49.
53. Information from Jill Smith.
54. *Farmland market*, no 25, February 1986, 53.
55. Ibid, no 31, February 1989, 44, referring to a sale the previous December.
56. Ibid no 32, August 1989, 40.
57. Opinion of James Linington, partner in G.W. Finn auctioneers.
58. Marks, 32.
59. *Farmers weekly* 20/11/1992, 10–11. Information from Jenny Cornelius.
60. BBC Radio 4 news report, March 1993. Information from Jenny Cornelius.
61. Garrad, 186.
62. KF 1965, 125.
63. KF 1968, 63.
64. TT 31/10/1972, 2 B–D.
65. Information from Peter Linington.
66. Information from Jill Smith.
67. Information from Mary Tyrrel and William Friend.
68. KF 1953, 402.
69. Document sent to EGQ, now in KA Ramsgate.
70. Information supplied by late Martin Jackson, then NFU secretary.
71. Information from Jill Smith.
72. KF 1976, 150.
73. KF 1981, 28.
74. Information from Mary Tyrrel and others.
75. NFU branch minutes 9/11/1971.
76. Information from Mary Montgomery, Jill Smith, Peter Dyas, Mary Tyrrel, Martin Tapp, Ann Linington, Tessa Tapp, Michael Smith and Clerk to River Stour (Kent) Inland Drainage Board.
77. Weekly lists of planning applications put out by Thanet District Council.
78. *Sic*. Information supplied by Department of Employment, Mill House, Margate, on 8 April 1993.
79. TT 24/10/1972, 1 F–G.

80. ITG 2/5/1975, 18D; also 9/5 and 16/5, letters to editor.
81. KF 1984, 130.
82. PRO MAF 68/5907; Grigg, 98.
83. Grigg, 104.
84. EGQ diary.
85. KF 1948, 70.
86. 6,500 remained May 1994, 1,268 having been sold since January 1986.
87. RQ.
88. Information from Jill Smith and David Steed.
89. Information from various sources, particularly in 1993 from Eric Humphrey, then Kent area organizer of the RAAW section of the TGWU, and Bob Lawrence, who gave a non-Union view. For the 1% ownership of homes by farm workers, see also *Farmers Weekly* 5/4/1991, 86. Roger Hobcraft for report on EKTC.
90. Garrad, 67–71.
91. Ibid, 68.
92. KF 1951, 130.
93. KF 1965, 125–129.
94. Information from Michael Smith.
95. KF 1952, 171.
96. EGQ interview with Brian Lovelidge, *Milk Producer*, vol 17/2 March 1970, 72–75.
97. *Farmers Weekly*, 20/4/1961, Paul Attlee article.
98. Information from Peter Linington.
99. Information from Michael Smith.
100. ITG 4/1/1957, 4C.
101. EGQ diary.
102. Information from Peter Linington.
103. EGQ diary.
104. KF April 1965, 129; also KM in March 1965.
105. Information from Jill Smith.
106. EGQ diary.
107. KF 1956, 428.
108. Thanet branch NFU minutes.
109. KF 1961, 199.
110. Information from Jill Smith. *Farmer & Stockbreeder* 18/5/1945.
111. *Farmers Weekly* 20/9/1946.
112. KF 1948, 137, Information from Jill Smith and David Steed.
113. Information from Peter Linington.
114. Information from Michael Smith.
115. EGQ papers; author.
116. KF 1954, 90.
117. Garrad, 69.
118. *Farmers Weekly* 27/1/1961.
119. EGQ papers; information from Michael Smith.
120. EGQ diary.
121. Garrad, 69.
122. ITG 6/10/1950, 5D.
123. ITG 19/10/1951, 8C.

124. ITG 3/11/1967, 9 E–F.
125. EGQ diary; also paper he read to the British Institute of Industrial Management at Norwich on 18 November 1954.
126. EQQ diary.
127. Garrad, 69–70.
128. EGQ papers and diary; author.
129. EGQ diary.
130. Catalogue with prices, now in KA Ramsgate.
131. Letter of 21 September 1971 W. Fowles, accountant of Broadstairs – EGQ.
132. Script for Southern TV film of Monkton Court farm made on 15/12/1972, supplied by Michael Smith.
133. Garrad 68, but in fact the decennial agricultural return figures for this crop never regained their pre-First World War level.
134. *Farmers Weekly* 31/8/1973, article by Jack Sarl.
135. *Farmers Weekly* 28/4/1961, article by Paul Attlee.
136. *Poultry World* 15/2/1962, article by Peter Henderson; Michael Smith's account of the farm for visitors; script of Southern TV film 15/12/1972.
137. ITG 7/3/1947, 3F.
138. Script of Southern TV film 15/12/1972.
139. Report for the formation of Vegetable Growers (Kent) Ltd, 1964, supplied by Richard Tapp.
140. Information from Peter Linington.
141. ITG 2/10/1959, 1G.
142. ITG 27/2/1953, 3F; author's recollections; Lukehurst, 148, quoting *Geography* no 38 (1953) 135–141. The winds reached 175 mph in the Northern parts of the North Sea and Irish Sea, but were not so strong as that here.
143. Lukehurst, 187–189.
144. Dudley Stamp, L. *The land of Britain: its use and misuse*, 1st ed London, 1943, Part 85, 598.
145. ITG 12/3/1954, 4C.
146. Lukehurst, 209.
147. Script of Southern TV film of Monkton Court farm 15/12/1972.
148. Lukehurst, 238.
149. Information from David Steed.
150. Government White Paper quoted by Lukehurst, 235.
151. Viz. for instance article by B.P. Mann and S.D. Wrattan, in *Crop Protection* 1992, vol 11/6, 561–571, which explains a computer-based advisory system for control of summer pests of oilseed rape in Britain, to enable farmers to judge as accurately as possible when pesticides are needed. This was hopefully an example of convergence of interest of those with a direct financial stake in the commercial success of farming and the ecologist!
152. Dr J. Lopez-Real of the Department of Biological Sciences, Wye College, was involved in these experiments, together with Advanced Recycling Technologies, a Suffolk-based firm, to which Thanet District Council leased the site for 5 years in 1993.
153. Article in the *Vegetable Farmer* 1992. The first reservoir at Nether Hale cost £16,000.
154. Information from Jill Smith.

155. Information from Peter Linington; article in *Crops* 23/10/1985, on the Linington farms.
156. Information from Michael and Philip Smith.
157. *Farmers Weekly* 14/11/1980, 83–85.
158. ITG 2/3/1979, 5A.
159. *Guiness Book of Records* 1986; EKT 21/5/1980; 4; KG 11/9/1981, 1; information from Tessa Tapp.
160. Information from William Friend.
161. Information from David Spanton.
162. ITG 9/2/1990, 19.
163. Information from Peter Linington, William Friend, the late Martin Jackson and other farmers.
164. Ploughing match catalogue in author's possession.
165. Garrad, 125.
166. Catalogue in author's possession. Edwin Baxter II, grandson of the first.
167. ITG 26/10/1956, 2D. Catalogue of match in author's possession.
168. Match catalogue in author's possession.
169. ITG 28/10/1966, 1A.
170. ITG 2/11/1951, 2C.
171. 1957 match catalogue; EGQ.
172. Match catalogues. 234 of the 1956 entries in the Women's Section were for a childrens' handwriting competition.
173. EGQ.
174. ITG 22/10/1971, 19, 20.
175. ITG 27/10/1972, 8A; TT 24/10/1972, 5 A-E.
176. Information from Ann Linington; match catalogues; ITG 27/10/1972, 8A; TT 24/10/1972, 5 A-E.
177. Match catalogues; ITG 26/10/1973, 4; TT 23/10/1973, 5 A-B.
178. Information from many sources.
179. ITG 26/10/1973, 4; TT 23/10/1973, 5 A-B.
180. Small, 1.
181. Ministry of Agriculture and Fisheries, *Agriculture in the UK 1994*, London, 1995; ibid, News Release 33/96, 31 January 1996.
182. Information from Sandwich branch of G.W. Finn & Sons, auctioneers.
183. ITG 15/9/1995.
184. *Agriculture in the UK 1994*.
185. Ibid.
186. The *Times* 1 February 1996.
187. ITG 21/7/1995; 15/9/1995.
188. Information from Geoffrey Philpott.
189. ITG 14/7/1995, 5.

Conclusion

1. EGQ.
2. J.C. Gilham, *Minster Abbey, Minster in Thanet*, Thanet 1988, 11.

3. One can imagine some farmers or landowners might have allowed this, or turned a blind eye. Buckland, 259
4. Information from Mr J.D. Sykes. Brynmore Green, *EFFs, LULUs and NIMBYs*, Wye College Occasional Paper no 90/2, fig 3.
5. K 12/10/1872, 3B.
6. Observations. Letter to author from I. Tittley of the Natural History Museum dated 24/11/1993.
7. English Nature reports ISBN 185716 140 8, 1994, and ISBN 185716 141 6, 1994.
8. Information from Martin Jackson, secretary of the Thanet Fishermen's Association, 1993.
9. For example, ITG 24/10/1914, 8C; 10/11/1995, 3; *Thanet Extra*, 9/2/1996, 1, quoting Dr Peter Evans of the Seawatch Foundation.
10. EGQ.
11. ITG 4/2/1933, 4F.
12. ITG 6/2/1937, 8A; 5/2/1938, 5 F, G.
13. K 2/6/1900, 6F; 7/7, 2E.
14. But they were reported decreasing nationally already in 1934, through rat poison – ITG 31/3/1934, 15D.
15. KFJ May 1948, 70.
16. KF 1985, 174. British Trust for Ornithology figures.
17. KF 1982, 402.
18. It is still there with the date on it.
19. J.F. Cook, "A spatial model for identifying nitrate protection zones over an aquifer", *SEESOIL, Journal of the SE England Soils Discussion Group*, 7/1992, 51–53, citing MAF/WOA 1989, *Nitrate sensitive zones scheme, A consultative document*.
20. KF 1986, 413.
21. KF 1990, 28.
22. Southern Water news release no 49/local a, November 1991.
23. A.D. Hall and E.J. Russell, *A report on the agriculture and soils of of Kent, Surrey and Sussex*, London, 1911, 186.
24. William Marshall, *The review and abstract of the County Reports to the Board of Agriculture*, York, 1818, 5/420–421.
25. Marshall, *The rural economy of the Southern counties*, London, 1798, 2/5.
26. Hall and Russell, 143.
27. Weir H., Catt J.A. and Madgett P.A. "Postglacial soil formation in the loess of Pegwell Bay, Kent, England", *Geoderma. An international journal of soil science*, 5/131. I am indebted to Dr Paul Burnham for this reference.
28. Letters to the author from Dr Burnham dated 31 July 1992 and 12 April 1996. Alagoz, Z. "Soils of limestone terrains in SE England and Mediterranean Turkey, with particular reference to transported material". Unpublished PhD thesis, Wye College, University of London, 1995.
29. Information from David Perkins.
30. Lecture by Paul Bennett to the Friends of Quex on 20 November 1995.
31. Information from Mary Tyrrel and David Steed.
32. Weather reports on the back page of the *Times* daily.
33. JKFU May, 1921, 139.

Illustrations

1) The former medieval chapel at Manston Court farm, before conversion to a dwelling.
2) 1913 ploughing match, West Northdown. Old Kent wooden plough
3) 1913 ploughing match. Margate Mayor Leon Adutt making speech. W.J. Gardner centre. F. de B. Collard in top hat.
4) An unknown ploughing match winning team, probably 1913.
5) Barzillai Sackett.
6) Ploughing match 1924. M.P. Harmsworth making speech.
7) Taking broccoli to the station in Cornish crates, 1920.
8) Ploughing match 1955 Monkton Court.
9) Ploughing match 1961 Ozengell Grange.
10) Ploughing match 1955 Monkton Court. Marjorie Smith with her Irish smile presenting prize to fastest finisher, Tom Ovenden. See Supplement p. 366.
11) Ploughing match committee 1948. L-R W.J. Gardner. E.G. Quested. Brian Egerton. Lady Northbourne (prize presenter). Lord Northbourne. H.A. Smith. James Lamont. Michael Smith. W.G. Gardner.
12) Land girls threshing at Woodchurch, 1944.
13) Harvest 1932.
14) Guernseys at Woodchurch, showing their hierarchy. The boss cow leads them to pasture, closely followed by her two nearest rivals. (Before de-horning).
15) Above Minster, where the Thanet Way now is, 1911.
16) New housing advancing over Northdown, 1989.

Illustrations

(1)

(2)

(3)

(4)

(5)

(6)

(7)

(8)

(9)

(10)

(11)

(12)

(13)

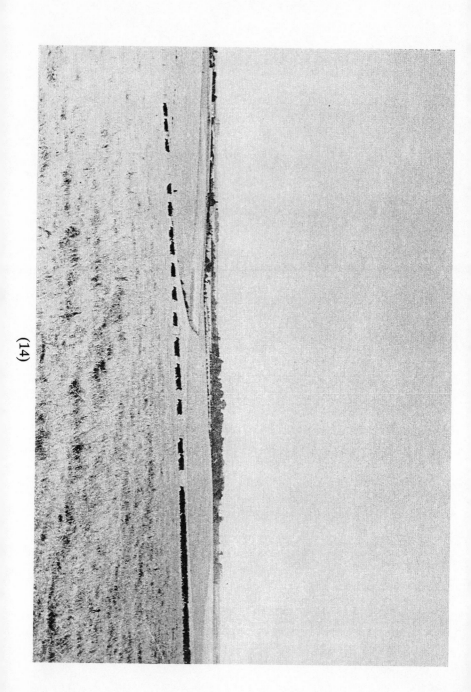

(14)

(15)

(16)

Index

Supplement

In Memoriam

We have lost two people who were an example to many and to whom this book was in debt. Penny Ward died in 1998 and Ann Linington in 2000; thankfully tribute was paid to both in the first edition. I also regret to record the death of Mrs Elizabeth Haighton, a correspondent who in early life lived at Hengrove and Twenties, and who had hoped to provide some recollections for this edition.

Thanks and apologies

Dr Joan Thirsk did not complain, but was poorly introduced in the first edition. She was and remains a famous authority on agrarian history, general editor of the multi-volume Cambridge University Press *Agrarian History of England and Wales*, and editor of much respected work continued in retirement. Oxford's failure to give her a chair appears one of the most extraordinary examples of the glass ceiling.

P.23

My apologies to Reg and Rex Goodban (long since delivered in person) for stating that their farm no longer existed under the name of Spratling Farm. The farmstead is still there next door to Spratling Court.

Illustration No.10

My apologies again: it was Tom Ovenden, the fastest finisher, receiving a prize at the 1955 ploughing match, not George Hewett. My thanks to those who rang to tell me.

P.46 para.3 line 3

I am grateful to Jim Mills for giving me a copy of a map from Lambarde's *Perambulation of Kent* (not in the reprint I used) showing beacon sites in existence well before the Armada. They were at Gore End, above Minster, St. John's and near St. Lawrence as well as the Beacon Road area of Broadstairs. The map is widely known in reproduction, often without attribution to Lambarde.

Corrections

P.48 para 4

Lambarde's figures for household numbers are not for 1563, but for the 13th year of Elizabeth I, 1570 or 1571 as she came to the throne on 17 November 1558 (Lambarde p.11, 1826 reprint of London 1576). Before 1752 the year began 25 March.

P.91 para.1

William Pitt the younger was out of office when he came to Thanet in 1803, in his role of Lord Warden of the Cinque Ports. He became Prime Minister again in 1804.

P.104 end of para.2

Woodchurch and Cheeseman's farms were bought by John Powell Powell of Quex in 1841, not 1837 as had been supposed, and for £7,750. They had been advertised for sale by auction in 1837, but evidently withdrawn. (Whitfield archives U/1063 T.69).

Errata

Page 2 line 27   For "probably tribal groups" read "probably tribal, groups".

Page 2 penultimate line	For "It looks as Thanet" read "It looks as though Thanet"
Page 44 line 2	For "There paucity" read "Their paucity"
Page 80 line 34	For "*diplotaxis muralis*" read "*Diplotaxis muralis*"
Page 80 line 35	For "*brassica muralis*" read "*Brassica muralis*"
Page 119 line 3	For "Tradtional" read "Traditional"
Page 125 line 1	For "*Lepidium (Cardaria) Draba L.*" read "*Lepidium (Cardaria) draba L.*"
Page 170 line 20	For "3-4, 000" read "3-4,000"
Page 229 line 28	For "*Lepidium Draba*" read "*Lepidium draba*"
Page 276 line 24	For "*Arenaria Interpres*" read "*Arenaria interpres*"
Page 280 line 34	For "*Lepidium Draba*" read "*Lepidium draba*"

Additional Information

Pp 2-3. Archaeology can now produce more general pictures of conditions in Southeast England in the various prehistoric ages than it could earlier. A fascinating example is Dr.David Perkins Ph.D. thesis "An exploration of the evidence for the existence of a cultural focus in the form of a 'Gateway Community' in the Isle of Thanet during the Bronze Age and early and middle Iron Age' (Institute of Archaeology, University College London 2000). The gist of it is that the Wantsum was an important sheltered part of the route from the Continent to the Thames in the Bronze Age, until the Iron Age development of sailing craft able to tack into the wind and move safely round the North Foreland. Control of the Wantsum from our relatively high island enabled a population of perhaps several thousand to survive here, and their leaders, secular or priestly, to organize the raising of the 380 known and postulated total of over 600 barrows made here between 2000 and 600 BC. The people also cultivated the good soil in the valleys and coastal areas of a Thanet which Dr.Perkins estimates to have been perhaps 25% larger than now, due to land since lost to the sea.

P. 12

The name Leubucus has been identified as a Frankish man's name by Susan Kelly ("Trading privileges in early medieval England", *Early European History* 1/1,1992, 7). It now looks more likely that the Abbess Eadburgh who corresponded with St.Boniface was not from St.Mildred's Thanet. (Barbara Yorke, "The Boniface mission and female religious in Wessex", *Early European History* 1998, 150-153).

P.20, para.2

Woodchurch From carved stone incorporated into the stables, Anthony Swain, a Canterbury architect and specialist in medieval churches, estimates the probable date of St.Nicholas-at-Wode as the end of the 12th century. William de Wode, a minor knight floreat ?1189-1207, or his father, are plausible movers of the project. William tried to build a windmill "on his own free tenement of Monkton" adjoining Acol (Woodchurch and Acol being part of the Monkton parish). Christchurch Priory disputed it until at least 1204. William was plainly a locally prominent, assertive character, who also took part in Grand Assizes (legal enquiries) in 1202, 1203 and 1205. He was also listed in a rental of 1207 as owing the Priory five marks. There was another windmill in the 12th century, owned by the Archbishop at "West Hallemot", possibly Downbarton, and the Thanet Archaeological Trust has now found remains of another dating from the 12-14th century on the site of the Asda store at Westwood, then under St.Augustine's overlordship. (E.J. Kealey, *Harvesting the air: windmill pioneers in 12th century England*, University of California Press 1987, 223-225, citing a number of secondary and medieval sources. Information from David Perkins).

Two members of T.A.T., Jenny Price and David White, have investigated crop marks south of Woodchurch, finding amongst other things a medieval pewter candle snuffer. They hope to make a dig in the derelict parts of the farmstead. Jenny convincingly suggests that Christchurch Priory must have backed the building of the church because it enhanced its authority close to the farthest boundary of Monkton parish with Minster parish under St.Augustine's overlordship.

P.41 third paragraph. Ozengell Grange.

Ozengell Grange was not mentioned as a property of St.Augustine's as it was not in William of Thorne's list. But Charles Cotton shows that at the Reformation it was known under this name and was collecting tenants' tithes for the Vicar of St.Lawrence. (*The history and antiquities of the church and parish of St.Lawrence*, London and Ramsgate 1895, 11, 203). Possibly the apparent late emergence of the Grange in this way was connected with improved production by tenants of larger farms after the end of feudal exactions in the 14th/15th centuries, but this is speculation and underlines how much we need more basic research into St.Augustine's role in medieval Thanet.

P.47 paras. 1 and 2. Spread of Protestantism

Margaret Bolton has material from parish baptismal registers showing the replacement of saints' names by biblical ones in St.Lawrence between the 1560's (37.6% biblical) and the 1650's (53.7% biblical), proof of the spread of more pronounced Protestant views. She also has an interesting account of Peter Johnson, the Puritan vicar of St.Lawrence. (Margaret Bolton, "St.Lawrence: church and community", 1995, and information from her). Sabine Pollmann's University of Kent M.A thesis (1998) "An exploration of religious practise and piety in the parish of Minster in Thanet 1460-1560" reveals a Minster population still either Catholic or neutral, with a very few overtly Protestant wills or names.

P.48. 16th century population rise.

Margaret Bolton is preparing a new publication on the Elizabethan population of Thanet, which she estimates rose by nearly 3/8ths between 1560-1569 and 1600-1609, her researches being still under way. In St.Lawrence parish between 1560 and 1609 28.2% failed to reach 16, and life expectancy for those that did was 40.6 years for women and 44 for men. She shows how the 16th century was racked by epidemics, often flu. (Information from Margaret). These figures indicate there had been some life improvement for the working class of St.Peters by the second quarter of the 19th century (see p.143).

P.43-44 and note 32 chapter 3. J.P's in the 16th century

There is new information on the role of the Crispe family. Sir
Henry (knighted 1553) was JP 1539-75, and sat in the Quarter
Sessions 1561, 1564, 1569, 1571 and 1573. He rarely appeared at
the Assizes. Nicholas Crispe was JP 1559-64. The Richard Crispe
JP 1585-98 was from Whitstable, so Thanet had none after 1575,
though the numbers in Kent as a whole rose. (Michael Zell, "Kent
Elizabethan JP's at work", AC CXIX 1999, 7,8,27,32).

Pp 64-65. Example of 17th century land value

In 1616 Gallens (later called Gallows, finally Garlinge farm) of
120 acres was sold by William Johnson of Fordwich and Edward
Lamming of Canterbury to William Lamming for £1,200. In 1689
after two further sales, one at least between family members, and
mortgaging at least twice and some twenty various transactions, it
was sold for £1,800 including repayment of mortgages to the
wealthy John Evanson, a London sailmaker (perhaps the equivalent now of the owner of an aircraft engine factory). He left it to
the Royal Bethlehem Hospital in his will. All evidence points
to this being a prime farm, on flat land, with considerable coastal
access. (Bethlehem Hospital archives Box 6.)

Ch.2 p.61-2, Ch. p.77-79, etc
New crops in 17th -18th centuries

Turnips were known in Thanet by the 1680's – William and Elizabeth Payne of St.John's flung one at tithe collectors on one
occasion (Joan Thirst, *Alternative agriculture*, Oxford 1997, 70).
But Dennis Baker showed they were not a normal crop.

Hasted mentions a vineyard at Quex gardens (2nd edition 1800,
X, 302) and one must have been tried at Woodchurch farm at
some point, as a half-acre field bore this name, though apparently
without vines, in 1757 and still in 1808. (Whitfield archives, U1063
T69). A Sackett's Hill farm lease of 1712 required there to be 20
acres of sanfoin by the end of the lease (21 years?), showing
landlord concern for its spread. (Whitfield R/U 1196 T3 Bundle 3).

P. 85, last paragraph
Use of chalk for building

One of the very few precise references to this comes from 1757,
when the chalk wall round the yard at Garlinge farm fell down,

and the tenant Edward Bing, had "trouble keeping my stock in"!
(Bethlehem Hospital archives box 6).

Position of women

Both male owners and tenants of Garlinge farm in the 17th and
18th centuries appeared impressively literate, but when Elizabeth
Jenkins signed as co-vendor with her husband William in 1689, she
wrote like a small child in un-joined up letters. Sarah Taddy's letter
to the Governors of Bethlehem Hospital in 1728 about the death
of Roger, her father, the tenant, was reasonably good but not up
to the male average. (Bethlehem Hospital archives box 6). Some
contemporary tenants were much less educated. (See below).

Ch.4, p.77, para.1
An example of early 18th century land value

Sackett's Hill farm of "100 acres more or less" was sold for £1,021/
10/- in 1714. The rent was £48 in 1712. It had been mortgaged for
£500 in 1705, assigned to George Jessall, merchant of Ramsgate,
then to Thomas Curling, mariner of Ramsgate in trust for John
Curling. (Whitfield R/U 1196 T3 Bundle 2 and 3).

  The mid-18th century agricultural depression was reflected in
local rents. In 1728 the rent of Garlinge farm was £80 for 120 acres
(as in 1692) for 21 years, but the tenant was in arrears and it was
reduced to £75. He was still in arrears in 1756. (Bethlehem box 6).
The tenants of Woodchurch and Cheeseman's farms were in
arrears in 1759 and 1761. The Woodchurch tenant, George May,
was trying to right matters, and wrote to his landlord "My Mesh-
enger ... wheare at the Fountain" (Inn in Canterbury) "by 3
o'clock fryday" with an instalment. (Whitfield U1063 T69).

P.71 para.1
Farmers "paultering" a wreck

The Garlinge farm tenant Stephen Evers reported to his landlord,
the Royal Bethlehem Hospital, that a Danish light ship (sic) came
ashore and broke in two just the other side of Margate in winter
1742/3. "The farmers went with their wagons, horses and servants,
broke it up and carried all away." Evers' son brought some back to
their farm, which worried his father greatly. (Bethlehem archive
box 6).

Ch.4, p.79, para.3
Larger inland farms share coastal plots to stack seaweed

Woodchurch shared a square acre of ground at West Bay, Westgate, with Cheeseman's, Street and Westgate farms for the stockpiling of the precious "weed and oar and dung", and this probably continued until Westgate was built up. Garlinge farm was outstanding in having apparently a considerable amount of foreshore, only gradually sold for building between the late 1860's and 1920's. (Bethlehem archive box 6).

Good reputation of Thanet farmers with an aristocrat in the North

John Kedman of Minster, who married Susan Peal of St.Nicholas 1769, went to work for the 2nd Marquis of Rockingham as Master Farmer on his Yorkshire estates in 1769. With another Kent farmer named Wellard he was asked to improve the estates, and was said to be "cleaning the land exceedingly well and in a few years would increase its value". (Information from Mrs. Jean Sanders in Yorkshire, quoting Wentworth Papers in Sheffield Archives).

Wheat supplants barley

The instructions given in leases by the landowners became more stringent towards the end of the 18th century as land values and wheat prices rose. At Garlinge farm in 1692 the tenant, Roger Taddy, was only required to grow 20 acres of wheat, but by 1788 the tenant John Tomlin had to sow 1/3rd wheat and 1/3rd barley, oats and clover, leave 1/3rd fallow, thenceforth follow the round tilth, with much higher rent for any land put to industrial crops (hemp, flax, rape) or brickmaking. (Bethlehem archive box 6). In 1784 John Bridges at Chambers Wall farm, St.Nicholas was buying 18 quarters of seed wheat to 9 of barley and 3 1/2 of oats. He was growing pillbeam wheat on the marsh in 1787, and eggshell wheat on higher ground. This is one of two references to his marsh crops. (Whitfield R/U 1231 E7)

Inheritance in gavelkind

Examples have been found of this lingering almost into the 19th century. The children of the gentleman farmer John Friend, died 1793, were co-heirs in gavelkind, and John Sidders, yeoman of

Birchington, died 1818, was one of two sons and gavelkind heirs of Thomas, yeoman of Birchington. (Whitfield R/U 487 T46, R/U 1063 T6).

Fire Insurance

This evidently came in much earlier on the leading farms than had been supposed. The Governors of Bethlehem and Bridewell Hospitals insured Garlinge farm in the City of London from 1788, and the County Fire & Provident Society opened an office in Ramsgate in 1811. (Bethlehem archives box 6; KG 30/7/1811,1)

P.92-3
Crushing of the 18th century smallholder/labourer

John Bridges' (Chambers Wall farm) "new" account book at Whitfield illustrates this. Take the case of William Elgar, who was paid £18 for boarding an unspecified number of yearly servants in 1784, and £13 for boarding four in 1785 – unexpectedly early for boarding outside the farmhouse in Thanet. Mount was paid in sacks of maltings and faggots in lots of 100 for his labour in 1784, and 9/- a week in 1785, with 24 legs of pork at 4/4d and two quarters of wheat at 3/8d. In 1790 Bridges agreed to pay Elgar 10/6 a week and find him a house, indicating that his smallholding had been given up. He was still sold pork that year, but in 1795 October meal, and also given one guinea because of the high wheat price. (Whitfield R/U 1231 E7).

P.95-6
Use of workhouse labour

Bridges was using workhouse labour in 1789 already – John Coleman being paid 7/- then for work done by the poor. In 1800 the Overseer Thomas Busbridge paid Bridges £10/16/- for a man to replace Thomas Young for 18 weeks (12/- a week). (Whitfield R/U 1231 E7).

P.97
Machinery

In June 1794 John Bridges allowed his shepherd 2/4d for "three long days with the machine". There is no indication what kind of machine.

Pp.78-79, 80.
Use of corn drills

Their use was not universal here even in 1817, so Arthur Young's prediction in 1770 was way out. (*Thanet Magazine*, November 1817).

Chs. 6, 7 and 8.
Encroaches by the sea

Garlinge farm, 120 acres in 1695, was only 112 in 1772. In 1835 6 acres were reported lost to the sea, in 1855 the sea was said to be encroaching considerably. This seems to have continued till the first sea wall was completed in1879. There were also intermittent losses to the sea at Cliffsend farm. (Bethlehem archives box 6 and Kent agents' report books).

Pp.130-132, 135
Farmers' difficulties in 19th century

John Cramp, the tenant of Garlinge farm who had reported to the Parliamentary Commissioners in 1833, and said he was going to feed his stock entirely on carrots in 1830, went bankrupt in 1846. Mrs. Louisa Paramor, tenant in her own right at that farm 1862-1892, was behind with the rent in 1879 and 1888-90, and said 1888 was the worst year she had known – she had no hops. (Bethlehem archives, Kent agents' report books). No such details were found before for these periods, but there must have been many such cases.

A spate of burglaries in 1848

In September that year 30 were reported from farmhouses in two months, done by a London gang. Nearly all farms were "fitted with large bells" and 39 special constables sworn in. (KG 12/9/1848,4E). Later the gang were arrested and farm crime was not a problem again until the late 20th century.

P.157
An overlooked ploughing match competitors' dinner in
December 1849

This was overlooked in the first edition. The reporting was markedly less condescending than for the 1862 one (p.140 1st edition), which underlines the wave of religiosity and pomposity of the 1850's and 1860's. It is unclear if there were other such dinners before or after. (KG 11/12/1849,2F).

P.172
Military service of the gentry

Major Percy Powell-Cotton served in the Northumberland Fusiliers before going into the Militia in 1890. (Information from Brian Fagg).

Pp.135, 167 and 202
Early dates for modern sanitation and telephone in farmhouses

Cliffsend farm was provided with mains water and a WC indoors in 1888 and Garlinge farm with a bathroom in 1909. Garlinge farm tenant William Hedgecock installed a telephone himself in 1900. (Bethlehem archives Kent agents' report book).

P.165
Reasons for spate of farm sales in 1904

There was record rainfall in June-August 1903 after ten years below average, in 1904 a cold backward spring and a hot, dry July and August – disastrous seasons with crops generally below average. (Bethlehem archives Kent agents' report books).

P.172
Quex Hospital in World War 1, Thanet's only rural voluntary hospital

Of 1,961 patients (mainly sick Australian and Canadian soldiers) only 3 are said to have died. They suffered mostly from pneumonia, trench fever (malaria?), and bronchitis. (Talk to Friends of Quex by Hazel Basford 11 February 1999).

Pp.187-188
Difficulties caused by World War 1

It was very hard to get women to work on the land in 1915 as large numbers of troops were billeted locally. In 1917 no labourer would live or work at Cliffsend farm for fear of air raids and bombardment. In December 1918 it was still impossible to get cattle cake and the Government only supplied inferior pig meal. All farm implements and horses were 100% dearer and very hard to obtain. (Bethlehem archives Kent agents' report book).

P.195
Great Depression of 1930 plus

An accurate indication of the effect in Thanet is the Royal Bethlehem Hospital's reduction of the rent of Cliffsend farm by 10% for 1930-32, and 15% for 1932-33. The full rent was restored in 1934. George Spanton, the tenant, was highly esteemed by the Hospital's agents. He had pedigree cattle and pig herds by 1925. (Bethlehem archives Kent agents' report book).

P.204
Role of a farmer's wife in World War II

I regret not having mentioned that my mother, Olive Quested, was a V.A.D (voluntary unpaid nurse) for years, looking after Dunkirk and Battle of Britain casualties in Margate Hospital in 1940, later other troops and civilians, and finally returned POWs of the Japanese at Haine Hospital. She always cycled to work.

P.262
Dutch elm disease

The great loss of trees in Kent was apparently due to almost total lack of control over it. In Sussex the loss was far less. (*Times Weekend Supplement*, 30/9/00, 21, article by Andrew Morgan, author of *Trees of Sussex*, Pomegranate Press 2001, working on a similar study of Kent).

Illustration No.2

Thomas Page, ploughman, and J. Woodcock were probably with Bar Sackett's wooden plough at the 1913 ploughing match, as the winners of that class. (ITG 8/11/1913, 3E).

Illustration No.4

Charles Smith was probably the ploughman and William Drayton his assistant, as winners of the four-horse iron plough class and champions. The smartly dressed young man was probably the manager of Cobb's Thorne farm, or one of the family. (1913 ploughing match, ITG 8/11/1913 3E).

The Environment

The District Council's air pollution survey gives no local black spot analyses, as it finds Thanet's overall quality within the theoretical median for the Southeast. Vehicle air pollution is noticeable on many roads, from badly-maintained engines. Concern remains over Southern Water's determination to pump partially treated sewage water from Margate and Broadstairs into the sea from an enlarged works on an open space in a residential area at Foreness. But an improvement in seawater off the north shore is proved by the resurgence of bladderwrack (*Fucus vesiculosus*), which now grows even on the Nayland rock, always bare in my family's memory back to 1900 at least.

Farmers plough back all residues of crops, but only three apply the Council's free seaweed. Efforts to compost this for local use by Wye College and the Council have been abandoned. At least one stable manure heap on farmland has been removed by order of the District Council due to urban smell complaints. Andrew Lamont, owner of Crumps farm livery stables at St.Nicholas, has wiser neighbours and is applying horse manure generously to his small arable area, aiming to restore it to pre-1939 condition. Chalk shows on the surface in many places where it was not seen before the last few years, and in the Shottendane valley it is acute in one place. Most farmers will not use weed or dung because it corrodes their machinery.

Rooks at Quex have largely moved their nests outside the park to escape culling, but are reduced to 27 nests. Those at Monkton seem to hold their own better. Other birds decline in numbers still, though surprisingly corn bunting, robin and green woodpecker are increasing in Kent and even in Thanet. (Information from Tim Hodge of the Thanet Ornithological Trust). Foxes were much reduced by mange, which has led to a great increase of rats in central farmland. (Information from Arthur Burbridge). A very few partridges and hares are still seen.

The high level of nitrate in the water from the Sparrow Castle pumping station on the Birchington-Manston road led to this being from 2000 used entirely for agricultural irrigation – 12 million gallons per annum for Quex Park estates, a useful saving of drinking water. (Information from Anthony Curwen). But in 1935 this was top quality water.

Some remarkable hedge planting has been done, notably by the

Ursuline College pupils led by Paul Wells, and Robert Montgomery. Plans are cherished by some to extend these by creating
hedge-lined bridle paths round field margins, to cater for the
many riders and lead the mass of Thanetonians to appreciate their
countryside more.

Position of Thanet farming early 2001

There is general gloom. Taking average net income of general
cropping farms as 100 for 1989-90 to 1991-92, the provisional net
income for 1999-2000 was 50. Total U.K. subsidies funded by the
Intervention Board and MAFF rose from £2,740.5 million in 1995-
96 to a forecast £3,026.3 million in 1999-2000. Cereal subsidies by
the Intervention Board, MAFF and other departments were £12.2
million in 1995-96, forecast to rise to £58.2 million 1999-2000.
(MAFF, *Agriculture in the U.K. 1999*, London 2000). 24,000
farmers and farm workers were forced out of their livelihoods in
1999. (Times 19/12/00, 2)

Since then things have worsened, but true to form, Thanet
farmers have so far escaped the worst. Only one has left the
industry, though Mike Welham, secretary of the Ash & Thanet
branch NFU, forecasts that more will. There is only one part-time
smallholding left in Minster, whereas forty years ago there were
about thirteen. (Information from Denis Neville). But there are
still farms of many sizes, from the 2,000 plus acres of the Tapps to
the 70 of Arthur Burbridge and his daughter Tina – dedicated
farmers if ever there were.

Farm workers are now only a little more numerous than farmers.
It proved impossible to find out much about them from the paid
staff of the RAAW section of the T&G (TGWU) in Kent, in 1993
it was easy to do so. It seems there may not even be a branch any
more here, but thankfully the redundant farm workers find it
reasonably easy to get new work due to their high skills and good
reputation. Some work for contractors, whom farmers increasingly
employ, some are self-employed on contract work. Some farmers
employ gang labour as needed, so far not Eastern European.
Only one farmer was said to be still using local casual labour
(traditionally female) in 2000. It seems unlikely there will be any
more like George Knight, Somali farm foreman who retired in

1999, having been Kent County champion ploughman in 1988 and twice East Kent champion. (ITG 22/1/99).

Since 1989 the agricultural returns for Thanet have been subsumed into a general report for Southeast England, so our farming history's factual basis has disappeared. The NFU journal has become commercial with no reports from Kentish districts. Rural Thanet has been semi-obliterated for the agrarian historian, and perhaps in the eyes of government.

Land prices have stayed buoyant, partly because of potential development rights. About £3,000 an acre is still said to be current for good land for agricultural use, £5,000 or more for horse paddocks, and £100,000 or more for building, the average in the Southeast being £7-8,000 (*Southeast Farmer*, November 2000). 42 plus acres between St.Peters and Margate were advertised for £140,000 (£3,380 per acre) in February 2000 (ITG 25/2/00) and said to have fetched about the asking price. There is demand for old farm houses: Manston Court farmhouse and farmstead sold for the guideprice of £490,000 (*Extra* 19/3/00).

Much more wheat and a little barley have been grown in the past two years, encouraged by subsidy. Two large farms – one of them Quex Park farm, part of the trust set up to preserve Quex Park and the Powell-Cotton museum – have gone over entirely or mainly to corn, using contractors. The unusual rainfall over the past winter has delayed wheat sowing – hundreds of acres were reported not sown in mid-February. Only about 200 acres of cauliflower were grown with 14 producers in autumn 2000, another informant at Christmas said there were only ten. Some oilseed rape and linseed are sown as break crops, but far less rape than ten years ago. It has brought much disease (altenaria).

The fall in potato prices starting in 1999 put most Thanet farmers out of early potatoes. The Tapp family continue, as sole suppliers of Kent Veg., and Quex Park contrary to earlier reports is growing 54 ha in 2001, but none on the marsh now, and no first earlies. This year's varieties at Quex are Colmo, Premier, Marfona, Estima, King Edward and Piper. In June 1997 Quex Park farm "entertained all the big-wigs of the potato world, including supermarkets and consumer magazine representatives." (Information from Richard Tapp and Anthony Curwen. *Adscene* 27/6/97). A few collards and peas are also said to be grown. David Steed stopped growing wheat and grass seed, but Rex Goodban still grows some parsnip and wallflower seed. Peter Dyas at Sevenscore and Jonathan Marsh, manager of Cleve Court farm, both grow onions.

Trinity Growers is believed to be the only grower-owned cauliflower co-operative in existence. It concentrates on spring cauliflower now, and in the 2000-2001 season grew 112 cultivars, of which 53 were produced. Robert Montgomery grows a larger number of cultivars, of which a quarter come from Trinity. Large new packhouses were built in recent years at Elmwood farm (Philpotts), Woodchurch (Quex Park estate) and Monkton Road (Robert Montgomery), but the Woodchurch one is now to be a grain store, Quex Park having given up cauliflower.

Seed purchases and marketing have changed. Tozers, with its representative David Kemp at Minster, is now the only English seed firm. Most cauliflower growers sell to supermarkets. Richard Tapp retired as chairman of Kent Veg., which now has no Thanet members except the Tapps. Wantsum Produce, with Robert Montgomery as Chairman, sells 60% to supermarkets, 30% to wholesalers, 5% to processors and 5% to the Intervention Board. There are also two smaller co-operative marketing firms, not farmer owned. Veg U.K. established about 1980 sells for 'all the local farmers', and Invicta established in 1999 sells for 'most local farmers'.

A small new trend is seen in livestock husbandry. Quex Park now has 90 breeding beef cows, with three bulls and progeny, to a total of 220-290 on average. They are mostly kept on the marshes near Sandwich. Mary Tyrell continues her goat herd, which in 2000 won best Kent goat and highest recorded milk yield at the Kent show, following on many other awards. The Smiths at Nether Hale gave up sheep, but there are currently at least five small flocks, some kept as a sideline by people not primarily farmers.

There is still some involvement in the wider world. In 1999 Anthony Curwen served on the NFU national vegetable committee, Richard Ash on the potato one and Rex Goodban on the seed. Jill Smith is chairman of the Kent Royal Agricultural Benevolent Institute county committee, which raised £52,000 in 2000, and was the first such to win three of the four awards by RABI annually to the counties. David Kemp won the cup, for organizing Quex fair. Peter Smith was chairman of Canterbury Farmers' Club in 2000 and as secretary of the Kent Farmline won a prize of a website to serve the charity. Martin Tapp and Peter Dyas are on the Stour River Internal Drainage Board, Martin being chairman and also chairman of the Environment Agency's Kent Flood Defence Committee. He has been on the Agency's Area Environment Group for Kent since December 1996. David

Steed was on the Southern Region Environment Protection Committee in 1998 and 1999. David Steed and Rex Goodban were ploughing judges and David Ash and Anthony Curwen root judges at the East Kent Ploughing Match in 2000, Thanet farmers being in demand for such jobs. The Association has 14 Thanet members.

Non-agricultural income seems increasingly valuable. Wives' separate professions, conversion of obsolete farm buildings to housing or business units and ever more horse paddocks all help. Windfalls can come, even double ones: one farmer with a bowl-shaped field was able to make it flat when the contractors for the Ramsgate harbour road had nowhere else to put a mountain of excavated chalk. Good land continues to be sold, sometimes in massive chunks for business parks, sometimes in nibbles for small housing developments or the enlargement of industrial sites or caravan parks. The two farm shops do well, and the farmers have no interest in farmers' markets, though David Steed advocates a system of franchised farm shops. Organic farming is likewise dismissed, though something may depend on the results achieved by Christopher Reynolds, 1999 chairman of Kent NFU, on the organic farm he has started as well as his conventional one near Hythe. Opinions are divided on GM crops, Richard Tapp having written strongly in favour of them in *Southeast Farmer* in June 1999, and David Steed opposing them at the CPRE farm forum in Thanet District Council offices in September 2000. The farmers' main hopes seem to rest on new crops of the future, on subsidies and on selling land for building. Many are said to be trying to get their land downgraded to facilitate this, on grounds it is reported of insufficient water retention – though in the current pluvial period this seems rather an advantage. The reputation of our soil must still hold, as the Duchy of Cornwall has bought Abbey farm Minster, but Thanet District Council, faced with empty business parks, no ferry to France and uncertain success for the airport, is eager to expand its council tax base. The British public, with its "country gentleman syndrome", is eager for homes in the country. Perhaps the only hope of largely preserving Thanet's once famously good land lies in a wise reform of the CAP, combined with realization of the Thanet Country Park project, but such things may lie at the end of the rainbow.

The national disregard for Thanet agriculture now seems all the sadder in the light of the most recent research reinforcing our knowledge of its famous past. Archival material in the Public Record Office recently discovered by Joan Thirsk shows that in

1560–1580, under Elizabeth I, five of the only 14 Kentish farmers with over 300 animals lived in Thanet, and in 1576 William Mussared of St. Nicholas died in occupation of 209 acres of sown arable and 782 animals, implying at least 400 acres of pasture. In 1600–1620 three of the largest farms in Kent were respectively in Minster in Thanet (310 acres), Monkton (277 acres) and St. Lawrence (204 acres). (Joan Thirsk, "Agriculture", in Michael Zell ed. *Early Modern Kent 1540–1640*, Maidstone, 2001, pp. 76, 79, 81).